Darwin's Air War
1942-1945

An Illustrated History
Commemorating the Darwin Air Raids

Bob Alford

The Aviation Historical Society of the Northern Territory
Darwin, Northern Territory, 2011

2ND EDITION.
FIRST EDITION PUBLISHED 1991
REPRINTED JULY 1997 AND JULY 2001

ISBN 978-0-9807713-0-5

CONTENTS

INTRODUCTION

John Grey Gorton learned to fly in England while at Oxford University. He joined the RAAF in 1940 and subsequently flew fighters on four fronts, including Singapore and Darwin. After a distinguished service career he became Prime Minister of Australia in January 1968, the first former RAAF member to attain that position.

This is a book which needed to be written. The Aviation Historical Society of the Northern Territory is to be congratulated on bringing together the history of the first aerial attack on Darwin and the subsequent events until the raids posed no further threat to Australia.

After all, the raid of 19 February, 1942, was the first attack by any power on Australian soil and as the bombs rained down on Darwin, and on the ships in the harbour, no one knew that it was not the beginning of the invasion of the continent of Australia. It probably would have been if the Japanese had not been stopped at Milne Bay, in New Guinea, which is the furthest south they ever got. The exodus from Darwin as a result of the attack was not good for Australia's morale. Hundreds and hundreds of people fled south and arrived in southern states full of foreboding. But the troops remained in Darwin and American and Australian fighter pilots fought off the invaders when and where they could but this did little to diminish the damage done in the initial raid and the sixty three which followed it.

I came to Darwin with the 77 Squadron of the RAAF when the raids were practically over. We operated from a strip in Batchelor and began operations by fitting our tents in the scrub which surrounded the strip. We saw little action although Squadron Leader Dick Cresswell scored the first kill for the Squadron when he shot down, by night, a bomber, but there was little else for the rest of the Squadron to do apart from scrambles to intercept non-existent raids, and doing sweeps, and flying top cover for the destroyers which were bringing back our troops from guerrilla operations in Timor.

Darwin, or the surrounding countryside, was the base for Hudson bombers and Beaufighters which struck back from Darwin. For the first few days of 1942 nobody knew what was to come and this book reminds us that we did not know and so we remain the vast, relatively empty continent, for the moment.

[signature]

1991

THE AVIATION HISTORICAL SOCIETY
OF THE NORTHERN TERRITORY

The Northern Territory has an exciting history of aviation, from the earliest balloon ascent over Darwin (then Palmerston) by Professor Burns in 1891, the 1919 arrival of the Vickers Vimy from England, the record breaking flights of the 1930s and its own Flying Doctor to the air operations of World War II and the post war era of Vulcans, Concorde and modern military and civilian aircraft. For many years enthusiasts attempted to preserve tangible reminders of this history, however much of their work was destroyed by Cyclone Tracy on 25 December 1974.

The Aviation Historical Society of the Northern Territory was established by a small group of enthusiasts in 1975. The group sought to preserve aviation relics salvaged following the destruction caused by Cyclone Tracy. The Society was formed as, and remains, a non-profit organisation managed by a committee elected by the membership. Its main aims are to record, acquire and preserve a collection of the Northern Territory's aviation heritage and display this collection to the public through the Australian Aviation Heritage Centre.

The original museum facility, first opened to the public in 1988, was located in a pre World War II naval victualling building leased from the Northern Territory government. It is now used by the Society as an archive, restoration and storage facility. The building still bears the scars of Japanese strafing attacks and is a Registered NT Heritage Place.

For some time during the 1980s negotiations were carried out between the United States Air Force and Northern Territory government to acquire a Boeing B-52 bomber. Included was a plan to build a facility to house and display it along with the Society's collection of aircraft and other artefacts. This was achieved in June 1990 when the new Darwin Aviation Museum was officially opened with a fully refurbished B-52 on permanent loan from the USAF as the centrepiece.

The Society and museum facility, the Australian Aviation Heritage Centre, are fully independent of other bodies. The museum is a fully accredited Northern Territory Regional Museum recognised by the Northern Territory Museums and Art Galleries Board. The Society provides assistance to like minded organisations and individuals, principally in the areas of research, education and the promotion of historical tourism.

The Society has undertaken a variety of projects including the refurbishment of a de Havilland Dove, a CA-27 Sabre, a B-25 Mitchell bomber recovered from the Tanami Desert, the construction of a replica Mk VIII Spitfire and a range of displays exhibiting significant elements of the Territory's aviation history. A Mirage IIIO (A) fighter was refurbished voluntarily by members of No. 75 Squadron at RAAF Tindal Air Base.

Recent projects undertaken by the Society include the relocation of the historically significant RAAF Darwin water tower/control tower from the base to the Aviation Heritage centre and the aquisition of Auster, and Nomad aircraft and a Bell 47 helicopter for restoration and display.

The bombing of Darwin on 19 February, 1942, was a significant event in Australia's history. The Aviation Historical Society of the Northern Territory is proud to display this and the Territory's unique aviation history for all Australians. This book complements those displays in telling the story of Darwin's Air War.

ABOUT THIS BOOK

This work follows on from the successful 1991 publication of the same name. Published by the Aviation Historical Society of the Northern Territory the original drew on information available via the range of sources available at the time.

Over the intervening years, and particularly following the 50th Anniversary of the Darwin bombing activities in 1992, the 50th Anniversary of the end of World War II events as part of Australia Remembers and the annual 19 February commemorative activities in Darwin and elsewhere, much new information has come to hand, primarily through those who served, the veterans themselves, who have provided their stories, papers and photographs.

The publication of a range of books, articles and other papers on this chapter in Australia's history, access to material held in national repositories, the continuing release of material on the Internet, the opening up of Japanese records and continuing research in this area and again, the veterans, has seen a huge amount of material from which to draw in expanding and improving *Darwin's Air War*. The amount of information on Japanese operations in particular has provided valuable data not previously available and which has questioned what has tended to become conventional wisdom over the years.

It was no coincidence therefore that the Aviation Historical Society of the Northern Territory decided that it was opportune to republish *Darwin's Air War*. The process was to be a simple one. This new work would draw on, and draw together, information provided by those who served in the North Western Area of Operations including the American, Australian, British, Dutch and Japanese forces. It would also include photographs not generally published previously to complement a number of those used in the initial work and would include the unique series of colour transparencies taken by a young American pilot serving at a roadside airstrip south of Darwin in 1942.

This new work covers the broad spectrum of military aviation in Australia's north during World War II and it is hoped that this expanded publication creates further interest in a period of danger in Australia's history; a time when air battles were fought over Darwin and when many, too many, young lives were lost in fighting Darwin's Air War.

ABOUT THE AUTHOR

A former President, Historian and now honorary Life Member of the Society, Bob Alford is well known for his research, writing and artistic skills and has assisted many individuals and organisations seeking information on the Territory's aviation history. He was involved in the organisation of the 50th Anniversary of the Darwin bombings in 1992 and was appointed Northern Territory Chair of the Australia Remembers commemorative activities in 1995.

Brought up in country Victoria, Bob later served in the RAAF as an Armourer for twenty years in a variety of overseas postings. Retiring from the RAAF in 1986 he undertook the location and documentation of WWII sites including aircraft crash sites. Bob was appointed Director of the National Trust in 1993 before opening a heritage consultancy in 1999. He also served as Chair of the NT Heritage Advisory Council for five years. Bob retired to Thailand with his wife, Pat, in 2007, though he maintains a strong interest in researching and documenting the Territory's rich aviation heritage.

EXPLANATORY NOTES AND ABBREVIATIONS

Explanatory Notes

Where possible, metric measurements are used with the exclusion of altitude readings, which follow international convention in stating heights in feet. Where imperial measurements are quoted in documents, publications or other source material these figures are retained to reflect the original. Metric measurements are quoted to the nearest whole figure.

With a large discrepancy in both Allied and Japanese figures regarding combat victories and losses, the term 'claim' is utilised in describing combat figures. Where figures are quoted in documents, publications or other source material, the terms quoted in them are used for accuracy in reflecting the original.

Although the Allied names for Japanese aircraft were not introduced until mid-1942, they are used throughout the text in acknowledgement of their usage and the familiarity to many readers. Where technical descriptions, such as A6M2 Rei Sen are used to describe the Mitsubishi A6M2 Type O 'Zeke', are quoted in documents, publications or other source material, these terms are retained to reflect the original.

Japanese names are presented in the context in which they are written and used. That is, the given name followed by the family name; for example, Akira Eguchi, Susumu Akasaka. The Japanese terms for naval and army flying units are also used in lieu of the Allied equivalents, which varied in their designations between services, and are presented in italics. The Japanese unit designations are detailed at Appendix 4.

Abbreviations listed below are used throughout the text and follow those used in source material and in conforming to usage at the time. In the case of ranks, and particularly those of the RAAF, post war abbreviations are used. Where abbreviations differing from those provided are quoted in documents, publications or other source material they are used to accurately quote the original source material.

Abbreviations

A-A	Anti Aircraft
AAHC	Australian Aviation Heritage Centre
AASL	Anti Aircraft Searchlight
AAU	Air Ambulance Unit
ABDACOM	American-British-Dutch-Australian Command
AC	Aircraftsman
ACH	Area Combined Headquarters
ACM	Air Chief Marshal
ACS	Airfield Construction Squadron
AD	Aircraft Depot
Adm	Admiral
AFB	Air Force Base
AGH	Australian General Hospital
AGWAR	Adjutant General Department of War Washington
AHSNT	Aviation Historical Society of the Northern Territory Inc.
AIF	Australian Imperial Force
AirCdre	Air Commodore
AM	Air Marshal
AMF	Australian Military Forces (Army)
AMM	Airplane Maintenance Mechanic
AMS	Air Materiel Squadron
ANAM	Australian National Aviation Museum
AOB	Advanced Operational Base
AOC	Air Officer Commanding
APU	Auxiliary Power Unit
ARD	Aircraft Repair Depot
ASR	Air Sea Rescue
ASRF	Air Sea Rescue Flight
ASWG	Australian Special Wireless Group
AVG	American Volunteer Group
AVM	Air Vice Marshal
AWA	Amalgamated Wireless Australasia
AWC	Allied Works Council
AWM	Australian War Memorial
BD Squad	Bomb Disposal Squad
BDU	Bomb Disposal Unit
Bn	Battalion
Bomb. Gp	Bombardment Group
BPSO	Base Personnel Staff Office
Brig	Brigadier
Brig-Gen	Brigadier-General
Bty	Battery
CAC	Commonwealth Aircraft Corporation
Cal.	Calibre

Explanatory Notes and Abbreviations

Capt	Captain	ICS	Interceptor Control Squadron
CAS	Chief of Air Staff	IFF	Identification Friend or Foe
CFI	Chief Flying Instructor	Intell	Intelligence
CGS	Chief of General Staff	IntellO	Intelligence Officer
CMF	Citizens Military Forces	JAAF	Japanese Army Air Force
CO	Commanding Officer	JNAF	Japanese Naval Air Force
Col	Colonel	KLM	Dutch Air Lines
Colln	Collection	KNILM	Dutch Air Line Netherlands East Indies
Comm. Unit	Communications Unit	Ku	Kokutai
Coy	Company	LAA	Light Anti-Aircraft Battery
Cpl	Corporal	LAC	Leading Aircraftsman
CPO	Chief Petty Officer	LCpl	Lance Corporal
CRTC	Combat and Replacement Training Centre	LORAN	LOng RAnge Navigation
		Lt	Lieutenant
CSIR	Council for Scientific and Industrial Research	LtCol	Lieutenant Colonel
		LtCdr	Lieutenant Commander
CSU	Constant Speed Unit	MG	Machine Gun
DAP	Department of Aircraft Production	Maj	Major
DCS	Dokuritsu Dai Shijugo Chutai (Direct [Independent] Command Squadron, JAAF)	MajGen	Major General
		MFCU	Mobile Fighter Control Unit
		MID	Mention-In-Despatches
DFC	Distinguished Flying Cross	MRS	Medical Receiving Station
DFM	Distinguished Flying Medal	MV	Motor Vessel
DMR	Dept. of Main Roads (NSW)	MWS	Mobile Works Squadron
DSC	Distinguished Service Cross	NAC	National Airways Corporation (New Zealand)
DSO	Distinguished Service Order		
EATS	Empire Air Training Scheme	NAOU	North Australian Observer Unit
EFTS	Elementary Flying Training School	NCO	Non-commissioned Officer
EM	Enlisted Men	NEA	North Eastern Area
FCPO	Flight Chief Petty Officer – Imperial Japanese Navy	NEI	Netherlands East Indies (Indonesia)
		NEIAF	Netherlands East Indies Air Force
FCU	Fighter Control Unit	NT	Northern Territory
FEAF	Far East Air Force	NWA	North Western Area of Operations
Fld	Field	OBU	Operational Base Unit
FlgOff	Flying Officer	OC	Officer Commanding
Flt	Flight	OCU	Operational Conversion Unit
FltLt	Flight Lieutenant	OFI	Oil Fuel Installation
FS	Fighter Sector	ORs	Other Ranks
FSgt	Flight Sergeant	OTU	Operational Training Unit
Gen	General	PatWing	Patrol Wing US Navy
GHQ	General Headquarters	Pln	Platoon
GP	General Purpose	PltOff	Pilot Officer
Gp	Fighter Gp	PO	Petty Officer
GpCapt	GpCapt	PO1c	Petty Officer 1st Class
GR	General Reconnaissance	PO2c	Petty Officer 2nd Class
HAA	Heavy Anti Aircraft	PO3c	Petty Officer 3rd Class
HARS	Historical Aircraft Restoration Society	POW	Prisoner of War
HQ	Headquarters	PRU	Photo Reconnaissance Unit

EXPLANATORY NOTES AND ABBREVIATIONS

Pvt	Private
QM	Quartermaster
RAA	Royal Australian Artillery
RAAF	Royal Australian Air Force
RAE	Royal Australian Engineers
RAF	Royal Air Force
RAN	Royal Australian Navy
RC	Replenishing Centre
RCM	Radio Counter Measures
RDF	Radio Direction Finding - Radar
Regt	Regiment
RFC	Royal Flying Corps
RNEIAF	Royal Netherlands East Indies Air Force
RSU	Repair and Salvage Unit
R/T	Radio Transmitter
SFTS	Service Flying Training School
Sgt	Sergeant
SNCO	Senior Non-Commissioned Officer
Spr	Sapper
Sqn	Squadron
SqnLdr	Squadron Leader
S/Sgt	Staff Sergeant
SWPA	South West Pacific Area
TAF	Tactical Air Force
TAIU	Technical Air Intelligence Unit
T/Sgt	Technical Sergeant
USAAC	United States Army Air Corps
USAAF	United States Army Air Forces
USAFFE	United States Armed Forces Far East
USAFIA	United States Army Forces in Australia
USAT	United States Army Transport
USFEAF	United States Far East Air Force
USN	United States Navy
USO	United Services Organisation
WAAAF	Womens Auxiliary Australian Air Force
WAG	Wireless Air Gunner
WgCdr	WgCdr
WOff	Warrant Officer
W/T	Wireless Transmitter

Darwin's air war arguably commenced at 1043 hours on 22 December 1941 when nine Boeing B-17 Fortress bombers of the USAAC's 19th Bomb. Gp took off from Batchelor airfield to bomb enemy vessels in the Gulf of Davao and Lingayen Gulf in the Philippines. It was the initial response by the Allies against the Japanese from Australian soil. Though each aircraft carried only four 500 lb (227 kg) bombs and only four made the attack the following day, the use of a Northern Territory airfield in those early days of the war against the Japanese was the culmination of a defensive build up that had been in the minds of strategists for some 30 years.

In 1883 the first of many Japanese pearlers arrived in Darwin and settled quietly in their own enclave as just another element in the cosmopolitan make up of the north, but it was from 1892 that a threat from Japan was in the minds of Australians. The American entry to the Philippines was applauded as the possible forging of an alliance against the nation they most feared. The alliance failed to materialise but in September 1908 a visit to Australia by Roosevelt's 'Great White Fleet' saw pro-American and anti-Japanese sentiments voiced when the Premier of New South Wales, G. C. Wade, stated that Australia looked to America "...as her natural ally in the coming struggle against Japanese domination", no doubt in the shadow of the Japanese destruction of the Russian fleet four years earlier.

In the event, Japan was an Ally during World War I. As part of her spoils of war Japan gained control over German mandates in the Pacific - the Marshall, Caroline and Mariana groups - allowing domination of the western Pacific basin and thus an extension of her reach toward northern Australia. These post-war territorial gains further added to Australian concerns and Japan's aggressive build up of her bases in the Pacific and later, the brutal campaigns in China and Manchuria in the 1930s, only exacerbated them.

In 1919 Viscount Jellicoe visited Australia and was requested by the Hughes government to assess the military situation and formulate a plan for the defence of the Pacific. His recommendations included the establishment of a Far Eastern Fleet with its main base at Singapore and Australian bases at Port Stephens, Cockburn Sound and at Bynoe Harbour west of Darwin. The Australian government rejected Jellicoe's plan as over reactive and too expensive, opting instead to maintain the Thursday Island naval coaling station and sentinel over the strait between Australia and New Guinea as Australia's most important northern base.

Jellicoe's report was some years behind that of Field Marshal Viscount Kitchener, who had assessed the strategic situation in 1911 and found Darwin's one strategic advantage was as a landing place. In his report he had stated prophetically that when "...railway communications with other portions of the Commonwealth has been established, the importance of Port Darwin will be so greatly increased from the commercial and strategic points of view that it will be sound policy to provide fixed defenses [sic] to protect the port against attack...I would recommend two batteries each of two 6-inch Mk VII guns, one on the east point and one on the west point..."

Both reports sat, apparently unheeded, until Jellicoe's report was revisited at the 1923 Imperial Conference and from it came the 'Singapore Strategy'. It was a plan that would see the end of Darwin's role as a major naval base. It was instead to become the end of the so-called Australia-Singapore line; a site for naval fuel storage facilities but not as a naval base. Singapore would be developed as a base to receive the British Fleet should any problems arise, while Australia and New Zealand were to look after any 'smaller' problems such as minor invasions or landings until Britain's might could be brought to bear on any adversary.

Whilst Darwin was perceived only as a strategic naval refuelling facility, even planning for its development saw little if any thought given to the threat of airpower. Instead, the proposed fuel tanks were to be erected behind and on Stokes Hill as protection against naval bombardment and in turn protected by a battery of coastal guns. Nothing it seemed had been learned from the dangers of aerial attack that had emerged from World War I.

Despite the warning signs, the erection of the tanks proceeded. Approval was granted in 1924 and foundations for the first four tanks were commenced in 1926. By 16 July 1928 No. 1 tank received 7,896 tonnes of oil from the tanker *War Krishna*. Other tanks followed and by mid-1941 nine tanks carried 63,402 tonnes of oil. By 2 December that year another two tanks had been completed increasing the capacity of the OFI by a further 12,058 tonnes.

THE DEFENCE BUILD-UP

A further assessment of defence preparedness was made in 1928, this time by AM Sir John Salmond RAF, who was to advise on the organisation, equipment, training and the role of the RAAF. Passing through Darwin, Salmond was appalled at the exposure of the oil tanks to air attack, but, as a strong believer in the much vaunted Singapore Strategy, he suggested that defence against raids by only small forces was required, along with a modest increase in RAAF strength to be based in the south. He effectively ducked the issue of any RAAF presence in the north and in effect left the RAAF as the 'Third Brother', subservient to both the navy and army; in their eyes anyway.

Defence planning in the 1930s saw an upgrading of the military presence in the north and despite the navy's push to establish Darwin as a base, military strategists decided that the protection of the OFI was an army responsibility. A committee, including Maj T. R. Williams CMG DSO, was despatched to Darwin and recommended two 6-inch guns and 3-inch anti-aircraft guns, only to meet disagreement from the strategists who recommended four 6-inch guns, with lights, along with the anti-aircraft guns.

As a result Williams was again sent to Darwin following cabinet approval of the so-called 'Emergency Scheme for the Fortification of Darwin' on 17 May 1942, this time he was to command a 'Darwin Detachment' of RAA and RAE troops to implement the scheme. On 2 September 1932 Williams, four officers and 42 troops of the 'Darwin Detachment' arrived in Darwin aboard a small flotilla comprising HMAS *Australia*, HMAS *Canberra* and the seaplane carrier, HMAS *Albatross* – the entire Australian fleet less its two submarines.

Members of the Darwin Detachment sent to construct Darwin's fortifications in 1932. Photo: Alford Colln.

Work proceeded quickly, with the army using gangs of unemployed and prisoners in the construction of fortifications at East Point and at Emery Point along with accommodation for a garrison to follow. Concrete pouring was completed by January 1933 and the first gun mounting was installed later that year. Another followed and both guns were proof fired on 22 May 1934. By 1936 four 6-inch guns, two each at East and Emery Points, along with their ancillary command posts, magazines and searchlights were installed. An anti-aircraft battery of three 3-inch guns was installed and further defence works followed.

A worsening international situation, particularly in Europe, and no doubt with an eye to Japan's continuing aggression in China, saw further increases in defence works and yet another appraisal of Darwin's defences. In 1936 CGS, MajGen John Lavarack, inspected the defences and Darwin's hinterland, partly by air, in a RAAF Tugan Gannet. Among his conclusions were that, despite a number of natural barriers, mostly mangroves, "...no obstacles exist anywhere that would make an approach to Port Darwin by an enemy land force impossible." He also warned of the potential of the Japanese pearling fleet to cause problems in defence. "...each carries a crew of from 10 to 12 Japanese [and]... some of them carry qualified navigators...it is certain that a considerable portion, if not most, of the Japanese have had either Naval or Military training. The crews could, of course, be increased and military stores provided without our knowledge."

Lavarack also concluded that "...at the present time no bombardment or air attack on the port would be necessary, since the cheapest and most effective form of attack would be a landing... [by] a small force...if the operation were successful reinforcements and further supply via Port Darwin itself would be simple, - if unsuccessful the small force...would be a negligible loss to the enemy."

But, while dismissing air attack, Lavarack made the point that when "...the R.A.A.F. squadron is stationed in the area, it will be adequate in [defence against]...the scale of attack envisaged." He had earlier commented on the anti-aircraft defences, which "...must be considered in relation to the fact that it is intended eventually to establish a squadron of the R.A.A.F. at this station."

"Eventually" came quicker than Lavarack may have envisaged. The 22 January 1937 edition of the local

THE DEFENCE BUILD-UP

newspaper, the *Northern Standard*, reported that "An important proposal for the establishment of medium air bases...is being considered. The Federal Government plans to provide tentatively for the development for defence purposes of main aerodromes at Darwin, Brisbane, Evans Head and Sydney."

To date, any RAAF presence in the Northern Territory had been in a number of deployments to 'show the flag' from bases at Richmond or Point Cook, which were in the main *ad hoc* affairs, utilising the existing civilian facilities of Darwin's Civil 'Drome at Parap. Others had been in the form of searches for lost airmen, geological and photographic surveys, and even these operated mostly from airstrips in central Australia.

RAAF Hawker Demons led by Squadron Leader Charles Eaton (left) were involved in the successful search for Sir Herbert Gepp's de Havilland Rapide in Central Australia in May 1937. Photo: Alford/AHSNT Colln.

Things moved quickly after the news report. On 13 April 1937 the RAAF's Service Director of Works, WgCdr Hepburn, and Director of Signals, SqnLdr Wiggins, visited Darwin and selected a site for the new military aerodrome at the '4½ Mile peg' from Darwin on the northern side of the main north-south road and three km east of the Civil 'Drome. Initial surveys comprising some 1,320 hectares of land were completed by September that year.

On 20 December the Minister for Defence approved the purchase of the land at an estimated cost of £1,000. The total allocation for the development of the aerodrome was £282,000. Also it was discovered later, with some concern, that the two proposed hangars were themselves to cost a total of £95,000.

Despite the possible overruns, plans proceeded. In January 1938 WgCdr George Jones and SqnLdr Charles Eaton inspected the site and following their approval acquisition of the site was gazetted on 10 February.

Eaton was a well known figure in the Territory. He had been involved in the search and recovery of the ill-fated *Kookaburra* crew of Hitchcock and Anderson in 1929 and in the search for the *Golden Quest II* in 1931. Born on 23 December 1895 Eaton served with the RFC during World War I and migrated to Australia with his family in mid-1923. Joining the RAAF in 1925 he became a RAAF Instructor in 1930 and commanded 21 Squadron at Laverton from 1937-38. In between times he carried out the searches for *Kookaburra* and *Golden Quest II* and Sir Herbert Gepp, and flew in the 'Great Air Race' from Sydney to Perth in 1929 and was then seconded to oversee the development of the new RAAF station at Darwin.

Plans for the new RAAF station were quickly implemented. Noel Healey, a contractor from Dunmarra, won the tender for clearing the site at £14 per acre whilst tenders for water reticulation and sewerage, a power house and generators, barracks, workshops, stores, and offices were accepted between January and August 1939.

In April, Jones and Eaton had been advised by CAS, AVM Richard Williams, that they were to be appointed Station Commander and Squadron Commander respectively at the new station. Further, Williams advised, they were to act as a committee in providing information on all aspects of the station's development, something they had been doing for some time. A subsequent inspection by the pair on 18 May saw them submit a report to CAS that "...progress was continuing to expectations."

The 2 December 1938 edition of the *Northern Standard* also reported on progress at the site, and further reported that "Two Royal Australian Air Force Squadrons, instead of one will be established at Darwin by early in 1940 as a result of speeding up of the defence program." Events in Europe saw an urgent review of the situation however, and pressure was on the construction authorities to hasten works at the site.

In a Minute to CAS on 13 March 1939, WgCdr Swinburne commented that the station "...will not be ready for occupation until the next dry season at least, i.e., March 1940...It is recommended therefore that we use the civil aerodrome at Darwin as a temporary station until

THE DEFENCE BUILD-UP

the permanent one is ready." The recommendation was taken up and when Eaton was appointed CO No. 12 (GP) Squadron on 6 February 1939, the date of the unit's formation at Laverton, he and his Equipment Officer, FlgOff Arthur Hocking, were instructed to prepare the unit for deployment at short notice. A week after forming, the squadron had a complement of 14 officers and 120 airmen, while its aircraft strength comprised a mixed bag of four Hawker Demons and four Avro Ansons, both obsolete types in urgent need of replacement in such perilous times.

A further seven Ansons joined the unit whilst preparations for the move to Darwin continued. In March and April the coastal steamers, *Montoro* and *Marella*, transported squadron equipment to Darwin. On 1 July the movement of personnel began when an advance party under Arthur Hocking departed Melbourne aboard the *Marella* before transferring to the *Montoro* in Sydney for the trip north via Thursday Island and on to Darwin.

Comprising two officers and 30 NCOs and Airmen, the advance party arrived in Darwin on 24 July 1939, signalling the commencement of a permanent RAAF presence in Darwin and the Northern Territory. With the RAAF station still incomplete, the personnel were to share quarters in the derelict Vesteys meat works on Bullocky Point with the Darwin Mobile Force. Two days later a flight of three Ansons led by Eaton arrived at the Civil 'drome and on the 29th the Administrator, C. L. A. Abbott, turned the first sod for the temporary camp in a ceremony attended by all available personnel, locals and what media there was at the time. Eaton and his flight returned to Laverton shortly after, while construction began.

It was not for another month that the unit's Ansons arrived. Two flights touched down on the 30th after flying via Broken Hill, the town 'drome at Alice Springs and Newcastle Waters. Cec Fisher, an LAC Armourer, was aboard one of the Ansons, recalling that "To our pleasure Darwin...was not the flat, sandy area we had imagined, but a peninsula into Van Dieman's Gulf with little promontories and inlets, situated on a hilltop and almost surrounded by water – a pleasing sight. The excitement upon arrival...with low passes over the town, was tempered with a touch of reverence when it was realised that the landing approach over Fannie Bay headland was over the monument...to commemorate the arrival from England 20 years before... [by] Ross and Keith Smith and crew in their Vickers Vimy...

In our own way we, too, were making history – the first RAAF Squadron to be based in the Northern Territory."

Six days later the squadron's main party boarded the *Marella* bound for Darwin. At the same time five of the unit's new CAC Wirraway aircraft were flying north as 'C' Flight via Narromine, Winton and Daly Waters. They arrived over Darwin at 1030 hours on 5 September where, as Cec Fisher recalled, "...a crowd of a few hundred people, including the Administrator and his wife, had gathered at the aerodrome for an appropriate ceremony and to witness what had promised to be a spectacular display with the arrival of the Wirraway flight. They watched in horror as one of the first aircraft to dive over the aerodrome went into a spin and crashed on the tarmac killing both the pilot and air observer."

The aircraft, A20-5, was flown by FlgOff Arnold Dolphin and his Observer, Cpl Harold Johnson. The first Australian airmen to die on Australian soil in a war only two days old, they were buried at the Gardens Cemetery the following day.

Work on the temporary camp continued with the erection of two 'rag hangars' and a further 27 buildings including accommodation, administration and maintenance facilities, all under the collective title 'Temporary Hutted Camp' or 'Tin City Parap' as it was dubbed.

The hutted camp erected by 12 Squadron at Parap, 1939. Only the former Qantas hangar remains. Photo: Alford/AHSNT Colln.

Five bomb dumps were constructed near the Fannie Bay Gaol, involving "...the digging of sand...at Fanny [*sic*] Bay, filling sand bags and then constructing blast walls...this was followed by bringing...112 and 250 lb bombs down from Vestey's to be fused and stacked ready for use. More bombs and ammunition were sent by rail to Katherine in

THE DEFENCE BUILD-UP

case of emergency..." Cec Fisher recalled. Work also began on the practice bombing and gunnery ranges at Lee Point (Leanyer) and Casuarina Beach.

LACs George Perkins and Colin Eades cart 112 lb bombs to the 12 Squadron bomb dump at the Darwin Civil 'Drome, 1939. Photo: Cec Fisher.

Despite developmental works the squadron commenced operational patrol duties and training soon after arrival. On 4 December a weekly patrol over the Darwin-Derby-Wyndham-Broome sector commenced: the first regular coastal surveillance patrols over the desolate northern coastline. Reconnaissance patrols were also flown out over the Arafura and Timor Seas and Arnhem Land coast whilst closer to home the pearl luggers were under scrutiny. There was a distinct awareness that Japan would join the Axis Powers and the activities of the luggers in Darwin Harbour and at Frances Bay were constantly monitored and photographed by 12 Squadron aircraft.

With Australia at war with Germany and Italy from 3 September 1939 and with the growing threat from Japan, works at the new RAAF station were expedited. By 1 June 1940 work had progressed sufficiently to formally establish the site and in accordance with a Directive signed three days previously the aerodrome was declared 'RAAF Station Darwin'. It had a complement of 30 officers and 212 NCOs and Airmen under the command of now WgCdr Charles Eaton.

The same day saw the formation of the only operational RAAF unit to be formed in Darwin: No 13 GP Squadron. As a result most of the personnel and all of the Ansons of 12 Squadron's 'A' and 'B' Flights were absorbed by the new unit. The Wirraways were retained as 'C' Flight 12 Squadron and remained based at the Civil 'Drome. Number 13 Squadron, under SqnLdr J. R. 'Sam' Balmer, commenced operations

from the RAAF Station on 9 June while its Avro Ansons were retrospectively replaced by 12 of the new Lockheed Hudson light bombers then coming into service. Number 12 Squadron may have been the first to arrive but it lagged far behind in the re-equipment stakes and was forced to soldier on with the Wirraways for another two years.

A flight of 13 Squadron Hudsons over East Point, 1941. Darwin township is in the background, with the Civil 'Drome at centre left. Photo: Ken Nicholson.

The Hudsons had evolved from the successful Lockheed 14 airliner and were greeted enthusiastically by air and ground crews alike, though they were not without fault. "They would bite you if you didn't fly them pretty exactly. They had a bad habit of stalling and flicking over on their back if [they were] heavily loaded or flown too slowly," recalled Ron Barker, a 13 Squadron ground crew member who went on to become a pilot.

Construction at the RAAF Station continued throughout 1940, with the Airmens' and Officers' Messes opened on 12 and 13 October respectively. On the 20th a successful tender by Dan S. Hart saw the beginning of construction of a new gravel runway at Batchelor Aerodrome, some 100 km south southwest of Darwin. Further development of the satellite 'drome included the relocation of fuel and ordnance from Katherine, which was undertaken following a visit to Darwin by CAS ACM Sir Charles Burnett KCB, CBE, DSO as part of a meeting of the Darwin Defence Coordination Committee on 15 November.

In the same period the government initiated the development of new airfields at the Seven-Mile site south of Alice Springs and at Adelaide River, whilst improvements were made to existing 'dromes at Katherine, Daly Waters and at Tennant Creek: all to accommodate the expected

THE DEFENCE BUILD-UP

increase in RAAF traffic. In 1941 a series of AOBs was also established across the northern coastline at or near existing mission stations: at Drysdale in the Kimberleys, Bathurst Island, Milingimbi and Groote Eylandt.

Senior military staff, Darwin 1939. From left, FltLt Duncan RAAF, LtCdr A. E. Fowler RAN, WgCdr C. Eaton RAAF, LtCdr J. H. Walker RAN, LtCol H. C. H. Robertson CO, U/K and Maj Thyer, staff officer, 7 Military District. Photo: Alford/AHSNT Colln.

None was considered suitable for operations in GpCapt Frederick Scherger's view, as the "...runways...were only clearings in which the surface was rough, in many cases sandy, and usually unserviceable after rains." However, these isolated strips and their fuel caches did allow patrols to be extended and provided valuable 'away-from-base' training for aircrews, including digging their aircraft out of sand or mud. Both 12 and 13 Squadrons utilised the AOBs throughout 1941 as part of their coastal patrol and surveillance operations. A number of the missions were also equipped with radios to provide a coast watching facility and maintain contact with the AWA Coastal Radio Station 'VID' located in Darwin's Botanic Gardens.

The first Hudson fatalities occurred on 15 August when a 13 Squadron aircraft, A16-8, crashed into the sea off Casuarina during a gunnery exercise. Killed were FlgOff C. M. Davies, FlgOff C. G. Keely, Sgt M. A. Hipkins and LAC J. Currie. Three bodies were recovered and buried at Gardens Cemetery the following day. A few days later Hipkins' mother received a letter from him. "Dear Mum, we had a sham fight yesterday. On paper my plane was shot down. I am a dead'un" he wrote, perhaps prophetically. Unfortunately he was to be one of many.

The RAAF Station and associated air force developments were but a few of a number of defence projects that were completed between 1938 and 1941: Larrakeyah Barracks,

hutted camps at Stuart Park and Winnellie on Darwin's eastern outskirts and naval facilities at Coonawarra and HMAS *Melville*. Two military hospitals, 119 AGH initially at Bagot and later at Berrimah and a reticulated water system were also completed.

The latter was developed in a town reliant on wells from the earliest days of settlement in 1869. After public outcries in the 1930s, water was eventually run from the old Vesteys pumping station at Howard Springs from 1939. However it was insufficient for increasing needs in both construction and population – predominately the military. Instead a dam across the Manton River 60 km south of Darwin was commenced and despite labour disputes, contractual problems and poor equipment, the first water flowed in March 1941. Problems with supply persisted until the evacuations from Darwin in 1942 solved the matter satisfactorily – at least for the military.

Darwin itself also benefited enormously from the defence build up. New banks, the Commonwealth and Bank of New South Wales, were built while the streets were sealed, kerbed and guttered. The Hotel Darwin, Commonwealth housing, a new civilian hospital and private housing were all constructed and all required labour that was outstripped by demand. Darwin had been transformed, outwardly at least, from a rough frontier town to a large defence base prompting the *Northern Standard* to proclaim Darwin as arguably "...the most prosperous town in Australia..."

By late 1941 Australia had been at war for two years and spread her forces as far afield as Great Britain, the Middle East, Malaya, Singapore, New Guinea and on remote islands in the southwest Pacific. The RAAF had few operational aircraft at its disposal for service in Australia and those it did have were in the main obsolescent types, including the Anson, Wirraway and Hudson as 'front line' aircraft. Others were in the pipeline including the Curtiss P-40, Bristol Beaufort and Consolidated PBY Catalina. However the European Theatre was far more a priority in American and British minds than the Far East and Pacific, despite a growing Japanese threat. When war was declared the Prime Minister, R. G. Menzies, was quick to offer the Australian military to Britain, confident in an understanding that Britain would reciprocate should Australia be threatened, and that Britain's navy and Singapore were all powerful and impregnable.

THE DEFENCE BUILD-UP

Unfortunately Australia had been slow to realise that Britain's navy had been reduced to a two-ocean force: that of the western hemisphere and the Indian Ocean. Its capabilities in the Pacific were questionable as was Singapore's supposed invincibility. Changes in Britain's interests in the Middle East and Mediterranean also took precedence over her dominions to the east. Rather than being a launching pad for Britain in the Pacific, Singapore had become little more than a passive barrier, hopefully blocking any Japanese ideas of expansion into the Indian Ocean. Australian assessments to the contrary were ignored and the result almost two years later was a debacle.

The newly constructed Bank of New South Wales and Commonwealth banks at left, with the older Commercial Bank (the 'Stone Bank') at right, 1941. Photo: Alford/AHSNT Colln.

Thus, the ludicrous Singapore Strategy held. The Americans seemed equally blind to the threat, even though events in the Pacific must have sounded the alarm bells. By May 1940 the situation in the Pacific had deteriorated rapidly. Germany had given Japan a free hand in the Dutch East Indies and the Vichy French had allowed Japanese control of Indo-China.

In October the ruling Japanese Prince, Kanoye, was replaced by a military government under Hirohito and a subsequent statement clearly indicated that the Japanese considered East-Asia and the South Seas as their interest alone. Japan continued its expansionist policies and prepared for war, but by mid-1941 she was isolated by a trade embargo imposed by Britain, America, the Dutch and China. The Japanese had not helped in having signed a Tripartite Pact with Germany and Italy in May that year.

As late as February 1941 the Americans had dismissed the need for long range heavy bombers in the Pacific and

regarded "...as inadvisable the establishment of air bases in the Pacific." In a matter of months however, and based on General Douglas MacArthur's belief that the Philippines could be defended, the decision was urgently reviewed and they began to search for air routes to the Philippines for the USAAC's Boeing B-17C and D bombers, whilst avoiding the Japanese-held Micronesian islands.

In August 1940 two Catalina flying boats of the US Navy's Patwing 10 flew a group from Honolulu to investigate possible staging airfields at Rabaul, Port Moresby and Darwin. Both Darwin and Port Moresby were recommended and Capt Floyd J. Pell USAAC organised the Darwin end. Pell also conducted a survey of airfields in the northwest to determine the availability of high octane fuels and report on the condition of, and facilities at, the airfields he visited. His report was not encouraging as there were few that could be relied upon.

A Boeing B-17C of the 5th Bomb Group, Hawaiian Air Force USAAC at the RAAF Station in late 1941. Photo: Alford/AHSNT Colln.

Shortly after, the B-17s began flying staging flights over the Pacific. The first, nine B-17s of the 14th Provisional Squadron, Hawaiian Air Force, departed Honolulu on 5 September bound for the Philippines via Midway and Wake Islands, Port Moresby and Darwin, landing there on the 10th. They flew on to Manila two days later. Seventeen more from the 19th Bomb. Gp made the trip during the next few weeks, though not without problems.

The runways at the newly developed Darwin RAAF Station were not surfaced and this negated its use, particularly when one B-17 sank through the surface. Scherger, who had been appointed as station commander during September, replacing Eaton who was posted south, reported that "...

surfacing was still proceeding." One B-17 commanded by Capt W. E. McDonald took over a week to effect an engine change at the RAAF Station and following repairs taxied out for take off only to break through the runway crust and damage two propellers; a further week was lost in flying in, fitting and testing new items.

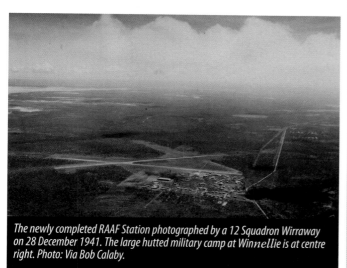

The newly completed RAAF Station photographed by a 12 Squadron Wirraway on 28 December 1941. The large hutted military camp at Winnellie is at centre right. Photo: Via Bob Calaby.

September also saw all leave for RAAF personnel in Darwin cancelled as the international situation worsened. Number 13 Squadron under WgCdr J. R. McDonald, who had replaced 'Sam' Balmer, remained involved in operational activities including flights to Ambon and Koepang, visits to the AOBs and, in late November, a futile search for the ill-fated HMAS *Sydney*. Last seen heading out to sea and reported by Gunner Des Lambert at the observation post on Rottnest Island, the ship disappeared. It was a further 67 years before *Sydney* was again seen, by Australians anyway; this time on the sea floor after having been sunk by the German raider, *Kormorant*, on 19 November 1941.

Four Hudsons of 2 Squadron from Laverton staged through Darwin on a familiarisation flight to the proposed AOBs in the NEI on 26 September and were followed by a further four on 8 November. The RAAF, even if poorly equipped, appeared at least to be preparing for any crisis that might arise.

The Americans too, were making attempts to make up for lost time. In early November MacArthur had appointed MajGen Louis H. Brereton Commander FEAF and on 6 November ordered him to proceed to Australia to survey the Trans-Pacific Air Ferry Route from Australia to the Philippines and Java, whilst also assessing an extension to Singapore and China. Brereton was also instructed to prepare bases in northern Australia and the Malay barrier through which the USAAC could operate. "...MacArthur was far sighted", Brereton wrote, "Never at any time did he fail to realize [*sic*] that, if a campaign in the Philippines was unsuccessful, it would be essential...to provide adequate defense [*sic*] of Northern Australia, the Dutch East Indies, and the Malay Peninsula."

Brereton departed Clark Field in the Philippines by air on 11 November, arriving at Batchelor 14 hours later. Disappointing was probably the kindest word he would have chosen to describe conditions there, writing that the "...facilities at Batchelor were rudimentary. Nothing was being done at Batchelor Field or at Darwin to prepare [them] for the transit of heavy bombers. We had already brought out 35 heavy bombers...via the trans-Pacific ferry route...and there were three out of condition, including one wrecked at Batchelor Field owing to the condition of the runways".

Fortunately Brereton had unlimited authority to initiate action and obtain funding, but it was even more fortunate that "GpCapt Scherger, RAAF, in command of the station at Darwin, was energetic, efficient and very impatient. With his able assistance and that of Brigadier Blair, the local commander, I was able in less than two days I spent there to initiate work on the Batchelor Field runway in a hurried attempt to prepare [it] for additional bombers due any day from the States. It was the old problem of trying to beat the rains."

Brereton went on to Port Moresby and Rabaul before meeting with ACM Sir Charles Burnett regarding a range of requirements including the transit of aircraft from Townsville and Brisbane to Darwin. Basing his requirements on three Fighter Gps, a heavy bomber group and three bomber reconnaissance groups along with the associated service groups, improvements to a number of airfields was also agreed to, including Daly Waters and an American camp at Batchelor. In the event, the route from Brisbane to Darwin via Charleville, Cloncurry and Daly Waters became known as the 'Brereton Route', though not always as a compliment: many commented on following the trail of aircraft wrecks across the remote outback to get to Darwin.

THE DEFENCE BUILD-UP

In Darwin from late November the 13 Squadron historian recorded that the "...sense of something about to happen increased...Sketchy daily shortwave radio news broadcasts received in Darwin...particularly from KZRM Manila, reinforced rumours of an impending Pacific war, and induced heightened feelings..." On 2 December Signal A88 from AOC Northern Area directed that 13 Squadron prepare to move to the NEI at 36 hours notice. At the same time 2 Squadron, which had also re-equipped with 12 Lockheed Hudsons, was preparing to move from Laverton to Darwin under WgCdr F. Headlem.

Six days later the wait was over. In the early hours of 8 December Australian time, the Japanese struck at a number of targets throughout the Pacific and Asia. The first was a land attack on Shanghai and a seaborne assault at Kota Bharu on Malaya's far north coast an hour and a half later. There the Japanese invasion force was attacked by Hudsons of the RAAF's No. 1 Squadron in what was the first hostile action by the Allies in the Pacific war. Though eventually forced to withdraw as a result of enemy attacks and aircraft losses, the unit managed to inflict considerable losses on the Japanese force.

Hudsons of 1 Squadron RAAF at Daly Waters during the move to Singapore in May 1941. The unit was the first to engage the Japanese landings at Kota Bharu on 8 December. Photo: Alford/AHSNT Colln.

The attack on Malaya was followed across the International Dateline an hour and a half later, on Sunday 7 December. A few minutes before 0800 hours Japanese carrier-borne aircraft of the 1st Attack Fleet began a devastating attack on the huge American US naval base and airfields at Pearl Harbor on Oahu Island. Over the next hour continuous bombing, strafing and torpedo drops effectively reduced the American fleet and aircraft there to ruins. The casualties were largely US Navy personnel; those killed totalled 2,403

whilst the wounded accounted for another 1,178. Eight battleships were sunk or severely damaged and others damaged, whilst a total of 193 aircraft at the naval base and at the USAAC base at Hickham Field were lost.

Part of the devastation wreaked by carrier-borne Japanese aircraft at the Pearl Harbor and other American installations on Oahu Island, 7 December 1941. Photo: Via Ghyslaine Miller.

Attacks on Thailand at Singora and Pattani in the south, on Singapore, the northern Philippines, Guam, Hong Kong and Wake Island followed over the next six and a half hours, while Midway Island was bombarded from the sea later in the day. The attacks were well coordinated and having relied on the duplicity of the Japanese in Washington and elsewhere for their success, it was a "...day of infamy..." as the American President, Franklin D. Roosevelt, stormed. The Japanese had all but neutralised the Allied forces on the Pacific and the first 24 hours of war saw a sudden realisation by the Allies of the gross underestimation of the Japanese capabilities and of the weaknesses in their own forces.

The only positive note, if there could be one, was that the American aircraft carrier fleet had not been at Pearl Harbor and remained intact. It was a miscalculation that saw Admiral Isoroku Yamamoto comment "...Nekubi o kaite wa ikeni" ("It does not do to slit the throat of a sleeping man.")

In Australia the mood following news of the attacks was one of shock, but also in realisation that the wait was over. Australia's role had suddenly changed from that of fighting in distant theatres for Empire to that of a nation threatened for the first time in her European history. It was a matter of when, and not if, the Japanese would move south through the NEI, and when they did Darwin would be called on to become a vital link in the coming conflict.

CHAPTER 2

DESPERATE TIMES
The RAAF in the NEI, ABDACOM and withdrawal

In Darwin the Hudson crews and squadron personnel were on standby to move forward, and in the period 5 to 10 December 1941, 2 Squadron moved to Koepang in Dutch Timor whilst half 13 Squadron's aircraft moved to Laha across the bay from Ambon - only to be greeted with news of the Japanese attacks on Hawaii. The remaining six aircraft joined 13 Squadron at Laha shortly after and the unit occupied the primitive airstrips at Namlea on the larger island of Buru west of Laha, and, for a short time, Babo in Dutch New Guinea, before moving back to Laha.

The units began operations immediately. On 10 December 13 Squadron was briefed to attack the flying boat base at Tobi Atoll in the Carolinas. The CO, WgCdr McDonald, and his crew aboard A16-69 perished in an early morning take off, when, as FltLt Arch Dunne, recalled, "...we were taking off about 3 o'clock in the morning and he said that he'd go off first, he would slow up and wait for us. He was going to come back to about 110 knots...I said 'Crikey don't do that, it's much too dangerous. You just keep going and flash your lights...keep the speed up and we'll catch up.' I took off and...was just coming up to him...with the fellow in the tail

turret flashing an Aldis lamp...all of a sudden he was almost flying backwards alongside me. I turned away smartly and my co-pilot Bill Ross said, 'He's dropped a flare.' I said, 'Oh Lord, he hasn't dropped a flare, he's dropped himself'...he slowed down too much and she just...spun out."

The tricks of the Hudson at low speed and a pilot new to the aircraft, not the enemy, had taken the first crew to die on operations. They were the first of many for the Hudson units over the coming months. The scant remains of WgCdr J. R. McDonald, FlgOff R. G. Pope, and Sgts W. R. Foreman and W. J. Nagel were buried in what became the Ambon War Cemetery.

Arch Dunne took over the lead for the mission and as Ron Cornfoot, the pilot of A16-96 recalled, "...we found Tobi Is. but no Jap flying boats, so we bombed the secondary target, the wireless station, and turned for home – Ambon."

At the same time 2 Squadron commenced operations from the airfield at Penfoie outside Koepang. Four aircraft under FltLt R. W. B. Cuming attacked a Japanese W/T ship, the

Hudsons of 13 Squadron at the RAAF Station, 1941. Both 2 and 13 Squadrons fought a losing battle against the Japanese before being withdrawn to Darwin in February 1942. Photo: AHSNT.

DESPERATE TIMES

Nanyo Maru on 8 December causing it to be grounded and abandoned.

Operating from at best rudimentary airfields as they were, both Hudson units were forced to rotate their aircraft through Darwin for major servicings and repairs. Conditions for aircraft and personnel at the NEI bases were primitive with no protective revetments, camouflage or repair facilities. Stores of all description were lacking and food was extremely basic - mostly hard biscuits, and beans or fish in tomato sauce ('Goldfish'), resulting in a variety of complaints including diarrhoea and dysentery. Malaria and dengue fever also took their toll on air and ground crews alike. The arrival of 19th Bomb. Gp B-17s staging through Ambon on the flight to Batchelor from the 16th also put a strain on resources and extra supplies including fuel had to be rushed in. All the while the Japanese were advancing and the squadrons were only delaying the inevitable.

Despite the odds, the Hudsons and their crews kept up the pace, carrying out missions far beyond the limits of men and aircraft. With the toll on endurance of man and machine, and enemy action, came appalling losses. On New Year's Day A16-29 crashed into the sea near Ambon killing three of the Turnbull crew; one, Sgt B. E. Haack, survived. The others remain missing.

Ron Cornfoot was involved in a combined strike by Hudsons of 2 and 13 Squadrons on 12 January, and remembered that "An hour before dawn... [WgCdr J.] Ryland (McDonald's replacement as CO), Dunne and I set off again from Ambon while Rob Cuming, Sattler, Barton, Hodge and Gorrie left from Namlea planning to meet over Menado for a concentrated attack. Trying to confuse the Japs we made a wide sweep and commenced our bombing run from the north. I was in formation with Ryland and Dunne at 8000'... Bill Morley...was to release our bombs two seconds apart as soon as he saw Ryland's bombs go...I knew I would have to hold '96 steady for at least 30 seconds trying to ignore the flak bursting around us. It was most nerve wracking, particularly when Reilly, my Wireless Operator, passed me up a scribbled message...from one of the Namlea Hudsons reading 'Zekes attacking am on fire.' Glancing quickly to the right I saw a ball of flame going down – one of my friends. I thought that 30 seconds would never end."

"Of the five Hudsons from Namlea, Rob Cuming was the only survivor...Later [FltLt M. P.] Maurice Willing had gone

up to Menado on reconnaissance and also never returned," Cornfoot recalled. Two Japanese pilots of the newly arrived 3 *Ku*, FCPO Yoshimi Sasaki and PO2c Shoichi Shoji, flying Mitsubishi A6M2 *Zekes* claimed the Hudsons of Barton and Hodge, while three Nakajima E8N *Dave* seaplanes attacked and downed Gorrie's aircraft. PO2c Takeshi and his observer, FCPO Yoshimaru Kizaki, claimed the 'kill'. Sattler's crew in A16-7 was attacked by two of the seaplanes and both *Zekes*, crashing into the jungle and killing the crew. They were buried by the inhabitants of a small village in the Tonando District.

There was only one survivor from the four aircraft lost that day; FlgOff E. D. G. Howard, the co-pilot in the Hodge crew managed to parachute to safety and evade the Japanese before being captured and interned as a POW for over three years. He was lucky; most others were executed.

FltLt R. W. B. Cuming's crew comprising FlgOffs R. H. Martin and P. H. Richards and Sgt J. Bessell-Browne lasted only another eight days before they and seven passengers heading to reinforce Namlea and Ambon were all killed when their aircraft A16-79 crashed on take off.

January 12 had been a black day for the units, with a loss rate of 80 per cent for the Namlea crews. Those crews lost were "...all experienced Hudson operators and their loss was a bitter blow to squadron morale and operational effectiveness", Bob Dalkin, a Hudson pilot wrote, "...This plus the loss of Willing a week later, confirmed, if any confirmation were needed, that the unescorted Hudson, though a valuable and useful aircraft, was no match against the Japanese Zero and other types of enemy fighter aircraft."

On 11 January the Japanese landed in force in the Celebes and during the following days the Hudsons flew some 30 missions against the Japanese force. "It was a matter of getting back and refuelling... [and] getting out again as fast as you could. There was no room for pattern bombing...or formation [flying]. Targets were anything you could see," recalled Arch Dunne.

Even as the Hudsons, by then operating as a combined unit under WgCdr E. D. Scott at Halong, a flying boat base near Laha, continued harassing an advancing enemy, the airfields at Laha and Namlea were under attack from strafing Japanese fighters. Seven Hudsons were either destroyed or damaged to the extent they were unflyable between 20 and 30 January. Aircraft A16-71, '33, '66, '125, '121 and '123 were caught at Laha while A16-59 was lost at Namlea.

In ten weeks 17 Hudsons were lost including A16-61 and the FlgOff G. G. Mitchell crew on 14 February when their aircraft cashed near Koepang in a severe tropical storm. In all 40 young lives were lost. A further four headquarters staff; WgCdr E. D. Scott, FlgOff H. G. Verey, Cpl F. W. Gaskin and AC.1 F. A. Evans were executed by the Japanese at Laha on 6 February.

By late January 1942 the RAAF position in the NEI was all but untenable. WgCdr J. Ryland had flown to Darwin on the 9th to confer with the RAAF Station Commander regarding the supply of equipment and spares so as to continue operating. However the Japanese were moving rapidly and the aerodromes from which the Hudsons were operating were under constant attack by fighters and bombers flying from their newly occupied bases in the Celebes. Damage to fuel and ground installations weakened the RAAF units even further. It was time to go.

Even then, operations continued. Lloyd Edwards a 13 Squadron Sgt WAG, who had arrived on 24 January was transported to Halong on the evening of the 27th and at dawn next day "...we boarded the Short Sunderland [sic] A18/13 for our return to Darwin to take over a replacement aircraft... we took over A16/68...and immediately resumed our patrol duties the final one...commenced [at] LaHa [sic] 3.40 pm and ended at Namlea 10. pm January 29...It was during this evening that the evacuation of the 13 Squadron ground staff from LaHa [sic] [and] Ambon commenced, the final lift of which was about mid night."

From 20 to 31 January almost all the air and ground crews were taken by Hudsons to Darwin. Though battered and badly in need of repair, the aircraft carried well in excess of the normal crew numbers. The last to go were 2 Squadron ground staff based at Namlea. Lloyd Edwards recalled that, "There were only three aircraft involved...F/Lt Law-Smith was first to take off with about 26 ground staff aboard. He was followed by F/O Finlayson, who, because his aircraft had been damaged...could only take about 16. I was deputed [sic] to ensure all our 21 passengers were stripped down to a pair of shorts and a shirt. We took off at 4.30 am...I believe that the Japanese landed there at 11.0 am [sic] that same morning."

Some stayed behind. Following the demolition of equipment and as much of the base as possible, and the departure of the last three aircraft, SqnLdr McFarlane set out with the remaining officers and airmen heading for the south coast of Buru. After two weeks of heavy going to reach a prearranged rendezvous with a flying boat, they finally made it on 12 February. The Short S23 Empire flying boat, A18-13, flown by FltLt J. M. Hampshire arrived the following day to find the party waiting and flew them to safety. They were lucky as Hampshire had already flown in once. The second trip was a last attempt at rescue.

At Koepang 2 Squadron was also in dire straits. The Japanese were also closing in on Timor and evacuation was undertaken on the evening of 18 February after NWA HQ signalled WgCdr Headlem to withdraw the squadron. There were personnel enough for seven or eight full Hudson loads and four Hudsons departed Darwin for Koepang at 0300 hours to find a rapidly deteriorating situation.

In all six Hudsons departed Koepang at 0330 hours and arrived at Darwin on the morning of the 19th. However, it seems a further evacuation attempt was made. Bob Dalkin wrote that "In the very early hours of the 20th... two Hudsons staged through from Daly Waters to arrive at Koepang at first light, but they were too late...enemy troops were unloading from various vessels, paratroopers had been dropped, there was activity at the airfield and the two aircraft were forced to make a hasty retreat."

As they had at Ambon, some stayed behind. Twenty nine officers and airmen under FltLt Brian Rofe took to the jungle and after making contact with men of the AIF's Sparrow Force, evading the Japanese and facing death and sickness eventually made it to a beach in mid-April. They were rescued on the nights of 17 and 18 April by an American submarine, the *Searaven*.

Again, they were lucky: the day following the Darwin raids of 19 February a mixed 2 and 13 Squadron headquarters group under FltLt W. D. D. White were executed on Ambon by the Japanese. White, SqnLdr J. F. Anderson, FlgOff F. N. Meyer, Sgts I. W. Read and J. Baker, LAC L. D. Walker and AC1 J. A. Harris all died along with 226 members of Gull Force AIF.

The return of the Hudson units to Darwin saw an end to RAAF operations in the NEI and a retraction of forces to the Australian mainland, leaving only the remnants of the AIF's Sparrow and Gull Forces to fight on. Ron Cornfoot doubted that the Hudsons "...delayed the Japanese drive south for more than moments," recalling bitterly that "...losses were terrible in proportion to the numbers of Army and Air Force involved. The Army 'Gull Force' on Ambon virtually had nothing to fight with – no air or sea protection – and were captured to spend years as prisoners...from the R.A.A.F. point of view...we lost about 70% of the original aircraft and crews – precious Hudsons and precious crew members...Empty bunks in our barracks were...very prominent."

Elsewhere the Allies were also on the back foot. The Japanese were advancing rapidly and Japanese air units were by then based in the NEI. In early January 1942, Tokao *Ku* a heavy bomber unit of the 23rd *Koku Sentai* detached 23 Mitsubishi G4M1 *Bettys*, or *Rikko*, to newly captured Jolo Island in the Philippines and commenced operations on the 8th. The unit then moved 33 *Bettys* to Kendari on 1 February, where it joined the *Kanoya* and 1 *Ku*s. Operations commenced on 3 February with a raid on Perak airfield on Surabaya, following which, one *chutai* returned to Kendari whilst two *chutai* of 18 aircraft were detached to Balikpapan. On 18 February, Takao *Ku* attacked shipping in Surabaya harbour and on the 19th Japanese forces landed on Bali.

Fighters were also on the attack with aircraft of the battle-hardened 3 *Ku*, also part of 23 *Koku Sentai* moving from the Philippines as the Japanese advanced. Other units included the Tainan *Ku* and its *Zekes* and Ki-43 *Oscars* of the army's 1st, 11th and 64th *Sentai* scattered from Palembang south during February to the end of the campaign, along with the 59th *Sentai* and its *Oscars*, which remained until mid-1943. The 3 *Ku* had been based at Kendari in the Celebes from 25 January and on the 26th its Mitsubishi A6M2 *Zekes* attacked Timor. The main force moved to Balikpapan on 2 February to prepare for the campaign over eastern Java and the following day 27 *Zekes* along with a further 27 from the Tainan *Ku* met Dutch and American aircraft, claiming 39 of them. More were destroyed on the ground and over 90 Allied aircraft were claimed as destroyed though the figures remain unconfirmed. Following its successes over Java, 3 *Ku* was transferred to Koepang. Both the Takao and 3 *Ku*s were to become regular visitors to Darwin over the coming two years.

On Java meanwhile the newly formed ABDACOM under British commander, Gen Sir Archibald Wavell, and his American army deputy, MajGen George H. Brett, were pinning their hopes on reinforcements to the NEI, and particularly Java, to combat the advancing Japanese. A vital element of the defence of Java was air power, and Darwin, rapidly becoming a more strategically important centre, was a vital link in getting aircraft to the front.

Refuelling a Mitsubishi A6M2 Zeke of the 3 Ku on Timor, February 1942. The nimble Zekes effectively ruled the skies during the first months of the Pacific war. Photo: Bernard Baeza.

The town's importance had been emphasised as early as 22 December 1941, when the US Army's Chief of Staff, Gen George C. Marshall, directed that it be used as an American army and navy base. This followed a report in14 December 1941 by MajGen Dwight D. Eisenhower to Marshall that "...our base must be Australia, and we must start at once to expand it and secure our communications to it. In the last we dare not fail."

Part of the response was the relocation of the 19th Bomb. Gp from the Philippines to Batchelor in December 1941. With only a handful of bases remaining for operations the situation was becoming desperate, "I decided to request authority to remove the remainder of the bombers to Darwin...with the intention of operating from the two fields there, using Del Monte and Clark as advance bases," Brereton wrote. "General Sutherland approved the plan... not as a withdrawal of forces but to facilitate maintenance in order that the remaining planes might be used to the best advantage." MacArthur immediately agreed with the plan and while only 14 B-17s survived by 20 December they were withdrawn to Batchelor.

Two bombing missions were flown from Batchelor on the 22nd and on Christmas Day, with two aircraft lost on the mission of the 25th. The mission of the 22nd was the first flown against the Japanese from Australian soil with nine serviceable aircraft of the 93rd Squadron taking off at 1045 hours bound for the Gulf of Davao where they were to bomb

DESPERATE TIMES

seven Japanese ships. Each dropped its four 227 kg bombs but an overcast sky prevented any damage assessment.

The following day they were to bomb the Japanese landings in the Lingayen Gulf on Luzon. By take off time from Del Monte only six aircraft had been fuelled and armed. Shortly after take off the lead aircraft, 40-3062, developed engine trouble and Lt Parsel in 40-3074 took over. Another aircraft, 40-3067, had to abort with engine trouble and flew directly back to Batchelor. With Maj Combs and Lt Coats out of the mission, only four aircraft made the target and again cloud prevented an assessment of the results. The remaining three took off some time later and bombed Davao with mixed results before flying back to Batchelor. All nine B-17s had returned to Batchelor by the evening of the 23rd, after an absence of over 30 hours, some having flown 25 hours of that time. All crews were awarded the American Silver Star.

Another mission was flown from Batchelor on Christmas Day with the aircraft staging through Del Monte prior to attacking Japanese forces. Two aircraft were lost when Japanese fighters intercepted them over Davao, killing Sgt James Cannon a crewman aboard Lt Schaetzell's aircraft, 40-3062, and wounding Sgt Spaziano. Two others in Lt Mueller's 40-2072 were wounded. Cannon was buried in Grave 112 the following day at Darwin's Gardens Cemetery. Seven days later 12 of the Group's B-17s were ordered to Java and along with elements of the 7th Bomb. Gp, a mixed unit of B-17s and Consolidated LB-30s, engaged in futile missions in an attempt to stall the Japanese. By 1 March it was obvious the Japanese could not be stopped and the 19th was again on the move back to Australia. Of the 12 aircraft flown to Java only three returned and one of those was destroyed in a landing accident.

Despite these early missions by the Americans, reinforcements for Australia's forces, and ABDACOM, were slow in coming. For some time Australia had been agitating for reinforcements in the face of the Japanese advances. In mid-December the Australian Prime Minister, John Curtin, was advised by the US representative to Australia that the arrival of American troops by convoy was imminent. What was not mentioned was that the arrival was more one of expediency. The convoy had been diverted from the Philippines and the cargo and personnel were destined for the campaign on Java. But they were reinforcements nonetheless.

On 22 December, the day of Marshall's directive, the USS *Pensacola* convoy docked in Brisbane. Aboard the ships in the convoy, the *Holbrook*, *Meigs* and *Admiral Halstead*, were some 2,600 USAAC personnel including 48 pilots, the 147th and 148th Field Artillery Regiments, elements of the 7th Bomb. Gp and Gen Chennault's AVG *en route* to China. Eighteen P-40E fighters, 52 Douglas A-24s assigned to the 27th Bomb. Gp (Light), seven million rounds of .50" ammunition, 5,000 bombs, general purpose weapons and several thousand drums of aviation fuels and oils made up the manifest. Pilots, observers and ground crews of the 27th Bomb. Gp were awaiting the arrival of the A-24s in the Philippines as was the 34th Pursuit Squadron at Del Carmen Field, which was to replace its Seversky P-35s with the P-40s. They never arrived and the men were used as ground troops during the ill-fated campaign to hold the line.

Boeing B-17E, 41-2452 of the 19th Bomb. Group USAAF. A Java veteran it was involved in the first attempt at evacuating Gen Douglas MacArthur on 12 March 1942. Photo: Charles Schaedel.

The *Holbrook* sailed shortly after, bound for the Philippines with the 147th and 148th Regiments aboard, however Brett followed up Marshall's directive and diverted the vessel to Darwin, where she arrived on 5 January. Meanwhile the A-24 and P-40E aircraft in Brisbane were transported to an assembly depot at RAAF base Amberley where American and Australian mechanics uncrated and assembled them for test flying. By 12 January 15 of the P-40Es were ready for combat and were assigned to a newly designated 17th Pursuit Squadron (Provisional), with some pilots joining up after evacuation from the Philippines.

Assembly of the A-24s did not proceed so smoothly however. During assembly it was discovered that important components were missing, including trigger motors,

DESPERATE TIMES

A Douglas A-24 of the 27th Bomb. Group USAAF en route to Darwin, February 1942. The type was not a success in the Darwin area. Photo: Via Ted Ezzy.

solenoids, gun mounts and self sealing fuel tanks – all integral parts for an aircraft going into combat. Despite searches the items could not be located and the Group Armament Officer, Lt 'Zeke' Summers became more frustrated. The Group CO, Maj John H. Davies, suggested that those "…Americans responsible should be subject to trial for criminal negligence."

A number of the missing parts were manufactured locally and by 23 January enough aircraft and pilots were considered ready to be organised into combat squadrons. From the available aircraft and personnel the 91st under Capt Ed Backus, the 16th under Capt Floyd W. 'Buck' Rogers and the 17th under Capt Herman F. Lowery were formed. The 91st departed for Darwin on 4 February, flying via the 'Brereton Route'. From Darwin they flew on to Koepang in groups, three on the 9th and the remainder on the 11th of the month. The first three were met by small arms fire by 2 Squadron personnel. Damage to pride was more than that to aircraft and repairs were effected during the night to allow the flight to Java.

The other two squadrons were not far behind. Aircraft of the 16th Squadron departed for Darwin on 13 February, and it was on the Cloncurry-Daly Waters leg that they ran into trouble. On the morning of the 15th Constable Jack Stokes had completed his normal patrol around the Maranboy tinfields between Katherine and Mataranka when he spotted nine aircraft circling the police station residence before flying off. A telephone call informed him that the aircraft had all made emergency landings at the Maranboy airstrip, 11 km away.

Enlisting the help of local identity Ted 'Cowboy' Collins they drove towards the railway and airstrip and found one A-24 on its nose after hitting a tree stump. None of the other crews were injured and the aircraft were relatively undamaged. They had missed Daly Waters and low on fuel had landed on the tiny airstrip. Following minor repairs and hand refuelling they headed off for Katherine and on to Batchelor where they landed on 18 February. Meanwhile the aircraft of the 17th Squadron were at Daly Waters waiting to fly on to Darwin and Koepang.

On arrival at Batchelor on 18 February GpCapt Scherger denied the 16th permission to fly on in light of the probability of an attack on Darwin in the very near future. It was a wise decision. The 17th cooled its heels at Daly Waters before

DESPERATE TIMES

flying to Batchelor on the 21st where it joined the 16th and 12 Squadron RAAF in flying patrols.

The Provisional squadrons equipped with the P-40s were also headed north, though their destination was the Philippines. Between 12 January and 2 February 173 P-40Es had been delivered by convoys, unloaded, uncrated and assembled ready for assignment to the new Provisional squadrons being formed. The *Polk* arrived on 12 January with 55 aircraft. The SS *Mormac Sun* brought 67, the *Mariposa* 19 and *Coolidge* 32.

The first of the new Provisional Squadrons was the 17th. On 14 January Maj Charles A. Sprague was "...instructed to organise the 17th Pursuit Squadron (Provisional) with 17 P-40E type airplanes, 17 Pilots, 17 Crew chiefs, 17 Armourers, 1 Line Chief and First Sergeant, and three Radiomen", the unit diarist recorded.

Two days later the unit was ready to leave for the Philippines. However, the air route had been severed and instead they were deployed to Java and ABDACOM. They departed in two groups the following day with Sprague leading under escort of a Beechcraft flown by Capt 'Pappy' Gunn and the second led by Capt Walter Coss under escort by a RAAF Fairey Battle. Two didn't make it out of Queensland. At Rockhampton Lt Carl Giess ground looped in 40-667 after landing without flaps, while Lt Bryan Brown's landing gear collapsed on landing at Cloncurry, damaging 40-663. A third, 41-5334 flown by Lt Kruzel also had its landing gear collapse after a training flight at Darwin. The remaining 14 aircraft left for Java on 26 January, leaving Kruzel's aircraft at Darwin while he took that of Lt Irwin who was ill. On arrival at Java they came under ABDACOM control.

Next came the 20th Pursuit Squadron (Provisional) under Capt William Lane Jr. Twenty five aircraft departed Brisbane under escort by a B-24A, 40-2374, on 20 January and lost two *en route*; one flown by Lt Bernard Oliver scraped a wing on landing at Cloncurry and was left there. Lieutenant Allison W. Strauss flew a replacement to Darwin and two flights left Darwin on 4 February. The first flight lost eight aircraft when they were intercepted over Koepang, and the second flight of ten aircraft lost one on landing at Lombok. Only 15 made it to Java.

The last to fly the route via Darwin was the 3rd Squadron (Provisional). Commanded by Capt Grant Mahoney, the unit was hastily manned by what veterans of the Philippines remained with most being inexperienced pilots from the USA. The unit departed for Darwin on 6 February with 25 aircraft, losing two *en route* at Daly Waters and three more damaged at Darwin. When the 3rd left for Java two pilots and aircraft remained; Lt Robert J. Buel and his aircraft '54' and Lt Robert Oestreicher. They were to fly on once expected reinforcements arrived; they never came and the two remained at Darwin.

Only eight aircraft of the 3rd eventually reached their destination. Of the first flight, eight pilots, low on fuel and lost, crashed or baled out along the Timor coast. Seven were picked up by the RAAF and one was killed. The other flight of nine aircraft reached Java, but the losses caused a major rethink on ferrying fighters by air. In the event the Japanese solved the problem for them. They invaded Timor on 19 and 20 February and the route was severed. ABDACOM's future looked very tenuous indeed.

The ferry flights sent pilots and aircraft to a lost cause. While the three provisional squadrons, the A-24s of the 27th Bomb. Gp, B-17s, B-24As and LB-30s of the 19th and 7th Bomb. Gps flew what missions they could in battered aircraft under primitive conditions and in a rapidly deteriorating situation, they provided at least some resistance to a confident enemy in attempting to hold the Malay Barrier. In effect they were able to achieve little more than a stalling action, as did the Dutch in their obsolete Brewster Buffalos, Curtiss Wright CW-22 fighters, Douglas B-18 and Glenn Martin bombers.

The British and Commonwealth Squadrons including RAAF and RNZAF units were also badly depleted and when Singapore inevitably fell on 15 February 1942, despite Churchill's duplicity in continually maintaining its impregnability, ABDACOM was all but finished. Wavell closed his headquarters on 25 February and went to India with Brereton, effectively ending ABDACOM's futile campaign, though it lingered on before it formally came to an end when the Dutch surrendered on 9 March.

Evacuations of ground personnel commenced on 20 January, followed by what air echelons remained on the 26th. At 0300 hours on 2 March Lt Kelsay flew the last USAAF aircraft, an LB-30 AL515 with 38 men, the remnants of the 7th Bomb. Gp, from Java. Their destination was Broome in Western Australia.

DESPERATE TIMES

Meanwhile in the Darwin area, 12 Squadron had deployed to Daly Waters on 5 February in accordance with Operation Instruction 16/42. Two days later they were again on the move, with 'A' Fight ordered back to the Darwin Civil 'Drome, 'B' Flight to the RAAF Station and 'C' Flight to Batchelor where it joined the B-17s of the 19th Bomb. Gp, and two weeks later, the A-24s of the 27th Bomb. Gp.

Boeing B-17E serial 41-2497, Tojo's Nightmare, served in Java with the 19th Bomb. Group and later with the 43rd Bomb. Group. It is seen here at Daly Waters in mid-1942. Photo: AHSNT.

Six hundred kilometres south of Darwin the pre-war civil aerodrome at Daly Waters was transformed into an operational base during February 1942 and on 15 March became RAAF Station Daly Waters, before becoming 56 OBU, one of nine such units in the NWA. First developed in 1929 by Larkin Aircraft Company as a terminus for the Birdum-Daly Waters air mail run, Daly Waters later became an unlikely international hub as passenger aircraft from interstate and overseas staged through the tiny settlement – much to the delight of the pub owner, Bill Pearce who refuelled both aircraft and passengers.

An advance party of 13 Squadron personnel had moved into the airfield on 4 and 6 February, followed two days later by what remained of 2 Squadron's 'A' and 'B' Flights, a RAAF maintenance party and 'A' and 'C' Flights of 13 Squadron. A squadron servicing party also arrived to undertake all Hudson servicings in the NWA in conjunction with 2 Squadron personnel.

In Darwin itself, those who remained were expecting a raid. Fortunately most had been evacuated following a 10 December 1941 notice in the *Northern Standard* advising citizens that "The Federal War Cabinet has decided that women and children must be compulsorily evacuated from Darwin as soon as possible, except women required for essential services. Arrangements have been completed and the first party will leave within the next 48 hours...Darwin citizens will greatly assist the war effort by cheerfully carrying out all requests..."

According to many who made the trip, being cheerful was very difficult indeed, particularly in having to contend with the heat and very poor conditions aboard a number of the ships employed in the evacuations, which were mostly coastal steamers. But, despite being torn from family and home, they would at least be safe for the duration of the war.

During the period 19 December 1941 to 15 February 1942, 1,414 people were evacuated by sea. The *Koolinda* took 225 on 19 December, the *Zealandia* 530 the following day and *President Grant* left with 222 aboard on the 23rd. On 10 January the *Montoro* took 187, followed on the 26th by *Koolama* with 173. The *Koolinda* took the last 77 on 15 February, the day Singapore fell.

Evacuees from Darwin aboard the President Grant, December 1941. By February 1942 only 63 females involved in essential duties remained in Darwin. Photo: Barbara James.

Others went by air, road and rail; a Guinea Airways Lockheed 10 flew the last out on the evening of the 18th. Darwin had been reduced to just over 2,000 people, 63 of whom were women employed in essential duties.

Enemy air activity was also increasing in the region. There had been at least two alerts in Darwin, one on 28 January when an unidentified aircraft was picked up by searchlights and another on 8 February due to intense air activity over Timor. The Japanese were also moving forces towards Timor, planning to attack the island on 20 February.

DESPERATE TIMES

Darwin's role in the conflict escalated dramatically on 9 February when Vice Admiral Kondo Nobutake, Southern Area Fleet Commander, relayed Secret Telegraphic Order No. 92 from Rear Admiral Isoroku Yamamoto to Vice Admiral Chu'ichi Nagumo, commander of the 1st and 2nd Carrier Divisions, *Dai 1* and *Dai 2 Koku Sentai* of the Mobile Fleet, the same force that had attacked Pearl Harbor only weeks previously:

"...Owing to our air attacks at the beginning of February, the enemy, with its main base in Java, lost most of its naval and air strength...it appears that a part of the enemy strength is already taking refuge in the vicinity of Port Darwin. Intelligence shows that part of the U.S. air reinforcements, together with British and Australian forces are based there. At an opportune time the carrier task forces will conduct mobile warfare...endeavouring to annihilate the enemy strength in the Port Darwin area and to intercept and destroy enemy naval and transport fleets, at the same time attacking enemy strength in the Java Sea area from behind. For the surprise attack on Port Darwin on February 19, the task force will advance to the Arafura Sea..."

The following day a Mitsubishi C5M2 *Babs* of 3 *Ku* took off from base 333 (Ambon) at 1020 hours to carry out a reconnaissance of Port Darwin. Flown by PO3c Takahashi Takeshi with his Observer, PO1c, Yoshimaru Kizaki, the aircraft carried out its mission over Darwin between 1335 and 1400 hours before conducting a similar exercise over Bathurst Island. Landing back at Ambon at 1710 hours, the crew reported that they had spotted three aircraft in the air and seven on the ground, whilst some 18 ships were in the harbour. For those remaining in Darwin, it was now a matter of when and not if, an attack was to take place.

Camouflaged Wirraways of 12 Squadron prepare to fly out on a patrol from the Darwin Civil 'Drome, 1941. Photo: Alford/AHSNT.

There were no modern aircraft in Darwin in the lead up to the raids and those aircraft that were there at all were not capable of combat, comprising only obsolescent Wirraways and some of the battered Hudson bombers of 2 and 13 Squadrons following their withdrawal from the NEI.

It was only in the few days leading up to the raids that any fighter defence was at Darwin and even that was a result of changing circumstances and "...a typical army *snafu*," according to one of the American pilots, John Glover. Two P-40Es provided the sole fighter defence to the 15th of the month. These were the aircraft left behind by the 3rd Pursuit Squadron (Provisional) and their pilots, Lts Robert J 'Blackie' Buel and Robert G. Oestreicher.

P-40Es of 'B' Flight 13th Pursuit Squadron (Provisional) at Richmond RAAF Base on 13 February 1942 during the flight to join the USS Langley heading for Java. The Langley was sunk by Japanese aircraft on the 27th. Photo: Rick Hanning.

The 13th and 33rd Pursuit Squadrons (Provisional) had been ordered to join up with the USS *Langley* convoy at Fremantle in Western Australia by General Barnes on 10 February. They were the last of the provisional squadrons to form, with P-40Es landed from the USAT *Monroe* on 30 January. The 33rd Squadron under Maj Floyd 'Slugger' Pell, no stranger to Australia and the north, staged through RAAF bases during the flight from Brisbane, passing through Richmond in NSW before flying on to 3 Bombing and Gunnery School at West Sale in Victoria. Locals also recalled a number landing on the Princes Highway as they ran short of fuel.

The short hop to Laverton was little better. Only three landed there whilst eleven went on to Point Cook. Another, Lt Charles Hughes in aircraft '94' force, landed at Point Cook short of fuel some time later. Continuing on, the squadron got as far as Port Pirie before being ordered north

DESPERATE TIMES

to Darwin, with the intention of deploying it to Timor at a later date. In the meantime Pell was to provide fighter protection for Darwin and Java bound convoys.

Accidents *en route* depleted the unit. Lieutenant Richard Pingree was forced to remain at Port Pirie to await repairs but crashed in 41-5366 shortly after take off and was killed the day the Japanese attacked Darwin. Another, Lt Bryce Wilhite, was also forced to remain at Port Pirie with an unserviceable aircraft before returning to Amberley via Laverton. Staging through Oodnadatta, Alice Springs and Daly Waters, the unit lost more aircraft. Lieutenant Jess Dore had a flat tyre at Alice Springs and Lt David Latane also remained at the central Australian base while the remainder flew on. Lieutenant Bob McMahon hit a grader on the strip during take off at Daly Waters damaging the undercarriage on 41-4376, but elected to fly on to Darwin.

Lieutenant Richard Suehr was forced to put his aircraft down approximately 60 kilometres south of Darwin near the Marrakai Track. Alerted by Lt McMahon, the RAAF Station despatched a Douglas A-24 of the 27th Bomb. Gp, which dropped tinned food and supplies to Suehr. The first night he slept on the wing of his P-40, before heading north. After walking for some ten days, swimming a large river and finally locating the railway line he was picked up by train and taken to Darwin. His aircraft was later salvaged by the 43rd AMS based at Adelaide River. Suehr was lucky; he had missed the decimation of his squadron four days after his forced landing.

CHAPTER 3

19 FEBRUARY 1942
The first raids – Australia under attack

On 15 February 1942 Pell flew his depleted force into Darwin only to find the *Houston* convoy, for which he was to provide fighter cover, had sailed for Timor. On board the eight ships, four of which were cargo vessels, were the US Army's 148th Field Artillery Regt, the Australian 2/4 Pioneers, and AIF anti-tank troop and a number of specialist units along with their equipment and explosives.

Pell also found a P-40 and its pilot at the RAAF Station; Lt Robert Oestreicher reported that he had been out trying to locate the convoy and his fellow pilot, Lt 'Blackie' Buel.

Buel had been ordered out to intercept a Kawanishi H6K *Mavis* flying boat that had been reported shadowing the convoy. The USS *Houston* had broken radio silence at 0215Z hours to report the intruder. The enemy aircraft, flown by Sub Lt Mirau, continued shadowing the convoy for a further three hours at 13,000 ft before dropping a number of 60 kg bombs at 0448Z hours and turning for the 21st *Koku Sentai* base at Ceram.

With Oestreicher on patrol and out of contact, due presumably to the short range of the radio sets, the USAAF Operations Officer Lt Hewitt 'Shorty' Wheless, a 19th Bomb. Gp pilot, ordered Buel out to intercept. That was the last Buel and his P-40E '54' were seen but for those in the convoy as he flew over to intercept the *Mavis*. Buel located the flying boat and attacked it from astern only to be met by 20mm cannon fire from the navigator, Lt Marekuni Takahara, who expended a drum of 50 rounds. Both aircraft were hit and Buel plunged into the sea, while the flying boat had caught fire and was also headed for the water, its pilot and radio operator dead.

Takahara recalled the mission that was "...to find any convoy that might be leaving Darwin to reinforce Timor. Five flying boats, based in Ceram, took part in the reconnaissance...a convoy was discovered by our crew...at 1030. This was reported by radio and we were told to keep the vessels in sight...Our fuel eventually began to run low and we had to head for home, but before departing 60 kg bombs were released. Vigorous anti-aircraft fire was returned from the ships but we [were] unharmed. Relaxing after this...the crew were just about to have lunch when a single-engined fighter...approached. All the crew rushed to their posts and I...manned the 20mm cannon in the tail..."

The flying boat hit the water and Takahara recalled six crew members including himself, Amamoto, Okimoto and Sichishima escaped the wreckage though Sichishima died of his injuries two days later. They landed on Melville Island and spent two weeks foraging before being captured and sent across to Bathurst Island Mission. Following interrogation and medical attention at Adelaide River they were taken to Cowra POW camp in New South Wales where another navy pilot, Hajime Toyashima, was interned under the alias Tadao Minami.

The last known photo of Lt Robert 'Blackie' Buel's P-40E, No. 54, before he was lost attacking a Japanese Kawanishi H6K flying boat on 15 February 1942. Photo: Ken Tinkler.

The following day the *Houston* convoy was attacked by a flight of Japanese bombers, however they were repelled by anti-aircraft fire. Despite the Japanese reporting damage to three transports, the convoy remained intact, however ABDACOM ordered it back to Darwin in light of the risk in continuing on.

At Darwin, a C-39 transport aircraft with ground crews had arrived on the 16th. The mechanics and pilots carried out repairs and servicings on the P-40s in readiness for the trip to Timor, even as Pell put up patrols. Aircraft left behind by other units were cannibalised for spares or restored to flying condition. Lieutenant Bob McMahon's P-40 was a write off following his incident at Daly Waters and a second aircraft, 41-5376 *Barhootie the Cootie II/'Mac'*, fared no better when it was damaged in a landing accident. He managed to get a third aircraft serviceable, however Major Pell's aircraft, tail number '3', was not so obliging: it remained unserviceable with a coolant leak.

On the 18th Pell briefed the pilots, advising them that they were to depart for Java the following day at dawn.

That evening the convoy entered Darwin harbour and anchored. Both the *Houston* and USS *Peary,* an old four-stacker destroyer, departed almost immediately heading for Tjilatjap. *Peary* returned early on the 19th after having burned up fuel chasing a possible submarine contact.

The harbour was full of ships, some 47 in all, ranging from the 34.5 tonne RAN motor boat *Coongala* to the 12,770 tonne USAT *Meigs*, an American transport vessel. Most were carrying military equipment and explosives. The RAAF Station was also becoming crowded. On 18 February, an LB30 AL521, assigned to the 7th Bomb. Gp in the ill-fated Java campaign flew into Darwin with BrigGen Patrick Hurley aboard on his way to USAFIA HQ in Melbourne. The aircraft was captained by 1st Lt C. B. Kelsay, with Lt Laubscher as co-pilot.

A number of RAAF Hudsons, the P-40Es of Pell's 33rd Pursuit Squadron, a B-17E, 41-2417, *San Antonio Rose II*

of the 7th Bomb. Gp, the LB30, at least two C-39 transports, and three 'hangar queens' – aircraft under repair - including the A-24 of Capt Floyd 'Buck' Rogers and two P-40s, plus two of McMahon's wrecked P-40s out on the airfield were all at the base. When the 2 Squadron Hudsons flew in from Koepang early on the 19th the numbers swelled further.

Lieutenant Robert McMahon's second attempt at getting a serviceable P-40E, *Barhootie the Cootie II/"Mac"*, failed when he hit obstacles during landing. Photo: A. H. McEgan.

In the early morning hours of 19 February Adm Nagumo's two Carrier Divisions had reached an arranged launch point some 350 km north west of Darwin. A weather reconnaissance aircraft was sent up at dawn and it arrived over Darwin at around 0730 hours. Despite apparently being able to send, the radio was unserviceable and no report was received by Nagumo. The day was clear however and Nagumo ordered the strike.

The flight crews and their aircraft were ready for the mission. From before dawn the mechanics on board the carriers *Akagi* and *Kaga* of the 1st Carrier Division and *Hiryu* and *Soryu* of the 2nd Carrier Division had been arming the aircraft, running engines, topping up fuel tanks and carrying out last minute checks. The pilots and crews had been briefed by Capt Minoru Genda, the Pearl Harbor and Darwin operations' architect, and Cdr Mitsuo Fuchida the attack leader. By 0845 hours 19 February 1942 the force of 36 Mitsubishi A6M2 *Zekes*, 71 Aichi D3A1 *Val* dive bombers and 81 Nakajima B5N1 *Kate* level bombers were ready to be launched and seven minutes later the order was signalled.

Fuchida led his 18 *Kates* from *Akagi* while Lt Heijiro Abe led another 18 from the *Soryu*. Eighteen more under LtCdr Tadashi Kosumi launched from the *Hiryu* and the last 27,

19 FEBRUARY 1942

led by LtCdr Takashi Hashiguchi, lumbered into the air from the *Kaga*. An escort of 18 *Zekes* in two flights of nine aircraft launched from the *Soryu* and *Hiryu*, led by Lts Iyozo Fujita and Sumio Nono respectively.

Next went the *Val* dive bombers; eighteen each flew off the *Soryu*, *Akagi* and *Kaga*, led by LtCdr Takashige Egusa and Lts Takehiko Chihaya and Shoichi Ogawa while the last 17 under Lt Michio Kobayashi departed the *Hiryu*. Their fighter escort comprised two flights of 9 *Zekes* from the *Kaga* and *Akagi* under Lt Yasushi Nikaido and LtCdr Shigeru Itaya.

Fuchida set a course of 148 degrees and the force headed for Darwin.

At much the same time a land based bomber force was preparing to depart bases at Ambon and Kendari to follow up the attacks by the carrier-borne force. Twenty seven Mitsubishi G4M1 *Bettys* of the Kanoya *Ku*, 23rd *Koku Sentai* at Kendari were to be led by LtCdr Toshiie Irisa, whilst LtCdr Takeo Ozaki was to lead his force of 27 Mitsubishi G3M1 *Nells* of the 1 *Ku*, 23rd *Koku Sentai* on Ambon. The Kanoya *Ku* departed at 0635 hours, followed five minutes later by the 1 *Ku* and headed for Darwin.

The first casualty that day was a PBY-5 Catalina, Bu No. 2306 of the USN's Patwing 22. Flown by Lt Thomas Moorer and his crew on aircraft 22-P-18, the lumbering PBY was clearing the north western tip of Bathurst Island when nine *Zekes* attacked. Flyer 1c Yoshikazu Nagahama led the attack, setting "...my plane afire, destroying [the] port engine and putting large holes in fuel tanks and fuselage" Moorer reported, "...I endeavoured to turn into the wind but all fabric except starboard aileron was destroyed and it was discovered that with one engine and all fabric missing from port side an indicated speed of 110 knots was necessary...to keep the plane straight and level. There was no alternative but to land...and this was rendered even more hazardous [in] that the float mechanism had been destroyed by gunfire... At this time I glanced back and observed large streams of fuel pouring from both tanks and the fire extending along port side. Small balls of fire were bouncing around and noise caused by bullets striking the plane was terrific."

Moorer landed, striking "...the water at a great force but after bouncing three times managed to complete the landing." The crew quickly abandoned the flying boat but

were prevented in inflating their two life rafts by burning fuel. They waited until the attacking *Zekes* flew off, inflated the rafts and set off for Bathurst Island. They were later picked up by the Filipino blockade runner, the *Florence D*, which was in turn attacked and sunk. Moorer, his crew, less AMM2c J. C. Schuler, who it was assumed had been killed when the *Florence D* was bombed, and the remaining crew of *Florence D* were later rescued and returned to Darwin.

The second casualty was a Douglas C-53 of the USAAF's 22nd Transport Squadron, strafed as it sat on the Bathurst Island airstrip adjacent to the mission. Six *Zekes* from the *Hiryu* had split from the main force to silence any messages from the mission warning of their course to Darwin and strafe targets of opportunity.

They were too late. Father John McGrath had made his way to the radio shack and transmitted on frequency 6840 to the coastal radio station, VID. Lou Curnock, the operator, logged McGrath's message: "0935 hours 8SE (Bathurst Island) to V.I.D. (Darwin Radio) Huge flight of planes passed overhead bound Darwin." "Roger," Curnock replied, "Roger stand by." Curnock telephoned RAAF operations and reported the message, logging it "phoned to R.A.A.F." He then tried to re-establish contact with Bathurst Island but it was off the air, seemingly jammed by the Japanese. The message to RAAF operations apparently went no further.

At around 0938 hours Pell was back over Darwin after having departed for Timor at 0915 hours with the 19th Bomb. Gp B-17 navigation aircraft *San Antonio Rose II* flown by Lt Clarence L. McPherson. Pell was flying Lt Robert Vaught's aircraft '28' after commandeering it and ordering the Lieutenant back to Brisbane to join up with another unit. Some minutes into the flight deteriorating weather over Koepang threatened to bar their way and Capt Louis J. Connally a USAAF operations officer and 19th Bomb. Gp pilot advised Pell to return to Darwin while the B-17 continued on.

Meanwhile Fuchida's force crossed the coast near Koolpinyah east of Darwin at 0945 hours before turning to the northwest over Noonamah on the run in to Darwin. At 0955 hours the formation approached from the southeast and still there was no alarm. Three minutes later the first bombs were released on Australian soil.

19 FEBRUARY 1942

The only viable defence at Darwin was Pell's force. When the P-40s arrived over Darwin Pell left aircraft to provide top cover. Oestreicher later reported that five 'B' Flight remained aloft while Pell led his 'A' Flight to the RAAF Station to refuel and Bob McMahon recalled that they had "...been airborne for 23 minutes plus 5 minutes taxi time – we'd mucked around a 'bit long' for me...I intended to pitch off on our next circuit back toward the field – when Pell pitched off to the Left and headed down – the rest (4 Aircraft then followed) standard operational procedure was for the 2nd flight to orbit...until the 1st was parked, to avoid being jumped in the landing pattern."

The remains of the P-40E, tail number 28, Maj Floyd J. Pell was flying when he was killed on 19 February 1942. Photo: Shane Johnston.

The first warning of enemy aircraft came when, according to Oestreicher, he spotted the attacking *Zekes* and shouted a warning to his flight. Two of the Americans were shot down in quick succession with one of the pilots killed. Japanese pilot, Flyer 1c Yoshikazu Nagahama, who had proceeded independently after downing Moorer's PBY, downed Lt Elton Perry, and followed by Lt Max Wiecks, who baled out some 16 km out to sea. Over many hours he drifted to shore where he spent an uncomfortable night in mangroves before walking into an Australian camp and being taken in by Australian soldiers.

Perry was the first airman downed over Australia and his death was witnessed by personnel of the 2/14th Australian Field Regiment at Nightcliff. However, as the unit diarist reported "...the first plane to be shot down, a US Kittyhawk, was observed by members of the Regiment, but it took some time to convince Headquarters...that the event had occurred."

Bob McMahon had parked three bays from the southern end of the north-south runway and was writing up his aircraft's technical status when "a crewman ran out and yelled the Japs are here!, then ran back to his slit trench. I called him back and asked him how he knew...at that time a Bren Gun Carrier...came up with Peres on it. He jumped off and ran toward me pointing up (his chute on)...He jumped back onto the carrier and rattled off..."

Even as the Japanese struck, Pell attempted to lead his flight into the air but was attacked almost immediately by a *Zeke* and died after parachuting from his aircraft at only 24 metres. Warrant Officer Leon Bushby of the 19th MG Bn was at Camerons Beach when he saw a lone aircraft at low level with two others above and then heard the sound of gunfire, followed by an aircraft hitting the ground. The pilot's parachute hadn't had time to open when he hit the ground and was dead when Bushby arrived. A small book in the chest pocket of the dead airman read, 'Floyd Joaquim Pell USAAC.'

A keen illustrator, Lt Bob McMahon sketched his attack on a Nakajima B5N2 bomber attacking the US Navy PBY-5 Catalinas on Darwin harbour, 19 February 1942. Image: Bob McMahon.

Lieutenant Charles Hughes followed Pell and was killed even before he gained flight speed, crashing just north of the RAAF Station. Lieutenants Robert McMahon, Jack Peres, Burt Rice and John Glover succeeded in becoming airborne but were attacked immediately by enemy fighters.

Peres' aircraft, 41-5368 '189' and his remains were located in September that year, near Gunn Point, still in his aircraft and identified by his engraved watch. Perry has yet to be located, and whilst parts of Hughes' aircraft were found during roadworks in the mid-1960s, his remains have yet to be located. Lieutenant Walker, another member of the first flight was wounded, but managed to land at the RAAF Station, narrowly missing Lt McMahon as he was 'scrambling'; only to see his aircraft strafed and burnt shortly afterwards as Lt Vaught was preparing to take it into combat.

Rice parachuted from his stricken aircraft and was protected from Japanese aircraft strafing him by Glover. He landed safely in swampy country on the eastern side of the Howard River in Shoal Bay. Glover's aircraft, 41-5456 '36', was damaged in combat whilst protecting Rice and he crashed on the RAAF Station suffering facial injuries, though he claimed one Japanese aircraft.

Anti-aircraft defences were scattered around Darwin. These 3.7-inch A-A guns of the 14th A-A Battery were sited at the Oval on Darwin's Esplanade. Photo: Alford/AHSNT Colln.

Believed to be Lt Robert Oestreicher's P-40E at the RAAF Station on the afternoon of 19 February 1942. Photo: Bill Bartsch.

McMahon was able to stay in the air long enough to attack a *Kate* strafing three US Navy Patwing 10 Catalina flying boats before having to bale out of his burning aircraft. He parachuted to safety and was picked up in a creek on the western side of Darwin harbour by some mechanics of the US Navy's Patwing 10. On the harbour Seamen Ed Aeschliman and Tom Anderson were on a scaffold working on the port engine of Catalina 10-P-41, next to two other PBYs when the Japanese struck. Both dived into the water as *Zekes* began strafing the flying boats. Another seaman Herb Casey took to a raft and got the others aboard but it was attacked and overturned.

Aeschliman made it to some mangroves and watched a P-40 pilot parachute into a grove some distance away. A few moments later a whaleboat from the American seaplane tender, *William B. Preston*, picked them up. After searching they found "...1st Lieutenant Robert F. McMahon, still in his parachute, hanging from a mango tree. McMahon had been shot in the leg, and though conscious, was unable to free himself." McMahon was cut down and taken to 119 AGH at Berrimah where he joined the surviving 33rd Pursuit Squadron pilots.

Glover and McMahon identified Pell's body when it was brought to the facility that afternoon, whilst one of Glover's two watches was returned to him by an Australian nurse after being found in the wreckage of his aircraft.

Oestreicher reported that he remained in the air and "...after flying among the clouds for about half an hour I spotted two Series 97 dive bombers...heading for Batchelor airfield. Intercepting them at about fifteen hundred feet I fired and saw one definitely burst into flames and go down. The other was smoking slightly as he headed for the clouds...At approximately 11:45 I landed at the RAAF Field with my left tire [sic] and wheel shot up...Later...a report came through that a coast artillery battery had located both planes within a mile of each other. These were the first confirmed aerial victories on Australian soil." Despite Oestreicher being awarded the two enemy aircraft as destroyed, research has disproved both.

On the Airfield and in the town, the Japanese had created havoc. In just over forty minutes they had inflicted heavy damage, even in the face of heavy anti-aircraft fire from the batteries of the 14th and 2nd A-A Btys at the Oval, Fannie Bay, McMillans and Coonawarra, along with small arms fire from strategic points around the town. Machine gunners of the 19th MG Regt perched on the oil tanks put their lives at risk to keep up the defensive fire, while HMAS *Katoomba*, captive in the floating dock, put up an intense barrage. Troops at the Stuart Park and Winnellie camps and at scattered sites around Darwin fired on the attackers with whatever was available including WWI vintage Hotchkiss machine guns, .303" rifles and side arms.

19 FEBRUARY 1942

The Japanese crews were intent on their mission to eliminate Darwin and its port as an Allied base. Lt Takayoshi Morinaga, a graduate of the Yokaren Military School and a veteran of bombing raids over China in 1937 and the attack on Pearl Harbor was an observer in a *Kate* over Darwin. He recalled that he was carrying "...an 800 kg bomb...I was told to drop it on military headquarters and government buildings...I picked a building, dropped the bomb and saw a huge explosion." SubLt Sadao Yamamoto, also an observer in a *Kate* from the carrier *Soryu* bombed a "huge white and round shaped structure. I judged it to be one of the military barracks." Another, *Kate* pilot Tekeshi Maeda, remembered the excitement of the damage inflicted on Pearl Harbor and "After that, I'm sorry to say I had to attack Darwin. It was a simple mission. I dropped bombs and then I went home."

The remains of Roy Edwards' de Havilland Puss Moth, VH-UPN, lie forlornly on the tarmac of the Darwin Civil 'Drome following the raids of 19 February 1942. Photo: Alford/AHSNT.

Of the 47 ships in the harbour that morning 21 were sunk or badly damaged whilst the *Florence D* and *Don Isidro* were both sunk off Bathurst Island: 23 ships in all, of which the USS *Peary* bore the disproportionate loss of life. Ninety two seamen went down with the ship after she was bombed and sunk.

The town was also badly hit with severe loss of life. The Post and Telegraph Office was hit by large bombs and destroyed, killing nine of the staff including the Postmaster, Hurtle Bald, and his family. Many other buildings were in ruins and services were cut. Emergency services were quickly on the scene and the medical staff at the recently opened hospital at Kahlin and at 119 AGH at Berrimah worked tirelessly to treat the wounded.

The numbers of those killed on the harbour and in the town remained guesswork for some time. Bodies were recovered from the water for some days and buried in shallow, mostly unmarked, graves on Mindil and Kahlin beaches. Eventually it was accepted that 252 persons were killed and at least 350 wounded; perhaps the final figure will never be known.

The Civil 'Drome at Parap was also attacked though there were no lives lost and damage was minimal in comparison. The Guinea Airways hangar was damaged by strafing and a de Havilland Puss Moth aircraft VH-UPN owned by Darwin identity, Roy Edwards, was destroyed on the tarmac. A 12 Squadron ammunition store was destroyed by fire, a Wirraway, A20-232 damaged by shrapnel and a fire tender destroyed. Bruce Beales, an observer with 12 Squadron was walking to his aircraft after Operations Staff at the RAAF Station had ordered two Wirraways up on a harbour patrol at 0945 hours. "...our aircraft was hidden in the scrub on the opposite side of the field... [it was] a bright sunny day [and] we looked up to see three aircraft zooming around...we thought they were Americans" he recalled, "...until suddenly we realised they were firing at each other. We hastened our pace and then broke into a run as 'Val' dive bombers proceeded to strafe and then bomb our quarters. Fortunately they did not find our aircraft..."

Gunner Peter Roberts was at East Point during the attacks on the 'drome recalling that they were used to watching "...the Americans playing tag...dog fighting...Next thing there was a splash...then a second splash. Then we realised it was more than just fooling. Then a rumble of bombs...in the city itself [and] on the harbour...we knew it was on! But, by the time we were in our trenches Zeros were overhead...we started firing at the aircraft with .303s. Ten Zeros...followed up...strafing the civil 'drome...they seemed to fly in a circuit, coming from the civil 'drome down East Point...bank... drop down over Dudley Point and go in low to attack. It was absolutely to a pattern...a pre-conceived plan of attack...at only 150 to 200 feet when they banked over us."

At the Civil 'Drome, Aeradio operator, Bruce Ackland, had been watching aircraft "...having what appeared to be a dogfight to the north...no alarm had been sounded but felt wary...the clerk asked the R.A.A.F. on the T/printer – "Is it all clear?" The answer came back, "All clear now." I walked from the clerk's office...& heard drone of many aircraft. Looked in direction of aircraft & saw three large formations...No alarm had been given...the Ack

19 FEBRUARY 1942

Ack started to fire & that was first initial indication that aircraft were hostile...We rushed to aeradio shack and sent QQQQ...bombs were falling at R.A.A.F. 'drome by now... Mac and myself made haste to trench at our quarters... Large explosions were coming from R.A.A.F. & town. No alarm had been sounded. At 1020 Civil 'Drome was bombed. There had been a bit of machine gunning before that. Several bombs fell about 75 yds away from us...had more machine gunning after that - at times plane was no more than 200 ft up. Could see pilot distinctly...Could not work [radio] gear so went in car to VID and started to clear a damage report when someone yelled – 'It's on again.'"

Appearing in a Japanese wartime magazine, this photo purportedly shows Mitsubishi G4M1 *Betty* bombers on their way to Darwin for the noon raid on 19 February 1942. Photo: Bob Piper.

As Fuchida's force was heading back to the carriers, the 54 land based bombers of the 1st and Kanoya *Ku*s were on their way to Darwin and their target, the RAAF Station, which had also been damaged during the first raid. Flying Officer C. Saxton, the Station's Operations Officer, recorded that in the initial attack, "The first bomb was a direct hit on 13 Squadron hangar, immediately followed by a direct hit on 12 Squadron hangar which at the time housed U.S. aircraft... Telephone lines were intact except to the hangars, among the gutted wreckage of which, ammunition was exploding and aircraft, petrol and oil drums burning. The All Clear was sounded by Operations Room at 1040K..."

A further report on the raid noted that the "...force making the initial attack on the R.A.A.F. Station consisted entirely of escorted dive-bombers... [with] the advantages of height, overwhelming superiority of numbers, the element of surprise and the lack of fighter opposition...the Japanese aircraft flew so low that the faces of the pilots could be seen quite plainly...It was evident that the attack was fully rehearsed."

At approximately 1157 hours Saxton received a telephone message from the A-A HQ stating that "Two formations of bombers have passed over Larrakeyah and are heading for the 'drome." The alarm was sounded and a Verey signal fired at 1158 hours; exactly two hours after the first bombs had fallen on Darwin.

The temporary graves of four RAAF members killed at the RAAF Station, 19 February 1942. Photo: A. H. McEgan.

Murry Lawson was a young Fitter IIE with 2 Squadron and only recently arrived at Darwin. "...looking up we saw 54 heavy bombers, two flights of 27 each which pattern bombed the aerodrome. I heard the bomb bursts getting closer and closer – then they finally stopped."

Some 200 bombs of varying capacity were estimated to have been dropped in the noon raid and as Saxton later reported, "It was this raid which caused the majority of the casualties. The hospital, recreation hall, officer's and sergeant's [sic] messes, equipment store and many houses in the married quarters area were wrecked. Electric supply and telephone lines were just so many pieces of scattered, broken wire, water mains were wrecked in many places and the 'drome appeared a shambles."

Despite the damage to aircraft buildings and infrastructure, and fears by the Station Commander WgCdr Sturt de B. Griffith, amazingly only seven lives were lost at the RAAF Station during both raids. WgCdr Archibald Tindal, the Area Armament Officer, was killed by an attacking *Val* as he stood on the parapet of a trench firing a machine gun. Six others, members of Transport Section were killed when their trench collapsed; LACs L. A. Barton, P. S. Latham and A. V. L. Schulz and ACs S. G. Smith, F. Nealyon and Cpl R. Simons. All were buried on site before being moved to Berrimah and later Adelaide River War Cemetery. The

RAAF's present frontline airfield south of Katherine was developed in mid-1942 and named for Tindal.

A P-40E lies among the ruins of the 12 Squadron hangar at the RAAF Station. The hangar later became Darwin's postwar airport terminal. Photo: A. H. McEgan via David Vincent.

Aircraft losses as a result of the raids were severe. Nine of the 33rd Pursuit Squadron's P-40s and four pilots were lost, three PBY-5 Catalinas were strafed and burnt on the harbour, while five Hudsons, A16-57, '63, '72, '78 and '135, two Beechcraft C-45s, the LB30 AL521 and three 'hangar queens', two P-40s and an A-24 of the USAAF, were destroyed. The PBY-5 of Moorer's and the Douglas C-53 transport on Bathurst Island along with Roy Edwards' Puss Moth added to the loss: twenty six aircraft in all.

When the Japanese struck, AL521 was parked on the tarmac adjacent to the 13 Squadron workshops hangar. It was strafed and destroyed on the ground, killing the flight engineer, S/Sgt H. M. McTavish and wounding Sgt L. Beck, the upper gunner. Only the engines and outer wings remained intact. In his diary entry for the day, Hurley's Aide-de-Camp, Lt Bob B. Glenn, recorded that when "...we arrive at the airfield, we are shocked at the destruction we see. The Liberator bomber we left there yesterday afternoon is now four smoking engines laying on the ground with a twisted mass of framework strewn around behind them."

One aircraft managed to escape the bombings. The QANTAS flying boat VH-ADU, *Camilla*, was moored at the civil wharf and had been fortunate enough to have been obscured by the smoke from the adjacent wharf and the MV *Neptuna*. It remained virtually unscathed and after a quick check by Captains Hussey and Crowther, took off just minutes before the M. V. *Neptuna* and its load of explosives blew up at the wharf.

To add to the Hudson losses, A16-142 was written off after it force landed in Lake Woods south of Newcastle Waters that evening. At around 2200 hours A16-142 was to fly to Daly Waters with 16 ground personnel of 2 Squadron. One was Lloyd Edwards who was suffering from malaria and was being transported to hospital at the remote airfield. The aircraft encountered a severe electrical storm and after a while the pilot, FlgOff Lamb, realised he'd overshot Daly Waters. Making out what appeared to be a field he force landed, only to find it was a shallow lake. "...the plane did a complete ground (water) loop and aquaplaned some distance before stopping," Lloyd recalled. All waded to shore and after spending the next three days on the edge of Lake Woods south of Newcastle Waters Station, they were rescued by the manager and some drovers.

They were flown back to Daly Waters aboard A16-45. Unfortunately during salvage operations some time later FSgt P. L. Schroeter of 2 Squadron died on 9 March as a result of injuries he received at the site.

Other Hudsons evacuated ground crews to service the dispersed aircraft at Daly Waters that evening. One flown by WgCdr J. Ryland made the trip without incident, despite encountering an electrical storm and running short of fuel, while A16-142 force landed. Another, A16-18, flown by FltLt Ivor Black was forced to land at Katherine. Murry Lawson was aboard Black's aircraft and recalled that he was among a group about "...to board the aircraft at about dusk when an air raid red alarm sounded. Needless to say we disembarked very rapidly and headed for the scrub...happily it was a false alarm...by the time the plane was reloaded, with 24 of us on board, it was quite dark...We took off [and] no sooner had we become airborne then we were picked up by searchlight. This was a very eerie feeling...we hoped that the AA gunners weren't trigger happy – everyone at that time was well keyed up."

Japanese losses incurred in the raids were ridiculously small in comparison. Of the 188 Japanese aircraft involved in the initial raid, seven losses were admitted to by Fuchida, though he was vague as to the actual numbers. It seems all were as a result of ground fire but for the two claimed by Oestreicher and since disproved. Only two, and possibly a third have been confirmed as lost that day. None of the heavy bombers involved in the noon raid were lost.

19 FEBRUARY 1942

As they landed back on the carriers, each aircraft was inspected for battle damage and any hits were recorded. The *Zekes* from the *Akagi* suffered three hits, the *Kates* none and the *Vals* one, while the *Kaga* recorded four hits, seven hits and six hits respectively. On the *Soryu*, the *Zekes* suffered no hits, the *Kates* four and the *Vals* ten. The *Hiryu* recorded seven, four and two hits respectively. However, the *Kaga* reported one Val as "1 self-destruction" and the *Hiryu* one *Zeke* as "1 self-destruction."

fire put up by LCpl Fred Terrone and Spr Dick Spedding at the 1/54th AASL Bty site near Holmes Jungle and crashed nearby at Ironstone Knob. The two crew members, pilot and *Shotai* leader, Flyer 1c Takezo Uchikado, and observer, FCPO Katsuyoshi Tsuru, from Fukuoka Prefecture, were buried on site in a rough sapling fenced grave. Their epitaph was an old jam tin punched with the words 'Unknown Japanese Airmen Died 19.2.42.' They were relocated to graves AD 10 and AD 11 in the Berrimah War Cemetery later that year.

Warrant Officer Katsuyoshi Tsuru, the observer in the Aichi D3A1 Val, 3304 shot down at Ironstone Knob, was killed along with the pilot, Takezo Uchikado. Photo: Tsuru family via Bob Piper.

Lance Corporal Fred Terrone and Spr Dick Spedding at the site of Val 3304 they were credited with shooting down. Photo: AHSNT.

Further to these two losses, another two have been confirmed. One, a *Zeke* from the *Kaga* flown by Flyer 1c Yoshio Egawa, suffered damage to its undercarriage over Darwin and ditched near a destroyer. He was rescued whilst a second aircraft, a *Val* from *Soryu*, was also badly damaged over Darwin and similarly ditched near a destroyer rather than attempt a landing. Both crew members, Flyer 1cs Takeshi Yamada and Kinji Funazaki, were rescued and returned to their carrier.

Of the two aircraft confirmed as lost over Darwin one, a *Val* dive bomber, No. 3304, coded AII-254 was hit by small arms

Des Lambert, a gunner with 2 HAA Bty at the Coonawarra navy base recalled travelling to the crash site two days later, when "...I received permission from Major Nigel Sutherlan, O.C. of 2nd A.A. Battery to search for the wreckage which fell in the bush a mile or so from Berrimah. Accompanied by Bombardier James Glennie I walked along the railway line for some distance then headed towards the bush on the other side of the line. We came across some ambulance drivers camped near a gravel road: they directed us to the crash site. The wreckage was in a hole and parts of one or two of the crew buried nearby. A soldier was busy with a hacksaw trying to remove the three-bladed propeller. Borrowing a machete, I hacked off part of a wing tip as the O.C. wanted a trophy for the orderly room. An officer arrived, driving an [sic] utility truck, and drove us back to Berrimah with the large "trophy". I decided to leave the pilot's helmet on the fuselage, which became a mecca for many souvenir hunters, until there was little left." Des also prised off the aircraft manufacturer's plate confirming the type and production number, *Kitai Bango* 3304.

Members of the 56th Class, Oita air group, 1941. Hajime Toyoshima, one of 19 class members graduated in July 1941, is second from right in the middle row. Photo: Bob Piper.

The other aircraft lost and perhaps the most publicised of those captured during the war was a *Zeke*, No. 5349, BII-124 from the *Hiryu*. Flown by Flyer 3c Hajime Toyoshima. The aircraft had its oil tank holed by a .303" round over Darwin and it was over Melville Island heading back to the carriers that the engine seized and the propeller sheared off.

Selecting a lightly timbered valley Toyoshima carried out a very successful wheels up landing, striking his face on the gun sight but otherwise unharmed. Watched by members of his flight, they radioed his position to the carriers. A floatplane was despatched to rescue him, at one stage landing off a beach, however the search was abandoned when Toyoshima failed to appear. After wandering aimlessly for some days Toyoshima stumbled across a camp of young Aboriginal women and children. Despite his efforts at befriending them the group abandoned him during the night.

Mitsubishi A6M2 manufacturer's number 5349 under guard by RAAF Cpl Ellemor and Tiwi Islanders. The tail code BII-124 confirms it as belonging to the carrier Hiryu. Photo: Bob Piper.

Toyoshima was captured next day by a young Aboriginal tribesman, Matthias Ngapiatulawai and some other young men. He went willingly and was transported across Apsley Strait to the mission. Sergeant Les Powell, an army engineer recalled him being brought across by canoe and then "... disarmed him of a .32" automatic which had seven bullets in the magazine (found out later). We took him round to our quarters, then...fixed his wounds...fed him and removed his boots and coveralls. A message was sent to Darwin informing them and requesting an aircraft, which came two days later...At night we used to sit around the table interrogating him in Pidgin English. Quite a nice fellow."

It was during later interrogation by Joe Dacosta of Australian Army Intelligence, himself part Filipino and educated in Toyoshima's Kobe Prefecture, that Toyoshima mentioned he'd been hit 'over the big silver camp'. Investigations narrowed it down to two members of the 19th Infantry Bn at Winnellie camp, Sappers Tom Lamb and Len O'Shea. They were credited with the 'kill' and commended as were Terrone and Spedding.

19 FEBRUARY 1942

Toyoshima was subsequently taken to Darwin and following interrogation transported to Cowra POW camp in New South Wales via Adelaide River, Alice Springs and Port Pirie, where he was issued the first POW number, PJW11001. Toyoshima became a ringleader in the unrest at Cowra and blew the bugle to signal the break out of August 1944. He died by his own hand after being wounded.

As the Japanese landed back on the carriers and Fuchida reported on the raid, Nagumo must have been very pleased at the success of the mission. For only a handful of losses they had effectively eliminated Darwin as a forward base and a hindrance to their invasion of Timor – for the time being at least. "It seemed hardly worthy of us", Fuchida said later, "...if ever a sledgehammer was used to crack an egg it was then". But even then, Nagumo wanted to mount a second strike.

Fuchida argued against it, fully aware of the devastation they had caused. There was no need he countered; it would be like "...snatching a fan from a geisha". Any thoughts of a second raid were forgotten.

The overkill was even more pronounced in the amount of bombs dropped in the two raids. The *Vals* and *Kates* dropped 82,550 kg of bombs during the first raid whilst the G3M *Nells* and G4M1 *Bettys* added a further 32,050 kg in the noon raid. This equated to two and a half times the number of bombs and 83 per cent of the tonnage dropped on Pearl Harbor on 7 December 1941.

Darwin probably should have taken some perverse pleasure in being afforded so much attention. As it was the survivors were too busy burying the dead, tending the wounded and trying to restore some order to the shattered town, harbour and airfields.

The remains of one of five Hudsons destroyed during the 19 February 1942 raids on Darwin. Photo: AHSNT.

CHAPTER 4

AFTERMATH
Initial defences, airfields and Australia reinforced

On the day following the Darwin raids, newspapers and radio carried the story to a shocked Australia, already reeling from the fall of Singapore and the enormous loss of Australian forces only five days previously. The government of John Curtin tried to put on as brave a face as possible with the Prime Minister declaring that "...a severe blow has been struck on Australian soil...though information did not disclose details of casualties, it must be obvious that we have suffered. We must face this test with fortitude and fight grimly and unflinchingly. Australian forces and civilians conducted themselves with gallantry. Darwin has been bombed but it has not been conquered..." Brisbane's *The Courier Mail* reported.

There was confusion in Darwin itself, understandably so, and much has been written on the aftermath of the raids predominately in an attempt to sensationalise reported breakdowns in discipline and panic, rather than acknowledge the many acts of bravery by civilians and servicemen alike. AM Frederick Scherger who was in Darwin on the day of the raids and saw things first hand argued that he "...didn't find it unusual at all. It happened elsewhere in the world...the civilian population knows nothing of what is about to happen...[they] will be shocked beyond belief when it does happen and the first principle they work on is that absence of body is a lot better than presence of mind."

As it was, a majority of military and civilian personnel reported for duty soon after the raids and were employed in a variety of tasks, none of them pleasant.

As a result of the devastating raids, Justice Lowe of the Victorian Supreme Court was commissioned by the Commonwealth to conduct an enquiry into the supposed 'Day of Shame' that has been so widely misrepresented. His hearing was held 'in camera' for much of the process, thus allowing those with a grudge to vent their spleens and denying those vilified the right to answer their critics, the Administrator, C.L.A. Abbott, in particular. In the event this prevented its release until the post war years.

For many years the death toll from the raids has been the subject of much discussion, mostly revolving around the misleading information released by the authorities. Had they read the 31 March 1942 edition of *The Courier Mail* and no doubt other affiliated newspapers they would have seen the death toll reported as being at 240; very close to the final figure of 252.

For many years also, the debate over Japanese plans to invade Australia has raged. The Australians and the Americans knew through breaking the Japanese code that invasion was not a prospect but both the Australian government and Japanese were quite content to let the threat remain and use it accordingly – it was good propaganda for both sides and served the Curtin government's political agenda well. The Japanese even went so far as to produce Japanese invasion money in sterling, the Australian monetary unit at the time, though it was also the currency of British territories in the Pacific.

Certainly the perception of an invasion was very real, and the Australian military prepared numerous plans to counter any incursions. The Japanese navy was in favour of an invasion and had drawn up tentative plans, whilst the army assessed the situation and determined it would need ten divisions to do so and even then any progress relied on the ability of the navy to supply it. But as early as 10 January the Japanese had decided that Australia's potential as a huge supply and support base was to be negated by isolating it from the British and American forces, whilst lines of communication between India and Australia and Australia, Britain and America were to be cut. Despite pressure from the navy, a joint Army-Navy liaison meeting in Tokyo on 7 March ruled the proposal for an invasion out completely. The 'invasion money' made good souvenirs, as did fake maps showing the supposed invasion routes.

On 20 February 1942 the surviving 33rd Pursuit Squadron pilots were allocated a ward at 119 AGH. There McMahon, Wiecks, Glover, Walker and Rice attempted to gain some understanding of the previous day's events. Oestreicher came in for heavy criticism of his tactics, particularly in response to queries "...as to how did they get jumped by surprise," Bob McMahon wrote, continuing that they "...agreed that the other driver's [Oestreicher] actions (or lack of) attributed to it, as they were circling to the Left headed North East to North. Oestreicher peeled off over them, headed to the South East in about a 40° dive – they were wondering what was wrong with him – when his belly tank came off and about 3 seconds later called 'Zeros' but didn't give any direction – They thought at first he was diving on some but...he dove [sic] directly away from the attacking Zeros and when the rest of the Flight looked around they all had Zeros on their Ass!! and according to Walker when last seen Oestreicher was headed directly for the cloud cover at Batchelor...and was not seen in the fight again."

AFTERMATH

Notwithstanding, Robert Oestreicher was credited with shooting down two dive bombers purportedly located by Australian army personnel. The only wrecks that day would have been the P-40s of the 33rd Pursuit Squadron (Provisional) and the sole Japanese aircraft, *Val* 3304, at Ironstone.

Gen Barnes also reported the action the following day and in a signal entitled *Operations: Java Campaign* to AGWAR HQ USAFFE, stated that the flight encountered bad weather and turned back. Once over Darwin Barnes reported that Pell "...LEFT TWO ON PATROL 15,000 FEET, SEVEN LANDED STOP RT FREQUENCY JAMMED AS REPORT APPROACH ENEMY AIRCRAFT BATHURST ISLAND RECEIVED STOP SEVEN GROUNDED AIRCRAFT TOOK OFF AS AIRDROME WAS ATTACKED STOP THESE SEVEN AND ONE HIGH PATROL SHOT DOWN STOP OTHER HIGH PATROL LANDED SLIGHTLY DAMAGED...PILOT LOSSES FOUR MISSING BELIEVED KILLED COMMA SQUADRON LEADER KILLED COMMA OTHERS SAFE UNQUOTE."

As a result of their actions, all the American fliers were awarded the American DSC, and all but the four killed that day went on to other units. Oestreicher, whose aircraft '22' was the sole survivor of the day's combat, flew to Daly Waters in the afternoon of the 20th reportedly on the orders of Wheless and Connally, and was ordered to RAAF Amberley. Escorted by a Lockheed Lodestar he severely damaged his aircraft on landing at Cloncurry and flew on as a passenger in the Lodestar. He later served in the Darwin area as a pilot with the 7th and later, 9th Pursuit Squadron, 49th Pursuit Gp under Colonel Paul 'Squeeze' Wurtsmith and was assigned tower and general duties at Batchelor.

Confident of their success, the Japanese failed to follow up their advantage following the initial raids and while they consolidated their bases and available forces in the NEI the Allies continued their program of dispersal for the aircraft it had managed to retain. While 2 Squadron was effectively on strength at the RAAF Station most of its aircraft were at Daly Waters after evacuating ground crews on the evening of 19 February. The HQ unit of 13 Squadron moved to Daly Waters on 27 February and Batchelor remained the base for 12 Squadron along with the USAAF's 19th and 27th Bomb. Gps.

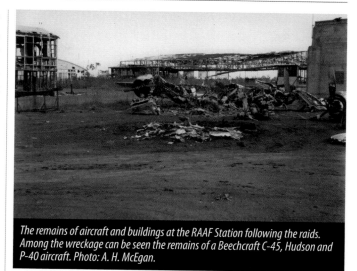

The remains of aircraft and buildings at the RAAF Station following the raids. Among the wreckage can be seen the remains of a Beechcraft C-45, Hudson and P-40 aircraft. Photo: A. H. McEgan.

The Americans had to contend with shortages of equipment and spares for their aircraft, though the A-24s of the 16th and 17th Squadrons continued flying patrols in conjunction with the 12 Squadron Wirraways. The American pilots and crewmen carried out their own maintenance often with the assistance of the Australians, as did the B-17 crews of the 19th Bomb. Gp. The A-24s weren't relied on to any extent as they were in poor condition and had time expired engines requiring overhaul or replacement. The aircrews persisted however, and continued patrols until March when they were ordered to Townsville. On 10 March crews departed Darwin aboard a Qantas flying boat to take delivery of fifteen replacements after they had arrived at Brisbane. Taking delivery from the 3rd Bomb. Gp they were flown to Batchelor. Operations with the new aircraft were short lived however; General Brett ordered them back to Townsville as part of a USAAF reorganisation and they were absorbed into the 3rd Bomb. Gp.

One of the A-24s remained after being 'acquired' by SqnLdr Brian 'Blackjack' Walker, CO of 12 Squadron at Batchelor. The aircraft had been resurrected by USAAF mechanics and fitted with a Wright Cyclone GR-1820 engine and propeller from one of the 19th Bomb. Gp's derelict B-17s. The propeller assembly was heavier and 12 inches larger in diameter than those on the A-24 and as Brian Walker related, "As soon as I started her up the tail came off the ground so...I shut her down & put a thinking cap on & of course they had the pitch control installed arse-about... we weighed the props by lifting them and guessing – the new prop we estimated was 70 lbs heavier with about 3 to 4 ins ground clearance hence we strapped 100 lbs of sand

AFTERMATH

into the rear luggage compartment & fired her up again [we] decided if you took off in the tail down position she'd be jake & of course marked the [throttle] quadrant where we got the right revs. She flew beautifully and no sooner had I gotten [*sic*] all the bugs out than my 3 U.S. enlisted men were posted...I was left with the aircraft so used it as a hack."

A '1000lb' Japanese bomb recovered on the RAAF Station after a Japanese raid. The bomb is a 250 kg Type 98 NO.25 type with filling of Hexanite and Anisol. Ray Jackson is at left. Photo: Ray Jackson.

Shortly afterwards Walker was posted to Sale in Victoria to form 30 Squadron and after convincing HQ that he should take the B-41 as it was called (part B-17 and part A-24) with him on the proviso USAAF officers approved it, he flew it south via Alice Springs. 'Blackjack' knew a number of the USAAF 'higher ups' and the approval was a formality. He "...kept it for several months... [but] sadly when the time

came to take 30 [Squadron] to New Guinea there was no one to fly the dear old Dauntless so I let the Yanks know and they came and took her away. She finished up polished silver as a Colonel's hack up in Townsville."

From 20 February 1942 work at the RAAF Station was carried out to clear the wreckage of aircraft and buildings in an effort to return it to operational status. Among those tasks was the recovery of unexploded and partly intact Japanese bombs, the latter to provide information on their construction, fuses and filling. A Bomb Disposal Unit was formed as part of 52 OBU at the RAAF Station, though the first bomb disposal course was not held until April that year. Among the members of the unit was LAC Ray Jackson, who remembered his squad being used as "...a utility unit [for the] location & digging up & defusing [of] Jap bombs, ranging from 50kg to 500kg...one of our B.D.U. Officers F/O Harry Belcher...was badly injured when a bomb exploded whilst they were examining it however he eventually survived." Among their other unenviable duties Ray recalled was to disinter the bodies of the six transport personnel killed in the second raid.

Members of the Bomb Disposal Unit watch on as one of many unexploded bombs is located on the RAAF Station. The long pole is used to indicate the angle of entry. Photo: Ray Jackson.

The BDU grew and became 6 BD Squad under FlgOff Ric Havyatt. Unit personnel disposed of Japanese bombs wherever they were found, mostly in Darwin and around the RAAF Station, but roamed far and wide. Ray Jackson and Harry Percival were involved in collecting and disposing of bombs during a three day trip in the Bynoe Harbour area in late 1942, working with Aboriginal assistants, Jacky, Jimmy and Jacko, and investigating the wreckage of a downed Japanese *Zeke*.

AFTERMATH

The unit later moved to New Guinea but the threat of unexploded ordnance remains in Darwin as development continues. A number of 60 kg incendiary bombs were unearthed in the 1980s and other finds are a matter of when and not if.

The most vital aspect of those early weeks and months following the first raids was the dispersal of RAAF and USAAF forces, meagre as they were, to areas where they might carry the fight to the enemy. A major problem was the availability of any operational aircraft; the RAAF had some 71 Hudsons, 13 PBY-5 Catalinas, 42 P-40E Kittyhawks and 126 Wirraways at its disposal and a majority of these were spread throughout Australia. The Americans were no better off, relying in the main on B-17s, A-24s and a handful of P-40Es.

As early as 23 January 1942 the Australian government had been aware of the urgent need for fighter aircraft after the Chiefs of Staff recommended that Prime Minister Curtin cable his counterpart, Churchill, stating prophetically that "Our experience at Ambon and Rabaul have emphasised the urgent necessity for fighter aircraft immediately. Japanese methods make it clear that without fighter protection…there is every prospect of carrier-borne enemy air attack destroying our extremely limited striking force on the ground…against our mainland aerodromes as well as at advance bases owing to lack of fighter protection and almost complete absence of gun defences. Make urgent representations to United Kingdom Government for immediate allotment to R.A.A.F. of up to 180 of Tomahawk, Hurricane II, or similar type."

After several cables and exchanges, including one from Churchill chiding Curtin of his lack of knowledge of the procurement process, an allocation of 125 airframes from the next British block was promised on the proviso that the Americans made up the balance. At least it had the potential to be a start, but the allocation failed to proceed. Instead the Americans came to the rescue with an initial issue of 140 P-40Es.

In order to disperse what aircraft were available, and with an eye on future defensive and offensive operations against the Japanese, an aerodrome development program, previously commenced in December 1941, was accelerated. FltLt John Yeaman, was charged with the initial selection and development of aerodromes in the region, along with

FltLt Brogan RAAF. They contacted Col Sverdrup of the American consulting engineers Sverdrup and Parcell regarding "… proposals outlined in a R.A.A.F. Instruction that five (5) major aerodromes were to be located between Adelaide River and Birdum…and as many roadside strips as possible (see R.A.A.F. HQ. File 175/6/3). The road strips were to be provided for the dispersal of aircraft from R.A.A.F. Darwin in the event of sudden Japanese raids. Full details of the aerodrome development for the defence of the area were given in signal W33 of 25 February," Yeaman wrote.

Between December 1941 and 17 February 1942 they selected a number of sites suitable for airfields including Hughes, Humpty Doo and Lake Deane. The latter two became fighter strips at the '34-Mile' (Livingstone) and '27-Mile' (Strauss) pegs on the North-South Road, whilst Hughes, named for the local Director of Mines became the home to the Hudsons of 2 and 13 Squadrons, 1 PRU and later, 2 Squadron and its Mitchell bombers.

Utilising the Australian style 'Swagman's hat', Tom Skillman of the American 43rd Engineers attempts to keep the myriad flies away during his time at Manbulloo airfield, 1942. Photo: Tom Skillman.

While the 19 February raids delayed the project, Yeaman's team moved to Katherine under authority of Signal W876 of the 17th. There they encountered considerable difficulties in the absence of roads and fuel, and the return of their command car which had been on loan from the 147th Field Artillery Regt at Noonamah. While at Katherine, the team selected a site on Manbulloo Station along with others south of the town, dubbed Kit Carson and Wilson by the Americans; the latter two became Tindal and Venn.

Most of the existing airfields in the region had been constructed prior to the war and were unsuitable for

AFTERMATH

military use. Katherine was one, along with Pine Creek, Birdum, Maranboy and a number of others. Improvements to the civil Aerodrome east of Katherine were commenced by the 808th Engineer (Avn) Bn US Army under Capt Chaffin. They had pushed a track through from Birdum, arriving on 19 February, but were severely handicapped by the inability of the North Australia Railway to move all their heavy equipment. Much of the work was done by hand until their plant arrived.

The arrival of the American 808th Engineer Battalion and its plant at Noonamah Siding in March 1942 was met by a very informal party of Australians of the 23rd Fld Coy RAE. Photo: Harry Geary.

In early March a second American engineering unit, the 43rd Engineer General Service Regiment (less the 2nd Bn) arrived at Katherine and commenced work at Manbulloo. In the following two months the two units had completed or improved 11 airfields, despite the primitive conditions at the work sites, accommodation and messing. Compacting of some runways and taxiways was carried out by rolling earth-filled 200 l drums.

Tom Skillman was with the 43rd Engineers at Manbulloo and remembered camping in "...2 and 8 man tents with dirt floors...with only a hand dug well for water...the flies were...terrible – I averaged swallowing at least one live fly a day...We swam in the river until we were getting an ear fungus that was very painful."

Eventually elements of the 808th and their plant moved north by rail to commence work on the roadside strips at the 28 and 34-Mile pegs and at Hughes. Harry Geary, a member of 2 Pln 23rd FldCoy, RAE, was at the rail siding at Noonamah south of the 27-Mile strip and remembered that in "...early March 1942 Two Platoon 23rd Fld Coy Engineers welcomed the USA Army 808 Battalion Engineers...on

that well laden train. However...we had no brass bands to welcome them GIs, only 'good day' Yanks. Our shirts and shorts were wet on clothes lines. Most of our blokes had lap laps on. Yanks must have thought we were a wild lot with no uniforms on... [our] visitors did arrive with Camel cigs for their new found Aussie mates [though]."

808th Eng Bn plant levelling the runway at the 34-Mile airstrip. The site was later named for Lt John D. Livingstone. Photo: Alford/AHSNT Colln.

By the time the 808th Engineers were ready to leave in mid-July they had cleared, graded and gravelled the airstrips at Katherine, Pine Creek, Burkeholder (later named McDonald), Fenton, the '34-Mile', Hughes and the '27-Mile'. None had been sealed due to an acute shortage of bitumen and oil though a couple had been oiled using salvaged sludge.

By September it was considered that the minimum airfield program was well advanced and it was thought that the 43rd Engineers could complete the Carson (Tindal) and Wilson (Venn) sites and construct a new airfield at Birdum prior to the onset of the wet season.

Australian RAAF units and authorities were also involved in the program, with the RAAF's Mobile Works Squadrons and Airfield Construction Squadrons units, the AWC and DMR (NSW) providing valuable assistance. The RAAF's 1 ACS commenced Coomalie Airfield in July, and sealed the airstrips at Livingstone, Strauss and Hughes. In concert with 1 MWS, the DMR (NSW) was responsible for sealing Batchelor, Fenton, Manbulloo, Daly Waters and Birdum.

Syd James was an LAC with 1 MWS, recalling that "One of our jobs...was to erect protection bays for the fighters.

AFTERMATH

To make one of these bays, lots of sheets of galvanised iron were required, so whenever we had time along with other crews, we went collecting the iron off buildings that had been bombed... Any timber we could collect, was very useful for the frame to nail the iron on to. The main frame was made from bush poles. The bays were also covered with camouflage nets, another one of our many tasks... We also dug up an underground petrol tank along with the pipe need to make an oil spray unit; with which we would oil the strip and keep the dust down. Many a night I've stood on the running board of the old truck (no idea where the truck came from) as it idled along [and] the oil sprayed out."

By year's end a dozen operational airfields were completed along the road to Katherine and the "Standards of occupancy established initially by U.S. Army Air Force in Australia, and affirmed by its successor, Fifth Air Force, for squadrons assigned to Northern Territory were met before the rainy season started in December 1942," the Office of the Chief Engineer USAFFE reported.

Long, southeast of Fenton, and Sattler at the '20-Mile' peg were the last and by the end of 1943 the number had increased dramatically to almost 50 airfields throughout the Territory, constructed in the main by the RAAF's 1, 8 and 9 ACS along with 1 and 14 MWS and the AWC. Not all became operational and though named for Australian and American airmen, many were little more than cleared strips allowing an aircraft to land if need be. But, while the RAAF and USAAF required airfields from which to operate, they also required adequate warning of approaching enemy aircraft. The requirement brought about the establishment of a number of early warning stations, the least publicised of which was a small site set up on the northwest coast of Bathurst Island and under the flightpath of approaching Japanese raiding forces.

Five days after the initial Japanese raids, 5 Fighter Sector was formed at Darwin with an establishment of seven officers and 47 ORs. Its role was to provide control of fighter operations and to coordinate the A-A defences.

Initially the new unit also provided radio watches for bomber and reconnaissance aircraft from the signals office that had moved from the RAAF Station to a remote location south of the main runway. Lieutenant Jesse Peaslee, a pilot and diarist with the 9th Squadron 49th Pursuit Gp later wrote that the "...only arrangement for aircraft control was an Australian radio crew who had an American airplane radio setup in a little tin building near one end of a runway." Commanded by FlgOff R. T. Thorogood, the unit was located in a most unfortunate site amid constant clouds of sand flies and it became known as Sandfly Gully. "...we established our first camp on the other side of the road from the entrance to the R.A.F. Base [sic] – some half mile or so in the bush." Cyril Holyoake, an Australian controller recalled, "When the...49th Pursuit Gp took over in May 1942, I and one other Australian were left behind...while the rest of the 10 or 12 members of 5 Fighter Sector proceeded to the Preston Town Hall, Melbourne where another Fighter Sector was established."

The Fighter Sector itself moved into the 119 AGH site and in March the coast watching facility on Bathurst Island was established to meet an urgent need for advance warning of enemy aircraft. Warning of aircraft up to 15,000 ft was required by LtCol Paul Wurtsmith, the Commander of the 49th Pursuit Gp USAAF then under training at southern bases, to allow his P-40s to gain enough height to intercept. 31 RDF Station at Dripstone north of Darwin was still under development and had yet to become operational. Even then the Bathurst Island site remained manned well after 31 RDF and other stations, including 38 RDF at Cape Fourcroy on Bathurst Island, became operational.

Bill Woodnutt, a LAC wireless operator, and two clerks, ACs McCoy and McKenzie, were sent to a site north of Cape Fourcroy near Point Fawcett at Wiyapurali, where they established a coast watching facility using antiquated RT1082/T1083 equipment under the call-sign '8X2'. From their rough bush camp they began transmitting vital information on approaching enemy aircraft to the Fighter Sector at Berrimah and its receiver '8X7'. They were ably assisted by Tiwi islanders, Louie and David, and "...there was a makeshift landing strip adjacent to the camp and Doc Fenton made several visits..."

It was a lonely existence but the airmen made a valuable contribution to the early warning system as the Radar facilities developed. On 26 April 1942, Wurtsmith wrote to AirCdre Blaidin commending (acting) Cpl Bill Woodnutt for "...the excellent performance of the W/T crew stationed at Cape Fourcroy, Bathurst Island. On this first day in operation the messages received from that station were letter perfect...This station has definitely proved its value and Acting Corporal Woodnutt [is] to be congratulated." Later in the year the group was joined by LAC Allan Stubbs, who had "...wandered down to the old Berrimah Hospital... an officer asked me...what I did before I joined up. I said, I played battery radios and came from the bush...I was on a boat that same day and landed at Cape Fourcroy..."

Bill Woodnutt did two tours at '8X2', operating the station until Christmas Day 1942, "...when 8X2 closed down and the members enjoyed a good sit down dinner with 38 RS (Radar Station) at Lubra Point." By that time Bill was reporting more raids on Timor by the Beaufighters of 31 Squadron than enemy activity. Before departing the island he performed one last duty and it had everything to do with the Beaufighters he was reporting.

A line up of 3 Ku aircraft on Timor, 1942, The first three are Mitsubishi C5M2 Babs reconnaissance aircraft, with A6M2 Zekes and a transport version of the G4M Betty at far right. Photo: Bernard Baeza.

On 29 December a Beaufighter crew abandoned their aircraft near Cape Helvtius north of Wiyapurali. The aircraft A19-71 of 31 Squadron had been hit during a low level attack on Japanese installations on Timor. With the controls partly jammed the pilot, FlgOff Ian 'Tiny' Wilkins and his observer, Sgt Bill Byrnes, were forced to bale out in sight of Bathurst Island. Both landed in the sea and it was with some reticence that Bill Woodnutt described the next few minutes. "As for my swim, believe me I was no hero. I did not want to do it. Sharks and crocodiles are [not] and never were my cup of tea. I was to learn...that there is a very fine line between courage and stupidity. Byrnes had not only jumped too early, but had jumped without his dinghy. My swim would have been a lot easier if I had not had to tow Tiny Wilkins' dinghy by the tow rope tied around my waist...I would need the dinghy in which to place Byrnes, who was a non swimmer. Also, thank God for

the intelligence of the P40 pilot [from 77 Squadron RAAF] who...flew over me, guiding me to Byrnes. In the heavy seas that were running it is very doubtful that I would have ever located what was simply a head and Mae West, without... that P40."

Woodnutt was awarded the MBE for his rescue and was later commissioned as Wireless Operator Air. The wreckage of the Beaufighter remained undiscovered for a further 58 years until it was located in May 2001: ironically during clearing operations for a new state of the art RAAF radar facility on the site of a wartime Loran facility erected in 1944 near Woodnutt's old camp.

The Japanese 23rd *Koku Sentai* commenced raids against Darwin in March, using *Bettys* of Takao *Ku* based at Koepang on Timor escorted by *Zekes* of 3 *Ku*, also operating from Koepang. Three *Zekes* covering a *Babs* reconnaissance aircraft were led by Lt Ichiro Mukai and raided the RAAF Station on the 4th, the day following the devastating raid on Broome by nine 3 *Ku Zekes* under Lt Zenziro Miyano.

The burning Hudson is believed to be A16-65 following the 4 March 1942 raid on the RAAF Station. At right is P-40E '36' force landed by Lt Glover of the 33rd Pursuit Squadron (Provisional) on 19 February. Photo: A. H. McEgan.

At that time 'B' Flight of 13 Squadron and some 2 Squadron Hudsons were operating as a single operational unit whilst attempting to reorganise in-between raids. A Hudson was damaged in the raid conducted on the 16th of the month, the day after Bob Dalkin had arrived at the RAAF Station on posting to 13 Squadron. Bob recalled that he was "...at about the intersection of the...runways [when] I stopped to watch a Hudson land...Just at that moment I heard shouting...followed by a not very effective air raid warning siren...within two minutes a formation of 14 Japanese... bombers was clearly visible...heading directly for the airfield.

AFTERMATH

Almost simultaneously a pattern of high explosive bombs started to detonate across the airfield...although I had started to run...I had no hope of gaining any cover...and as the bombs started bursting I flung myself flat on the ground... [later] when I raised my head...I saw that the whole nearby area was pitted with bomb craters...some hundreds of bomb fragments littered the immediate area, and it was the proverbial miracle that the only damage I sustained were my badly scratched knees...and my bloodied wrists and finger tips where I had unconsciously tried to dig my way into the gravel...I was more than a little shaken."

The Hudson he had been watching was an ex 14 Squadron aircraft flying in from Daly Waters by the Flt Lt Clive Forman crew. It was badly damaged; Sgt Gear was injured and Sgt John Forrest killed. "A short war for him." Dalkin commented.

The Japanese returned on the 19th, targeting the RAAF Station, the town and the Bagot A-A Bty. Two lives were lost, an aircraft damaged and a number of buildings partially destroyed.

Two days earlier Gen Douglas MacArthur and his family had arrived at Batchelor following an eventful trip by fast torpedo boats from Corregidor. From Del Monte they travelled aboard a 40th Recon Squadron, 19th Bomb Gp. B-17, 41-2447, flown by Capt Frank Bostrum. Members of his staff including Gen Harold 'Pursuit Hal' George of Interceptor Command came in on a second aircraft, 41-2429 flown by Capt William Lewis.

Gavin McEwin, an Aerodrome Control Officer at 53 OBU Batchelor remembered MacArthur's arrival in the aircraft "... carrying 50 or 60 people [sic]...We fed them and refuelled the aircraft, so that they could continue their flight south... He came out after the meal and climbed the ladder to the Tower to have words with me... 'I'm Douglas MacArthur, How are things going? Do you need anything which might make the job easier?' I asked him, 'Could I have the use of a Jeep to lay out the flare paths...?' He said, 'I'll see what I can do.' He climbed back down the ladder and they all boarded the aircraft...I gave them the green light and off they went." Gavin got his Jeep courtesy Capt Bob Morrissey of the 7th Pursuit Squadron 49th Pursuit Gp. He also got an electric flare path to replace the old kerosene or oil burning 'stink pots.'

The Japanese returned on 22 March, travelling as far inland as Katherine, while a 3 *Ku Babs* reconnaissance aircraft escorted by three *Zekes* was sent to reconnoitre Darwin. This time though, they were opposed not only by the A-A defences but by P-40Es of the newly arrived 9th Pursuit Squadron of the 49th Pursuit Gp USAAF.

The 49th Pursuit Gp and a number of its Curtiss P-40E fighters had arrived at Melbourne aboard the USATs *Mariposa* and *Coolidge* on 2 February after departing San Francisco on 12 January. Raised at Selfridge Field, Michigan, and officially formed on 20 November 1940, the Group trained on Seversky P-35 aircraft at Selfridge and later at Morrison Field, West Palm Beach Florida, before being assigned to the Pacific Theatre and Australia in January 1942.

From the Port Melbourne docks personnel were initially accommodated at Camp Pell at Royal Park before being transported to Camp Darley near Bacchus Marsh (named 'Backward March' by some). They were then transported to their respective squadron bases in NSW: the 7th Squadron at Bankstown near Sydney, the 8th Squadron at RAAF Fairbairn near Canberra and the 9th Squadron at RAAF Williamtown north of Newcastle.

A week after the Group's arrival they were advised in correspondence S.A.S. 1572 from AirCdre Bladin, Assistant CAS, that "The 49th American Pursuit Gp (80 P.40s.) has been temporarily allotted to come under operational command of the Chief of the Air Staff." The Americans confirmed it two days later on the 11th stating that the Group "...is temporarily assigned to operate under the control of the Commanding General, Royal Australian Air Force."

It was a unique situation and one that carried through to the operations of the USAAF as late as 1944 under both AirCdre F. M. 'Dad' Bladin and AVM A. T. 'King' Cole.

The Group's aircraft, some 111 of which had arrived earlier aboard the *Hammondsport*, were assembled and test flown at local bases and depots including Brisbane (Archerfield and Eagle Farm), RAAF Amberley, Laverton and Geelong. The pilots, most of whom had few if any hours flight time on fighters, carried out training flights in a small number of RAAF Wirraways assigned to each squadron for the purpose, and P-40Es, a number of them assigned to the Java campaign as they came on strength.

Some deployments to provide aerial defence were made to Melbourne, where Clyde Barnett, a pilot with the 8th,

AFTERMATH

recalled buying atlases to provide maps for both local and the expected cross country flight to the northern war zone. Cross country and local training flights were also carried out but accidents in the newly arriving P-40s were numerous and despite the best efforts of the Group Commander Col Paul B. 'Squeeze' Wurtsmith, they continued to deplete the available numbers of aircraft.

The accidents became such a concern that on 5 March Gen Brett of USAFIA sent a secret signal to the Adjutant General in Washington stating in part that:
CITE AGS 620...OVER 75% OF...PILOTS HAD ONLY A FEW HOURS OR NO TIME AT ALL IN P DASH FORTYS(.)...NINETYFIVE OF THE ONE HUNDRED AND TWO PILOTS OF THE FORTYNINTH Pursuit Gp HAVE NEVER BEEN IN A PURSUIT AIRPLANE...THE NUMBER OF ACCIDENTS HAS REACHED EXCESSIVE AND ALARMING PROPORTIONS(.)...MOST DUE ENTIRELY TO PILOT ERROR(.) DURING THE LAST WEEK FIFTEEN P DASH FORTY AIRCRAFT HAVE BEEN DAMAGED TO THE EXTENT OF NEEDING MAJOR REPAIRS...LENGTH OF TIME OFF PILOTING DURING TRAVEL SHOULD BE REDUCED TO MINIMUM(.) BETTER TRAINED PILOTS MUST BE ASSIGNED THIS THEATER(.) BRETT

Brett's request was not realised and the Group continued with those pilots it had along with veterans from the Philippines and Java campaigns who were trickling in. In a Special Order No. 54 of 9 March LtGen Brett relieved 11 of them from the 17th Pursuit Squadron (Provisional) to the 49th Pursuit Gp at Bankstown. Captain Walter Coss, and Lts Nat Blanton, George Kiser, Jack Dale, Joe Kruzel, Ben Irvin, Bill Hennon, Robert Dockstader, Lester Johnsen, Jim Morehead and Andrew Reynolds all added their experience. In time though, the young, inexperienced pilots proved themselves where and when it mattered most.

In the meantime, the accidents and fatalities continued. Pilot experience and mechanical failures accounted for most, but some could not be avoided. On 7 March Lts Richard Dennis and Monroe Eisenberg of the 8th Squadron

Pilots of the 8th Pursuit squadron 49th Pursuit Gp USAAF at RAAF Base Fairbairn ACT. The young American pilots proved themselves over Darwin during the raids of 1942. Photo: Clyde Barnett.

AFTERMATH

were driven off course by dense smoke during a flight from Laverton to Fairbairn. Both force landed but neither was hurt. A week later Lt Frank S. Stiertz tried to recover from a ground loop and take off, only to crash into a hangar. Unable to get out of the blazing aircraft Stiertz perished in the inferno.

The P-40E, serial 41-5455, was force landed on a beach in southern NSW by Lt Arthur 'Doc' Fielder of the 8th Squadron 49th Pursuit Gp on 28 March 1942. The aircraft was later salvaged and repaired. Photo: Bob Piper.

Far to the northwest at Daly Waters another young pilot lost his life as the 9th Squadron flew to Darwin. Lt Albert L. Spehr died as the squadron arrived over Daly Waters on the 17th. Spehr attempted a slow roll over the airstrip but the P-40E dived into the ground exploding on impact at the eastern overrun. Ron Buckingham, a 13 Squadron member, remembered the incident clearly, recalling Spehr's papers confirmed only nine hours on type and that he was a member of an amateur theatre club in El Paso Texas. Spehr was interred in the small pioneer cemetery opposite the old telegraph station next day, along with SSgt Collen Long who had died four days previously when a B-17 crashed on landing.

By 26 March the number of P-40E wrecks at the southern bases was extensive. Even with some having been repaired and others scrapped, there were still seven at Williamtown, four at Bankstown and five at Fairbairn.

Others fell victim to the weather and terrain. Two days later on the 28th, Lts John Musial, Arthur 'Doc' Fielder, Chester Namola and Neil Takala were part of a four aircraft practice gunnery sortie flying to Moruya in southern NSW when they encountered low cloud and fog. They flew further south, circling and trying to climb above the weather but the conditions persisted. Takala and Musial crashed in mountainous terrain, while Fielder and Namola force landed and their aircraft were salvaged. Musial and Takala were recovered and buried with full military honours at Canberra. Their aircraft, 41-5559 and 41-5602, were beyond recovery.

On 28 March 1942, the 49th Pursuit Gp squadrons received what probably confirmed their future. In a signal to the CO US Forces, Bankstown, Williamtown and Canberra, it was directed that "The red circle in the American insignia will be immediately painted white. Purpose is to avoid our aircraft being mistaken for enemy aircraft particularly by ground troops. All Australian forces will be advised..."

For a detachment of the 7th and the 9th Pursuit Squadron the advice was probably irrelevant. The 9th had departed Williamtown on 16 March and arrived in the Darwin area on the 18th. There they were based at Batchelor with aircraft standing alert at the RAAF Station pending completion of their permanent airstrip at the '34-Mile'. A detachment of nine aircraft of the 7th Squadron under Capt Bob Morrissey had headed north to Horn Island in the Torres Strait, where they were to provide defences against expected enemy air attacks. They didn't have long to wait.

The remains of P-40s left at RAAF Williamtown when the 9th Squadron moved to Darwin. The remains of seven aircraft were left at the base. Photo: Ron Robinson.

On 14 March the Japanese sent eight *Bettys* of 4 *Ku* from Vunakanau at Rabaul under Lt Shigeo Yamagata with an escort of 12 *Zekes* of the battle hardened Tainan *Ku*, recently returned from battles over Java and Bali, under Lt Shiro Kawai. The force arrived over Horn Island at 1020 hours and five minutes later the *Bettys* released 78 60 kg bombs. They were intercepted out to sea by Morrissey's P-40s though one, Lt William Redington, was forced to withdraw with unserviceable guns. The American pilots claimed four *Zekes* and one *Betty* in the combat, however the Japanese records list two *Zekes* flown by Lt Nobuhiro Iwasaki and Flyer 2c Genkichi Oishi. No bombers were reported lost by the Japanese.

During the combat Lt A. T. House in his aircraft, 41-5313, *Hiro's Poopy*, had his guns jam and dipped his wing into the rear fuselage and cockpit of a *Zeke* threatening Capt Morrissey. He managed to land his aircraft less a metre of the starboard wing. Lieutenant Clarence E Sanford became lost after the combat and after flying for some time, ran out of fuel and was forced to bale out. He parachuted into the sea off Bremer Island near Yirrkala Mission at the tip of east Arnhem Land, far to the west of Horn Island. Rescued by two young Aboriginal men, one of whom was Wandjuk Marika who went on to become a renowned artist, Sanford was eventually taken to Darwin by a Hudson bomber. House's aircraft was repaired and flown out.

Following his rescue, Lt Clarence Sanford was repatriated to the US and went on to fly a range of USAAF aircraft. He retired as a LtCol. Photo: USAF via Peter Callaghan.

On hearing of the combat and of the American claims, Col Wurtsmith produced a magnum of champagne, declaring it would be opened on the occasion of the Group's 500th victory.

First blood to the 9th Squadron came eight days later when Lts Clyde L Harvey and Stephen Poleschuk downed a Mitsubishi C5M2 *Babs* of 3 *Ku* six km north of Point Charles west of Darwin. Both crew members, pilot PO1c Shigiki Mari and his observer PO1c Shinobu Nagasawa

INTO COMBAT

were killed. Three escorting *Zekes* became separated from the *Babs* and one, along with its pilot, Flyer 1c Tokaji was reported missing. Nine *Bettys* from Takao *Ku*, led by Lt Yoshinobu Kusuhata, raided Katherine the same day dropping 84 60 kg bombs and causing one fatality, an Aboriginal man, Roger, who was hit by shrapnel as he sheltered behind a rock.

"...there were six men working out the front [of our store]," Anne Cox recalled, "They suddenly raced down our driveway and over the fence into the bush. We knew something was wrong and came outside. We heard an unusual drone. The planes were easily spotted in the eastern sky. They circled three times before they dropped their bombs. They bombed the aerodrome." Bert Nixon, a Katherine farmer also remembered the day. "I'd heard American and Australian planes, but these were different – they had a high pitched sing [*sic*] I thought, 'it's got to be the Japs' and when I looked up, there they were, nine of them in formation coming from the north-east."

Lieutenant Steven Poleschuk of the 9th Squadron and his aircraft, Huyebo, Russian for 'not worth much'. Poleschuk and Lt Clyde Harvey downed a 3 Ku C5M2 Babs aircraft west of Darwin on 22 March. Photo: Wilfreid Zeigler.

At the aerodrome the 808th Engineers heard the bombers at around 1330 hours and "They were finally spotted. There were 9 silver colored [*sic*] planes flying in perfect V formation at...approximately 20,000 feet...out at the [air] field, the crew on duty had been following the planes [and] when the bombs started coming down they all got into depressions or fell flat on the ground. ...Daisy cutters (anti personnel) fell within 10 yards of a group of men but...none were hurt...on further examination of the airdrome, about 85 bomb craters of varying sizes were located...if there had been any planes on the taxiway system they would have undoubtedly been destroyed."

One of many bomb craters at the Katherine aerodrome following the 22 March 1942 raid by Betty bombers of the Takao Ku from Koepang. Photo: Alford/AHSNT Colln.

The raid on Katherine was the furthest the Japanese raided inland and it was the first occasion in which 31 RDF Station at Dripstone became operational and was able to demonstrate the vital role it was to play in Darwin's aerial defences. Installed under the supervision of FlgOffs Hannam, B. L. Glassop and F. A. Hull under difficult conditions, not least of which were the lack of equipment and with little help from the RAAF, the system was finally calibrated with the assistance of Dr. J. Piddington of the Radiophysics laboratory and declared serviceable.

While the P-40s of the 9th Squadron downed the *Babs*, they in turn were aided by 31 RDF Station at Dripstone Caves, which became operational that day. John Scott, one of the mechanics at the site, remembered that the "...first enemy aircraft were located at a distance of 80 miles...the crew on watch were Bill Wellstead, mechanic, Fred Findlay and Kevin Wass, operators with Fred Findlay being on the cathode ray tube..."

INTO COMBAT

The effectiveness of the RDF set was treated with some scepticism initially and was considered quite rudimentary by the Americans as the air raid warning system "...was pretty much in the theoretical stage," wrote Lt Peaslee. "The radio locator was supposed to give an 80 mile warning, but due to technical reasons it was often not functioning. The enemy bombers were still slipping in without warning." Sandfly Gully "...had connection with 'fighter sector' an Australian intercept board which had connection with the radio locator" Peaslee continued, "The plan was for 'fighter sector' to plot the course of the enemy formation, plot the interception, call the squadron, giving orders to take off and the altitude of and vector to fly..." Difficulties with radio sets, their range and reception also caused a number of problems and, "...likewise the radio locator's tendency to give only ten to twelve minutes warning made it necessary for our pilots to fly away from the enemy in order to meet them at an equal altitude," Peaslee wrote.

Even then the American pilots were only provided the basic information. Clyde Barnett a pilot with the 8th Squadron recalled that "...at Darwin we had cloth grid maps which showed the coastline, islands, rivers and airstrips. The vertical grid showed letters and the horizontal grid showed numbers. The code changed daily. The primitive radar we had...could give us only coordinates of the enemy and either 'high' or 'low' (usually 'high'). We had to plan our own attack pattern based on enemy position information (from fighter sector)."

There were certainly limitations in those first days of 31 RDF operations, but with RDF, Sandfly Gully and Bill Woodnutt's team on Bathurst Island they at least now had some warning.

Number 31 RDF Station was the forerunner in the radar network, though conditions were at best basic for some months. Hal Porter, a young Flying Officer arrived there in May 1942, and described the mess as being "...under a tarpaulin at the side of a galvanised iron hut. Rice and goldfish [canned fish in tomato sauce]...were on the menu. The entrance to the station was between a gap in the six foot sandbag walls...the radar building was of corrugated iron...painted green and black...a few artificial trees and camouflage net reinforced the screening of genuine trees. Above the roof the aerial slowly turned dragging along artificial tree branches and trailings of Hessian." Compared to other comments Porter's were complimentary.

Despite technical difficulties, an initial lack of cooperation and poor conditions, 31 RDF Station and the chain of radar stations that followed were vital in detecting Japanese incursions. Photo: Alford/AHSNT Colln.

Once the teething problems had been either solved or adapted to, other stations followed. 105 RDF Station was established at Charles Point on Cox Peninsula and came on line on the 29th while 38 RDF Station was established at Cape Fourcroy on Bathurst Island, again under many difficulties made worse by its remoteness, poor access and lack of equipment. By the time 44 Radar Wing was established at Adelaide River on 12 December 1942, it comprised 31, 105, 38, 39 at Port Keats, 109 at Mount Woods, and 132 at Knuckeys Lagoon east of Darwin. Further stations were developed on the old Southport Road, at Fenton, Cape Van Diemen on Melville Island, and at Cape Don, Milingimbi, Yirrkala and the Wessel Islands.

From 22 March 1942, the Japanese encountered fighter opposition over Darwin for the first time. Bolstered by radar, the 3.7" A-A defences at the Oval, McMillans, Fannie Bay, Coonawarra and the 'Quarantine' along with the 102nd AA Bn (Coastal Artillery) US Army and their .50" guns, the P-40Es of the 49th Pursuit Gp would ensure that the enemy was no longer able to arrive unannounced or escape unscathed – or so the theory went.

The 102nd AA Bn had arrived by various means beginning in mid-March, with Battery B comprising six officers, 125 EM and 14 water-cooled .50 cal A-A machine guns assigned to the RAAF Station. Two unit personnel died when the Qantas flying boat, G-AEUF, *Corinthian*, struck debris after landing on Darwin harbour on 22 March. First Lt Edward O. Hubbard and Pvt Woodrow Ravenscraft were later awarded the Soldier's Medal for heroism in saving the lives of other men aboard the plane. The aircraft second pilot, Russell Tapp, was hospitalised for some months and

INTO COMBAT

received a Commendation for services to aviation after diving to try and rescue trapped passengers while the aircraft captain, Lewis Ambrose, was awarded a similar award for his work in maintaining the air links between Java and Broome.

Machine gunners of the American 102nd AA Bn (CA) manning their .50 cal. gun at one of the roadside fighter airstrips south of Darwin. Photo: Edward Rogers.

By 8 April 31 officers and 560 EM of the 102nd, along with their 49 .50 cal. machine guns and necessary equipment had been flown to Darwin. It was the first time an anti-aircraft unit had been flown into combat. The American Batteries were assigned to protect the RAAF Station and airfields south of Darwin.

The Japanese struck again on 28, 30 and 31 March and on 2 April with a combined force of 31 *Bettys* and 26 *Zekes*, with seven *Bettys* carrying 83 60 kg bombs, led by Lt Takeharu Fujiwara on the 28th; one flown by Lt Asihiro had its port engine shot up and it lagged far behind the others on the return journey.

Four *Bettys* and one *Zeke* were claimed by the 9th Squadron over the four raids, though only one bomber can be confirmed from the combat of the 28th, possibly that of Asihiro's. The Japanese claimed 17 P-40s and four damaged over the same period. The Americans lost Lt Clayton Peterson's aircraft, 41-5548, when Lt Robert McComsey was forced to bale out after being shot up over Darwin. The combined efforts of the P-40s and 31 RDF brought an acknowledgment from CAS Sir Charles Burnett; "QUOTE. PLEASE CONGRATULATE HUDSON PERSONNEL FOR GOOD WORK 27/3 AND RD/F PERSONNEL AND P40 PILOTS FOR EFFECTIVE INTERCEPTION 28/3. TAILS UP. UNQUOTE."

Two days later on the 4th, Takao *Ku* and 3 *Ku* sent over six *Bettys* and six *Zekes* to bomb the RAAF Station in what turned out to be a disastrous day for both sides.

The *Bettys* were from Takao *Ku*'s *Hikokitai-Sento-Kodo-Choso* 51st, 52nd and 53rd subdivision "...from the 5th *Chutai* of the Takao *Ku*, escorted by six Zeros," Japanese records confirm. They reached the Darwin area at 1348 hours and two minutes later reported an interception by seven P-40s, though 14 were airborne. At 1353 hours the *Bettys* released their bombs over the airfield in three two-plane elements flying in a V formation. At the same time, the last Japanese bomber on the right side of the formation caught fire and crashed. A minute later the last plane in the left side of the V was hit, caught fire, dropped out of formation and crashed. A minute after that, a third plane, the element leader of the left hand element, was hit, dropped out of formation and went down in flames. The three crews of Pilots FCPO Noboru Ashazawa (Nightcliff), Flyer 1c Shigeoshi Matsuda (T-361) and Flyer 1c Denichi Inada perished.

The three surviving aircraft made it home, all with some degree of damage and were reportedly written off. The leader's plane had one hole, his wingman three holes, and the surviving element leader on the right side of the formation had three bullet holes. The Japanese bombers' claim of three P-40s shot down by their defensive fire was subsequently disproved. The *Zekes* suffered no losses and claimed one confirmed kill, whilst claiming four P-40s destroyed. Allied claims were also extravagant, claiming one bomber more than the force that had been despatched. The first *Betty* fell into the shallows off Nightcliff and was claimed by the gunners of 14 HAA Bty at Fannie Bay, whilst another, coded T-361, crashed on Cox Peninsula. A third went into the sea, but was not recovered. The aircraft downed over

INTO COMBAT

Cox Peninsula was a straggler, damaged over the target and claimed by Lt John D. Landers.

Gunner Peter Roberts (right), an army mate and friends inspecting the wreckage of the Betty which crashed into the shallows off Nightcliff on 4 April 1942. Photo: Peter Roberts.

Lieutenant Cyril Molyneux, 2IC at West Point on Cox Peninsula described two of the aircraft, which were "...trailing whitish smoke and started to fall back from the formation. Within a short time...one plane exploded in a ball of fire and black smoke. The second one started to dive away and I lost sight of it because two more of the formation started to trail white smoke and fall behind and all attention was on the formation. One of the falling planes...could be heard coming down with engines screaming to an ear shattering pitch and finally crashing on Cox Peninsula where it started a fire. Next day I took a party out...and we soon located the wreckage. The main fuselage was fairly intact, one engine nearby, the other missing...One body outside plane and two inside. There may have been a fourth. I took personal papers from the body inside including photos (no doubt of his family) and sent these across to Darwin...next day a party went to the crash site with the M.O., Capt. H. D.R. Miller, and buried the Japanese with solemnity..."

Despite having at least two aircraft from which to gain vital intelligence information, little other than some personal papers including a bank pass book were recovered from the two aircraft. In a report on the recording of makers' plates the Directorate of Intelligence later wrote that "...the meager results from the *Betty*, number not yet ascertained, which crashed at WEST POINT, DARWIN, on 4th April, 1942...was the first to crash in any theatre of operations where it was available for identification and study. After gathering plates from all sources over a period of months, including plates intercepted in censorship, and those casually submitted by

Air Force personnel as individuals, only eleven component plates have become available. Neither the serial number of the aircraft, nor the organizational number and symbol usually found on the tail were recovered, notwithstanding that the aircraft serial number is usually found stenciled [*sic*] in upwards of 20 places on a *Betty* aircraft...In the case of the *Betty* from WEST POINT, souveniring probably played a major part in the destruction or dispersal of irreplaceable information. By the failure to obtain the necessary plate information, the opportunity for securing intelligence about the *Betty* aircraft and its production rates was postponed..."

From then on intelligence gathering was more detailed and yielded much more valuable information. But had the investigating officers walked 300 metres further they would have located the tail fin complete with the unit designation, T-361.

American and Australian personnel inspecting the wreckage of Lt John D. Livingstone's P-40E following his fatal crash at the 34-Mile airstrip on 4 April 1942. Photo: Alford/AHSNT Colln.

At the '34-Mile' airstrip the 9th Squadron was mourning the loss of Lt John D. Livingstone after he crashed on landing after combat. The aircraft 41-24873 crashed on the southern overrun and Livingstone "...was burnt and still sitting in [the] cockpit when I found him..." wrote the Squadron CO, Clarke Selman, many years later. Lt Grover J. Gardner had baled out of his '74' 41-5551 over the harbour and was rescued whilst a third aircraft, 41-5316, flown by Lt James A. Watkins nosed over after a forced landing at the RAAF Station. A 3 *Ku* pilot, FCPO Kiyoshi Ito, claimed one P-40.

The losses of the aircraft of Livingstone and Gardner were attributed to over exuberance on the part of the pilots after they flew across the RAAF Station shortly after three *Zekes* had strafed the area. Whilst they lowered their

INTO COMBAT

undercarriages as a recognition code, "P40s [sic] which flew across the aerodrome with wheels down shot at by our Ack-Ack", an annotation to the raid report reads. One of the 102nd AA Bty Sgts was so irate he was in tears, he related, and 'just wanted to punch someone.'

Livingstone was buried at the Gardens Cemetery in Darwin on 6 April. Eight days later the 9th Squadron moved from Batchelor to the '34-Mile' permanently, "...all except 30 men...the move was held up by the pilots' pet dog having a litter...and a grass fire that burned up a few tents", the unit historian recorded. A mechanic, Clint Palmer, also recalled that "...we had a brush fire that went through camp, all that was left was the tent pole, all personal items were destroyed and [we] had no extra clothes. There was no US army quarter master supplies, so could not get replacement clothes. Thanks to the Aussie QM [we] got some essential items."

Twenty one days after his death, the '34-Mile' was nominated as Livingstone Field under General Order AG 323.7 and officially designated under General Order 52 on 14 May.

The Japanese returned the day after their heavy losses of the 4th, though no damage and no losses were recorded. There was a lull for a further three weeks during which the remaining squadrons arrived in the Darwin area. The 9th Squadron's main ground echelon had arrived on 31 March and moved straight into the '34-Mile', whilst the 7th Squadron arrived at Batchelor on 6 April, where they remained for the rest of their tour.

An advance party of 25 men of the 49th ICS, the USAAF equivalent of a fighter sector, arrived at Noonamah ('Jungle Jump') south of the '27-Mile' strip three days later and commenced organising a camp area for the unit. Lt Joseph Field and four EM followed on the 12th while the majority of personnel were airlifted to Batchelor. The aircraft flew out on the 20th, 21st and 23rd. The flight of the 21st never made it.

After departing Daly Waters for Batchelor, the aircraft, a Lockheed 14, VH-ADY *Adelaide*, leased from Guinea Airways, overflew Batchelor and became lost. The crew, Captain Duncan Cameron and First Officer Bill Gray, were experienced pilots, but when night fell and fuel became short, they seem to have been looking for a place to land

near Annaburroo homestead. Whether they tried to land will never be known but they lowered the undercarriage and circled only to strike a ridge. The undercarriage sheared and the aircraft cartwheeled down the slope before catching fire. Both crew and ten passengers died in the inferno.

Despite extensive searches the aircraft was assumed as missing and the search called off on the 29th. It was another two months before the Annaburroo station owner, Harry Hardy, stumbled upon the wreckage. On 25 June Constable Joe Doyle wrote in the Pine Creek Police Station Day Journal, that he had "...the position in hand including... identification discs of the ten (10) American victims [and] the bodies of the two pilots..."

All were buried at Adelaide River on 27 June, Cameron and Gray as RAAF officers, while the ten passengers, Cpls Anthony Gattamelata and Ray Love, and Pvts William Bedord, John Faris, Walter Feret, Richard Schmidt, Buford Willard, Wyatt Wiley, Nick Hinich and Robert George were interred in the American section. A small headstone was erected to Wiley at the 'Jungle Jump' camp and inscribed, *TO The MEMORY Of W. WILEY LOST 4/21/42*; the property was later named 'Wiley's Rest.'

Pilots and ground crew of the 8th Squadron 49th Pursuit Gp on readiness at Adelaide River, April 1942. Photo: Clyde Barnett.

After an eventful trip across the continent north from Canberra and across Queensland via the Brereton Route, the 8th Squadron had flown to the airstrip at Adelaide River on 17 April. There they were to be based while they awaited the completion of their strip at the '27-Mile', but finally the three squadrons were together as a Group. HQ was based at the '35-Mile 'across Berry Creek, with the HQ Squadron flight of five P-40Es, a North American O-47 utility aircraft, 37-326, named *Pregnant Foose* and a RAAF de Havilland Tiger Moth at Livingstone 'strip.

INTO COMBAT

The lull in raids by the Japanese allowed vital works to continue as the Allies organised defences and aircraft dispersal, whilst maintaining the normal patrols, alerts, training and offensive missions as men and equipment allowed. Number 12 Squadron continued its mixed role, flying shipping patrols, searches and a variety of support sorties. Ranging from "...a Recco. of the Gunposts around BATCHELOR AERODROME..." to an "...aerial recco. for a suitable Bombing Range for the Squadron.", the unit flew 479 hours for the month, but losing Wirraway A20-90 on the 12th when it force landed on a salt pan in Bynoe Harbour.

The unit was also involved for over a week in searching, unsuccessfully, for the Lockheed 14, VH-ADY. While many of the unit's flights were considered 'milk runs' there were also the bread runs to fly. Jack 'Squizzy' Taylor recalled flying these sorties in conjunction with the daily patrols. "... we had a patrol – to be over Darwin at dawn – inspect the Harbour and boom, then fly along the coast to Daly River at zero feet to see if there were any boats or footprints in the sand indicating a landing...Peron Is was manned by the Army – we delivered bread and mail each morning by bombing their cook-house. The Army then asked [us] if we could pick up outgoing mail – a 6 ft long hook was rigged up under the fuselage and lowered and retrieved by the observer – their mail was suspended on a line between two 6 ft poles stuck in the sand. We would then make a low pass and collect their mail. W/O Mitchell was my observer on one trip [and] he told me when we landed he did not bother to lower the hook – but we still picked up the mail."

The requirement for aerial medical services, particularly in transporting patients from remote stations was realised when an Australian produced Wackett Gannet, A14-6, of 2 Air Ambulance Unit arrived at Manbulloo. Crewed by Sgt Frank Smallhorn, Cpl Phil Bronk a medical orderly, and AC George Booth, the aircraft was a detachment of 2 AAU, which had formed at Fairbairn on 1 March 1942. They arrived at Batchelor on 25 April: Anzac Day.

The same day saw the Japanese return over Darwin, though ten days previously a *Babs* escorted by four *Zekes* flew towards Darwin on a reconnaissance mission but went unreported. The raid was met by the three squadrons of the 49th flying as a Group for the first time.

12 Squadron pilot, FlgOff Jack 'Squizzy' Taylor, and his observer prepare for a patrol from Batchelor in their 12 Squadron Wirraway, 1942. Photo: Jack Taylor.

A force of 27 *Bettys* escorted by 14 *Zekes* led by LtCdr Katsumi Goro of Takao *Ku* took off from Koepang at 1100 hours (Japan Time). They had been preceded by a *Babs* to reconnoitre Darwin. The force was reported over Bathurst Island at around 1400 hours and 50 P-40s were scrambled to intercept. The *Bettys* dropped their bombs, some 150 of various types, at 1430 hours and they were intercepted as they slanted down on the run to the northwest and home. In a running battle out to sea, the P-40s claimed 10 *Bettys* and two *Zekes* while the Japanese claimed nine P-40s. The available Japanese records confirm four *Bettys* and a *Zeke* lost that day.

One *Betty* only just made it back to base. A crewman, Lt Takeharu Fujiwara, wounded and with four crew dead on board, flew back to Koepang and belly landed the aircraft.

INTO COMBAT

A damage assessment recorded over 180 bullet holes in the aircraft. A fifth could be added to the 49th's scoreboard.

Zeke pilot PO1c Shiro Murakami failed to return to his base and is suspected to have been the victim of Lt Bill Hennon, who "...saw ack-ack fire over Darwin and shortly later [*sic*] saw the bombers and Zeros at 23,000 feet...the Zeros (six in number) were above, about 1,000 feet, and slightly behind. One of the Zeros dove, but fired out of range and headed out to sea. I followed him, came up behind and opened fire at 100 feet...He exploded. I was so close...that parts of the destroyed plane struck my ship but caused only minor damage. I saw the Zero falling in six or seven pieces, all in flames. The main section struck the water and burned for a time...Engagement took place at 16,000 feet about 20 miles northwest of Darwin...I flew back over Darwin, but observed no enemy so I returned to my base..."

A second *Zeke* claimed was the subject of a report by Lt Donald Morse of the 8th Squadron, who was at best ambivalent, having reported only firing at it and claiming it without any further observation. But the 8th took the honours in downing the bombers. Lieutenant James Morehead flying 40-681, *Cisco Kid*, claimed three, Lts Ed Miller and Richard Dennis two each and Lts Mitchell Sims, James Martin and Clyde Barnett one each. Whilst claims totalled ten, and with only four confirmed, it is difficult to determine the successful pilots, though the combat reports indicate that Morehead had two confirmed, whilst Barnett and Martin could claim one each.

Morehead also narrowly missed downing a *Zeke*, recalling that "...inexperience caused the loss of this 'kill'." Referring to himself as M, he continued, relating that he "...carefully lined up the cowling of the radial engine...in the cross hairs of his sight and squeezed the trigger. Six tracers went out and neatly bracketed the Jap on both sides, just as the Zero pilot jerked his plane upward before M could adjust his fire. Careful adjustment...would have bagged the Jap."

Inexperience may have robbed Morehead of a *Zeke*, but it also told on the pilots as they returned to their respective bases. In a scenario similar to that of Lt Sanford on 14 March, Lt Ed Miller refuelled his aircraft, 41-24816, at Batchelor but instead of flying east south east strayed far to the west and force landed at Drysdale Mission in the remote Kimberleys. He bent a propeller blade and had to wait for a replacement. Forced to enjoy the hospitality of Father Serafin Sanz and the monks at the mission there, he was probably sorry to leave. Lieutenant 'Eck' Sims aircraft, 41-5648, was hit and lost oil, forcing him to land at the Bathurst Island Mission. He was returned to Adelaide River and his aircraft was later repaired and returned to service the following day.

Lieutenant Martin landed at Darwin, refuelled, took off "...and got lost and went to Pine Creek, then in here. (Adelaide River)" Lieutenant Barnett in 41-35171 headed east and "...found Lt. Herbert along side me. We flew for about twenty minutes...and he said he had only 20 gallons of gas left. We struck land south of Daly Rivers [*sic*] and flew NE until we hit Batchelor and I landed at Adelaide River." An over enthusiastic Morehead tried a couple of victory rolls over Adelaide River and with "....flat tires [*sic*]...the thrills of the day were not yet over. As [it] touched down the nose... started over and the tail...went straight up in the air, hung for a minute and dropped back down without going on its back."

Lieutenant Barnett found a number of 7.7mm rounds in the mainplane and tailplane of the aircraft he flew that day. It later became Morehead's aircraft '51', *L'il Ace.*

The Japanese returned two days later and the successes of the 25th were overshadowed in what turned out to be a black day for the 8th Squadron. As on the 25th, a *Babs* preceded the raid to reconnoitre Darwin and it was followed up by 17 *Bettys* and 21 *Zekes* from Koepang. Led by Lt Hirata Tanemasa, the force was over Darwin at 1237 hours and they were intercepted by P-40s from all three squadrons. The Americans claimed three bombers and four fighters though only one *Betty* can be confirmed. Two Wireless Air Gunners, Sgts J. B. Rohr and D. C. E. Upjohn were killed at the RAAF Station as they sheltered in a slit trench.

Despite the Japanese claims of 19 P-40s destroyed, the American losses can be confirmed. Captain Allison W. Strauss the CO of the 8th Squadron was shot down over Darwin whilst Lt Owen Fish, also of the 8th was downed in his aircraft, 41-5329. Strauss was last seen being fired on by *Zekes* and observers at Emery Point reported seeing a "...P/40 [*sic*] crash in the sea about 3,000 yards to the N-W...the landing gear was down and motor cut off, and firing long bursts. A motor launch went out immediately but no traces of plane were observed. An oxygen container was later washed ashore..."

INTO COMBAT

Lieutenant Fish was observed to come down in a dive, level out and then slow rolled before spinning into the sea three km south southeast of Swires Bluff. Observers were "...of the opinion the pilot was still alive when he made slow roll at 3000 ft. A motor launch went out immediately and found portions of the plane, an identification card and fragments of a body. The...card was that of Lt. Fish." In a thus-far unexplained twist, Strauss is recorded as being buried on 1 May, whilst Fish remains anonymous.

Captain Allison W. Strauss, CO of the 8th Squadron 49th Pursuit Gp – killed over Darwin 27 April 1942. Photo: Strauss family via Gerry Wood.

Both Strauss and Fish were later awarded the Silver Star under General Order No. 36 of 10 August 1942, as was Lt John D. Livingstone, lost following the 4 April raid.

Lieutenant Stephen Andrew of the 7th Squadron was forced to bale out and Lt James Martin of the 8th force landed in shallow water off Gilruth Point on Cox Peninsula, after having his engine damaged in combat. He descended "...to two or three hundred feet, lowered my flaps and fired all my guns. This slowed me down to a speed of about 65 miles an hour. I landed safely."

Finding his radio was still working Martin called in his position. After spending a night in the bush he was rescued next day by the Dellissaville Aboriginal settlement

superintendent, Jack Murray, and four Aboriginal trackers including 'Turtle'. "That man him little bit hungry now alright," 'Turtle' reported, "We fella been catchem crab now... [and] cookem alonga fire...We get bit alonga American man alright. He bin talk: 'This is real eating boys.'" Martin was no worse for wear but in his report he advised "...all pilots to carry a supply of extra water and food in their planes...Suggest...more cooperation in combat...more team work. Also suggest that all dogfighting with Zeros be prohibited as much as possible." He went on to perfect his landing technique two months later.

Lieutenant Andrew spent some hours in the water, with four P-40s flying top cover. He finally made it to shore on Cox Peninsula near the P-40 of Martin's. Attracting the attention of a group of Australian soldiers under Lt Cyril Molyneux he was taken to their camp at the Point Charles lighthouse where they spent the night. Next day he and Martin were transported to West Point and on to Darwin and their units.

An unannounced visit to the area on 29 April by BrigGen Harold 'Pursuit Hal' George turned to tragedy as George and his party arrived at Batchelor. George had been ordered vide Special Order No. 1 of the 22nd to proceed immediately by aircraft to Darwin to "...assume command of all USAAF [units] in the Darwin area."

Brigadier General George's aircraft, a C-40 No. 519, was flown by Philippines veterans Capt Joe Moore and Lt I. B. Jack Donalson. Captain Allison Ind, George's Aide, stood in as the radio operator whilst *Time Life* magazine correspondent, Mel Jacoby, also accompanied the group. An Australian officer requested a ride from Daly Waters to Darwin and when the aircraft landed at Batchelor, George maintained that was the destination. This was denied and George, caught out, decided to 'have a look around.'

It was a fatal decision. As the group moved from the aircraft a pair of 7th Squadron P-40s scrambled, for no apparent reason, the subsequent inquiry found. The lead aircraft, 41-5621, flown by Lt Jack Dale slewed across the path of the second aircraft, tail number 32 flown by Lt J. W. Tyler and its slipstream in turn made Tyler's aircraft uncontrollable. Tyler slammed into the C-40, hitting BrigGen George, Mel Jacoby and Lt Robert D. Jasper of the HQ Squadron. Jasper was killed instantly, whilst Tyler and a Pvt Lambert suffered head injuries, lacerations and shock.

INTO COMBAT

George and Jacoby were transferred to the station hospital and then to 119 AGH at Adelaide River. Despite the best efforts of the medical staff Jacoby died an hour later whilst BrigGen George lingered a further four hours. He was taken to Melbourne and buried with full military honours. The 49th Fighter Gp newsletter, *The Forty–Niner*, described him as "...one of the finest men anyone could care to know. He was certainly a real leader of men and he held the respect of every person...under his command."

The wreckage of Gen George's C-40 transport aircraft lies in the 'boneyard' at Batchelor following the accident on 29 April. At least three A-24s of the 27th Bomb. Group are visible. Photo: Alford/AHSNT Colln.

After the losses of 25 and 27 April the Japanese failed to appear over Darwin for a further seven weeks. The Allies were able to catch up on vital servicings and equipment, while the 8th Squadron moved into its new base at the '27-Mile'. During early May a number of the 196 Squadron personnel including 33 Officers 163 EM began moving north and on "...May 11, installed themselves in the new camp at the newly-completed '27-Mile' strip southeast of Darwin. With the exception of a small camp at Connelly [Camp Connelly, in the present suburb of Winnellie] to maintain operations at the Fighter Sector, the 8th Sq was now the most advanced base of the 49th..." The '27-Mile' 'strip was known as Strauss Field from 14 May when Livingstone's name came into effect at the '34-Mile'. Captain Mitchell E. 'Eck' Sims was promoted to take command of the 8th Squadron.

As they occupied the new strip, personnel began adapting to the new conditions, though the unsealed runway and taxiways caused a number of problems that remained throughout the strip's wartime use. James Morehead later wrote that after "...our move from Adelaide River, we went to a strip bulldozed alongside the highway...Taxiways

were built that led from the end of the runway into the woods to revetments covered with camouflage netting... when landing the planes would immediately start kicking up dust...This was not so bad on the runway that had a sprinkling of oil, but on the taxi strip and in the revetments, it was thick as pea soup for several minutes...dust settled on the mechanics, the tools, spare parts, oil and hydraulic fluid containers, the airplane and its canopy."

The P-40E, West Palm Beach Playboy, of Clyde Barnett's in its revetted insert at Strauss, July 1942. This aircraft replaced his previous P-40E, '55' Janet, after its loss on 16 June. Photo: Clyde Barnett.

The dust also played havoc with engines, instrument pitot probes and armament; the P-40E was armed with six .50" calibre Browning machine guns which required regular servicing. The dust did however dictate the careful maintenance of aircraft and weapons according to Joe Cunningham, an Armourer with the 9th Squadron, who wrote that "...the guns are badly out of line due to the length of time they have been fired and regular dropping...for thorough cleaning. The guns have been completely removed every third day, bolts removed, polished and cleaned. The freezing and jamming caused by tremendous amount of dust and improper oil has almost entirely disappeared due to careful repeated cleanings and use of graphite based grease instead of oil. The armament section equipped a truck with detachable lights on fifteen foot drop cords in order to do night maintenance...the armorers [*sic*], as other departments are handicapped from lack of supplies..."

Similar conditions were encountered at Livingstone and to a lesser extent at Batchelor and through it all the ground crews serviced aircraft systems, weapons and carried out engine changes, allowing the pilots flying hours to 'slow time' the replacement engines. The efforts of the 'groundies' under quite primitive conditions were largely

INTO COMBAT

unsung, however the *Hammond Times*, a Californian newspaper, did report that the repair crews were doing the impossible. "Leisure and days off are unknown to the men", it reported, "They work from dawn until late at night, often around the clock to get wrecked planes back into combat... the squadron's equipment was still en-route, so hand made tools were manufactured...a total of 44 planes was salvaged in the first seven months and the mechanics did everything but overhaul motors."

Written of the USAAF ground crews, and the 43rd AMS in particular, the description was a common one and indicative of the efforts of USAAF, RAAF, RNEIAF and later the RAF to keep the aircraft operational.

The 43rd AMS had arrived in the Darwin area during March 1942 after arriving aboard the *Mariposa* with the 49th Pursuit Gp and joining them at Bacchus Marsh and Bankstown. The unit's introduction to the Northern Territory was one of trepidation; "...all this Sector is infested with buffalo fly, ticks and sand flies, while there are many crocodiles in the river," one member wrote, "[but] we found a use for these ant hills, broken into small bits and moistened, the substance is spread on the tent floor and packed tightly to produce a concrete-like floor..."

The 43rd AMS was initially assigned a site across the Adelaide River opposite and six km from the airfield from which the 8th Squadron was operating. However it was considered unsuitable. Instead they relocated to a site on Mount Bundy Station only two km north of the airfield on 16 April. Utilising whatever materials they could salvage in the area or acquire from Darwin, the unit constructed a number of specialist workshops, offices, quarters and messes – along with its own water system. The unit became all but autonomous, relying only on Base Section One at Adelaide River for food, provisions and clothing. They also had the assistance of the local Aboriginal people, as did most units, "They were a big help to us in recovering our planes", the unit historian wrote.

One of the unit's first tasks was to salvage the remnants of the 33rd Pursuit Squadron (Provisional) aircraft from the 19 February raids, along with the aircraft of Lt Suehr near Marrakai. Of the wrecks they assessed only four were eventually made airworthy; the others provided only spares, though "It was said that airplane parts were worth more than diamonds along the Australian front."

The unit's primary task however was to maintain and repair the P-40Es of the 49th Pursuit Gp, along with facilities for the supply of spares for a range of USAAF aircraft operating in the area. Commanded by LtCol Horace Diamond, and with Lt Manuel Burke Von Wald among his staff, the unit earned itself a reputation for efficiency in keeping the 49th flying.

Among its many other tasks was the salvage of crashed aircraft and in some cases the remains of the pilots. Lieutenant Ed Miller died when his aircraft, 41-24816, went into an uncontrollable dive from 10,000 feet and crashed near Strauss on 5 June. Crew Chief Bob Baden and Miller's close friend, Lt William C. Herbert went to the site; Herbert was later hospitalised for despondency over Miller's death and evacuated home.

Five days later Lt William Payne died under similar circumstances when his aircraft, 41-5557, crashed near Brocks Creek. Payne had only recently been hospitalised for yellow jaundice, but had also suffered from the effects of high altitude. "He said in confidence that he blacked out more than he told the C.O..." wrote Lt Bob Oestreicher to Payne's family, "I know and I'm sure you do that Bill was unconscious when he hit...It was useless to try to bring back what was left because it was a mere handful." The day following Payne's death, Lt Donald Dittler was forced to abandon 41-5621 when the engine caught fire over Brocks Creek. Dittler parachuted to safety and was returned to his unit at Batchelor. The aircraft was that flown by Lt Jack Dale the day BrigGen George was fatally injured.

These aircraft were a few of the many the 43rd AMS salvaged. In their time at Adelaide River, unit personnel either travelled to or salvaged almost fifty P-40s, along with other types. They ranged from aircraft crash sites as close as their own airstrip to the Daly River, where, after considerable effort they towed out 41-5449 'Minnesota Gopher' which had been force landed by Lt Harold J Martin on 13 June; it was later handed over to the RAAF. The 9th Squadron alone had 26 aircraft lost, crashed or involved in accidents from 24 March to 11 September.

Little wonder the *Hammond Times* reporter wrote so glowingly of the efforts of the mechanics.

The 43rd AMS remained in the Territory long after the departure of the 49th Fighter Gp. In early 1943, Diamond

INTO COMBAT

A P-40E being serviced under primitive conditions at the 7th Squadron's base at Batchelor. Squadron and 43rd AMS mechanics earned a well deserved reputation for their professionalism. Photo: Shane Johnston.

and Burke Von Wald moved it to Fenton where, as the 43rd Service Squadron, they maintained the B-24 Liberators of the 319th Squadron and later the 380th Bomb. Gp.

For the pilots having been involved in training flights and practice scrambles from 27 April, the calm was broken at 1120 hours on 13 June, when 27 *Bettys* and a large force of *Zekes* was plotted by the RDF stations at 180 km bearing 289°. In all 36 P-40s intercepted and in the ensuing combat four P-40s were either lost or damaged.

The P-40E 41-5513 of HQ Squadron pilot, Captain Robert Van Auken, was hit during combat and caught fire. Van Auken baled out at 800 ft and reported being strafed in his parachute. Landing on the southern tip of Melville Island he swam to shore and was later picked up by 'Old Johnnie' and two Aboriginal men after walking some eight kilometres. They took Van Auken by canoe to Darwin where he was hospitalised at Kahlin Hospital; he was later transported to the 4th General Hospital in Melbourne. Van Auken's aircraft was found "...buried ten feet in the mud; one box of

ammunition was the only thing recovarable"

Another pilot reported being strafed while parachuting that day. Lieutenant Pierre L. Alford of the 8th Squadron was attacked and his aircraft 41-25181 caught fire. Alford baled out east of Darwin and was spotted by Lt Earl Kingsley who reported that two "...planes attempted to strafe the parachute. I was still above them and could see tracers from both planes as they passed near the parachute. I dived on them to prevent their strafing again. It was later I found out that the parachute was Lt. Alford." Alford's aircraft crashed on Gunn Point only a few kilometres north of the wreckage of Lt Jack Peres' P-40E downed on 19 February; it was a further three months before Peres was found. Alford was later picked up by an Australian vessel and returned to Darwin.

Lieutenants Charles Johnson and Monroe Eisenberg had their aircraft damaged in combat and subsequently landed at Strauss airstrip, Johnson with a wound to his arm. Two Japanese *Zeke* pilots, FCPO Katsuji Matsushima and

INTO COMBAT

Flyer 1c Mikio Tanakawa were posted missing though no claims were made by the P-40 pilots. They lie in the water somewhere between Darwin and Timor, along with the crews of Hudsons and other aircraft.

The Japanese mounted raids over the following four days, claiming 35 P-40s in combat over the period. Twenty seven *Zekes* on the 14th, followed by 27 *Bettys* with an escort of 21 *Zekes* along with two sorties by *Babs* reconnaissance aircraft each escorted by three *Zekes* on the 15th and 27 *Bettys* with 27 *Zekes* in escort on the 16th. An unescorted force of nine *Bettys* returned on the 17th.

On the 14th the raiders were detected at 105 km distance, bearing 325° at 1253 hours. The P-40s intercepted and while the Japanese reported no losses the Americans claimed four *Zekes*. One P-40E, 41-5565, *Rosemary*, the usual aircraft of Lt Wilson Chapman, was flown by Lt Keith D. Brown and was shot up by *Zekes*. Brown baled out of the burning aircraft over the '11-Mile' transmitters of HMAS *Coonawarra*, breaking a thigh and suffering severe burns. Stan Goodwill, a young naval rating at Coonawarra recalled "...an American pilot was shot down over us & parachuted. The poor devil was terribly burnt from the waist down... whether he survived I'll never know." Brown survived and after landing was "...treated by M.O.s and Orderlies in [the nearby] hospital of the 2/12 Fld Amb. Brown can't say enough about the wonderful treatment received from the 2/12. He was also awarded the Purple Heart", reads a photo caption of Brown on a stretcher shortly after his ordeal. The medal would have provided little compensation for the time Brown spent in Hospital in Brisbane before being evacuated to America.

Next day the Japanese were reported heading for Darwin at 1135 hours and on arrival they targeted the wharf and oil tanks, damaging the railway line, a number of vehicles and several buildings including the *Army News* office. The Japanese suffered no losses despite claims of six *Zekes* and a bomber damaged. Twenty eight P-40s were scrambled and following a running fight out to sea two P-40s were lost.

Lieutenant Claude S. Burtnette of the 7th Squadron was forced to bale out after a 20mm round exploded in the starboard wing, taking the ammunition covers and most of the aileron. Jumping over Quail Island, Burtnette landed in the water some distance from shore and started swimming while Capt Bill Hennon flew cover. Later two 12 Squadron

Wirraways flew cover and after two and a half hours he reached shore. The Wirraways returned and later Hennon flew over and dropped a message. Burtnette was picked up that evening by the RAN lugger *Kuru* and returned to Darwin.

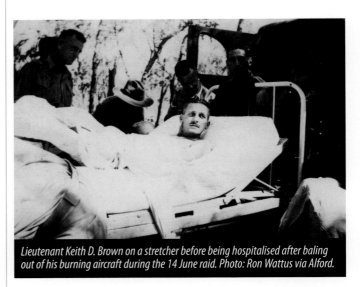

Lieutenant Keith D. Brown on a stretcher before being hospitalised after baling out of his burning aircraft during the 14 June raid. Photo: Ron Wattus via Alford.

Lt Clarence Johnson wasn't so lucky. After attacking a *Betty* he was in turn attacked by a *Zeke*. After firing on another bomber, his engine then caught fire and he baled out over Bynoe Harbour, losing his boots and a map of the food caches along the coast. He landed near a spring and set up a small camp. He did everything right for a time but impatience got the better of him and he wandered away, at one stage swimming from side to side across a river, "...so that I would not miss any camps or food stores which might be on either side."

After five days he was in dense mangroves and thought he heard a motor. In desperation he climbed a tree and saw a small launch. He fired his gun and yelled with no effect until the motor stopped and they answered. He was found by Jack Murray and his trackers from Delissaville and returned to Darwin via the lugger HMAS *Ibis* commanded by Lt Sodersteen. One of the trackers, Jack Mulberry, recalled that following the rescue they cooked tea and stew for Johnson; "That one white man he close up bugger up... him properly hungry bugger. He bin eatum tucker no more little bit."

Despite his rescue it was sheer good fortune that Murray and his trackers were in the area and more so that Murray stopped the engine only on the insistence of tracker Willie.

INTO COMBAT

"...I learned they were a searching party looking for me," Johnson reported, "...they had searched for two days. They later told me they had no idea I was there and had not heard my calls until the motor was stopped."

In his report Johnson recommended a number of do's and don'ts including wearing coveralls, strap-on boots a knife and gun, and in hindsight what he should have done. "Never wander off unless you know exactly what you are doing and always carry a compass" he wrote, "Don't throw away any equipment...don't get excited or hysterical; use your head; But don't drive yourself and use all your energy in one day...a slow steady pace will make your energy last much longer." He was right on the last point; he had lasted five days.

Twenty seven *Bettys* under escort by 27 *Zekes*, one flown by FCPO Kyoshi Sekiya on his first mission with 3 *Ku*, appeared at 25,000 ft and bombed Darwin at 1231 hours on 16 June, injuring eleven, severely damaging the Bank of New South Wales, destroying army equipment, hitting two oil tanks and damaging the Coastal Radio Station VID. Eighteen P-40s of the 8th and 9th Squadrons intercepted though the Japanese reported no losses.

Against claims of one bomber and a *Zeke*, three 8th Squadron P-40s and a pilot were lost, while three others force landed. Lieutenant Andrew Reynolds of the 9th Squadron force landed his aircraft 41-25180 near Berry Springs after the coolers were damaged in combat while Lt John Fisher crash landed his aircraft 41-5560 at Batchelor. Both were salvaged by the 43rd AMS and removed to Adelaide River for repairs. Lieutenant Robert McComsey of the 9th Squadron saved the salvage crews some travel time: he force landed his badly damaged aircraft 41-24832 at the 147th Field Artillery range just north of Adelaide River.

Lieutenant Chester Namola and his aircraft 41-5553 simply disappeared. Flying wing man to Lt Randall Keator, Namola was last seen as the four plane element attacked the bombers southwest of Bathurst Island near Gunn Point. "We started in to attack and before reaching the bomber formation three Zeros dropped their belly tanks, and...we could not get to the bombers, so we dived away from them, and that is when I lost my wing man..." Keator reported. Namola remains missing.

Lieutenant James Martin forced landed at Cape Gambier on Melville Island after his engine overheated following combat. He used his technique of landing on water as he had on 27 April and after swimming ashore and walking some distance to fill his water canteen he returned to the aircraft. He was rescued the following day by a naval vessel replenishing food dumps. "The plane bearing the name *Janet No. 55* was later discovered about 30 yards in the water...a note with the name of the pilot, Lt. Martin was found in a dead tree...also parts of his parachute," reported John Gribble from the Snake Bay settlement. Martin had been flying Lt Clyde Barnett's aircraft 41-5543 '55' named 'Janet' after his wife.

A flight or Shotai of G4M1 *Bettys* of the Takao Ku approach the coast. Photo: Bernard Baeza.

Lieutenant Bruce Harris was apparently hit after heading west to head off and attack the bombers. Turning towards land over Fog Bay he noticed he had only 38 l of fuel remaining and decided to land. He put down southeast of Point Blaze however the undercarriage collapsed and the aircraft caught fire. After resting, Harris decided to walk to a food cache to the north, leaving a note and carrying water, rations and a medical kit. On the fourth day he arrived at a beach where he was spotted by a 12 Squadron Wirraway, which dropped water.

In the meantime a de Havilland Tiger Moth flown by FltLt Pye had located Harris' P-40 on the 18th, landed and found his note. Returning to Batchelor, Pye took an Aboriginal tracker, 'Smiler' Fejo, on board and flew out again. After being dropped at the site, 'Smiler' followed Harris' tracks until the next day when the tracks ran out at aircraft wheel marks. Correctly surmising that Harris had been picked up and waiting for the aircraft to pick him up, 'Smiler' found "...geese feeding grounds, so I cut down three short stick[s] so I can throw them...Two sticks I hit two geese...Carried geese back to swag...got knife, cut two very short sticks,

INTO COMBAT

and set down and made fire stick. Then I cooked the geese." Indeed Harris had been picked up by Pye two hours after being found by the Wirraway; had he stayed he may have learned some of the survival skills of the Aboriginal people who had so much to offer Allied airmen downed over such a hostile environment.

Almost ten months later, Ross Stagg, a young Spitfire pilot in similar circumstances, found Harris' P-40 during his three week ordeal in the area.

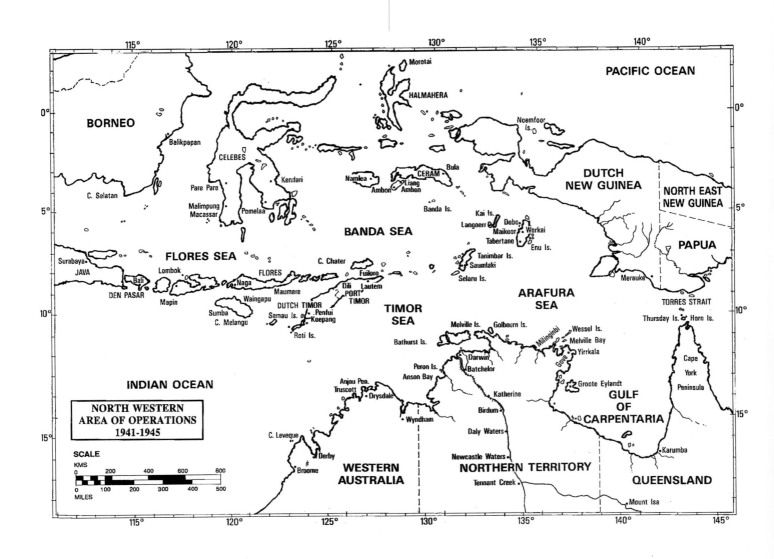

CHAPTER 6

CHANGES IN THE AIR
Reorganisation, Americans depart and the RAAF takes over

The day following Lt Harris' rescue a simple message was transmitted from the mission at Milingimbi by the Reverend Arthur Ellemore, "...Sergeant Frank Smallhorn, Corporal Phillip Bronk, AC1 George Booth; crew of Gannet A14-6 reported missing 19th May; now alive and well at this mission..."

The message marked the end of an epic 33 days of survival in a remote and inhospitable part of the Territory. It had commenced at 0700 hours on 19 May when the aircraft had departed 2 AAU's base at Batchelor, bound for Groote Eylandt. From there they were to evacuate an airman suffering from dysentery. "We had been flying for about 2 hours when I noticed the magnetic compass was behaving in an extraordinary manner," Smallhorn recalled, "...it was swinging very wildly covering an arc of 30 degrees or more both to port and starboard...The directional gyroscopic compass was U/S, and had been for some weeks. We were over 'tiger' country and had no idea where we were...the weather had changed...with heavy black cumulo-nimbus... [and] a ceiling down to less than 1000 feet, and very poor visibility...I decided to force land and spotted a likely looking site, on a swampy piece of ground covered with reeds and kunai grass 3-4 feet high."

Corporal Bronk and Sgt Smallhorn ponder the meaning of life after their forced landing on 19 May. They and AC1 George Booth survived 33 days before being rescued. Photo: George Booth

Smallhorn attempted to land on what to George Booth "...appeared to be a well grassed plain." It wasn't, and the aircraft somersaulted, though the crew escaped uninjured. The following few days were spent taking stock of their

resources and constructing a raft from the aircraft's fuel tanks. They then set off down a river, probably the Cato, on their raft, named *Santa Maria*. Attacked by crocodiles and continually beset by mosquitoes and sand flies the trio suffered appalling conditions before they eventually "... floated out of the river mouth and landed on Elcho Island." There they were taken in by an Aboriginal group under the leadership of the elder, Matui. They were fed for some days before being rowed across to Milingimbi via Howard Island. From Milingimbi they were flown to Darwin by Avro Anson and a brief period of hospitalisation before returning to duty. Their time with Matui and his group was an experience remembered by the three airmen for many years.

By mid year the strategic position in the NWA had improved to the extent that a number of units were able to move north and by July the reorganisation included the establishment of I RSU, 1 MWS, 5 and 9 RCs and 2 BPSO among many others. As the Australians began to plan for an increased presence, the RAAF's 1 MRS moved from its site at the 'five-mile' waterhole south of Daly Waters to a new site at the Batchelor turn-off on the main north-south road and opposite a developing Coomalie Creek airfield. Sited on a slope overlooking the Batchelor road, 1 MRS occupied the former hospital facility of the 135th Medical Regt. From there the unit provided medical facilities for the combat units and airfields south of Darwin.

Operational RAAF squadrons in the area comprised 12 Squadron, which had moved temporarily to Pell from 15 July, 2 Squadron at the RAAF Station and 34 (Transport) Squadron at Hughes. Number 34 Squadron had formed at the Civil 'Drome four days after the 19 February air raids and was initially equipped with two de Havilland DH 84s. Under command of FltLt J. W. Warwick, the unit moved to Daly Waters in March and carried out supply flights to Milingimbi, Batchelor and Darwin before again moving, this time to Batchelor, on 13 May.

Equipped with two Avro Anson and two de Havilland Tiger Moths the unit moved to Hughes on 15 July before relocating to Manbulloo on 27 August. The unit's aircraft were allocated to 6 Comm. Unit on 13 December and later in the war 34 Squadron operated C-47 aircraft in a variety of transport and supply roles.

CHANGES IN THE AIR

By mid year also, 5 Fighter Sector had developed into a more efficient unit with both Australian and Americans involved in the development of a reliable plotting system. Working with the Australians, the personnel of the "... [49th] Interceptor Control had fitted into the combat scheme..." the unit historian recorded. "At the advent of the war an Australian radio locator had been in operation [but] it supplied...inefficient air warning. The members who had formed the nucleus of the unit were familiar with plotting work...personnel acquired from the 31st Pursuit Gp knew radio's relationship with plotting...[and] between [them] was enough information to reorganize [sic] the Fighter Sector and relieve the Australian unit..."

The RAAF also saw the need for a more efficient system and Flying Officer Northey proposed that a standby fighter sector be built into trucks to provide a mobile unit. The idea was met with immediate approval and the 49th ICS provided 22 trucks, waterproofed them and fitted them out with plotting boards, radios and control facilities. With provision for five radio circuits it was the first mobile fighter sector in the RAAF and remained in use until late 1943. The Australians gained experience working with the Americans and took over operations when the fighter sector was handed back to the RAAF later in the year.

The operations room at the Fighter Sector, Berrimah. The use of trucks in providing a mobile unit is evident. Photo: AHSNT Colln.

RAAF personnel also constructed a new facility for the fighter sector on a small rise opposite the former 119 AGH site. They moved in on 17 August while the Sandfly Gully facility was shut down and relocated to the old hospital. Soon after the new fighter sector had been commissioned, all radar stations and observer posts were placed under 5 Fighter Sector's control. This was to provide a centralised

point for the collection and dissemination of information to the defences, which included the A-A and AASL btys.

With a lull in the air raids, the opportunity was taken for visits, inspections and medal presentations by high ranking Allied officers. In late June Generals Brett and Richardson spent several days in the Darwin area inspecting and visiting the American units. On 8 July Brett was again in the area, this time at Livingstone for the presentation of medals. "The ceremony was unique in that it was performed on a fighting strip in the front lines" the 49th's historian recorded, "...from which several of the pilots had taken off to perform the deeds for which they were to be honored [sic]. A large crowd of American and Australian airmen formed a hollow square around the general and the men receiving the awards. P-40s lined the field and a flight of Hudson bombers circled overhead."

In all, 4 DSCs, 12 Silver Stars and 5 Purple Hearts were awarded, while a DFC with Oak Leaf Cluster was awarded to Maj Hervey Whitfield, a weather officer. The Australians were also involved and the Hudsons were no coincidence: a DFC was awarded to FltLt Robert Dalkin of 13 Squadron.

The parade at Livingstone airstrip, 8 July 1942. RAAF pilot, FltLt Bob Dalkin was awarded a DFC for his daring raid on the Japanese base at Penfoie on 30 March. Photo: Wilfreid Zeigler.

Four days following the awards ceremony, Lt John S. Sauber was killed and Lt George E. Preddy badly injured in a training accident over Manton Dam. Commanded by Lt I. B. Jack Donalson, the 9th Squadron flight comprised Lts Dick Taylor, George E. Preddy and John S. Sauber.

During the flight the aircraft were over Manton Dam when Sauber dived on Preddy's aircraft in a mock attack.

CHANGES IN THE AIR

Sauber's aircraft struck Preddy's P-40 and both aircraft fell to earth. Donalson later recalled that "Sauber...looked at me and signalled [sic] he was starting his pass and I could see clearly that he was too close to have room to maneuver [sic] ...before he could break off the pass he collided with Preddy." Sauber is thought to have been either killed or disabled in the collision. His aircraft crashed and burned after rolling down into a small gully. Donalson "...circled, until Preddy landed - [we] returned to the base - got help and went to the crash site and recovered Preddy and the remains of Sauber [whose] body was still in what was left of the cockpit."

Preddy was more fortunate. He bailed out and parachuted to safety, badly injuring his leg on a tree as he landed. He recovered at a hospital in Melbourne before being transferred to the European Theatre, where he went on to become America's leading ace, until he was shot down and killed by American anti-aircraft fire on Christmas Day, 1944.

A 9th Squadron mechanic demonstrates his artistic skills on the P-40 '74' Kip of Lt Sid Woods at Livingstone airstrip. Photo: Wilfreid Zeigler.

The lull in the raids didn't last long. The Japanese returned in late July, though they were conducted by flights of three *Bettys* operating independently at night. Over six nights from the 25th they targeted Darwin town, the RAAF Station, Vesteys and Knuckeys Lagoon. Whilst damaging or destroying some buildings and infrastructure with no losses to themselves, in effect they achieved little other than to keep the area awake.

On 30 July 1942 three *Bettys* took off for Darwin at 0103 hours, damaged several buildings and returned to Koepang at 0650 hours. Four hours later 26 *Bettys* and 21 *Zekes*

departed Koepang heading for Darwin and the RAAF Station. They were plotted at 1209 hours at 258 km giving the 27 P-40s time to gain height for an interception. The P-40s "...made contact with the Japs and exacted a heavy toll of six Zeros and three bombers", the Group historian recorded, "...with so many other enemy ships damaged that it was assessed as highly probable that as many as twenty planes did not return to their base." One P-40, that of Lt Gene F. Drake, was lost when he was attacked by two *Zekes*. Drake baled out and was rescued by a patrol boat later that day.

The Japanese dropped 160 bombs on and around the RAAF Station damaging a 2 Squadron Hudson, cratering the runway, cutting land lines and destroying fuel stocks. Despite the claims by the American pilots, the available Japanese records list one *Zeke* as being lost. Equally extravagant, the Japanese pilots claimed 17 P-40s destroyed in combat.

The USAAF almost lost another P-40 when Lt Jim Morehead took off to intercept an early morning raid by three *Bettys*. Disoriented by the black out over Darwin and the airstrips, "...all of M's plans had become unglued. His hope of avoiding punishment for the unauthorised flight by bagging a Jap *Betty* bomber was dashed...he would be lucky to get his own skin back to earth," Morehead wrote. Fortunately he was able to convince Hughes controllers to turn the runway lights on and he made a successful landing, his "...first in a P-40E. Last and not least in this sad mission came the chewing out by the Sq. and Group commanders. Oh, for the life of a fighter pilot!!!"

August saw a major change in the make up of Darwin's aerial defences when 77 Squadron RAAF flew in to Batchelor on the 19th. Flying P-40E Kittyhawks, the Australian unit was to work in conjunction with the 49th Fighter Gp. The aircraft and pilots had been preceded by a contingent of ground staff who arrived on the 17th and commenced setting up a camp and making arrangements for the arrival of the P-40s. Rumours were already circulating among the Americans that they would be transferred in the near future and as if to give them at least some credence, a General Order was received from HQ in Melbourne on the 22nd disbanding the HQ, and HQ Squadron of the 49th and a number of other groups.

CHANGES IN THE AIR

Three weeks passed before the next raid on 23 August. Twenty seven *Bettys* escorted by a like number of *Zekes* departed Koepang at 0830 and 0855 hours, this time heading for Hughes airfield. Intercepted out to sea by 24 P-40s they lost four *Zekes* and a *Betty* before they arrived over Hughes at 1242 hours. The 3 *Ku* lost Lt Tadasune Tokaji, PO2c Nobutoshi Furukawa, PO2c Itsuzo Shimizu and PO3c Yoshiyuki Hirata. One *Zeke*, a Nakajima produced A6M2, manufacturer's number 916, crashed on land in the Bynoe Harbour area; 18 P-40s were claimed by the *Zekes*.

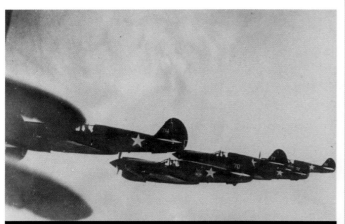

A flight of 9th Squadron P-40s. Aircraft '70' Scatterbrain is that of Capt George Manning and sports the 'bunyip 'emblem he devised when serving with the 7th Squadron. Photo: Alford Colln.

The USAAF P-40 pilots claimed seven *Bettys* and eight *Zekes* while Lt Frederick O'Reilly force landed his aircraft 41-35941 *Stew Head II* on a beach in Finke Bay east of Darwin. Damage to Hughes included the destruction of Wirraway A20-599 and a Brewster Buffalo A51-6, both on strength to the newly arrived 1 PRU. The runway was cratered and 250 drums of fuel and other stocks including ammunition were lost.

Another P-40 was lost the following day when Lt Lawrence Hansen's aircraft 41-24868 caught fire during an air test west of Batchelor. Hansen baled out and the aircraft crashed near a branch of the Finniss River.

After the claims of the 23rd, American HQ was jubilant. MacArthur was moved to signal Wurtsmith his congratulations "FOR GENERAL KENNEY STOP MY HEARTIEST FELICITATIONS TO INTERCEPTING UNITS OF DARWIN YESTERDAY STOP THAT IS THE WAY TO DO IT END" A more personal, and possibly more relevant, signal of the 25th read, "QUOTE SET UP THE BEER ON ME DAMN GOOD WORK QUOTE WURTSMITH UNQUOTE"

and "I DESIRE TO ADD MY CONGRATULATIONS TO THOSE ALREADY RECEIVED...FOR THE EXCELLENT TEAMWORK DISPLAYED...MY REGRETS THAT COL. WURTSMITH'S REQUEST TO SET UP THE BEER CANNOT BE CARRIED OUT. SIGNED COL. HUTCHINSON..."

Soon afterwards the Group was awarded a Presidential Citation and in effect it was timely as it was the last raid the P-40s were to intercept before moving from Darwin

Personnel of 3 Ku pose alongside A6M2 Zeke X-152. The aircraft is a Houkoku or presentation aircraft as evidenced by the markings on the fuselage side. Photo: Bernard Baeza.

Number 1 PRU had arrived from Laverton on 19 August equipped with a mixed bag of aircraft including Wirraways, three Republic P-43 Lancers, two Brewster Buffalos and later the F4 version of the Lockheed P-38 Lightning. The aircraft were, in the main, discards, lacking the range and performances required by reconnaissance aircraft and were not a success in the NWA. Bladin considered that among the aircraft "...Buffalos were not suitable for the task in hand and would not be used in operations." Fitted with three F24 focal cameras they were instead relegated to flying local photographic sorties. Whilst three of the type, A51-4, '5 and '6 were on strength, only '5 and '6 made it to the NWA. A51-4 lasted only three days before crashing at Laverton on 16 June. A51-6 was lost in the 23 August raid on Hughes and A51-5 crashed near Derby on 25 September, bringing their shortlived careers to an end.

The P-43 Lancers were no better. A56-3 crashed at Coomalie on 3 January 1943, while A56-4 was plagued with mechanical problems and saw little operational flying. The third, A56-5 was badly damaged in a landing accident at Coomalie on 14 December; both survivors were returned to the USAAF 5th Air Force in August the following year.

CHANGES IN THE AIR

The Lightnings were allocated to the unit from October 1942 and fared little better, being progressively written off in accidents. A55-2 lasted only three weeks before it crashed three kilometres west of Strauss and the pilot, SqnLdr Cridland, killed during an asymmetric approach to Hughes on 20 November. A55-3 flew a number of sorties as far as Timor before it landed at Batchelor with its undercarriage retracted and caught fire on 10 December 1943. Despite technical problems A55-1 flew a number of sorties over Timor and the NT before being destroyed by fire at Coomalie on 1 September 1944.

A55-1, one of three Lockheed F4 model Lightnings allocated to the RAAF after moving over its wheel chocks in high winds at Coomalie on 10 January 1944. Photo: AHSNT Colln.

The unit needed more reliable aircraft if it was to fulfil its role, however any replacements were some months away. From January 1943 it was relegated to providing photographers to fly with the B-24s of the 319th Bomb. Squadron of the 90th Bomb. Gp USAAF.

August also saw the Japanese commence night raids on a regular basis. Flights of three *Bettys* from Takao *Ku* came over at irregular hours, ranging from 2145 hours to 0529 hours, from the 24th to the 31st. No intercepts were made and damage was confined to buildings and infrastructure, whilst the Coastal Radio Station, VID, was severely damaged on the night of the 27th.

The following month saw the commencement of an increased Australian role on Darwin's defence when the 49th Fighter Gp began moving out. The changes in the NWA were part of Gen George Kenney's move to form an independent American Air Force, though the idea had been initiated in Washington to 'create a separate, entirely American Air Force for serving outside the Australian mainland.' Kenney made the idea his own and formed the 5th Air Force. He gave Wurtsmith 5th Fighter Command, moved the 49th Fighter Gp to join the 35th Fighter Gp in New Guinea, and ordered 76 Squadron to Darwin from Milne Bay. The untried 77 Squadron was ordered to Darwin from Pearce in Western Australia.

The first of the 49th Fighter Gp squadrons to go was the 7th, when aircraft and a number of ground personnel departed Batchelor for the Group's new base at 'Maple', the code word for New Guinea, on 9 September. Ralph Boyce, an armament mechanic with the 7th Squadron, and later a writer for *Stars and Stripes*, recorded the departure of Lt Wilson 'Chip' Chapman's aircraft *Rosemary III*. "...an Australian flew Rosemary. I do not know his name but he is [a] tall, competent looking flying officer with a bristling red moustache...He lowered his lanky frame into the cockpit...& kicked the energizer. When the engine roared to life smoothly...a little smile crept out from under the moustache...A wink at me on one wing and a smile at Wilding and Gordon on the other & he gave her the gun & taxied out...to disappear from view on the early morning mists..." The pilot was Flt Lt Cruikshank of 77 Squadron.

The ICS was next to leave under Movement Order 68, ordering the unit to Townsville. Departing their camp at 'Jungle Jump' on the 13th, two officers and 137 EM travelled in trucks on what was loosely called the north-south road and Barkly Highway, while two officers and 33 EM left by sea the following day. The balance had to suffer the luxury of travelling by air.

P-40s of the 7th Squadron over the Batchelor area. The lead aircraft, '10', is that of the squadron CO, Capt Bob Morrissey. Photo: via Gordon Birkett.

As the 8th Squadron at Strauss was preparing to move to 'Maple', a number of RAAF personnel visited Livingstone

CHANGES IN THE AIR

Pilots of 77 Squadron at Livingstone airstrip, late 1942. A future Australian Prime Minister, John Gorton, is standing, 4th from left. Photo: Alford/AHSNT Colln.

and Strauss before sending crews to make a number of improvements to the camps and dispersal areas. On 11 September "...the 77th Squadron for the first time joined with squadrons of the 49th in the daily patrol schedule."

That day also saw the 49th FG issued with a belated Movement Order No. 70 from HQ USAAF ordering them to "...depart from Darwin by water to 'secret destination' in a permanent change of station." Clyde Barnett recorded that Strauss was visited by the CO of 77 Squadron and the CO of an Operational Training Unit in Victoria on the 15th. There they discussed tactics with the 8th Squadron pilots and inspected the camps and airfield.

Two weeks later on 25 September the ground crews departed aboard the MV *Sea Witch*, while the pilots also learned that the squadron had been assigned an airfield "...the closest to Kokoda and the furthest of four from Port Moresby". On the 30th Barnett packed his aircraft and the following morning he was "...Up at dawn and ready to leave at 0800...No one knew about it as Eck (Sims) had forgotten

to tell them...Eck led Blue Flight, the first to leave - have two RAAF pilots, one in Ben Duke's #59 and one in Keator's #68 *Spodessape*. The RAAF pilots fly very close formation... had times of 1 hr 50 mins from Strauss to Daly Waters and 3 hr 20 mins from D.W. To Cloncurry."

The 9th Squadron was not far behind them. "...all available men are packing equipment ...Only a skeleton crew of mechanics and radio and armament men are kept on the line..." the unit historian recorded on 28 and 30 September, "...our ground echelon is moving supplies to the docks at Darwin ready to load on short notice. All 25 planes in good shape, [with] 20 pilots available."

"...at the end of September orders came through for us to leave also - pilots and crew chiefs by air via Townsville - others by way of water via Horn Island" Squadron pilot and Operations Officer, Jesse Peaslee recorded, "...The air echelon departed en masse one morning about October 7 - 25 P-40's and two transports. It was an uneventful flight to Charleyville [sic]..."

CHANGES IN THE AIR

And so, the aerial defence of Darwin was from then in the hands of the RAAF. The 49th Fighter Gp had come to Darwin at a time when the Australian forces were stretched to the limit and had played a crucial role in blunting the Japanese raids. During the period from its arrival in Darwin the Group claimed 70 enemy aircraft and assumed that a number of other enemy aircraft failed to make it back to their bases. The RDF stations scattered along the coast, the coast watchers and Fighter Sector had also played a key role in combating the Japanese.

The Americans lost four pilots in combat, one of whom remains missing, and four as a result of accidents. Fifteen aircraft were lost as a result of combat; forced landings and accidents accounted for many more and kept the 43rd AMS mechanics busy. The actual losses by both sides were in sharp contrast to the wildly extravagant claims: the Japanese had claimed 135 P-40s destroyed including nine over Horn Island on 14 March.

On 2 October 1942 General Order 50 was issued by the Chief of Staff on behalf of the Secretary of War awarding the 49th Fighter Gp a second Presidential Citation "for outstanding performance of duty in action during the period March 14, 1942, to August 25, 1942. Charged with the air defense of the area near Darwin...this unit, though greatly outnumbered...intercepted the enemy on every attempted attack and extracted toll far out of proportion to its own losses..."

Strauss and Livingstone strips were not idle for long. The aircraft and personnel of 77 Squadron moved into Livingstone on 16 September even as the 9th Squadron was preparing to leave, while 76 Squadron, relieved from its pivotal role in the Milne Bay battle, was posted to the Darwin area under SqnLdr Keith W. 'Bluey' Truscott. The unit's P-40Es arrived at Batchelor on 30 September, where servicings were undertaken by 77 Squadron groundcrews until the move to Strauss on 9 October.

Seemingly confident in its ability to mount raids on the Darwin area at will, the Takao *Ku* continued with night raids throughout September and October, seemingly more in nuisance value than inflicting serious damage. The raids were regularly mounted in the early hours before dawn; from 0341 hours on 25 September to 0220 hours a month later on the 27th. One RAAF and four army personnel were injured at Batchelor on 24 October, whilst the RAAF

runway, Don Hotel, several houses and infrastructure including power and phone lines were damaged during the other raids.

Three weeks passed before the next raid on 23 November though reconnaissance sorties had been flown by *Babs* on the 21st and 22nd. On the 23rd the Japanese paid the price. Five *chutai* each of three *Bettys* took off from Koepang at 2225 hours on the 22nd with a total of 150 60 kg bombs. They arrived over Darwin at varying intervals between 0300 and 0429 hours and heights ranging from 18,000 to 29,000 feet. One *chutai* was intercepted by SqnLdr Dick Cresswell at 0505 hours when he spotted them silhouetted against the cloud east of Darwin at 24,000 feet.

"They turned sharply to port when first attacked and in doing so starboard aircraft became detached" Cresswell's combat report reads, "...Opened fire from tracers seen to enter starboard engine and top of wing, which caught fire. Third attack made from above on starboard rear quarter. Tracers entered mid-wing section. E/A exploded...about 16,000 ft."

The aircraft, manufacturer's number 5414, tail coded T-359, crashed north of Koolpinyah Station, narrowly missing the homestead where coincidentally the owners, Oscar and Evan Herbert, were hosting a 77 Squadron barbecue. PO1c Kiyoshi Akamatsu and his nine man crew perished.

The P-40E A29-113 of SqnLdr Dick Cresswell, CO of 77 Squadron. Cresswell downed Betty 5414 over Koolpinyah east of Darwin on 23 November 1942. Photo: Ian Parker.

In contrast to the missed opportunities afforded by the 4 April *Betty* wrecks, Intelligence personnel seemingly left no stone unturned in the investigation of this latest aircraft to fall into their hands. Personal belongings including a glove bearing the name Hachigo were recorded though the name was not among those of the crew members, while papers gave them much valuable information, including the Takao *Kokutai* aircraft tail numbers, test flight readings and unit dispositions. A projection of the aircraft construction sequence was also able to be prepared from some 75 data plates recovered from the wreckage.

A more poignant find was not so much personal but a time line to the aircraft's demise; a record of the flight leading up to the interception by Cresswell, which when translated read,

"22 Nov. DARWIN night attack.
     Departure 23 – 30 min.
     Landed -------- hours---------
     Fuel carried 4500.
     (*990 Imp. Gals.*)
     Total consumption.
     Consumption/hr.
     Lubricating oil right 130 left 125.
     Quantity consumed.
       "   "   /hr.
     Altitude 3,000 metres.
     (*9840'*)
     Speed 150 knots.
     (*173 m.p.h. A.I.S. 208 T.A.S.*)
     Fuel pressure left 0.36 right 0.4
     Oil pressure   7   6
     Cylinder temperature 190 190
     Exhaust temperature 740 730
     Oil temperature left 70 right 70
     Supply pressure
     Revolution 1800..."

Reconnaissance sorties comprising a single *Babs* under a three aircraft escort were flown from the 24th to the 27th and again on the 29th. A single raid, the last for the year, was flown on the night of 26-27 November. Fourteen *Bettys* arrived over Darwin at 0320, 0356 and 0446 hours bombing the Darwin, Strauss, Hughes, Coomalie and Batchelor areas. One Hudson was badly damaged and two slightly damaged at Hughes and the runway was cratered while two houses, phone lines and the water main from Manton Dam were also damaged. A *Babs* escorted by three *Zekes* flew a reconnaissance sortie on 3 December, the last for the year, though it was unreported.

By year's end the NWA had developed considerably with the Allies preparing to take a more offensive role, notwithstanding the efforts of the Hudson crews. The heavy day raids of the earlier months had declined dramatically to night raids though the Japanese remained far from being a depleted force. The 23rd *Koku Sentai* had some 42 bombers available in the Celebes and a further 62 on Timor. The fighter force, both army and navy, was similarly equipped. A new airfield was also under construction at Fuiloro west of Lautem – some 200 kilometres closer to Darwin than Koepang.

The crash site of *Betty T-359* at Koolpinyah. Photo: Alford Colln

New equipment and units arrived in the Darwin area during the last quarter of the year, while others relocated from rearward areas. Number 2 Squadron moved to Hughes on 18 August joining 13 Squadron and 12 Squadron returned to Batchelor and established itself at the former USAAF 7th Squadron site west of the airfield in October. Soon after the unit began re-equipping with the newly introduced Vultee Vengeance dive bombers, with the first two, A27-8 and A27-11, arriving on the 30th.

Coomalie airfield was completed by the end of October though drainage problems persisted, and on 12 November the aircraft and personnel of 31 Squadron moved in from Batchelor to begin strikes against the Japanese in the islands to the north. Formed at RAAF base Forest Hill Wagga on 14 August and equipped with the powerful strike fighter, the Bristol Beaufighter, the unit became an enigma to the enemy, seemingly able to strike at will. The unit was joined at Coomalie by the remnants of 1 PRU on 6 December.

A further unit, 6 Communications Flight (later 6 Comm. Unit) was formed at Manbulloo on 15 December under the

CHANGES IN THE AIR

A Vultee Vengeance of 12 Squadron in flight over the Northern Territory coast. Photo: Alford/AHSNT Colln.

Northern Territory's legendary Flying Doctor, FltLt Clyde 'Doc' Fenton. Equipped initially with five de Havilland DH 84s, a DH 89 and three Tiger Moths, they commenced vital ration, medical and mail runs – and of course the *Army News* - to remote outlying units including radar stations, airfields and the NAOU, or 'Knackeroos' as they were known.

To the north the Japanese had also reorganised their forces. Photo reconnaissance duties had been taken over by the sleek Mitsubishi Ki-46 II *Dinah* of the Army's 70th *Dokuritsu Dai Shijugo Chutai* (DCS), or Independent Command Squadron, under Capt Shunji Sasaki, and commenced operations from Lautem on Timor's north coast on 24 October.

Whilst the C5M2 *Babs* remained with *3 Ku/Ku 202* for a time they were phased out of operations over the Darwin area, giving way to the army's *Dinahs*.

The navy's attack force, the 23rd *Koku Sentai* underwent an organisational change from 1 November. Takao *Ku* was redesignated 753 *Ku* while retaining its G4M1 *Bettys*, and 3 *Ku* was redesignated Air Group (*Kokutai*) *Ku* 202. Early in the New Year the updated A6M3 Mk II *Hamp* began to trickle through to the fighter units, though the A6M2 Mk I *Zeke* remained in service and was preferred by its pilots. The floatplane unit, 36 *Ku*, was similarly redesignated the 934 *Ku*.

The Japanese Army Air Force also maintained a presence in the region with the 7th *Hikoshidan* headquartered on Java. Under it came the 3rd and 9th *Hikodan* comprising the 59th and 75th *Sentai*, and the 7th and 61st *Sentai* respectively. The Nakajima Ki-43 I *Oscars* of the 59th carried out a number of interceptions of Beaufighters, Hudsons and Liberators from detachments at Dili and Lautem though in many cases they were misidentified as 'Zeros'.

In the Darwin area meantime, it was up to the obsolescent Hudsons to carry the offensive while RAAF units either commenced operations with new types or re-equipped.

CHAPTER 7

STRIKING BACK
Hudsons take the lead – and pay the price

Despite the retraction of the Hudson squadrons to Daly Waters, both 2 and 13 Squadrons initiated an offensive against the Japanese a month following the 19 February 1942 raids on Darwin. The Hudsons, what there were of them, were hardly ideal but they were the only bombers the RAAF had that were capable of striking against the enemy, while the USAAF had only its weary B-17s.

Daly Waters itself posed problems both in terms of logistics and the appalling conditions there. The Hudsons were forced to refuel at the Darwin RAAF Station or stage through Drysdale Mission in the Kimberleys of Western Australia *en route* to their targets and on occasion they were sitting targets as the Japanese raided Darwin.

Personnel of 2 Squadron clowning around at Daly Waters, 1942. From left, Don Landers, Reg Lewis and Charlie Mudge. Photo: Murry Lawson.

The remoteness of the airfield itself inspired much adverse comment. "Daly Waters was the pits" Murry Lawson a fitter with 2 Squadron commented, a sentiment echoed in the diary entry of Lt George Preddy as the 9th Squadron passed through on 16 March. "That's the worst place I've ever seen…" Preddy wrote, "The heat and flies are terrible. Luckily, the mosquitoes aren't bad." After having endured the flies at Alice Springs, Bob Foster, a pilot with 54 (RAF) Squadron thought otherwise, though he did have an incentive. "Nice place," he commented dryly, "…and my best recollection was that the station commander…had a large refrigerator in which he kept about two dozen bottles of beer, ice cold Castlemaine XXXX…it was a glass of beer I will remember for the rest of my life."

Despite the flies, the powdery dust that lessened the life of engines, armament and equipment, poor food and primitive facilities, conditions gradually improved over time. Replacement air and ground crews, spares and new aircraft saw morale and efficiency enhanced to an extent, though the improvement in morale didn't linger as operations took their toll on aircraft and crews.

Operations commenced soon after the first raids, though in light of available aircraft and crews they were initially confined to reconnaissance sorties. The first offensive mission was led by FltLt Bob Dalkin of B Flight 13 Squadron on 17 March 1942, in an attack on Koepang. Only three aircraft were available between both 2 and 13 Squadrons. Arriving back at Drysdale Mission after a successful night's work, Hudson A16-5 flown by FltLt Dick Overhue was damaged taking off for Darwin; the army demolished it with explosives on 4 April.

On the 20th A16-100 force landed short of fuel off Cape Fourcroy Bathurst Island. The crew of PltOff John Venn were all uninjured. "What a pity…" wrote Bob Dalkin, "A few broken limbs would have been splendid as we saw their aircraft blown to pieces at Ambon three weeks later. Venn was aged 20."

Three days later Hudson, A16-109 of 2 Squadron was attacked by fighters and spun into the sea near Koepang with the loss of Sgts J. G. Wright, D. G. J. Horsburgh and J. R. Maddern. The pilot, FltLt J. L. MacAlister, managed to parachute to safety but on the recommendation of a Dutch doctor, Dr. Hekking, at Tjamplong, he surrendered and spent the war as a POW.

On the 30th Bob Dalkin led a four aircraft strike on Koepang, leaving a trail of destroyed Japanese aircraft. Approaching the target, Dalkin recalled "Coming in low and fast…we found the whole of Koepang lit up…with taxiway flares, runway flarepath and aircraft with navigation lights switched on. There were many aircraft on the ground… with some flying on the circuit area…the very number of aircraft around was in my favour and on the spur of the moment, and to the horror of my crew when I called 'no shooting yet' – I throttled back, put some flap down and approached slowing down, with the airfield on my left… at the right speed I raised the flaps, climbed…above and behind a couple of aircraft in the circuit – opened the bomb doors, turned downwind and into wind towards the

STRIKING BACK

flare path, selected some parked and taxying aircraft as the aiming point, got the bombs away, realised that I was too low...and with the explosions felt that awful thump. Not quite knowing if we were still in one piece, one quick turn to give the crew a chance with their .303s, and then it was low level...to the nearby flying boat base at Hansisi. There were some aircraft on the water, and these were attacked with gunnery, one solitary 45mm gun was firing at us...and the rear gunner shouted that the fire was passing between the forward stub aerial and the...fins...I came very close to digging a wing into the sea. It was quite a night."

The Japanese no doubt learned from that, and Dalkin was awarded the DFC.

Not all missions were that successful and the toll mounted. In the period to 17 June, 13 Hudsons were lost, nine of them on operational missions. Thirty three crew members died, three of them in air raids on Darwin. Others died in fiery crashes or at the hands of the Japanese; some simply disappeared. Most were in their early twenties, though one, Sgt J. G. Wright, was an old man at 32. There were many more to follow through the remainder of 1942 and into 1943.

Flight Lieutenant Bob Dalkin briefs his Hudson crew prior to another mission over the NEI. Photo: Alford/AHSNT Colln.

Hudson A16-105 was with 2 Squadron only seven days before it was attacked and lost over Koepang on 13 April. The crew survived the subsequent crash landing though two, Sgts W. D. Witham and Sgt H. F. Hearle, were injured and captured. Apparently nursed back to health, they were bayoneted to death and bundled into a rough grave on 10 May. The pilot, FltLt H. O. Cook, and second pilot, PltOff V. C. Leithead, 'took to the jungle' and were eventually rescued

by the submarine USS *Gudgeon*. Leithead's luck ran out on 21 August 1943 when his Beaufighter A19-63 was involved in a mid-air collision over Taberfane.

WAG, Lloyd Edwards had joined FltLt Forman's crew following the death of Sgt Forrest in the raid of 16 March. With another WAG, Sgt 'Dusty' Miller and second pilot, PltOff L. Angel, Forman's crew flew a number of sorties during March and April. Lloyd's last mission with 13 Squadron was that of 13 April, the shipping strike in Koepang harbour. "During the bombing run we were attacked by a number of Zero fighters" Lloyd recalled, "Cook's plane was so badly damaged that he had to crash-land away from the harbour...Sgt Gitsham, the tunnel gunner in Blanchard's crew was also injured but managed to shoot down one of the attacking Zeros. We were also badly shot up and Miller, who was in the turret was mortally wounded." Lloyd Edwards later joined the crew of FltLt Dick Overhue and later served on B-24 Liberators with him. He flew 470 hours with 13 Squadron.

The day following A16-105's loss, A16-137 failed to return from a mission to Koepang with the loss of PltOffs P. G. Taylor and A. J. V. Lockley, along with Sgts K. A. Orchard and D. Thompson. On the 23rd FlgOff R. I. Blanchard and his crew of Sgts D. Jacobs, D. V. Woods and O. B. P. Grey in A16-182 also failed to return from a night reconnaissance and bombing mission to Koepang.

In between attacks on Koepang and Japanese shipping, among other tasks, Bladin directed the Hudsons to continue reconnaissance of enemy ports to report any invasion fleets, to prevent any build up of enemy forces around Ambon and Koepang, and to maintain resupply drops to the 2/2nd Independent Company on Timor. One daylight reconnaissance, a high risk undertaking, by SqnLdr 'Tich' McFarlane on 11 May, confirmed two new runways and some huts under construction at Laha, while Namlea remained unused.

Two days later the Venn crew's luck ran out. Flying A16-196, PltOff J. H. Venn and Sgts L. A. Omsby, W. J. James and B. A. Kilpatrick were part of an eight aircraft mission led by SqnLdr McFarlane to attack Japanese shipping in Ambon harbour. McFarlane split his formation as they neared the target, leading the FltLt Fraser, FlgOffs McCombe and Sharp and PltOff Venn crews low towards the harbour. Despite

STRIKING BACK

heavy A-A fire, Venn made a mast high attack on a 3,318 tonne vessel the *Taifuku Maru*. As the bombs detonated the aircraft exploded and went into the sea.

The other flight, led by Bob Dalkin, dive bombed their targets and despite some damage made it back to base. The vessel attacked by Venn was sunk whilst a 2,121 tonne vessel was hit and another near missed. Venn's crew and an aircraft were lost, though one crew member managed to survive the explosion.

Omsby somehow survived, only to be captured and later executed. "The fact that one member of this crew survived... and was later treated in the Japanese Naval Hospital has now been established beyond doubt" the post war searcher party file reads, "The survivor was...Omsby. As next of Kin believe that all members were killed in the crash, this item is to be treated as strictly confidential. Endeavours to locate the body of Omsby have so far been unsuccessful. War Crimes, Tokio [sic] are carrying on the investigation." In the harsh reality of war, Venn, James and Kilpatrick were probably lucky as they didn't have to suffer at the hands of the Japanese.

McFarlane led another shipping strike, to Halong Bay, on 22 May. Eight aircraft from both squadrons attacked a destroyer and four merchant vessels in the face of heavy A-A fire, before being attacked by *Zekes* of 3 *Ku*. Two aircraft, A16-174 and '187 were shot down, and crashed into Ambon Bay. Local natives managed to recover the body of PltOff A. W. Moss from A16-174 and another, Sgt P. C. Roll, was buried on a nearby beach; FlgOff P. G. Brooks and Sgt C. A. Vercoe were never found and were later reclassified killed. The locals were unable to reach A16-187, though the pilot, PltOff G. W. Allchin, and Sgt J. L Montgomerie survived and were taken prisoner; they were later executed and buried adjacent to a mass grave containing 11 AIF members. The remaining crew members of A16-187, PltOffs K. F. Kerstin and W. G. McLay were presumed killed in the crash.

The Gill crew was lost over Timor on 2 June. The aircraft, A16-108, was strafing ground targets when it collided with A16-143 and crashed in flames. The crew of PltOffs R. L. Gill and D. G. Campbell, and Sgts L. R. Kealley and S. L. Inglis were recovered from the wreckage and interred at Koepang in January 1946 before being relocated to the Ambon War Cemetery. A16-143 was badly damaged in the collision, however it was flown back to Darwin by FltLt Lindsay Trewren.

A16-132 went missing on operations in the Timor Sea on 17 June. Only the body of the pilot, PltOff G. R. Crawford was found. PltOffs C. V. Cantor, and B. V. Long and Sgts L. R. Hayward and M. McGuire remain missing.

Other aircraft were written off as a result of accident or through combat damage. A16-176 ground looped following a take off accident on 7 May and A16-184 crashed on take off from Darwin three weeks later on the 30th. A16-175 ran short of fuel returning to base after an attack on Penfoie by six Hudsons on 15 June. The aircraft was ditched close to shore and the crew were later picked by a Hudson which landed on the beach.

Meanwhile the Hudson squadrons had moved forward from Daly Waters in late April, with 2 Squadron relocating to Batchelor and 13 Squadron moving into Hughes. Bladin, had also relocated his HQ to Berrimah on 11 May so as to remain adjacent to the main telephone cable running between the RAAF Station and his wireless unit rather than rely on temporary, and vulnerable, land lines.

By May the Americans had also consolidated their forces to an extent with the arrival of the 49th Pursuit Gp in March and April. The 27th Bomb. Gp had moved to Townsville where it was absorbed into the 3rd Bomb. Gp, leaving the 19th Bomb. Gp and a number of USAAF units including Air Base Groups, the 135th Medical Regt, the 808th and 43rd Engineer Regts, ordnance companies and the 102nd AA Bn among others. The 38th Bomb. Gp's ground echelon was scattered throughout the Territory and at one stage boasted that the American war effort was being directed from "The porch of the Birdum Hotel..." the Group's regular reports stated.

South of Birdum the 19th Bomb. Gp had used Daly Waters briefly, but not without incident. Boeing B-17D, 40-3079, *The Gazelle*, had flown in to Batchelor from the Philippines on 19 December and was a veteran of the Christmas Day mission before being ordered to Java on 1 January 1942. It was transporting Cols Nichols and Hoyt from Batchelor only days after its return from Java when 1 and 2 engines failed and the aircraft crashed on landing at Daly Waters on 14 March. Staff Sergeant Collen Long was killed in the accident while the pilot, Capt Skiles, lost an eye and three others were injured. Long was interred in the small cemetery opposite the old telegraph station before reburial at Adelaide River on 20 August.

STRIKING BACK

Another B-17, 40-3067, had been lost six weeks earlier after it had been badly damaged during a mission over the Celebes, with its port outer engine nacelle holed among other damage. The crew managed to fly the aircraft back to Batchelor, only to be ordered to fly it to Laverton for repairs. It was the following morning, 28 January, that disaster struck. Len De Grussa, a gunner with the 22nd HAA Bty sited at 'Stump Hill' only a few metres from the western threshold of the runway, recalled that he and his gun crew "...watched the plane as it attempted to take off...as the B-17 appeared to lift off...both port engines failed, the plane crashed and [it] slewed directly towards our Battery of four 3 inch guns. Less that a hundred yards from... [us] it hit a huge tree stump...at this precise moment the navigator jumped...getting crushed against the tree stump. Unfortunately he was killed outright." Lieutenant Francis McAllister was interred at the Gardens Cemetery in Darwin the following day.

Another followed on 16 March, this time as part of the operation to evacuate Gen Douglas MacArthur from the Philippines to Australia. B-17E 41-2507 was one of three that departed Batchelor in the first evacuation attempt, however it struck problems taking off from Del Monte after the MacArthur party failed to arrive. The pilot, Lt Henry Godman, ditched the aircraft off Mindanao, though two crew members, SSgt Frank Lyle and Sgt Allen G. Whitehead, were killed. The remainder made their way back to Del Monte and on to Batchelor.

Australian personnel inspecting the remains of the B-17C, serial 40-3067 which crashed at Batchelor on 28 January 1942, killing Lt Francis McAllister. Photo: Charles Schaedel.

During June a detachment of the American 135th Medical Regt under Lt Thuerer established a facility near 'Jungle Jump' south of the Noonamah siding to provide medical facilities for the units in the area. It was a fortuitous move. The night of 27 June saw another B-17 accident, when again, an aircraft was badly damaged during a mission to Kendari. Attacked by several Japanese fighters during a running battle, the aircraft was badly damaged. The pilot, Lt Weldon Smith, managed to get the aircraft, 41-9014, back to Darwin but it crashed nose first and turned on its back. The 49th ICS at nearby 'Jungle Jump' and 135th Medical Regt personnel rushed to the scene. "[The] arrival [of] Lt. Thuerer proved to be extremely timely" the unit historian wrote, "...his instruments had scarcely been unpacked when a B-17 bomber out of gas and unable to negotiate a landing in the dark, smacked through the trees a mile from camp, portions...were strewn all along the hundred yard path...and foreward [sic] ...fuselage [was] torn off and set aflame...The crew were all injured, three fatally... These men provided the first and most serious cases to require treatment from the 135th's efficient staff." Sergeants Glover Burke, Robert French and West Bryson were interred at Adelaide River the next day.

The remains of Boeing B-17 aircraft of the 19th Bomb. Group in the 'boneyard' at Batchelor, 1942. Photo: Alford/AHSNT Colln.

A fifth, a B-17E, was lost at Batchelor on 12 August and again the pilot was Lt Weldon Smith. The aircraft crashed on take off and was subsequently scrapped. Smith and his crew were uninjured.

Another B-17 unit, the 64th Bomb. Squadron of the 43rd Bomb. Gp had arrived in the Territory on 22 May when personnel and equipment arrived at Daly Waters. By the 30th a camp had been established and communications installed: "...the squadron was ready to commence their training and begin operations" Sgt John Morrill, the unit historian noted. The status quo remained through June and July until the CO, Major Jack Bleasdale, joined the squadron on the 15th. Five days later the squadron was advised that it was to move to Fenton airfield, "...in the near future."

A week later the unit was advised that four B-17s had been assigned to it and on the 30th two crews left for Charleville to pick them up. One arrived at Daly Waters later that afternoon. From 31 July personnel began the move to Fenton and by 2 August all but the RAAF and four US Army weather personnel were at Daly Waters.

Major Bleasdale flew another B-17E, 41-2656 *Chief of Seattle* into Fenton on the morning of the 3rd and a third aircraft came in that afternoon. The fourth aircraft, 41-9207 arrived on the 5th, though it needed an engine change. The following day two B-17s were ordered to Townsville and ten days later two more were assigned to the 19th Bomb. Gp 'for operational duty.' The *Chief of Seattle* was shot down during a reconnaissance mission on 14 August while serving with the 435th Squadron 19th Bomb. Gp. The tangible generosity of the people of Seattle who had donated $280,535 for its purchase remains missing. While the remaining pilots kept up their hours by flying P-40s of the 49th Fighter Gp, inspections by Gen Brett and other high ranking officers, concreting floors, constructing revetments, playing sport and attending meetings at least kept personnel employed, though the boredom must have been overwhelming. Entries in the unit history, ranging from "No change in events on this date...No change... Nothing eventful happened on this date...The Squadron Commander's pet parrot died today..." to "Several sacks of mail arrived and a large mail call was enjoyed by all" and "...pay for the month of June and July was gladly received but no one seemed to know what to do with the money." say it all.

At times they must have wondered why they were there at all, until 21 September when "A radiogram arrived...and ordered this squadron to prepare for a move...the order was not really news." But, finally it came to pass, and personnel began departing for Iron Range in north Queensland via Darwin on the 25th; by the 29th Fenton was deserted.

For over four months the squadron and its personnel had been squandered, with no operational duties and in effect no aircraft, though two RAAF officers, FlgOffs Coglan and Watkinson, had been seconded to set up operations and intelligence sections. No doubt there was some logic behind the squadron's move to the Territory, however it remains obscure.

In time, high unserviceability rates, accidents and losses involving the B-17s, along with a lack of maintenance facilities and spares, combat weary crews, and a shortage of operational aircraft saw the efficiency of the 19th Bomb. Gp suffer. As a result the unit was repatriated to the USA in November 1942 and its aircraft handed over to the 43rd Bomb. Gp.

In mid-1942 a unit was formed to gain intelligence into enemy aircraft and equipment. At the outbreak of the Pacific war the Allies had little up to date information on Japanese aircraft and their capabilities, despite a number of reports, not least of which those of LtGen Claire Chennault of the AVG 'Flying Tigers' in China, warning of a new aircraft more agile than any in the USAAC inventory at the time.

A new unit, the Technical Air Intelligence Unit, sometimes referred as the Allied Technical Air Intelligence Unit, was formed under the Directorate of Intelligence at Victoria Barracks in Melbourne in mid-1942. A joint USAAF/US Navy/RAAF venture it was based on the RAF's A. 1. 2G Section, which had a number of successes in assessing Luftwaffe aircraft and equipment. Initially staffed by one officer, Capt Frank T. McCoy of the USAAF and one clerk it was later joined by two RAAF personnel. McCoy remained as CO throughout the war years.

"ZEKE"

A carved wooden model of the Mitsubishi A6M2 Zeke used as a recognition aid by Allied pilots from late 1942. Photo: Arthur Morash.

TAIU's role was to investigate, monitor and evaluate Japanese aviation technical trends and development from what material was available – in essence the remains of crashed, damaged or abandoned aircraft. The Australian end was held up by FlgOff N. Clappison, the first RAAF

STRIKING BACK

officer posted in to TAIU and who later became the CO of the RAAF component. TAIU grew to some 100 Americans and 35 Australians serving throughout the SWPA and headquartered at the AMP building in Brisbane from 1943.

FlgOff F. P. Crook, who served his 'apprenticeship' in the NWA from late 1942 to mid-1943, followed the RAAF's Intelligence Officers of 5 Fighter Sector, including FlgOff C. D. Pender, who was active from the day of the first raids. Crook, whose main task was to examine wreckage and gather data plates – called 'tin canning' - fought a constant battle against souvenir hunters. Little did the 'collectors' realise that from these 'souvenirs,' information relating to a number of aircraft characteristics could collectively provide production rates, and a host of vital data.

The first essentially intact A6M2 *Zeke* to fall into Allied hands was aircraft No. 5349, which had been force landed on Melville Island by PO1c Hajime Toyoshima on 19 February 1942. A detailed examination of the aircraft was carried out and a subsequent report included its range and speed, the use of the Swedish designed Oerlikon 20mm cannon, American type compasses, Hamilton Standard type propeller and Type 98 gunsight. It also revealed its weaknesses in a lack of armour and self-sealing fuel tanks. From all this data the aircraft should have looked more vulnerable, however much of it was ignored in favour of a *Zeke* located in the Dutch Harbour area of the Aluetians almost four months later.

RAAF personnel inspect the wreckage of Mitsubishi G4M1 Betty 5414, T-359. The aircraft provided much valuable information for Allied intelligence. Photo: Owen Veal.

The second type to be thoroughly assessed, and the first for TAIU in the NWA, was *Betty* No. 5414, which was shot down on the night of 23 November. The lost opportunities of April when the identities and investigations of the two *Bettys* downed on the 4th were compromised, this aircraft was thoroughly investigated – to the extent that Crook revisited the site in December to search for the starboard engine, tail cannon and any papers that may have been missed in the initial investigation.

Other aircraft followed including '*Betty* 3677' downed on 6 July 1943, a Ki-49 *Helen* 174 at Koolpinyah and two *Dinah* aircraft, one, 2414 at Opium Creek east of Darwin and the other, 2273 on Bathurst Island; most of the TAIU records have seemingly long since disappeared, perhaps to be found in an archives some day.

In September 1943, then Major McCoy released Memorandum No. 2, in which a listing of all known Japanese aircraft wrecks in the SWPA appeared. Despite the claims by Allied fighter pilots the list for the NWA included only a handful of aircraft, 11 in all, though one, *Val* 3304 was erroneously listed as being on Yule Island.

A captured A6M3 Hamp outside TAIU's Hangar 7 at Eagle Farm in Brisbane. A number of captured Japanese aircraft were restored and provided valuable information to the Allies. Photo: Alford Colln.

Whilst those in the NWA were at least listed, the priority for TAIU was the SWPA; this was where they could salvage almost intact aircraft for reconstruction and flight comparisons with Allied aircraft from the secretive 'Hangar 7' at Eagle Farm aerodrome in Brisbane. TAIU became the predominant agency for the dissemination of technical reports, identification manuals, the allocation of code names to Japanese aircraft and the specialist examination of aircraft and equipment for the Allies in the Pacific to war's end.

STRIKING BACK

Meanwhile the Hudsons soldiered on despite appalling losses. A further nine were lost on operations to year's end, taking with them 32 aircrew. In all, the squadrons lost 99 officers and NCO aircrew in 42 aircraft from 8 December 1941 to 27 December 1942.

By the end of June the Japanese were estimated to have extensive forces at its bases on Timor, Ambon and Bali, whilst a number of *Bettys* of Takao *Ku* were moving west to the base at Kendari in the Celebes. A total of 59 fighters, 69 bombers, 12 flying boats and four observation aircraft were suspected of being available.

The Hudson squadrons were kept busy flying reconnaissance missions to try and keep track of the enemy movements, while at the same time mounting attacks on the enemy. Ambon, Atamboea, the Ermena-Tinar road system, shipping at Tenau and targets at Kefannaroe and Nikiniki were all attacked during June and July whilst supply drops were also carried out to resupply the beleaguered Australian Sparrow Force operating in Japanese controlled Portuguese East Timor.

On 18 August three Hudsons of 13 Squadron provided top cover for a Catalina despatched to evacuate wounded Sparrow Force personnel. Engine problems saw the Catalina forced to remain in the area until repairs were effected and it took "...all day, with the Japs just across the way at Dilli [*sic*]" wrote one of the 13 Squadron pilots, FltLt Trewren. "They finally got off and landed...successfully with the wounded."

Aircraft and crews were stretched but continued flying reconnaissance and offensive missions despite no clear target priorities being assigned by Allied HQ. In effect Bladin was forced to improvise and the situation was made worse by a lack of specialised aircraft that could provide up to date information on enemy movements. It was an *ad hoc* approach that resulted in an unnecessary toll on men and machines.

In some cases crews were flying on an almost daily basis. Flight Lieutenant Dick Overhue's log book entries show 20 flights in the first two weeks of June and 21 flights from 1 to 15 July. On the 9th he flew A16-210 from Darwin to Hughes, took A16-207 on a test flight and then flew from Hughes to Darwin; to round out the day he flew an "Afternoon raid on Dilli [*sic*] 4 x 250 special 4 x 25 incend. .5 A/A bullet through cockpit." The other six days were spent on bombing and

gunnery practice, travel flights, a patrol, bombing practice on a towed target, providing air support for a landing at Toeal and a reconnaissance to Ambon on the 15th.

Overhue flew with 13 Squadron from 14 August 1941 to 10 May 1942 and with 2 Squadron to 17 December, gaining a DFC during his 2 Squadron service. He later went on to fly B-24s with the 380 Bomb. Gp and 24 Squadron RAAF, earning a bar to his DFC. He was typical and others were no less deserving.

The first loss for the second half of the year was on 30 July when A16-234, a 2 Squadron aircraft failed to return from an armed reconnaissance of the Kai islands. The crew of FlgOffs R. C. Muecke and F. S. Moss along with PltOff L. M. Miners and Sgt J. E. Laman remain missing; the only clue to their disappearance, a combat report by a 36 *Ku Jake* floatplane pilot, Lt Kasuka Sasaki. "...the enemy made a rapid skilful...attack" Sasaki reported, "but...because of our counter attack the co-pilot was either killed or seriously wounded and because of the low altitude, the pilot didn't have time to recover...he crash landed on the sea." Sasaki was accompanied by his observer, PO2c Takemura and gunner Flyer 1c Uehara.

On 7 August WgCdr McFarlane led nine 2 Squadron Hudsons on a strike against transport ships off Timor's south coast. Attacking from the north the Hudsons left one transport burning despite A-A fire from an escorting *Azakasi*-class destroyer. All aircraft returned safely, but it must also have left a feeling of satisfaction to have had nine aircraft serviceable enough to undertake the mission.

A scene often repeated. A burial service for a 2 Squadron member killed on operations. Photo: Malcolm Long.

STRIKING BACK

Two weeks later 2 Squadron attacked Japanese forces at Maubisse near Dili in support of Sparrow Force and the following day a further five Hudsons led by FltLt S. Fraser in A16-178 set out to repeat the attack. They were intercepted by two fighters and A16-209 was attacked and set on fire. The pilot, FlgOff Sid Wadey, managed to take to his parachute, however the remaining crew members were unable to escape. PltOff S. W. Faull and Sgts W. R. Edeson, F. M. O'Reilly and W. H. Gould perished in the crash. Wadey was found seriously injured by natives who assisted him to a neutral Portuguese administration and from there he was taken to Sparrow Force and finally evacuated to Darwin on 27 September.

Meanwhile one of the remaining Hudsons became separated from the formation and was attacked. Flying Officer Neil Badger in A16-241 evaded the attacking fighter by flying at low level and through valleys to the sea. "Finally the Zero made two quarter attacks from astern, level to slightly lower than our aircraft, which was then 80 feet above the water" Badger reported, "On the second of these attacks when pulling away to starboard at 50 yards it was raked by our belly gun and crashed into the sea."

A month later on 25 September A16-241 of 2 Squadron flown by FlgOff R. R. James and his crew achieved a similar feat on their first mission. Attacked by four *Zekes* they managed to hold them off in a running battle of stall turns, island hopping through the clouds, sharp turns at very low level over the sea and a chase through the fog shrouded Timorese valleys.

The crew of B-26A Marauder 40-1430 Wee Winnie at Batchelor, November 1942. From Left, Sgt Nelson, Lt Robert, Lt Wells, Sgt Arrato, Sgt Pitcher and Sgt Tom Roberts RAAF. Photo: M. Roberts.

The crew, FlgOff R. R. James, PltOff R. D. Ryan, WOff H. E. Cutten, FSgts K. G. Keech and P. S. Reen and Sgt R. E. Norris survived only to be shot down over the Arafura Sea by a 934 *Rufe* flown by Flyer 1c Osamu Yoza on 24 April 1943.

September also saw reconnaissance sorties flown over the Aru and Trobriand Islands on the 3rd and on the 13th a pair of 13 Squadron Hudsons attacked supply vessels off Betano; two 305 tonne vessels were sunk in diving attacks and the next day eight aircraft attacked Japanese shipping off Saumlaki. One aircraft, A16-172 of 2 Squadron was lost as a result of enemy ground fire, killing the crew of FlgOffs K. L. McDonnell, V. Treloar and K. J. Ahern, along with Sgts G. S. Dobbs and G. Ward-Smith.

Missions continued throughout October, with A16-243 lost during a reconnaissance sortie over Koepang on the 1st. The crew of FlgOffs J. E. Alcock, P. C. Gunston and G. V. Boynton, and Sgts F. P. Kemp and W. S. Powell had operated from March and Alcock "was regarded as one of the best reconnaissance pilots the squadron had. He had carried out several very successful missions" FltLt L. Trewren wrote, "The idea was to photograph ships in the harbour and then take shots of Penfoie drome. When he saw the dust of the fighters taking off... we allowed five minutes and then headed for home. I think [he] was shot down...by fighters waiting for him, or he stayed too long after seeing them take off."

The following six days were confined to sea patrols and searches, before a strike by three Hudsons of 13 Squadron on the harbour and waterfront at Dili on the 10th. Fires were reported and reconnaissance sorties were flown to assess the damage over the following three days. Shortly afterwards three 13 Squadron Hudsons attacked Vila de Manatuto on Timor's north coast. Hudson A16-170 of 2 Squadron was lost when it failed to return from an attack on Koepang on the 25th along with its crew of PltOff R. K. Dunning and Sgts D. W. Francis, L. H. Fraser and M. L. Kenihan.

In early November the overworked Hudson squadrons were reinforced temporarily when twelve Martin B-26 Marauders of the 22nd Bomb. Gp USAAF arrived at Batchelor from their base at Reid River near Townsville on the 1st. Over the next four days they flew missions over Timor and Dili in particular, claiming six enemy fighters shot down in the process. They were supporting the Hudson squadrons who flew night missions to Bobonaro, Maubisse, Aileu and Bacau.

STRIKING BACK

The Marauders were in four aircraft elements of the 2nd, 19th and 408th Squadrons of the Group and comprised:
2nd Squadron; 40-1552 Lt McClaran, 40-1529 Lt Siegel, 41-7593 Lt Hitchcock and 41-1432 Lt Patterson
19th Squadron; 40-1498 Capt Allen, 40-1411 Lt Thompson, 40-1388 Lt Cooper and 40-1428 Lt Wenk
408th Squadron; 40-1540 Capt Michaelis, 40-1430 Lt Robert (with Sgt A. G. Roberts RAAF as navigator/bombardier), 40-1481 Lt Miller and 40-1515 Lt McCord.

A number of RAAF personnel served as navigators, bombardiers and co-pilots on the B-26 aircraft, including Sgt A. G. 'Tom' Roberts, who flew with crew of Lt Robert in 40-1430 'Wee Winnie'. His log book succinctly records the raids of 2 and 4 November;
"2.11.42 0800 B26 1430 Lt Robert Raid (4 500 lbs bombs) Batchelor Field – Dilly [sic] 5:00 [hours]
4:11:42 0900 B26 1549 Lt Robert Raid Rtd. Eng. Trouble Batchelor – Dilly 1:30"

One of the few B-26B models in service, 41-7593, was lost over the five day detachment. Flown by Lt Charles Hitchcock, the aircraft was hit over Dili by A-A fire as it attacked a cathedral suspected of being used as a supply dump on 2 November. The A-A fire was, according to the USAAF mission report, 'Moderate, medium accurate.' The report continued matter-of-factly, that "...Ship 17593 hit right engine, tore off landing gear, started fire...flew on one engine to within 40 miles of Darwin. Gunner Campbell killed in crash. Two others injured. Ship 1432 dropped life rafts. All of crew picked up by 0600L/4 by Navy lugger."

The B-26B, 41-7593 flown by Lt Hitchcock during the Batchelor deployment. It was lost off Bathurst Island after being damaged by A-A fire over Timor on 2 November. Photo: M. Roberts.

As with any incident there is a human side. Hitchcock later submitted a detailed report, relating that "Our right engine had been put out of action by ack-ack fire...at Dilli [sic] Timor. The left engine was not putting out full power from the time we had taken off...both engines were due for a change. We flew along for approximately 2-1/2 hours on the left engine...we were flying at...about 1000 feet above the water, when the remaining engine froze...Immediately Sgt. Simms (RAAF) my co-pilot, opened the escape hatches while I feathered the engine and trimmed the plane for a glide...the waves were not too large, but the swells seemed fairly large and rough...I let the plane skim over the water... for about 100 yards...the instant the plane stopped moving I lunged upward and out. I climbed up on the wing and noticed five other crew members...the plane seemed to float fairly well for about 1-1/2 minutes, time enough for me to climb in and pull out the other crew member, and also a life raft. Sgt. Campbell, the turret gunner, was killed in the crash. He was sitting under the turret, next to where the plane's fuselage cracked open...we had only one life raft, but Lt. Patterson dropped us another [from aircraft 40-1432] until a RAAF...Hudson...dropped us a large round Australian raft that saved the day until we were picked up 17 hours later."

Another B-26 dropped supplies later in the day and despite storms, HMAS *Forceful* set out from Darwin and picked them up at 0630 hours on the 3rd. Even as Hitchcock's aircraft struggled from Timor a group of Australians in Lancer Force (renamed from Sparrow Force in November) had been listening in on the drama. They radioed for news, "Did Hitchcock make it?" they asked, but heard nothing. Next day the B-26s flew over and Capt 'Bull' Laidlaw broke into the frequency to again ask about Hitchcock. The answer came that evening, "Thanks Diggers, Hitchcock made it. Stop. Crash landed Bathurst Island."

The detachment returned to Queensland on the 5th. The aircraft and Sgt Glenn A. Campbell remain in water off Cape Helvetius, close to Bill Woodnutt's old camp site. If there can be a positive to the incident, it was that it prompted the RAAF into basing two *Fairmile* Air Sea Rescue craft at Darwin.

Captain Franklin Allen summed up the deployment of the B-26s in a 7 November letter to his wife, stating, no doubt with due regard to the censors, "...Been quite busy lately in the business for which I am here. I'm ok." He also managed to

STRIKING BACK

photograph a group of 12 Squadron Wirraways, captioning one "...No 2 [*sic*] Dive Bomber Squadron (RAAF) at Darwin...they were real combat ships."

Far from being 'real combat ships' the Wirraways were obsolescent and were being utilised for mundane but important roles in the Darwin area. Jack 'Squizzy' Taylor remembered the early morning patrols, mail and bread deliveries to remote camps and on many an occasion, searching for missing aircraft, including a Wirraway, A20-503, which had crashed in the Daly River area on 3 October. The bodies of the crew, squadron acquaintances FlgOff Peter Hughes and his observer, Sgt Stanislaus Corcoran, were in the wreckage; they were recovered by 'Squizzy' and 12 Squadron personnel and interred at Adelaide River.

With the year drawing to a close the Hudson squadrons kept the pressure on with raids on Timor and the islands. Three 13 Squadron Hudsons raided Dobo on 23 November after briefly meeting a *Jake* floatplane some 120 km from the target. The Japanese pilot, Lt Masashi Tokukura broke off the action only to meet up with the Hudsons again as they departed. A brief combat between Tokukura and SqnLdr K. M. Kemp and his crew in A16-236 saw no result for either, though Kemp claimed a floatplane shot down.

Flight Lieutenant Arthur Cambridge and his crew at Batchelor. From left, Sgt Tom Gunn, Sgt G. 'Dusty' Rhodes, PltOff J. Grey, FltLt Arthur Cambridge and Sgt C. H. Cooper. Photo: Tom Gunn.

A further mission involving three aircraft ran into trouble on 4 December when A16-232 was attacked by a *Zeke* north of Laga. One crew member, Sgt G. J. Thame, was killed when the top turret and tunnel gun area received hits, while the aircraft and one engine were badly damaged. With the other two aircraft covering him, the pilot, FlgOff A. A. Cambridge, flew back to Batchelor only to find his

undercarriage jammed. Jettisoning his bombs Cambridge made a belly landing. The remaining crew, Sgt G. A. Cooper, Sgt T. I. Gunn and a RCAF officer, FlgOff J. M. Barnes were unhurt. Cambridge and Gunn remained together and later served on B-24s with 24 Squadron.

Christmas Eve 1942 saw the loss of the FlgOff G. P. Thompson crew when their 2 Squadron Hudson was downed by enemy fighters over Cape Lore on Timor. The remainder of the crew, Sgts G. P. Dunbar, K. G. Chote, R. M. Clark and R. M. West perished along with their skipper. Three days later A16-210 was also shot down by enemy fighters near Lavai on Timor. The crew of FlgOff M. W. Johns, PltOff J. F. Nixon and Sgts D. K. Tyler, K. Ross and J. C. Horseman remains missing.

For their efforts over the past year, 2 and 13 Squadrons were each awarded a U.S. Presidential Citation though they were slow in materialising: 2 Squadron received its award at a Colours parade in 1972 and 13 Squadron waited a further 18 years before it was similarly honoured in Darwin on 1 June 1990 – fifty years after its formation. Some 47 decorations were awarded to the Hudson crews in the NWA, ranging from DFCs, DFMs and DSOs to 11 Mentions-in-Despatches. There should have been many more.

In Brisbane's *The Courier Mail* of 1 January 1943, Noel Adams reported that the "Heroes of the air war in Northern Australia are two Lockheed Hudson squadrons, who have been battling with the Japanese ever since the Pacific war began...In spite of the heavy odds against them...these squadrons are still smashing Japanese bases and immobilising Japanese aircraft, troops and supplies... Among many members...who have been decorated are WgCdr John Ryland D.F.C...Flight Lieutenant Archie Dunne D.F.C...Flight Lieutenant R. Dalkin D.F.C...and Flight Lieutenant William Duckett White D.F.C...Fifteen flying strips...have been named after members of the two squadrons who lost their lives...WgCdr J. R. MacDonald, Flight Lieutenants R. W. B. Cuming, J. Turnbull, A. Barton, P. Hodge, G. Sattler, M. F. Willing, and J. L. MacAlister. Flying Officers P. Gorrie, P. Blanchard, P.G. Brooks, G. G. Mitchell, Pilot Officers J. A. Venn, P. G. Taylor and G. W. Allchin." Later an airfield on the far northeastern tip of Arnhem Land was named for an NCO, Sgt William Gove, though he was interred as a Pilot Officer.

STRIKING BACK

Adams went further in Melbourne's *Argus* newspaper, writing that "For over 12 months the 2 squadrons have shouldered the main burden of the air war in the north western area. But because their exploits, though often overbrimming with danger and high courage, are seldom on a spectacular scale, the public know all too little of them...This is the first time that 2 squadrons have been officially cited for their record of active service."

By the end of 1942 the two Hudson squadrons were all but depleted. The operations they had flown over the year had taken an appalling toll on men and machines; and they still had to face the dangers of the coming year.

So too, the crews of the newly arrived Beaufighters of 31 Squadron. At Batchelor, the unit was involved primarily in training and familiarisation flights before moving to Coomalie on 12 November. The squadron quickly established itself at the airfield, eager to get into action and five days later they flew their first operational mission; a six aircraft strafing attack against targets at Maubisse and Bobonaro on Timor.

The same day also marked the unit's first operational loss. Enemy fighters were active and A19-46 dug a wing into the

sea trying to evade a *Zeke* off Cape Batu Poetch. Squadron Leader D. C. Riding and his observer, WOff R. A. Clark, had no chance of escape and they were the first of 61 aircrew members to die in action, 43 of them listed as 'missing, presumed killed.' Some no doubt lie buried on remote islands, whilst three are known to have been captured. One, FlgOff C. A. Greenwood, survived to tell his story.

The squadron continued its strikes over November and December under the command of WgCdr Charles F. Read, whom the squadron personnel nicknamed 'Coomalie Charlie.' Read was a popular leader and remained as CO until September 1943 when WgCdr F. W. B. 'Bill' Mann took over. In its first two weeks of combat operations 31 Squadron flew 53 sorties, most of them low level strafing attacks using the considerable firepower of four nose mounted 20mm cannon and six .303" machine guns in the wings to advantage. Shipping escort duties were also conducted, covering HMAS *Castlemaine*, *Armidale* and *Kuru* against enemy aircraft attacks on 1 December, and later the corvette, HMAS *Kalgoorlie* and the Dutch destroyer *Djerk Hiddes*.

Only three days after the loss of the Riding crew, A19-69 of PltOff M. J. Morrison and Sgt A. F. Forest was last seen

A fine shot of Beaufighter A19-159 EH-M of 31 Squadron over its home base, Coomalie. Photo: Alford/AHSNT Colln.

STRIKING BACK

WgCdr Charles Read (seated in cane chair, centre) and some of the original aircrews and an army liaison officer (left, centre) at Coomalie in early 1943. Photo: Phil Biven.

diving from 7,000ft pursued by an enemy aircraft. They are believed to have gone into the sea some 229 km west north west of Cape Fourcroy Bathurst Island.

On 2 December 31 Squadron raided Penfoie aerodrome after staging through Drysdale mission on the 1st. Flying Officer Ken McDonald, the pilot of A19-57, remembered Drysdale with no great fondness, "Our introduction…was quite a shock. The mission buildings were on flat country near the river, but the only serviceable grass airstrip was cut into the side of a hill. Its outer extremity ended with a cliff, a sheer drop into the river…and the other end just finished where it ran straight into the hill. You landed into the hill and took off over the cliff regardless of the wind strength and direction. There was no choice….the surface [was] sandy and boggy [and] fuelling was from 44 gallon (200 litre) drums which had been scattered about the bush."

After a dawn takeoff, in which, "Remarkably, everybody got off safely and we set course for Penfoie…Intelligence [had] reported a large number of aircraft there and our task was to attack and destroy as many as possible. None of us had been anywhere near this end of the island before… so we hoped to catch them by surprise and make just one run over it and get to hell out as fast as possible." They did: approaching fast and at low level they caught the Japanese completely by surprise. "Now we could appreciate the awesome firepower of the Beaufighter's…guns, all firing together." McDonald wrote.

The attack by the six aircraft was over in two minutes and a column of smoke 500 m high and visible 80 km out to sea was reported by the crews: FltLt J. Stanley and Sgt H. Thorncraft in A19-9, McDonald and PltOff F. Magee in '57, Dennett and Meers in '59, Flt Lt P. Biven and Newport in '62, Kearney and Ramsay in '66 and Wilkins and Byrnes in '67. In their wake the Beaufighters left an estimated 13 bombers and two fighters destroyed on the ground, along with burning fuel dumps and other damage. Staging through Drysdale they eventually reached Coomalie after being diverted to search for the vessels *Castlemaine*, *Armidale* and *Kuru*.

There to meet and congratulate the crews was the AOC NWA, AirCdre 'Dad' Bladin. The following day, the Melbourne's *Sun* reporter, Merton Woods, reported 13 bombers and two fighters destroyed in less than a minute under the headline, *Devastating Raid on Timor*.

A week later a *Sun* War Correspondent wrote of the raid. Under the headline, *Commandos of the Air in Dawn Strike*, he reported that "Commandoes [*sic*] of the air best describes the Beaufighter personnel who one day last week, in a dawn strike on a Japanese aerodrome at Koepang (Timor), destroyed 21 grounded planes. This remarkably successful mission referred to by the Prime Minister (Mr. Curtin) in his review of the war situation in Parliament on Thursday, was carried out by daring young airmen who graduated...only a month ago."

It was a most successful raid, but it was early days for the squadron and the article and resultant publicity may also have raised expectations of a certain invincibility of men and machines.

The squadron's 100th mission was recorded on the 16th and a week later A19-22 with Sgt R. T. Hand and WOff M. C. Smith went missing on operations over Timor, just two days before Christmas. Even Christmas Day and the following two days saw no rest, with strikes on the Lavai-Laga areas on Timor, whilst the Japanese build up of forces at Fuiloro aerodrome was blunted by attacks on the 22nd, 23rd, 24th, 27th and 28th of the month. The squadron claimed one Japanese fighter shot down.

On the 29th two crews had lucky escapes when their aircraft were lost: both as a result of ground fire over Timor. PltOff G. Gibb and his observer, Sgt D. A. Webb, ditched A19-20 off Betano and swam ashore. They were found by Australian Lancer Force personnel and returned to Australia by HMAS *Arunta* on 10 January, none the worse for wear but for a bout of malaria. Both FlgOff Ian 'Tiny' Wilkins and his observer, Sgt Bill Byrnes, were forced to bale out of A19-71 in sight of Bathurst Island. Both were rescued by Cpl Bill Woodnutt, the coast watcher based at nearby Wiyapurali.

A further squadron was added to the NWA inventory on 5 December, when a mixed Dutch and RAAF party comprising five officers, 51 SNCOs and 140 Airmen along with 203 tonnes of equipment departed Canberra as part of 18 NEI Squadron's move to the NWA.

Beaufighter A19-82, EH-F, landing at Coomalie. The aircraft crashed on take off at Coomalie on 21 November 1943 and was written off two weeks later. Photo: AHSNT Colln.

Formed at Canberra on 4 April 1942, the unit was destined for the NWA as a means of maintaining a Dutch presence close to, and in missions over, their former colony. It was a unique mix of Dutch and Australian aircrew, along with RAAF and Javanese ground crews. Whilst aircrew were made up of escapees of the former NEIAF, KLM and KNILM pilots, manning problems saw the RAAF make up the difference, mainly in gunners, whilst the ground crews were also bolstered by the RAAF; at one stage there were 38 different nationalities and 18 different languages extant. When the unit moved north there were 173 NEI and 219 RAAF personnel in the unit; the Dutch overall commander was LtCol te Roller, whilst the RAAF personnel had their own senior officer.

Equipped with the North American Aviation B-25 Mitchell medium bombers, the unit had trained over NSW before being advised of its impending move north, though a number of its aircraft had been requisitioned by the 3rd Bomb. Gp as an operational priority. These were eventually made up and the unit was equipped with 19 aircraft in 1942, with a further 16 in 1943, 87 in 1944 and 28 during 1945; in all, the unit operated 150 of the B-25C, D and J models.

Nine B-25s departed Fairbairn on Boxing Day and by 18 January 1943 the squadron's move to McDonald north of Pine Creek was completed. There it came under the control of RAAF HQ NWA, relying on 9 Stores Depot and 14 ARD at Gorrie for stores, provisioning and major aircraft servicings.

STRIKING BACK

By year's end, the order of battle in the NWA boasted eight operational RAAF squadrons, excluding 18 NEI Squadron which was *en route*, and their established strengths as follows:

No. 2 Squadron at Batchelor, 18 Hudsons;

No.12 Squadron at Batchelor, 6 Wirraways and 18 Vengeances;

No. 13 Squadron at Hughes, 18 Hudsons;

No. 31 Squadron at Coomalie, 24 Beaufighters;

No. 76 Squadron at Strauss, 24 P-40Es;

No. 77 Squadron at Livingstone, 24 P-40Es;

No. 1 PRU at Coomalie, Buffaloes A51-1 and A51-3, Lancers A56-3 and A56-5 and Lightning A55-1; and

No. 6 Comm. Unit at Batchelor, five DH 84s, 1 DH 89 and 3 Tiger Moths.

The year 1942 had been a long one, but it was also one of dramatic change in the NWA; from the early months which saw rapid Japanese advances throughout the Pacific when even Australia herself was perceived as being under the threat of invasion to a change in fortunes by year's end when the Allies began to regain the initiative. Fortunately the Allies had also gained the upper hand elsewhere. The battles of the Coral Sea and Midway had been fought and won and any Japanese invasion plans of New Guinea thwarted, while a continuing build up of American and Australian forces saw new units established and others re-equipped.

Despite switching to night raids, the Japanese remained a force to be reckoned with. They had an estimated 334 aircraft capable of deployment in the NWA, mainly those of the 23rd *Koku Sentai* with the 753 *Ku* and 202 *Ku* and the floatplanes of the 934 *Ku*, along with the army's 7th *Hikoshidan*. The last raid for the year had been a desultory affair over Hughes, Coomalie and Strauss on 27 November but it was only a matter of time before the Japanese recommenced their raids in earnest.

Meanwhile, events 'down south' at Richmond RAAF base were moving closer to the arrival of the long awaited and much vaunted Spitfire Mk Vc aircraft of 1 Fighter Wing in the NWA, with personnel and aircraft of the Wing's 452 and 457 RAAF Squadrons and 54 (RAF) Squadron preparing to move north in early 1943.

The USAAF was also preparing to move a heavy bomber unit north in response to an Allied HQ request for the establishment of a strategic strike/reconnaissance force to operate against Japanese forces in the NEI, Ceram, Celebes, and western New Guinea area.

The earlier lack of organisation, equipment and resources had been largely overcome and with new aircraft and units arriving, 1943 must surely see a reversal in fortunes as the Allies mounted pressure on the Japanese to the north.

THE CLYDE H. BARNETT JUNIOR COLLECTION

These photos are part of a series of colour transparencies taken by Lieutenant Clyde H. Barnett Jr., a young American pilot who flew with the 8th Squadron, 49th Fighter Gp USAAF from Strauss Airstrip in 1942. A keen photographer, Clyde documented squadron life in Darwin and New Guinea, but it was not until 1946 that these unique historic records were returned to him by the censor. They were passed on by Clyde in 1983.

The 8th Squadron scoreboard, a Japanese 'Zero' horizontal tailplane, Strauss airstrip, September 1942.

Lieutenant Clyde Barnett, "ready for flying June '42" at the alert shack, Strauss airstrip.

Inside the Officers' Club at Strauss. Furniture was acquired from Darwin via the military authorities.

Lt. Clyde Barnett in front of his P-40E, West Palm Beach Playboy, the replacement for his original aircraft lost following combat on 16 June.

Lt. Clyde Barnett in the squadron jeep, Strauss Airstrip.

Lt. Clyde Barnett in the cockpit of his P-40E '55' "Smiley", Strauss airstrip, 1942.

Lt. Clyde Barnett prepares to to depart on a sortie. The Tiger Moth A17-494 was used by the 8th Squadron as a training and communications aircraft.

Home for Lts. Ben Duke, Marlin Smith, James Martin and Clyde Barnett over their six month stay at Strauss, 1942.

A P-40E of Yellow Flight taking off from the south end of Strauss.

Lt. Clyde Barnett in the squadron mess writing home, Strauss Airstrip.

Lt. Ben Duke, an 8th Squadron pilot and his crew chief, Strauss 1942.

CHAPTER 8

CHANGING FORTUNES
The Spitfires arrive and the enemy is under pressure

The year 1943 opened on a more optimistic note with the arrival of the Spitfires and personnel of 1 Fighter Wing. Commanded by GpCapt A. L. 'Wally' Walters, with WgCdr Clive Caldwell as Wing Leader, the Wing was the result of direct consultations, though some might say confrontations, by the Australian Minister for External Affairs, Dr H. V. Evatt with the British Prime Minister, Winston Churchill, and the British government. Evatt had met with the War Cabinet during his May 1942 visit and requested three Spitfire squadrons for the defence of Australia.

The request was refused, citing the dire need of both Malta and the Middle East for the tropicalised Spitfire Mk V aircraft. Further, the apparent willingness of the Americans to continue providing the P-40 Kittyhawks in growing numbers was put forward. Evatt, not to be put off, sought and won Churchill's backing. War Cabinet, probably with little option, endorsed the decision to send one RAF and two RAAF squadrons, noting that the symbolism of "...sending these squadrons from this country would be very great. Moreover, it must be borne in mind that while there were Australian squadrons fighting in this country...there were at present no United Kingdom units in Australia." In effect the two RAAF squadrons were constituted RAF (Article XV) squadrons and weren't signed over to the RAAF until late 1944 – and only then with British approval for the RAAF to take ownership.

In the event, forty eight Mk Vc Spitfires were allocated with an initial attrition replacement figure of five aircraft per month. The three squadrons, 54 (RAF), 452 and 457 RAAF Squadrons embarked on the *Stirling Castle* along with six aircraft, on 19 June 1942. They departed Liverpool the following day and put into Sierra Leone 10 days later. There, 42 of the Wing's allocated Spitfires were off loaded from the *Nigerstown* and diverted to Takoradi in Ghana for transport to the Western Desert. The convoy sailed into Melbourne on 13 August with six aircraft making up the entire fighter wing.

Replacements to make up the numbers reached Australia on 25 October and training intensified at Richmond RAAF Base and Camden aerodrome in NSW. The pilots needed all the training they could get as they had been out of action for some time. Even more than the lack of action due to the voyage however, was that, prior to their move to Australia, few had any combat experience at all and the squadrons had been involved in fighter sweeps rather than defensive combat for some months.

Of the three squadrons only six or seven pilots had any combat experience, though the new postings, WgCdr Caldwell and FlgOffs Adrian 'Tim' Goldsmith and John Bisley boosted Battle of Britain veterans FltLts Bob Foster and Robin Norwood of 54 Squadron, along with SqnLdr Ray Thorold Smith of 452 Squadron and SqnLdr Ken James of 457, both of whom had been made unit COs.

Squadron leader E. M. Gibbs, CO of 54 (RAF) Squadron and FltLt Bob Foster beside Spitfire Mk Vc DL-A at the RAAF Station February 1943. Photo: Malcolm Weatherhead.

Despite the arrival of new aircraft, the expectations of Churchill and the Australian Government of the Spitfires being in the NWA in the short term could not reasonably be met. It would be some months, and certainly not before January 1943, before they could make the move. In the interim it was up to the two P-40 Kittyhawk squadrons, 76 and 77, to defend Darwin until their arrival.

The first recorded enemy raid for 1943 saw two *Bettys* of the 753 *Ku* over Darwin at 2244 hours and a further two at 0015 hours on 20 January. No damage was reported and four P-40s of 76 Squadron were sent up to intercept

CHANGING FORTUNES

including FltLt J. A. Cox of 77 Squadron who was scrambled from Livingstone and despite firing at a *Betty* caused no visible damage.

The 76 Squadron CO, SqnLdr Keith 'Bluey' Truscott, claimed one bomber damaged when, "...soon after midnight 4 aircraft scrambled over Darwin" the squadron history sheet recorded, "A. F/L Kerville B. F/O... Tainton C. SqnLdr Truscott D, Fsgt Loudon at 0042K on 22nd S/L Truscott made head on attack on three *Betty*s with only 1 gun firing followed by a beam attack all guns jammed. *Betty*s fired from blisters and disappeared into cloud. Fsgt Loudon sighted 3 *Betty*s 300' below to starboard and behind and made a diving ¼ attack to point blank (range) getting in 1½ secs burst. The following day NW Area advised one *Betty* confirmed to Sqn Ldr Truscott."

Squadron Leader Keith 'Bluey' Truscott, CO 76 squadron (at the wheel) and fellow pilots, Strauss January 1943. Photo: Alford/AHSNT Colln.

At least one *Betty* was badly damaged that night. Aboard the aircraft flown by Masao Tanimura was a Japanese journalist, Shin'ya Saito, who described the flight, the biting cold, the time over Darwin and the attack by the P-40s. Damage was inflicted to the starboard engine and propeller whilst the port engine failed completely; all non-essential items were jettisoned while, "...one of the crew removed the [Shinto] talisman and stuck it between the adjustment tiller and the sunshade. Before my very eyes, two of the crew put their hands together and prayed for the propeller. I could not help from respectfully bowing my head to the white talisman." The aircraft made it back to Koepang.

A similar raid by two *Betty*s on the 21st saw them drop 28 60 kg bombs over the Darwin town and Frances Bay areas. Four P-40s failed to intercept the pair. A further raid

on the 24th was threatened, though the Japanese records confirm two *Betty*s of the 753 *Ku* departed Koepang for a raid on Darwin at 2327 hours, returning at 0612 hours the following morning due to weather, and without releasing their bombs.

The action on the night of the 20th was the first for some time for Truscott and after the hectic days of the Milne Bay battles, "This victory heartened him after weeks of boredom, because boredom is dangerous...it blunted the skills" his biographer wrote.

The statement effectively summed up the experience of both squadrons during their Darwin service. Accidents were frequent, some 20 in all, including a forced landing on Melville Island by FlgOff J. G. Gorton in A29-60 on 7 September the previous year, the loss of A29-62 following engine problems over Batchelor on 13 October and the rescue of the pilot, PltOff J. C. Griffiths, who parachuted to safety, and a jammed rudder cable on A29-142 at Strauss on 3 February, forced the pilot, SqnLdr Truscott, to run the aircraft off the 'strip.'

On the evening of 29 January the personnel of 76 Squadron embarked upon the MV *Maetsuyker* and sailed the following morning, bound for Onslow in Western Australia, where they arrived on 4 February. The squadron's aircraft had deployed to Drysdale Strip at the Kalumburu Mission from where they flew air cover for the ship and its cargo of personnel and equipment. However the boredom continued even with the change of locale; Truscott died on 28 March when his P-40 slammed into the sea off the Western Australian coast during mock attacks on a Catalina flying boat.

For 77 Squadron the boredom continued until 13 February, when the unit was officially tasked to move to New Guinea to participate in the defence of the Milne Bay area with 75 Squadron. The unit moved out at short notice and both Livingstone and Strauss were again vacant; and again, as they had when the 49th Fighter Gp departed, RAAF personnel moved in to carry out a number of improvements in anticipation of the arrival of the replacement units.

The Spitfires and personnel arrived in the Darwin area during January. Ground personnel of the three Spitfire units and those of 7 RSU arrived in Darwin aboard the MV *Maetsuycker* on the 25th. The aircraft came via the overland

CHANGING FORTUNES

route: Richmond - Mildura - Oodnadatta - Alice Springs - Daly Waters and on to Batchelor. A formation of 24 aircraft arrived at Daly Waters on the 18th under a Beaufighter escort while a QANTAS Lockheed Lodestar, VH-CAK, flown by Capt O. F. Y. Thomas conveyed a dozen servicing personnel to undertake any repairs *en route*. A number of unserviceabilities saw 7 RSU personnel travelling to remote airstrips to effect repairs. The remaining aircraft flew in over the following days.

The personnel and equipment of 7 RSU had arrived at Darwin by sea on 12 January and were transported to their base at the northern end of Pell airstrip at the 65-Mile peg south of Darwin. There they joined 4 RSU, which had occupied the southern end following their arrival from 1 November 1942. On arrival at Pell, 7 RSU personnel found "...43 tents pitched, 4 open messrooms, 2 kitchens, [and] 4 showers erected by [the] Mobile Works Squadron." The efforts of the RSUs were paramount in maintaining the supply of serviceable aircraft to the operational units, 7 RSU the Spitfire squadrons and 4 RSU a range of types and units.

The Spitfire squadrons remained at Batchelor before deploying to their permanent bases, 54 (RAF) Squadron to the RAAF Station on 25 January, 452 to Strauss on the 31st, followed by 22 aircraft and pilots the following day, and 457 to Livingstone on 1 February. The "Squadron's main party moved from Batchelor to Livingstone... [and] the aircraft were flown over...by the evening the squadron was more or less comfortably settled" the Unit History Record reflected, "...On the whole LIVINGSTONE is a better equipped camp than our former base, there being three excellent messes and a fine recreation hut for the airmen...supplied by the Salvation Army. Water is plentiful...and there are fine facilities for showers..."

The aircraft and personnel of 54 (RAF) Squadron were based at the RAAF Station with their camp area at Nightcliff, some five km from the base itself. "We had been a long time coming" Bob Foster wrote, "It was now late January 1943 and the war with Japan was now over a year old. By the time the promised Spitfire wing had been organised in June 1942 and it had finally arrived...seven months had come and gone, but at least we were in situ and ready for anything – so long as something, anything – happened... The war we had come to fight was starting to disappear in our neck of the woods."

Despite his misgivings, Foster was the first to draw blood for the wing. On 6 February, the 70th DCS sent a Ki-46 *Dinah* over Darwin and it was tracked by radar before Foster's four Spitfires were scrambled at 1205 hours. After being vectored onto the *Dinah* by 5 Fighter Sector, Foster, in BS181 *Yvonne* - the usual aircraft of FlgOff J. D. Lenagen - and his wingman, FSgt B. Mahoney, closed in on the aircraft before Foster fired "...two quick bursts at 300 yds., the first of which caused cannon strikes to be seen on port engine...a fifth burst, followed by a long burst closing to 100 yds., resulted in further strikes raking the E/A, the port engine of which caught fire, the flames spreading to the rest of the machine. The enemy spiralled down in flames and was seen by both White 1 and White 2 to hit the water burning fiercely." Lts Kurusuke Setaguti and Fumio Mori died as their aircraft crashed into the sea west north west of Cape Van Diemen off Melville Island. They were the first of nine *Dinah* crews to be downed over the NWA.

A group of 457 Squadron Fitters IIE hoisting a Rolls Royce Merlin engine at Livingstone, 1943. Photo: G. Williams.

Flight Lieutenant Bob Foster of 54 (RAF) Squadron beside the Spitfire in which he scored the first 'kill' on 6 February 1943: a Mitsubishi Ki-46 *Dinah*. Photo: Alford/AHSNT Colln.

CHANGING FORTUNES

The squadron record confirmed it as "A memorable day for the squadron, since it marked our first real kill in Australia...General jubilation." From then, however it was more a waiting game.

Training flights had continued once the squadrons had settled in to their new bases and with them came the first fatalities. Two 452 Squadron pilots, Sergeants E. E. Hutchinson and Stockley in BS184 and BR549 collided during an exercise involving dummy attacks on a 90th Bomb Gp USAAF B-24 on 27 February. Six days later FSgt P. F. McCarthy in BS158 was killed when he and BR535 flown by Sgt A. E. Cooper collided on landing.

Accidents and combat were to take their toll over the following months. During the period 23 January to 14 March alone, 22 accidents were recorded, nine of which resulted in the aircraft being written off. There were two fatal accidents, those of FSgt McCarthy, and a 452 Squadron pilot, FlgOff W. H. Ford in BS175 on 27 February. Ford was part of a six aircraft flight despatched to Wyndham in Western Australia to provide aerial defence against the Japanese attacking the ship MV *Maetsyucker*. He apparently became disoriented during a heavy storm and crashed into high ground in the Tabletop Range west of Batchelor. It took six days for a land party to reach the site and recover Ford's remains. The aircraft was beyond recovery and remains on a hill named Mount Ford for him.

During 1943 1 Fighter Wing recorded 239 accidents, 51 of these as a result of combat with 65 aircraft either written off or 'converted to components.' Of these incidents 22 resulted in fatalities, 13 of them as a result of combat.

Whilst the Spitfire squadrons were at Batchelor they had shared the airfield with 2 and 12 Squadrons, along with an advance element of three B-24D Liberators of the 90th Bomb. Gp. Led by Maj Harry Bullis with the Lts Charles Hesse, B. Coolidge and Hatfield crews, they were the precursors to the American heavy bomber commitment to the NWA.

Operating from Batchelor the small force comprising aircraft from the 319th, 320th and 400th Squadrons flew four armed reconnaissance missions over Menado, Kendari, Macassar and Ambon. They claimed a Japanese light cruiser and a 5,080 tonne cargo vessel during a mission to Ambon on 21 January, though a gunner on Lt Hatfield's crew, Cpl R. C. Rafferty, was killed during an intercept by Ku *202 Zekes*.

Four days later Lt Charles Hesse and his 320th Squadron crew were assigned a reconnaissance mission to Kendari, a 2,575 km round trip. No bombs were carried and a bomb bay fuel tank was installed.

After a five hour trip and a camera run over the Kendari airfield the B-24 was attacked by fighters, which left after a 20 minute running fight. Despite some damage and the news that they had failed to get any photos, Hesse headed for home. "...a short time later, we spotted a convoy consisting of one destroyer and three transport ships" Hesse wrote, "We kept them in view...and radioed its position and heading back to base. While we were near the convoy, a float-type two-seater biplane surprised us from above and behind. This antique looking craft dropped two small projectiles which did no harm. Then it proceeded to make a diving attack... [but] our tracer seemed to encircle him and he broke off his attack...apparently unhurt... [we] arrived at Batchelor about 7:30 PM."

Two further missions, bombing raids on Ambon on the 30th and 31st of the month, were aborted due to weather on the first attempt and engine problems on the second. On 2 February Hesse and his 320th crew received orders to join the 319th Squadron based at Fenton under the command of Capt Charles E. Jones. From Fenton the 319th and attached

Taken by a USAAF crewman, Cpl Charles McBride, and with a steady hand, this photo shows two Rufes climbing to intercept an Allied bomber. Photo: via Bob Livingstone.

CHANGING FORTUNES

aircraft of Hesse and the other crews carried out armed reconnaissance missions until July when the 380th Bomb. Gp arrived in the area.

The Nakajima Ki-43 *Oscars* of the Japanese Army's 59th *Sentai* and the *Zekes* of Ku 202, along with Mitsubishi A6M2-N *Rufe*, Mitsubishi F1M *Pete* and Aichi E13A1 *Jake* floatplanes of the 934 *Ku* based around the islands in the Ambon area provided headaches for the Allied crews of the Hudsons, B-25, Beaufighters and B-24s, despite continued harassing raids, particularly by 31 Squadron. The 59th *Sentai* had re-equipped with Ki-43 Model II *Oscar* in early 1943 and was based at Dili, from where they intercepted a number of raids. Unfortunately Allied aircrews tended to describe any Japanese fighter as a 'Zero' and the role of the unit has been obscured as a result.

The 934 *Ku* evolved from the 36 *Ku*, which had formed at Balikpapan on 20 July 1942 with 8-10 *Jakes*. It was redesignated 934 *Ku* from 1 November 1942 and moved from Borneo to Ambon on 14 March 1943 under Cdr Kenji Kumura. The unit was initially equipped with eight Aichi E13A1 *Jakes*, and eight *Petes,* and later with the *Rufe*, 10 of which arrived from Yokosuka on 18 March 1943.

The new unit operated initially from Ambon with 16 *Jakes*, 8 *Petes* and 24 of the new *Rufes*, which had been arriving in the area from February that year. From July 1943 a detachment operated from Taberfane with 12 *Rufes*, eight *Petes* and 16 *Jakes*. The main bases were at Ambon along with Taberfane and Dobo from June, though Taberfane was abandoned after an earthquake on 10 December. The unit then moved to Manokwari and was equipped with a number of Kawanishi N1K1 *Rex* seaplane/fighters late that year. The *Rufe* element was deactivated on 1 March 1944, while the *Jakes* moved to Macassar; the 934 *Ku* was disbanded on 1 October that year.

On 18 January, the date of its arrival in the Territory, 18 NEI Squadron had flown its first mission, an armed reconnaissance to Tanimbar Island in search of shipping. The following day, the 19th, the Kai Islands were targeted and the B-25s received their first combat damage when they were intercepted by *Zekes* and floatplanes of Ku 202 and 934 *Ku*. The B-25s claimed two *Zekes* and a *Jake* floatplane probably destroyed over Fuiloro and Dobo. On the 20th three B-25s led by Lt Gus Winckel raided Dobo and were intercepted by three patrolling *Pete* floatplanes.

The *Shotai* leader, Lt Yoshio Tamura, the CO of the Observation Buntai and his observer, PO2c Ichiro Ito, and the two other *Petes* pursued the B-25s out to sea but were outdistanced.

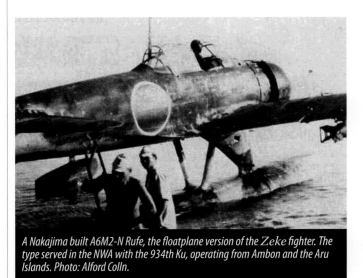

A Nakajima built A6M2-N Rufe, the floatplane version of the Zeke fighter. The type served in the NWA with the 934th Ku, operating from Ambon and the Aru Islands. Photo: Alford Colln.

The 934 *Ku* was also involved in the death of the Chair of the Methodist Northern Australian Mission, the Reverend Len Kentish, when a *Jake* bombed and sank the coastal supply vessel *Patricia Cam* on 22 January. Flown by PO1c Yamazaki with FCPO Ozawa and Flyer 1c Ninomiya as observer and gunner, the aircraft bombed the survivors in the water before strafing them. The *Jake* then landed and signalled Kentish aboard. He was flown to Dobo and imprisonment. The 18 survivors managed to reach safety though two died shortly afterwards. The remainder were rescued by HMAS *Kuru* on the 29th.

Len Kentish wasn't so lucky. He was interrogated and bashed under the control of Lt Mangan Sagejima, until raids by 2, 18 NEI and 31 Squadrons in late January and early February so badly damaged the floatplane base that the 934 *Ku* suspended operations for a time. Sagejima was enraged at the damage and on 5 February he, PO Kenzo Hoyama and a civilian, Shozuke Kohama, took Kentish behind the gaol where Hoyama beheaded him. It was not until postwar that Kentish's fate became known when the local natives provided information to the Allies. The three were tried and found guilty in Hong Kong in 1948; Sagejima was hanged and the others sentenced to life imprisonment.

On 31 January a dawn raid on Dili saw two B-25s force land on their return due to a shortage of fuel. Aircraft N5-134

CHANGING FORTUNES

landed at the Port Keats Mission southwest of Darwin whilst N5-139 force landed in the swamps of the Moyle River floodplains north of the mission. The crew was uninjured and erected a canvas awning to provide shade while they awaited rescue. Late in the day FlgOff 'Squizzy' Taylor in Wirraway A20-542 dropped supplies "...to [the] crew of crashed B-25 near Port Keats – aircraft then landed...and flew Sgt. in charge of land party to position for guidance."

Photographed by FltLt 'Squizzy' Taylor of 12 Squadron, B-25 Mitchell N5-139 lies on the Moyle floodplains north of Port Keats Mission following its forced landing on 31 January 1943. Photo: Jack Taylor.

A third aircraft landed on the small airstrip at 39 RDF Station at Port Keats. The "Dutch crew was very surprised & delighted to see us RAAF boys..." wrote Bob Meredith, a radar operator at the site, "...we then hand pumped enough petrol (hard work)...to get them back. All of us had to clear end of strip of tall trees...late in the day with a struggle [the aircraft] took off. Pilot did a wonderful job. Tuesday 2 February...Natives have found other planes...about 25 miles away, crews safe, formed a party to go out and rescue them. Rough country, crocodile infested...plane dropped them rations. Saturday 6 February...all the rescued boys flown out today." The crews were returned to their unit none the worse for wear.

The squadron suffered its first fatalities in the NWA on 5 February when N5-132 crashed and its bombs detonated north of McDonald airfield shortly after take off as part of a four aircraft flight ordered to Darwin for standby duty. The seven man crew of SgtMaj Schalk, SgtMaj Kessels, and Sgts Hiele, Janssen, Abeleven and Maarschalkerweert perished, along with the RAAF gunner, Sgt Harold Walton, who lingered for some hours before dying. Two RAAF passengers, Sgt D. L. MacPherson and LAC M. T. Palamountain, were also killed in the crash. Only recently married, Palamountain was hitching a ride to start leave.

Six B-25s carried out a further raid on Dili on 18 February and were intercepted by fighters with one aircraft, N5-144 ditched at sea. With the pilot and bombardier dead and the co-pilot badly wounded, the surviving crew of the downed B-25 took to a liferaft and were spotted by the remainder of the 18 Squadron aircraft, which by that time were running low on fuel and were forced to head for home. A Hudson later dropped supplies and they were eventually rescued by HMAS *Vendetta*. The B-25 claimed one *Zeke*, while further claims of one *Zeke* destroyed, one probable and three damaged were made following missions later that month.

Ten days later, warning of Japanese air movements led to a successful strafing attack, Operation COO 46, on Koepang by 31 Squadron. Staging through Drysdale on the 27th, eight aircraft: A19-57 with WgCdr Read and FlgOff Marr; '51 FlgOff Wilkins and Sgt McNamara; '62 FltLt Biven and Sgt Newton; '45 FlgOff Kearney and Sgt Ramsay; '16 FltLt Cohen and FlgOff Richards; '17 FlgOff McDonald and FlgOff Magee; '59 FltLt Dennett, and Sgt Meers; and '47 with FltLt Stanley and Sgt Thorncraft made the attack early on the 28th, leaving a number of enemy aircraft destroyed or burning on the airfield.

The warning had come from 51 Wireless Section, part of the ASWG, or 'Eavesdroppers', as they were known. The unit had established itself at two locations near Coomalie airfield in 1942, one on an ironstone ridge to the south and the other overlooking the Batchelor road to the west. From there they intercepted and translated the *Kana* code of the Japanese via receivers that were tracking each of their operators. They tracked the movements of 20 bombers of the 753 *Ku* between Kendari and Koepang over a three day period and later in April provided the itinerary of Admiral Isoroku Yamamoto to Allied HQ; the information led to the successful interception of Yamamoto's flight and his death in the jungles of Bougainville on the 18th. With regular interceptions of Japanese radio traffic the NWA was able to counter a number of Japanese operations before they developed.

The first real test for the Spitfires came on 2 March when 26 aircraft of both 54 and 452 Squadrons were scrambled to intercept a force of 21 *Zekes* sent to attack Coomalie airfield, seemingly in retaliation for the problems the Beaufighters

CHANGING FORTUNES

had been causing on Timor. Led by LtCdr Takahide Aioi, the *Zekes* of Ku 202, claimed six fighters destroyed and ten damaged without loss, while the Spitfire squadrons claimed three destroyed and one damaged. Neither side recorded any losses but for a Beaufighter, A19-31.

Lieutenant Commander Takahide Aioi led 21 3 Ku Zekes on the 2 March 1943 raid on Coomalie. Aioi served in China, on carriers, and over the Philippines, the NEI and Darwin. Photo: Alford Colln.

Ed Simmonds, an LAC radar operator recalled the incident, commenting that "I was on fatigues...at 44 Radar Wing, which was on a ridge just south of the strip. I saw three Zeros fly up the valley below me and they were so close that I could see every detail of the last plane and its pilot... They came in over Anson Bay that was not covered by radar, and they flew so low that the radar lobes would miss them. Later radar was installed on Peron Island..." One of the A-A gunners, Geoff Wisby of 'D' Troop 112 LAA Regt was at Coomalie and wrote that "There was no warning of enemy aircraft in the area and when O.P. was told of six unidentified planes that looked like Zeros, O.P. replied, No Yellow, No Red, treat as friendly...it was only when they were told their guns were firing they said take action."

It was too late. The *Zekes* had been and gone, destroying one Beaufighter, A19-31, the aircraft of McDonald and Magee, and damaging another. A19-31 had been on a familiarisation flight and after landing, the pilot, PltOff A. E. Longoni, had parked it at the end of the airstrip instead of its usual revetted insert. "The raid only lasted a few seconds" McDonald recalled, "When the all clear came through we could see some smoke rising from the strip. We...went to investigate... [and] almost wept when we found the smouldering remains of A19-31...we felt like wringing Longini's [*sic*] neck. The only item salvaged was a wing tip..." McDonald may have rued his desire to 'wring Longoni's neck'; both he and his observer, Sgt A. R. Dale in A19-79 died over Dobo when they were hit by A-A fire 13 days later.

Apart from the Beaufighter lost at Coomalie, the Spitfires also lost their cover. They had previously been referred to only as 'Capstans' with 'Marvel' engines to keep the fact that the aircraft were in Australia from the Japanese. News of the Spitfires' first clash was quickly announced, with the 5 March edition of *Army News* reporting that "The Prime Minister, Mr Curtin revealed to Australia and the world that the famous British Spitfire fighters were being used in the South-West Pacific Area, and that they had already successfully engaged Japanese planes in combat over Darwin."

While Churchill expressed satisfaction in learning "...of the ascendancy they have immediately established over the enemy...", Curtin's announcement and his claim of six enemy aircraft downed not only embarrassed the pilots, but had the potential to undermine any successes should the Wing make just one mistake. Indeed, General MacArthur had warned against focusing attention on the Spitfires before they had the opportunity to prove themselves.

Five days after the Coomalie raid, the 70th DCS sent over a *Dinah* crewed by Lts Yutaka Tonoi and Chokiti Orahara. Four aircraft of 457 Squadron were scrambled at 1100 hours to intercept near Bathurst Island. FltLt D. McLean and FSgt F. R. J. 'Darky' McDowell spotted the aircraft and attacked, each making two attacks from close range. The aircraft was seen to crash into the sea off Lee Point by 54 Squadron personnel. A notebook and some other items including oxygen bottles were recovered from the *Dinah*. Only 452 Squadron was yet to open its scorecard.

CHANGING FORTUNES

They didn't have long to wait. Over the three days 11 to 13 March *Ku* 202 had sent over single *Babs* reconnaissance aircraft and on the 14th a *Babs* preceded a force of 25 753 *Ku Bettys* sent to bomb Darwin; all were forced to abort the missions due to poor weather. Not so on the 15th however. Twenty two *Bettys* escorted by 27 *Zekes* departed Koepang at 0634 and 0645 hours, though three *Bettys* were forced to return to base. The *Bettys* carried a total of 256 bombs and targeted Darwin town and the oil tanks, destroying two tanks and buildings including the US Army HQ. They were met by 27 Spitfires and in the following combat they claimed 15 Spitfires whilst 1 Fighter Wing claimed six *Zekes* destroyed, two *Bettys* and one *Zeke* probably destroyed with three *Bettys* and eight *Zekes* as damaged.

The combat raged so close over Darwin that the A-A unit summary for the raid recorded "NOT allowed to engage." Cliff Taylor, a gunner with the 19th HAA Bty at Fannie Bay wrote that "...They clashed right overhead. Dogfights ranged from about 25,000 ft down to almost ground level with some of the Spits going straight at the bombers. Planes wheeling, milling, machine guns, cannon fire (the haze remained for nearly an hour), planes on fire, pilots baling out, men dying – it's hard to imagine that this happened in Australia. I shall never forget the air battles."

Japanese records detail two *Zekes* lost with one, PO2c Seiji Tajiri, listed as missing; the pilot of A6M2 *Zeke* No. 6540, Tajiri was downed by 54 Squadron pilot, FlgOff A. Mawer. Losses by 1 Fighter Wing were recorded as four lost, with another, BR468 of 457 Squadron, damaged but later repaired.

Three Spitfire pilots failed to return. A badly wounded FSgt F. L. Varney of 54 Squadron crash landed his aircraft, AR619, between two houses on Myilly Point and was rushed to the nearby Kahlin Hospital where he died early on the 16th. He was buried as a Pilot Officer; his commission had come through but had not been acted upon. Sergeant A. E. Cooper, also of 54 Squadron was seen to bale out of his aircraft AR620 but was dead when picked up, apparently having broken his neck when he struck the aircraft. A third aircraft BS293 of 452 Squadron was hit during combat and the pilot baled out and was rescued near Picnic Point on Cox Peninsula.

The fate of the fourth aircraft, BS231 of 452 Squadron, remained a mystery for a further 43 years, until in 1986

it was confirmed as being that of the 452 Squadron CO, SqnLdr Ray Thorold-Smith. Thorold-Smith, more popularly known as 'Throttle', disappeared during the combat and despite searches over the following days neither he nor his aircraft were located. He was later listed as 'missing, presumed killed.' Theories abound as to his disappearance and perhaps the cause will never be known. What is known is that the aircraft lies in mud in the western reaches of Darwin harbour, with nothing apparently untoward; the undercarriage is retracted, the propeller is in coarse pitch and the aircraft is settled in a straight and level attitude.

Spitfire Mk Vc BS231 at Camden NSW prior to deployment to Darwin. The aircraft was flown by SqnLdr Ray Thorold-Smith during the 15 March 1943 combat. Photo: Alford/AHSNT Colln.

What is also known is that the RAAF, 1 Fighter Wing and 452 Squadron lost a popular figure, one who was "...tall, rangy and loose jointed, very calm and collected" as Gavin McEwin, the duty controller at Batchelor, remembered, "[He] always looked as though he had fallen into his clothes rather than dressed." Thorold-Smith was replaced by SqnLdr Ron McDonald, the CO of 12 Squadron, following a hasty conversion from Wirraways.

Two weeks after the raid, the 54 Squadron historian recorded that "The navy's fishing activities in the harbour have resulted, among other discoveries, in the recovery of about five feet of the wing-tip of the Zero shot down by F/O Mawer on 15th March...which has been added to the squadron's relics..." The relic went on to become the squadron's scoreboard, listing its 'kills' from WWI to those during its service in Darwin.

By the end of March 1943, the Hudsons were facing the end of their service in the NWA. Both 2 and 13 Squadrons had commenced the new year with reconnaissance

CHANGING FORTUNES

missions and supply drops to Lancer Force on Timor. During January, 13 Squadron flew 82 sorties, recording a number of encounters with enemy aircraft including two *Zekes*, a Kawanishi H6K *Mavis* flying boat, a *Dinah* and a Mitsubishi Ki-21 *Sally*, the latter being badly damaged by the fire from Sgt R. G. Curtiss in A16-247; the crew of A16-227 survived a similar encounter on 3 March following a raid on Dobo.

The wing tip of a Nakajima built A6M2 Zeke 6540 downed by FlgOff G. A. Mawer on 15 March 1943 was recovered and used by 54 (RAF) Squadron as its scoreboard. Photo: Alford Colln.

Another encounter involved SqnLdr Kemp who had led three Hudsons to Dobo on 11 January. This time, instead of a *Jake* they had met on 23 November, they were intercepted by two *Pete* biplanes. The faster Hudsons outdistanced the *Petes* though Lt Tetsui Nakayama and his wingman claimed a Hudson damaged. Nakayama and his crewman were killed over Dobo on 2 February when their F1M2 *Pete* was shot down after attacking three 2 Squadron Hudsons led by WgCdr Jock Whyte. Seven days later a force of nine Hudsons raided targets on Timor and were intercepted by Ki-43 *Oscars* of the 59th *Sentai*. The CO, Maj Tsuguroko Nakao, was shot down and killed during the supposedly uneven combat with the Hudsons, though the 2 or 13 Squadron records fail to detail the encounter.

Even as 13 Squadron wound down, 89 sorties were flown in February, mostly in attacks on Dobo and the Aru islands, while a further 61 sorties were flown the following month. Dobo, Saumlaki and Langgoer were targeted, whilst supply drops to the men of Lancer Force were also maintained. February saw a further aircraft written off when A16-212 crashed on landing at Hughes during a heavy storm on the 27th. The pilot, Sgt K. Danks-Brown and a Flight Rigger, LAC Edwards escaped, however Sgt R. C. Robinson, Cpl

C. C. Jennings and LACs R. G. Bradley and P. R. Lazarus were killed.

The end came on 30 March. The final operation by the Hudsons of 13 Squadron was a six aircraft mission to bomb Timoeka on the southwestern tip of Dutch New Guinea and all returned safely. It was the end of a long operational career for the squadron over a two year period from 10 December 1941, when it flew its first offensive mission to Tobi Island, to 30 March 1943 with the Timoeka raid.

For the next week the unit flew army cooperation exercises before handing over aircraft and equipment to 2 Squadron. One, A16-227 'The Saint', had survived a 3 March combat with a *Sally* and was handed over on 15 April but lasted only six weeks before being written off in a landing accident at Milingimbi on 1 July. Squadron COs were also changed with WgCdr R. H. Moran posted in from 2 Squadron as the new 13 Squadron CO while WgCdr 'Jock' Whyte took over 2 Squadron.

By 12 April 13 Squadron was on the move. One hundred and eighty six airmen departed Hughes whilst 30 aircrew flew aboard the remaining six Hudsons to Batchelor. From Hughes personnel proceeded to Canberra, where they were to re-equip briefly with Beauforts before reappearing in the Territory. The personnel and aircraft of 2 Squadron moved to Hughes shortly afterwards.

From its first loss, that of A16-8 on 15 August 1941 to that of A16-212 on 27 March 1943, 13 Squadron had lost 25 aircraft and 54 Squadron members. Twelve aircraft were lost on operations whilst a further two were written off as a result of damage incurred during operations. Seven were lost on the ground as a result of enemy action, including the 19 February 1942 air raids, and four in accidents.

With 13 Squadron gone, the RAAF had one operational bomber squadron in the NWA. With that added responsibility came more missions and more losses for 2 Squadron and the toll continued until December 1943 when part of the unit was posted south to re-equip a flight with Beauforts.

The unit had started the year with shipping patrols, armed reconnaissance and offensive missions to Koepang and other targets on Timor, Timoeka in Dutch New Guinea, Maikoor, Taberfane and Dobo in the Aru Islands, and

CHANGING FORTUNES

Saumlaki in the Tanimbar Islands and Langgoer in the Kai Island group. Many were at extreme range and all posed extreme dangers.

Two crews were tragically lost on 19 April when A16-183 and '197 collided after take off from Milingimbi. Both crashed onto Rabuma Island just north of the base only minutes after take off and personnel at Milingimbi recalled hearing the resultant explosion, though many of the bombs remained intact until detonated by the RAAF in the 1990s. The crews were initially buried at the crash site before being interred at Adelaide River. Lost that day were PltOffs J. L. Barnes and J. L. Bassan, FlgOff K. R. Mills and FSgt H. H. Hadley in A16-183 and FltLt K. E. Daniel, FlgOff J. J. Laws, PltOff P. O. Butler FSgt T. W. Wilson and Sgt W. J. Gove in '197.

Flight Lieutenant Keith Daniel and his crew. From left, Daniel, Sgt Bill Gove, PltOff Les Jope, PltOff Jack Laws and Sgt Bill Wilson. Daniel, Gove and Laws were killed on 19 April 1943. Photo: AHSNT Colln.

Five days later the Kilgariff crew in A16- 217 flew a lone armed reconnaissance mission to Dobo, where they noted three *Jakes* on the water south of Taberfane. Kilgariff decided to make a strafing run, however they were attacked by a *Pete* floatplane flown by PO3c Yoshio Imada. The Hudson was able to find cover in low cloud and escaped.

On 28 April A16-241 disappeared over the Arafura Sea. Part of a seven aircraft armed reconnaissance of the Aru Islands, the aircraft was heard one and a half hours after leaving Milingimbi saying that it had one engine shut down and that it was 30 minutes out. That was the last heard from the crew comprising FlgOff R. R. James, PltOff R. D. Ryan, WOff H. E. Cutten, FSgts K. G. Keech and P. S. Reen and Sgt R. E. Norris. Two other crews were lucky: one aircraft had failed to take off and another had engine problems and aborted the mission.

The *Rufe* floatplanes of the 934 *Ku* struck on 7 May when they intercepted A16-171, one of a five aircraft mission, near the Maikoor River and with it went the Hicks, Jackman, Quinn, MacKenzie and Henry crew. Others were lost to A-A fire; A16-233 was downed by fire from the *Sugi Maru* north of Tanimbar on 8 September with FlgOff L. A. Martin and PltOffs M. C. Wettenhall and R. H. Williams killed. Two, Sgts M. A. Graham and J. W. R. Boannas managed to bale out but were captured and taken to Ambon where they were executed on 31 October.

The aircraft had been on a 'Horse' patrol, part of a new system of shipping patrol routes. 'Giraffe' was the area around Timor, 'Horse' around the Tanimbars, 'Jackass' between Timor and the Tanimbars and 'Koala' around the Aru islands. 'Gull', 'Heron' and 'Kiwi' were added to the patrol tracks on 1 January 1944. A16-178 was on a 'Horse' patrol on 16 October when, as happened so often, it failed to return. Lost were FlgOff J. P. Oldridge, FSgts D. N. Rumble and J. F. G. Cullen and Sgts F. R. Drake-Brockman and D. W. Petch.

From its first loss on 12 January 1942 to 31 December 1943, 2 Squadron lost 24 aircraft and 119 members on operations. Six aircraft were written off as a result of operational damage and a further seven due to enemy action including the 19 February 1942 air raids. Nine were lost in landing and other accidents. Twelve of those aircrew lost were executed as POWs; some after having been nursed back to health by their Japanese captors in just another part of the madness of war.

On 17 December 1943, RAAF Organisation Memorandum No. 404 laid out the future of 2 Squadron and confirmed that of 13 Squadron.
"1...No. 2 Squadron will be re-armed with Beaufort aircraft to replace the Hudsons...as follows.
2. The Beaufort aircraft of No. 13 Squadron...will move as early as possible into North-Western Area and will arm a flight of 2 Squadron. Beaufort crews of 13 Squadron will be transferred with their aircraft. As the Hudsons of 2 Squadron become due for repair or overhaul they will be withdrawn and replaced by further Beauforts, until the squadron is re-armed to a strength of 18 Beauforts plus one dual Beaufort.
3. Following the transfer...13 Squadron will be re-armed by the allotment of 9 Venturas (type B34) as they become available...
4. No. 13 Squadron will then consist of one flight of 9 type PV1 Venturas and one flight of 9 type B34 Venturas."

CHANGING FORTUNES

The crew of A16-199 prior to the last operational Hudson flight in the NWA on 8 April 1944. From left, Leo Zarnke, Bob Hebbard, FlgOff Roger Kuring (pilot), Ray Hilton and Jack Carolin. Photo: Ian Parker.

The news was timely as by late December 1943 there were only ten Hudsons remaining on strength: A16-154, '160, '177, '199, '203, '207, '215, '219, '226 and '230. They and their crews flew on into 1944, with a further two aircraft and crews lost on operations before the Hudsons were gone.

A16-230 was shot down during a reconnaissance of islands in the Banda Sea on 27 March 1944. The crew survived and made it to Loeang Island, where they were cared for by natives before being captured some time later. From Loeang they were transferred to Babar Island, though one, Sgt D. C. Beddoe, was shot dead after waving at a B-25 passing over the barge taking them to Babar on 24 May. The remainder went on to Tan Toey POW camp on Ambon. Squadron Leader J. L. Scott, and FSgts R. I. M. King, B. E. Wallace and K. C. Wright were executed on 16 August, despite Japanese claims of them having been transferred to Japan. Beddoe's killer, a Japanese Warrant Officer, was charged with his murder.

A mystery that remained unsolved until post war was that of A16-203. The aircraft departed Hughes on a routine convoy patrol on 3 April and failed to arrive at Milingimbi. Despite searches the aircraft was not located and the crew of PltOffs C. D. Brockhurst, R. J. Philpott, R. L. Black and H. J. Gillies, along with FSgt R. G. Frew were listed as 'missing presumed killed.' It was not until 1946 that the aircraft remains were located only a few kilometres away at Paddy's Landing on the Adelaide River.

The last of the Hudsons, A16-199, flew its last sortie on 8 April with the Leo Zarnke, Bob Hebbard, Roger Kuring, Ray Hilton and Jack Carolin crew. It was transferred to 3 Comm. Unit the following day; in what can kindly be seen as an oversight, no entry appeared in the Unit History Records to mark the end of an era in RAAF operations in the NWA.

Beauforts had begun arriving at 2 Squadron from January 1944 and by the end of March A9-361, '363, '368, '373, '375, '379, '386, '392, '388, '496, '508, '519, '540, '576 and '578 had been brought on strength. They had begun shipping and reconnaissance patrols in concert with the Hudsons from January and by April were mounting strikes on targets in Timor, including Penfoie. Despite a number of successful strikes the Beauforts did not last long and were replaced by Mitchells mid-year.

Other units had also been active from early 1943. The Beaufighters of 31 Squadron had been maintaining pressure on the Japanese with low level strikes on airfields, floatplane bases, shipping and Japanese infrastructure in general, often working in with 2 Squadron and its remaining Hudsons, along with 18 NEI Squadron, which had been involved in strikes against their old peacetime haunts in the former Dutch empire, the NEI.

One of the first missions flown by 31 Squadron was a four aircraft strafing attack on the road system between Bacau and Beco in Portuguese East Timor on 19 January, during which A19-67 was lost to ground fire. Both N. L. Thomas and Sgt D. E. van Hooten were killed in the crash and buried nearby. Nine days later the squadron CO, WgCdr Read flew a reconnaissance sortie over Dobo and claimed a *Jake* floatplane destroyed at the moorings.

Three days after Read's successful reconnaissance, FCPO Ogawa and his crew were patrolling north of Milingimbi when they spotted an Allied convoy. As they prepared to attack the ships Ogawa's crew spotted a lone Beaufighter and broke away into clouds. Both FltLt J. L. Stanley and his Observer, Sgt H. O. Thorncraft in A19-19 carried on with the mission. Another lone reconnaissance to Dobo was flown by FltLt Cohen in A19-78 on 3 February, during which a *Jake* was claimed destroyed at the moorings before a *Pete* intercepted the Beaufighter, which escaped.

The crew of FlgOff A. E. Longoni and Sgt A. R. Dale weren't so lucky; they were part of an attack on Dobo on 15 March when their aircraft, A19-79, was hit by A-A fire and crashed into the sea. Three days later the floatplane threat in the Aru Islands escalated when the vessel *Sagara Maru* arrived at Ambon with ten of the Nakajima A6M2-N *Suisen* Type 2 *Rufes* and 11 pilots. The unit, a *Suisen-Tai* of the 934 *Ku* had formed under Lt Toshiharu Ikeda during February and had sailed from Yokosuka on 11 March.

One Hudson, A16-217 met up with a *Rufe* on 24 April but managed to escape in clouds and another was intercepted

by PO3c Yoshio Imada's *Rufe* the following day. The FltLt J. S. 'Bunny' Austin crew in A16-204 managed to return to base. Austin died on 9 November 1943: not on any dangerous mission over Japanese-held territory – he'd flown many of those - but of blood poisoning as the result of an insect bite. A DFC was added to his Mention in Dispatches and a reporter later wrote that squadron members "...recalled the time Bunny stooged over Penfoie for an hour after leading the Hudsons in... [defying] the screaming ack-ack fire...to observe the bombing results – and then took his own aircraft in to bomb...*Yet Bunny was just a typical member of this Hudson unit.*"

On 26 April the *Rufes* opened their score when A19-59 was shot down after becoming separated from a second Beaufighter as they neared Taberfane. Three patrolling *Rufes* flown by PO3c Yoshio Imada, PO3c Hidenori Matsunaga and Flyer 1c Osamu Yoza claimed the 'kill'. The Beaufighter observer, Sgt C. W. Thompson, was killed whilst the pilot, FlgOff C. A. Greenwood, survived only to be captured; he served out the remaining war years as a POW.

From March to the end of May 1943, 31 Squadron flew 185 sorties, 37 in March, 49 in April and the remainder during May. Five aircraft were lost while 20 enemy aircraft were claimed as destroyed, a majority of these the floatplanes of 934 *Ku*. The B-25s of 18 NEI Squadron had flown a similar number of sorties over the period; 46 in March, 57 in April and 72 during May. They claimed two enemy aircraft destroyed but had lost five aircraft on operations and a further three in accidents from late March.

On 30 March N5-133 flew an armed reconnaissance to Kaimana and encountered heavy A-A over the target, cracking the nose perspex. Heading for home, the aircraft also spotted a seaplane wake before being attacked by two fighters, one of which they claimed as destroyed; the B-25 suffered a fractured fuel line and lost an engine. The aircraft captain, Lt Swane, advised 18 Squadron of the problems and force landed at Point Jarlheel on the northeastern tip of Melville Island. Lts Swane, de Wolf and Begeman, along with Sgts Rouvroye and D. Moore RAAF, were rescued and returned to their unit.

April saw a maximum effort by the B-25s with missions involving from five to seven aircraft regularly attacking targets on Timor and in the islands in concert with 31 Squadron and the B-24s of the 90th Bomb. Gp's 319th

CHANGING FORTUNES

Squadron. The month started badly however, with the loss of N5-140 on the night of the 5th. It was part of a three aircraft flight on standby duty at Darwin when it and N5-130 and N5-145 were ordered to carry out an armed reconnaissance of the north coast of Timor.

Almost immediately after take off, N5-140 crashed into the sea at Nightcliff, a short distance from the runway at the RAAF Station. The crew of SgtMaj Tijmons, SgtMaj van Wylick, FSgt Hill a RAAF member, and Sgts van Bremen and Weller, also a RAAF member, died in the crash. They were buried at Adelaide River on the 7th but for Weller; his body was later found in a 54 Squadron fish trap and he was buried the following day.

The mix of nationalities serving with 18 NEI Squadron is evident in this photo taken in late 1943. Photo: Ted Lewis.

The same day had seen LtCol Fiedeldij inspect Hughes airfield, no doubt with a view to realising his desire to extend the reach of his B-25s. For some time the limitations of McDonald in terms of range had been discussed. At the time the B-25s usually flew to Darwin to refuel and remain on stand by duty prior to flying out on missions. At times they flew into Batchelor, where Gavin McEwin, a duty controller there, recalled that when 18 Squadron flew in they "...would arrive, 3 or 4 of them, pull off the runway and park by the Tower. A pilot would get out and go into Station H. Q., return[ing] after about 10 or 15 minutes. All the time they were parked they would keep their engines running. The pilot would get back in the aircraft, then they would all taxy [sic] out on to the runway and take off, leaving great clouds of smoke behind them. I often wondered how long it would be before one of them pranged on take-off..."

By late April most missions were flown from Darwin, with a high number of travel flights recorded from McDonald

to Batchelor whilst preparations were made for a move to Batchelor. On 8 May the move began in earnest with the main party of eight RAAF officers and 256 RAAF ORs, along with all the NEI personnel travelling to Batchelor. Most went by air and the reminder by road, whilst all the squadron aircraft but for N5-143 were flown to their new base. In all some 260 tons of equipment was moved over 87 trips. N5-143 arrived at Batchelor on the 14th.

Preparing a B-25 Mitchell of 18 NEI Squadron for a mission at McDonald Airfield, February 1943. The unit served only a few months at the airfield before moving to Batchelor. Photo: Charles Eaton Jr.

For the Spitfire squadrons meanwhile, it had been some weeks since the last raid and some degree of frustration was beginning to set in. The 457 Squadron report for April noted that the month "...has been a heavy strain on the patience of both air and ground crews. Lack of action and days of monotonous routine and hot weather tend to make the squadron personnel a little restless as there are no facilities for enjoying brief respites away from service life." Had he waited a few days the entry may have been entirely different.

The Japanese mounted a raid on Sunday 2 May and it became one that remained contentious for some time and one that has been debated ever since.

After having flown in from Kendari the previous day, twenty five Bettys armed with a total of 90 60 kg bombs and 16 70 kg incendiaries departed Koepang at 0650 hours, followed by an escort of 27 Zekes 40 minutes later. Seven of the Bettys dropped out shortly afterwards and returned to base. Led by LtCdr Minoro Suzuki, the Zekes were lacking a number of experienced pilots following transfers to Rabaul in support of the Guadalcanal campaign. Air Officer Kiyoji Sakakibara, Lt Fujikazu Koizumi, FCPO Shigeo Sugio and NCO pilots Kunimori Kakikariya and

CHANGING FORTUNES

Yoshiro Hashiguchi had all gone, leaving LtCdr Takahida Aioi, Lt Sadao Yamaguchi and NCO pilot Kiyoshi Ito, along with some experience in NCO pilots Bunkichi Nakajima and Matsua Hagiri.

The enemy force was plotted over Bathurst Island at 0926 hours and at 0945 hours the Spitfires of 1 Fighter Wing were scrambled; 12 from 457 Squadron, 18 from 54 and 11 from 452 Squadron. By 1008 hours the Japanese were 32 km from Darwin, however the Spitfires were still climbing and a number had dropped out through engine, R/T or other problems including a cannon stoppage in the case of SqnLdr Ron McDonald. The A-A batteries opened up as the enemy approached Darwin, firing 219 rounds, however they failed to score any hits.

By the time the Spitfires had assembled and climbed to make their attack the enemy were about 64 km west of Port Patterson, heading northwest for home. In the following combat which, "...lasted approx. 15 to 18 mins..." The 452 Intelligence Officer reported, "...was a running one beginning 40 miles NW of Darwin out to 60 miles NW out to sea."

Whilst the Japanese suffered no losses other than some damage, they claimed 21 Spitfires destroyed. The figure was reasonably close to the actual losses for 1 Fighter Wing; 14 Spitfires failed to return to base through a variety of causes.

BR239 was damaged in combat and the pilot PltOff G. P. Farries of 54 Squadron baled out 32 km southwest of Peron Island. He was rescued along with Sgt W S Hardwick of 457 Squadron, who was forced to bale out of BS171 after it suffered CSU problems and the engine failed during combat. "We were taken into attack at 16,000 feet, diving to port out of the sun" Hardwick recalled, "On entering the dive my airscrew went into full fine pitch; the tachometer registered 4,000rpm and severe vibrations almost shook the engine from its mounts...I pulled out of the dive in an effort to reduce both the revs and the vibrations, but to no avail... With smoke pouring from my engine I switched 'OFF'...and prepared to bale out...With so many pilots reporting the same trouble, and no immediate assistance forthcoming from either Britain or the manufacturer, investigations were carried out locally. The 'Colonies' had to go it alone... [and] following...modifications the heavy losses of Sunday 2nd May were never repeated."

Sergeant Bill Hardwick at Livingstone. Forced to bale out of his Spitfire when the propeller CSU seized during the 2 May 1943 combat, he was rescued and returned to his unit the same day. Photo: Bill Hardwick.

BR480 also suffered CSU problems and the engine failed before action. The pilot, Sgt Cavanagh of 54 Squadron was able to force land on a beach six km southwest of Point Charles, where the aircraft was submerged in the rising tide. Similarly, BS221 suffered an engine loss before combat due to a CSU failure and glycol leak. The pilot, Sgt Fox of 54 Squadron abandoned the aircraft over Darwin harbour and was rescued soon after.

Aircraft BR526 of 452 Squadron had its controls shot away by a *Zeke* as FlgOff A. P. 'Tim' Goldsmith attacked a bomber. Goldsmith baled out and was rescued; the aircraft dived into sea 48 km northwest of Darwin. BR572 of 54 Squadron was ditched in the sea 6 km west of Point Charles due to fuel shortage. The pilot, PltOff G. Wall, was rescued by motor launch. Another loss due to fuel shortage was BR536, DL-H, which was force landed off West Point, and the aircraft was submerged by the rising tide. Flight Sergeant G. Spencer of 54 Squadron was rescued and returned to his unit.

BS191 was force landed on a beach 19 km south of Point Charles also due to fuel shortage, however the aircraft was recovered and repaired. The pilot, FltLt P. St J. Makin of 452 Squadron was rescued; the aircraft survived the war, was authorised for disposal in 1946 and sold in 1950. Flying Officer A. C. McNab of 452 Squadron was killed when his aircraft, BS162 crashed into sea due to a possible cockpit fire while returning to base following combat. He was last seen pointing down in to his cockpit by FlgOff K. Barker and FSgt B. Little before climbing suddenly, then diving and flattening out before hitting the sea. Neither pilot nor aircraft were recovered.

CHANGING FORTUNES

BS220 was crash landed at RAAF Darwin following combat by PltOff I. Taylor of 54 Squadron, whilst FlgOff G. L. C. Gifford in BS173 failed to return from interception about 96 km west of Darwin. The 457 Squadron pilot was presumed killed during combat. BS225 had its engine hit during combat with a *Zeke* and crashed into sea 96 km west northwest of Darwin, forcing PltOff K. J Fox of 452 Squadron to bale out and parachute to safety before being rescued. BS226 ran out of fuel even as it attempted to intercept the Japanese bombers, and the pilot, PltOff W. E. Nichterlein of 452 Squadron force landed in shallows off Darwin.

Personnel of 54 (RAF) Squadron salvaging what they can from what is believed to be Spitfire BR536, DL-H, which force landed off West Point on 2 May 1943. Photo: Alford/AHSNT Colln

BR547 suffered CSU problems and the engine failed prior to combat over water 16 km west of Fog Bay. The pilot, Sgt R. S. Stagg of 452 Squadron baled out and made land in his dinghy that evening. "Next day I guessed I was about 100 miles from Darwin" Stagg recalled many years later, "I thought I could walk that far so I struck inland...Some nights I found little mounds to sleep on...some I just lay buried in mud to get away from the mosquitoes. About the fifth night I tried to sleep...in a tree. But I fell out into waist-deep water."

When he failed to return Stagg was listed as 'missing presumed killed,' though searches by squadron pilots continued. On the fourth day Spitfires "...flew within 50 feet of me...I threw my Mae West in the air but they didn't see me." However, he didn't give up and spent many more days wandering aimlessly through mangroves and swamps infested with mosquitoes, sand flies and crocodiles. He got weaker by the day and at one stage contemplated suicide, but kept going.

Stagg later came across the P-40E that Lt Harris had force landed a year earlier, thinking it was a recent wreck and struggled on. It was on the 22nd day that he found an old cart track and shortly after was surprised to see an Aboriginal stockman, followed almost immediately by a European, World War I veteran and prospector, Bill Essex. Stagg was very lucky; Essex was on leave from the army and was due to return to his unit.

"When that living skeleton told me he was Flight Sergeant Ross Stagg I could hardly believe it" Essex commented, "...I knew he had been posted missing for three weeks...the poor beggar was in a terrible mess, and I was sure he was going to die." But Ross Stagg survived though he spent many months recovering. "That fellow just wasn't meant to die in the bush – that's all I can put it down to", Essex concluded.

Statistically the losses for the day put the major causes as combat and engine failure along with fuel shortages: five were lost as a result of combat (35.71%), four to CSU/engine failure (28.57%), four due to fuel shortage (28.57%), and one, that of FlgOff McNab, of unknown causes but probably as a result of combat (7.14%).

For WgCdr Clive Caldwell and 1 Fighter Wing however, worse was to come. Despite their own experiences in learning the hard way how to combat the Japanese fighters, the Americans were quick to criticise the Wing and its leadership for the losses. General George C. Kenney, commander of the U.S. Fifth Air Force, rather than pass the message on himself "...sent [AVM] Bostock to Darwin to talk with the kids and tell them that if they didn't stop that dog fighting business, I'd send them to New Guinea to serve with the Americans and learn how to fight properly." Whether Bostock passed on the message in full is unknown but at the Wing and squadron level there was anger at Kenney's attitude but also a realisation that errors had been made and they were trying to ensure it didn't happen again. Measures included early interceptions, the possibility of extra fuel and strict instructions not to dog-fight with the Japanese fighters.

The newspapers picked up on Communiqué No. 386 put out by MacArthur's HQ, which carried the phrase 'our air losses were heavy'. The papers carried comments including: "After a long succession of air victories over Darwin, our Air Forces suffered a severe reverse yesterday";
"Today's GHQ communiqué describing the action uses, for the first time, the phrase 'our air losses were heavy'. ";and
"They were suffered by defending Spitfires which took off 'in force', flown by RAF and Australian pilots."

CHANGING FORTUNES

The Japanese media also reportedly picked up the communiqué with the 6 May edition of the *Nippon Times* headlining its report, "*Port Darwin Raid Terrifies Anzacs. Poor show of Spitfires causes heated discussions – blame is put on bad weather. The question of why the Spitfires, considered by the anti-Axis camp to be the best fighter plane on the world, failed to show their power in air combats in the May 2 raid, has become the centre of much heated discussion in Australia...*"

Indeed it had and Prime Minister Curtin was urged to point out to MacArthur that the communiqué had provided information of value to the Japanese; MacArthur's response was to imperiously deny the accusation and in effect insinuated that the media had it in for him. But, to the pilots and NWA HQ it tended to confirm the view that this was MacArthur's and America's war and no one was going to steal the limelight. "I think it...gave General MacArthur another chance to have a go at us, and he seized it with both hands", Bob Foster commented.

Probably the most contentious comments came from CAS AVM G. Jones, who, seemingly without consulting anyone other than the media reports, and with an apparent axe to grind, concluded that Caldwell "...held his attack rather too long which led to the Spitfires being led further away...in this the Wing Leader placed too much reliance on individual pilots..." and that the engine problems were due to inexperience, while fuel shortages could "...only be attributed to an error of judgement on the part of the Wing Leader, bearing in mind the inexperience of a number of pilots."

Inexperience would certainly have been a factor as a number of the more experienced pilots were absent on leave or at conferences. Caldwell in fact had stated in his post combat report under the heading War Standing of Pilots that "Of the 95 pilots on strength...37 only had fighter experience prior to coming to this Area. Some half dozen [of these] could be classified as 'experienced'. Of the remaining 58...without previous fighter combat experience 45 had no operational combat experience whatsoever."

Notwithstanding, Caldwell and the controllers at the Fighter Sector had continually warned the pilots to constantly monitor their fuel state, and his subsequent report on the action attributes some of his pilots' failure to do so on inexperience and keenness.

Caldwell was awarded a DSO in June and some time later when he viewed his personal records at the insistence of GpCapt Walters, he noted that Jones had penned, "This officer is an Empire Air Trainee and as such is now considered sufficiently decorated thus as to have no further awards regardless of future service."

Late in the morning of 2 May Bladin ordered 31 and 18 Squadrons to attack Penfoie airfield, where he suspected the Japanese aircraft would return. The Beaufighters were to stage through Drysdale and hopefully catch the enemy as they attempted to land. They departed Coomalie shortly after midday, with one turning back after a hatch blew open, and after refuelling at Drysdale, took off for Penfoie. They hit the airfield line abreast at very low level and at 370 km/h. The CO, WgCdr Read, strafed two *Zekes*, one of them taxying, destroying them both whilst another hit two *Bettys* setting them both on fire. One Beaufighter's guns failed to fire. As they departed the area the Beaufighters were pursued by *Zekes*, which were forced to give up the chase thirty minutes later. The Beaufighters returned to Coomalie via Drysdale next morning.

Eight 18 Squadron Mitchells in two flights of four; N5-134, '131, '136 and '138, and N5-147, '146, '149 and '151 followed up the daylight attack and bombed the airfield after midnight, dropping bombs and flares at five minute intervals. Three bombs were reported to have hit buildings on the airfield. All the Mitchells returned safely; N5-147 lasted only three weeks before being hit by A-A fire over Saumlaki and crashing into the sea, taking with it Lts L. Bal, and P. Kruyne, Ensign A. B. Andele and Sgts C. van Ginkel, F.A. Hoogeweld and the RAAF member, Sgt R. P. Leehy.

From the raid of 2 May the Spitfire units had some respite from enemy raids over Darwin, though events further afield were to see a detachment deployed to Milingimbi, whilst the remainder cooled their heels in Darwin for some weeks. For the other units in the NWA the second half of the year promised little let up in their offensive missions against the Japanese to the north. But, it would also see a fading threat as the Japanese suffered losses in the SWPA and closer to home as the Allies continued their harassing raids.

CHAPTER 9
A SHOW OF FORCE
The Japanese a fading threat?

Despite losses of aircraft and personnel as a result of the offensive missions being flown by the RAAF units, notably the Beaufighters and Mitchells, along with the B-24s of the American 319th Squadron, the Japanese were still able to put up enough fighters and floatplanes to intercept a number of raids.

The raid by 31 Squadron on 2 May had been intercepted, though the Beaufighters had been able to escape and two days later a *Zeke* of Ku 202 intercepted a 2 Squadron Hudson on its return from a bombing mission over the Kai Islands. Six B-24s of the 319th Bomb. Squadron returning from bombing Babo were also intercepted over the target, probably by *Oscars* of the 24th *Sentai*, and again over Maikoor by *Rufes*.

A Nakajima K-43 *Oscar* of the 24th Sentai, which was found by Allied troops on Hollandia. The unit served briefly in the NEI before being assigned to New Guinea. Photo: Bob Livingstone.

Charles Hesse was leading one flight of B-24s and recalled that as they neared Dobo on the return trip, "Rick Vannucci called on the intercom...that it looked like some big birds were taking off from the water... 'They are floatplanes; look like fighters!' He counted six float-type Zeros (Rufes) and one float-type biplane." After a brief combat the *Rufes* departed and the B-24s headed for home. The Japanese pilots, PO1c Mitsugo Ichikawa, PO3c Toyu Inohara and Flyers 1c Katzuo Ikeda and Osamu Yoza claimed a B-24, however all returned safely to Fenton. Hesse's aircraft had fifteen bullet holes and shrapnel from a 20mm cannon projectile in one flap.

On 6 May Catalinas of 11 and 20 Squadrons attacked Babo, B-24s bombed Manokwari, the Kai Islands and Saumlaki, whilst the Mitchells of 18 Squadron raided Dili. The Beaufighters of 31 Squadron hit Taberfane at dawn,

destroying four *Rufes* and three *Jakes* at their moorings. Charles Hesse learned the same day that "...the Japanese seaplane base which we accidentally ran upon two days before, was attacked by Australian Beaufighters...Good work, mates!"

The Beaufighter strike on Taberfane had been led by SqnLdr G. W. Savage. They staged at Milingimbi on the night of the 5th and took off before dawn the following morning. Savage in A19-57 "...led the flight in from the river with the first pair in line abreast at 1,000 feet and the rest in sections of two. Saw ten monoplanes along half a mile of beach leading to Taberfane. The first three floatplanes were close in-shore and afloat, and the remainder, seven floatplanes, drawn up on the beach. Strafed the first one on the water...considered to be a Jake...which was seen to burst into flames and to sink at once. Then strafed and set fire to two floatplanes on the beach. These were single seater, radial engined monoplanes considered to be *Rufes*. On subsequent runs, strafed Taberfane village petrol dumps under the coconuts behind the beach and buildings...causing fires."

A group of floatplanes including A6M2-N Rufe, Aichi E13A Jake and Mitsubishi F1M2 Pete biplane types caught at their moorings. Photo: Alford Colln.

Savage had a bullet pass through the throttle quadrant and into the port fuel tank, however he made it safely back to base. The aircraft of FlgOffs W. J. C. Budd and F. M. McQueen, A19-60, failed to return. The raid by the Beaufighters was followed up next day by five 2 Squadron Hudsons with the loss of the Jackman crew following an intercept by PO3c Mamoru Imio and Flyer 1c Takaomi Oyama in two *Rufes*. Hudson A16-211, *The Tojo Busters* as also badly damaged by the *Rufes* and crash landed at Milingimbi.

A SHOW OF FORCE

On 9 May the Japanese raided Milingimbi, either in retaliation for the raid on Taberfane or in recognising its threat as a growing offensive base for Allied attacks in the area – or both. Seven *Bettys* took off from Babo at 0702 hours each armed with 12 60 kg 'daisy cutter' anti-personnel bombs. They struck Milingimbi at 1110 hours after being picked up on radar 30 minutes earlier, bombing the mission and shipping. A Beaufighter flown by FlgOff Delaporte attempted to intercept the bombers however his 20mm cannon stopped. One Aborigine, one AIF member and ten RAAF members were killed in the raid.

Personnel of 2 Squadron pose in front of Hudson A16-211, The Tojo Busters, at Batchelor, April 1943. The aircraft crash landed at Milingimbi on 6 May. Photo: Alford/AHSNT Colln.

With more raids expected, Bladin ordered a detachment of six 457 Squadron Spitfires to the island. Early next morning five were scrambled when unidentified aircraft were picked up, however it was a pair of Beaufighters returning from an aborted mission to Taberfane. Other aircraft were also picked up as the Spitfires were about to land - this time the aircraft were nine *Zekes* of Ku *202* from Rangool in the Kai Islands and the Spitfires hastily tried to gain height. A combat ensued with the unserviceable sixth Spitfire and its pilot, FlgOff F. D. 'Bush' Hamilton, remaining on the ground and providing an *ad hoc* controller's job via a chain of six airmen relaying messages to and from the radar hut.

Shortly after the two Beaufighters had landed three *Zekes* strafed the airfield and runway. Flight Lieutenant Phil Biven and his observer were walking from their aircraft when it was strafed. The Beaufighter, A19-72, on loan from the CO was destroyed; "...not the way to endear oneself to the CO..." Biven reflected. A second Beaufighter was damaged. Two *Zekes* were lost in the combat, one each to PltOff G. 'Grumpy' Morse and FSgt Rex Watson.

One of the Spitfire pilots, PltOff Bruce Little, had just landed with his aircraft, A58-81, after being hit in combat but took off again once he saw the strafing *Zekes*. He then lined up behind the last of the *Zekes* before it saw him and turned back. The two flew at very low level; 300 ft and below, each trying to get the upper hand. In the end it was the *Zeke,* as the Spitfire "...somersaulted, turned and rolled three or four times" Little recalled, "I retained consciousness throughout and when the Spitfire finally came to rest I was lying on my left side and could hear the Zero circling overhead." After a strafing pass the *Zeke* departed and Little trudged back to the airfield. His was the only Spitfire lost that day, however the Beaufighter and the 72-tonne supply vessel *Maroubra* were destroyed along with 36 tonnes of RAAF equipment.

The remains of Beaufighter A19-72 after being strafed by attacking Zekes during the 9 May 1943 raid on Milingimbi. Photo: Phil Biven.

The following day SqnLdr J. A. Madden was on convoy escort duty in Beaufighter A19-83 when a *Jake* flown by PO1c Hisao Yuga and his crew dropped a bomb on an Australian corvette as it entered the Wessel Islands. Madden shot the aircraft down and from then the *Jakes* were escorted by *Rufes*. On the 28th the Japanese again attacked Milingimbi with nine *Bettys* of the 753 *Ku* from Babo. Six 457 squadron Spitfires led by FltLt Peter H. Watson intercepted the force, downing four of them, though claiming only three. Two Spitfires were lost and one was damaged in the raid; FlgOffs F. B. Beale and A. H. Blake remain at the bottom of the Arafura Sea.

By early March, 12 Squadron had completed its conversion to the Vultee Vengeance aircraft, which has been described by its detractors as short in range, slow, and plagued by mechanical problems. Far from it, argued Cyril McPherson, a 12 Squadron flight commander with 603 hours on the

A SHOW OF FORCE

type. That "...unfortunate impression...was, in my opinion, completely unfounded...It had absolutely no vices; and stalled as gently as a Tiger Moth with not the slightest inclination to drop a wing or even to shudder...in all respects it was an extremely stable aircraft...During my term in 12 Squadron" McPherson recalled, "...we had four accidents that could have been called serious...and not one...was attributable to any weakness or failure in the airframe nor to any difficulty in handling the aircraft."

Pilot Officer Bruce Little was lucky to have survived both the attack by Ku 202 Zekes and the resultant somersaulting and crash of his Spitfire A58-81. Photo: Alford/AHSNT Colln.

The first of those accidents involved McPherson himself in A27-6, which he force landed at West Point on 23 March after the electrical fuel system failed. This was followed two months later on 23 May when Sgt J. Sheehan in A27-208 made a forced landing on what is now Dum-Im-Mirrie Island, also due to an electrical fault. A27-202 force landed at Batchelor on 10 June, and on the 30th A27-218 stalled and crashed shortly after take off at Batchelor when the undercarriage was raised too soon. From all these incidents the crews walked away uninjured.

The one fatal accident was that of A27-5, which crashed on take off from Batchelor on a ferry flight to 2 AD on 15 May. The pilot, FlgOff D. C. Wilmot, was killed and his passenger, Sgt Cotter of 31 Squadron, was badly burned and was rushed to 1 MRS. "I flight tested it...on 15 May, just prior to F/O Wilmott [sic] taking delivery of it to fly back to Laverton" Cyril McPherson wrote, "...it was subsequently discovered that the master connecting rod had broken causing the engine to seize up shortly after becoming airborne (how lucky was I?)"

A Vultee Vengeance of 12 Squadron demonstrating a dive bombing attack at Batchelor while interested squadron personnel look on. The type's service with the RAAF was brief. Photo: Jack Taylor.

On 18 March the CO, SqnLdr Ron McDonald, had been posted out to take over 452 Squadron, leaving Flt Lt J. E. Hooper as CO; Hooper was promoted to Acting SqnLdr the same day. Three months later on 18 June he was able to take the Vengeances on their first and only offensive mission from the NWA. With flight commanders, FltLts Cyril McPherson and J. B. Keys, 12 Vengeances each with a 454 kg bomb load flew to Bathurst Island where they refuelled. One failed to take off and the remainder headed out for Selaru in the Tanimbar Islands with an escort of 31 Squadron Beaufighters. Nearing the targets of Lingat and Werain the Vengeances split up into two flights; McPherson's flight bombed Lingat and Keys' flight attacked Werain. "The attack was most successful" the unit historian wrote, "...our flyers met with no interception and only ineffective ack-ack fire. All our planes returned safely."

The mission set a landmark for RAAF operations in the NWA; "...it was the only squadron of single engined aircraft ever to carry out a bombing attack on a Japanese base from mainland Australia," Cyril McPherson commented.

A SHOW OF FORCE

Any elation was shortlived however. A scant eleven days after the Selaru raid 270 personnel departed Batchelor for Darwin and on to a new base at Merauke in Dutch New Guinea. The base was meant to cover MacArthur's western flank, however this was at best questionable in the short term: when 12 Squadron arrived on 8 July they found that not one of the promised buildings had been commenced. Self help was the order of the day but with an extreme shortage of material, progress was very slow. The air echelon comprising 17 Vengeances arrived shortly after and 12 Squadron, after four years in the Northern Territory, began a new phase in its operational history.

The move by 12 Squadron to Merauke was a part of a directive by MacArthur to commence a 'show of force' from the NWA. Despite some earlier concerns, by mid-1943 the chances of Japanese landings in force along the NWA coast had become slim. With reverses at Guadalcanal and in New Guinea the Japanese were effectively on the defensive and fully aware of the risks involved in sea based operations in the face of land based aircraft.

With this in mind earlier considerations had included the seizure of islands in the Arafura Sea, the north of New Guinea, Borneo and the Celebes, however limitations in offensive forces, Japanese dispositions and areas of 'close waters' that prevented open sea operations saw them lapse. Instead MacArthur planned to thrust into northern New Guinea at Lae, using the NWA squadrons, including NWA based American units, to assist in not only confusing the enemy as to the target of his attack, but to pin the Japanese down to prevent any aircraft reinforcements being sent to the area.

Essentially the NWA squadrons were to mount the 'show of force' in attacks on airfields at Koepang, Kendari, Ambon and at Dobo among others. General Kenney wrote to AVM Bostock outlining the role of NWA in the operation, and Bostock in turn repeated the order to NWA and to NEA, who were to provide support for the NWA. In effect the order varied little from what Bladin and his squadrons were already carrying out; destroying Japanese coastal traffic, attacking airfields and bases and generally pinning the enemy down.

A further directive from Kenney on 4 August, in which he laid down the operational aims of NWA, again saw little in the way of any new initiative; instead it was unclear in its direction and caused frustration to those who had to send the aircrews out to risk their lives. "...our offensive, being entirely of a hindering nature, and not immediately aimed at territorial gains, appeared to comprise more incident than plan" one official historian noted. Perhaps, as has been wryly suggested, the Americans wanted any territorial gains to be theirs alone and in voicing a widely held view at the time, AVM Frederick Scherger commented that it was "...going to be an American war; [MacArthur] was going to have revenge on the Japanese. No way was there going to be historical praise to any other than Americans."

The offensive from NWA lasted through June and into July with almost daily attacks on Japanese forces by the remaining Hudsons of 2 Squadron, Beaufighters, Mitchells and the B-24s of both the 319th Bomb. Squadron and the newly arrived 380th Bomb. Gp USAAF. One mission flown by 31 Squadron was the last for FlgOff Ken McDonald before his posting to a training unit and it was another attack on the floatplane base at Taberfane.

Instead of the usual dawn strike this was to be at last light on 12 June, after staging through Milingimbi. "We were becoming familiar with the target, having visited it on a number of occasions" McDonald recalled, "As usual I had slept badly; if at all. Even after months of squadron life I never could sleep well knowing that I was due to go on a sortie the following day. Yet when I got up in the morning I was able to quickly shake off the lethargy and maintain concentration until the job was over, then I would collapse with nervous exhaustion. I think most of the aircrews shared similar experiences."

Flying at 20 ft above the water the Beaufighters approached Taberfane at 1730 hours; McDonald and two others provided top cover whilst the other six attacked the floatplanes and base. With no enemy aircraft airborne McDonald joined in and destroyed a *Jake* and two *Rufes* at their moorings. The return flight was eventful; a ruptured fuel line meant nursing the aircraft back to conserve fuel, avoiding Milingimbi and its lack of any night landing aids and hoping at best to be able to ditch near the Cape Don lighthouse. Instead they made Darwin and flew on towards Coomalie into "...a blue brown haze, then I smelt it. "Smoke! Those bloody fires down on the ground!"...grass fires were burning all over the place. They didn't do any harm...but by hell it was going to be hard to see that flarepath."

A SHOW OF FORCE

Realising they had probably overflown Coomalie, McDonald and Magee finally picked up the radio beacon signal and landed safely. They were lucky; fifteen months later the seasonal grass fires claimed three men and two aircraft in similar circumstances.

For McDonald and Magee it was their last trip before heading to 5 OTU, each with a DFC; others awarded DFCs included the CO WgCdr Charles Read and his navigator FlgOff John Marr, SqnLdr Gordon Savage and FlgOff Jim Kearney. A DFM went to FSgt E. 'Basher' Barnett.

Floatplanes of the 934th Ku at Taberfane under attack by 31 Squadron Beaufighters on 12 June 1943 and photographed by FlgOff Ken McDonald's observer, Frank Magee. Photo: Ken McDonald.

The lack of facilities encountered by Ken McDonald at Milingimbi had also been recognised, as had the absence of a base at Arnhem Bay in eastern Arnhem Land that may have assisted MacArthur's plans, but also would have facilitated both flying boats and land based aircraft. In correspondence from RAAF HQ in Brisbane on 5 June a number of NWA airfields and facilities were discussed including the provision of an OBU at Groote Eylandt to cater for the Catalinas, maintaining Milingimbi to operational requirements and the establishment of both an airfield and flying boat base at Arnhem Bay. A new airstrip at Drysdale was also discussed; the latter two became Gove and Truscott.

The Japanese conducted five major raids on Darwin and the Top End over the last half of 1943. The first of these was on 20 June, even as the 'show of force' was well under way, but on this occasion it was not the Japanese naval air units involved but the army, which had maintained a presence in the NEI from March 1942. Headquartered at Malang on Java, LtGen Einosuke Sudo, CO of the then newly formed

7th *Hikoshidan*, had taken control of the air units in the region including, the 3rd and 9th *Hikodan*. Both the 59th and 75th *Sentai* were under the 3rd whilst the 7th and 61st *Sentai* came under the control of the 9th *Hikodan* and all had recently converted to newer aircraft; the 59th to the Ki-43 II *Oscar* and the 75th to the Ki-48 II *Lily*. The 7th and 61st had been working out teething problems on their new heavy bomber, the Ki-49 *Helen*. It was a force of 59th, 75th and 61st *Sentai* aircraft that raided Darwin.

A reconnaissance sortie of the Darwin, Winnellie and RAAF Station was flown by the 70th DCS on the 17th, though 42 Spitfires failed to intercept the *Dinah* which had photographed a stockpiling of equipment bound for the 380th Bomb. Gp at Fenton and Manbulloo airfields. Two days later 51 ASWG operators monitoring the Japanese radio frequencies detected a large build up of aircraft at Koepang, which, along with the appearance of the *Dinah* on the 17th, signalled an impending raid. The Spitfire units were advised accordingly.

On the morning of the 20th the attacking force comprising 18 *Helens* with an escort of 22 *Oscars* under Maj Takeo Fukada, and nine *Lilys* departed Koepang. Nearing Bathurst Island the bombers climbed to 20,000 ft while the *Oscars* climbed to 27,000 ft; the *Lilys* stayed low and delayed their approach to mount a surprise low level attack. At 0945 hours 46 Spitfires were ordered up by the Fighter Sector at Berrimah, though a number were forced out with engine and other problems.

The *Helens* dropped their bombs over Darwin and the RAAF Station while the *Lilys* achieved complete surprise and attacked Winnellie, the RAAF Station and the Frances Bay ammunition storage facility at tree top height. Ben Walker, an LAC with 1 MWS at Winnellie recalled the attack and in particular the incentive it provided to dig deeper slit trenches as a result.

RAAF Sgt, Dick Dakeyne, a RCM operator with the 380th Bomb. Gp was also sheltering in a trench during the raid along with an American Sgt 'Stony' Marckley, when he heard Marckley call, "Dick, my leg is gone." "I had ...a look and it was nearly severed about mid-thigh" Dakeyne recalled, "I put my little knowledge of first aid to good use and then dragged him out of the trench...[and] went to try and find a driveable vehicle to take him in to the hospital..." What he failed to mention was that he had himself been wounded and as one newspaper reported, "…it was probably Dakeyne's quick thinking and courage which saved the American staff sergeant's life. Dakeyne was in hospital for five weeks." The entry in his log book reads matter-of-factly: "Wounded during air raid on Winnellie (out of Darwin). Off duty for 6 weeks."

At least seven of the nine Kawasaki Ki-48 Lily bombers can be seen in this photo taken during their low level attack on the Winnellie area and RAAF Station 20 June 1943. Photo: Alford Colln.

In the ensuing combat the Spitfires claimed eight heavy bombers, five fighters and a light bomber, all of which were described variously as *Bettys*, *Sallys*, *Zeros*, *Haps*, *Lilys* and *Dinahs*. A number barely made it to their bases before crash landing in friendly territory. Even the supposedly deskbound OC Wing, GpCapt Walters, claimed an *Oscar* destroyed and was posted south four days later – whether as atonement for having the temerity to take part in the combat or otherwise remains unknown. Caldwell then took over the Wing as OC and remembering the comments following the 2 May raid, and the apparent success of the Wing in the raid of 20 June, Caldwell commented, "…the quality of the Wing emerged and MacArthur had the infernal cheek to send a personal signal of congratulations." Such are the politics of war.

While the Japanese fighters claimed nine Spitfires destroyed and six probables, the Spitfires lost two pilots, both of 452 Squadron, and two aircraft damaged. PltOff W. E. Nichterlein was posted missing as was PltOff A. T. Ruskin-Rowe. Three weeks later Spitfire BS174 was located to the north of Koolpinyah Station; in it was the body of Tony Ruskin-Rowe. Bill Nichterlein and his aircraft, EE607, were never found and remain somewhere in Adam Bay near the Vernon Islands. The log book entry of FlgOff Keith Colyer of 452 Squadron recorded succinctly: "Darwin bombed. Wing destroyed 8 bomber, 4 fighter. 10 probs. & damaged. Self damaged 1 Zero. Nichterlein & Tony Rowe missing." Two Spitfires were claimed by Lt Shohei Inaba of the 59th *Sentai*. Despite the number of enemy aircraft claimed, the Japanese lost an *Oscar* flown by Lt Shigato Kiwata, suspected as being downed over the Vernon Islands by PltOff A. Mawer, and two *Helens*. One went into Adam Bay leaving only oil slicks, a fuel tank and personal effects including a Japanese flag and a Mae West with a red cloth and name tags. The other, manufacturer's number 174, crashed north of Koolpinyah station. Eight bodies were found and buried in shallow graves whilst "A thorough search was instituted but with the exception of a small printed book and signal message blanks, no further papers could be found. Parts which had been widely scattered were collected and the whole of the remains thoroughly combed. All articles of immediate intelligence value were packed and despatched to NW AREA", reported the RAAF Intelligence Officer. The majority of the wreckage was salvaged and forwarded on for assessment in Brisbane.

Eight Nakajima Ki-49 Helens of the 61st Sentai pass across the gunsight of PltOff Keith Colyer of 452 Squadron during the 20 June 1943 raid. Photo: Keith Colyer.

A SHOW OF FORCE

Lieutenant Kenjiro Matsuhara and six crew members were never recovered from the *Helen* wreckage in Adam Bay, nor was the *Oscar* pilot Lt Shigato Kiwata. The Capt Katsuhiro Ohta crew of eight from *Helen* 174 were reburied at the Berrimah War Cemetery on 29 June as 'Unidentified Japanese Airmen'. Ben Walker recalled going to the crash site as part of a team to disinter the bodies some days later and "...having to wear gauze masks soaked regularly in Citronella to beat the stench."

Two days later Capt Shigeo Nango led a force of *Oscars* of the 59th *Sentai* to attack Darwin once again and whilst the radar picked them up crossing the coast, heading south and then heading back out to sea, no intercepts or A-A fire were encountered; the 'raid' was not reported by the Allies. It was the end of any further army raids on the Australian mainland; the 7th *Hikoshidan* had been advised of a transfer to New Guinea the day before the raid of 20 June.

Aircraft of 753 *Ku* raided Darwin again on the 28th when nine *Bettys* escorted by 27 *Zekes* attacked the old Vesteys meat works at Bullocky Point, damaging buildings and a number of vehicles. No losses were recorded by either side though 1 Fighter Wing claimed four *Zekes* destroyed and the Japanese three Spitfires. Two days later the enemy returned, this time to attack the American B-24 base at Fenton. The day previously a *Dinah* had flown over Fenton giving warning of a raid in the following days.

At 0700 hours on 30 June 23 *Bettys* departed Koepang followed two hours later by 27 *Zekes* from Lautem. At 1120 hours they were picked up by radar as two separate plots about 32 km apart and 258 km west-northwest of Darwin. They were intercepted by 38 Spitfires 40 km west of Batchelor, however confusion led to the Spitfires attacking the bombers and thus leaving themselves open to the escorting *Zekes*. Despite being under attack the bombers turned southeast and pattern bombed Fenton at 1230 hours before heading north west and out to sea. The Japanese fighters claimed 16 Spitfires, whilst 1 Fighter Wing claimed four bombers and three fighters destroyed and a number of others as probables or damaged.

The Japanese recorded no losses, but for the Spitfires it was a bad result. Seven aircraft were destroyed and two pilots killed. Flying Officer J. C. 'Jimmy' Wellsman of 54 Squadron died in combat, while FlgOff W. J. Lamerton of 452

Squadron died of burns after his aircraft BR241 crashed and burst into flames as he landed at Strauss. Sergeants Holmes and S. C. Laundy of 54 Squadron and FSgt Col Duncan of 452 Squadron all baled out and were later rescued.

At Fenton the 319th Squadron and 380th Bomb. Gp had lost three B-24s and a Curtiss Wright CW 21B Falcon 'belonging' to Lt Shoupe, a pilot with the 319th. The B-24s, 42-40346 *Nobody's Baby* of the 319th along with 42-40393 *Black Magic* and 42-40486 *Dis-Gusted* of the 380th were destroyed. A petrol tanker, five tractors, a bombsight repair workshop, and 12 aircraft engines were also destroyed; one USAAF member was injured.

The burnt out remains of B-24 42-40393, Black Magic of the 528th Squadron, 380th Bomb. Group following the 30 June raid on Fenton. Photo Bob Livingstone.

Six days later the Japanese returned to Fenton following reconnaissance flights by the 70th DCS on the 3rd and 5th. The force comprising 21 *Bettys* from Koepang and 27 *Zekes* from Lautem was picked up by operators at 38 Radar Station at Cape Fourcroy at 1037 hours followed by 319 Radar Station at Fenton and the Fighter Sector ordered the Spitfires up a minute later. In all 33 Spitfires took off though 54 Squadron was only able to get four in the air "...owing to the deplorable state of so many of our aircraft for which no replacements have been forthcoming for months past", wrote SqnLdr Gibbs. Four others managed to get off but it was balanced out when four other aircraft had to force land due to engine and other problems.

The controllers at Fighter Sector put the Spitfires in an ideal position to attack and the Wing split up to attack the bombers and engage the fighters. In the combat that followed the Spitfires claimed eight *Bettys* destroyed, three *Bettys* and a *Zeke* as probables, with three *Bettys* and a

A SHOW OF FORCE

Zeke claimed as damaged. The Japanese lost one *Betty*, manufacturer's number 3677, which was seen over Fenton trailing the main formation, its port engine smoking at 1125 hours before crashing into a swamp on Welltree Station and killing the eight man FCPO Masao Kobayashi crew. The *Bettys* dropped their bombs five minutes later, cratering the main runway, setting grass fires that ignited the fuel dumps, damaging three B-24s and destroying a B-24, 42-40497, *Homma Homma Kid*.

For 1 Fighter Wing it was another bad day, with the Japanese wildly claiming 14 Spitfires; 457 Squadron lost three pilots while three others were able to bale out and parachute to safety. A total of eight aircraft were lost. Pilot Officer F. R. J. 'Darky' McDowell was found, still in his aircraft, 14 days later while FlgOffs F. D. 'Bush' Hamilton and N. F. Robinson remained missing and despite extensive searches, during which three other aircraft were located, it was a further 30 years before the wreckage of their aircraft were located; Hamilton's on Billabong Ridge and Robinson's some six kilometres away.

From 6 July the Spitfires faced only one further concerted raid, on 7 September, whilst the 753 *Ku* devoted itself to night raids for the remainder of the year. Sending over small sections of three and four aircraft they raided Fenton, Coomalie, Pell, and Long airfields along with Parap, Adelaide River and Batchelor on 13 and 28 August, 15 and 18 September and 11 November, the last bombing raid of the war over the NWA. Spitfires and the A-A batteries at Fenton, Hughes, Darwin and Batchelor failed to down any of the raiders, but for 11 November when one *Betty* was lost to 457 Squadron pilot, FlgOff J. H. Smithson. Searchlights illuminated the enemy aircraft, enabling Smithson to down one bomber though he claimed two, and was later confirmed as having shot down a second. He was later awarded the DFC for the action; the Japanese records confirm one aircraft lost but it was significant; aboard were the unit's second in command, Hikocho (Executive Officer) Cdr Michio Horii and the Hikotaicho (wing leader), Lt Takeji Fujiwara.

One constant in the enemy's intrusions over the NWA was that of their reconnaissance efforts, which had increased from mid-year. On 18 July the 70th DCS flew a reconnaissance sortie over the Fenton area and the Wing was scrambled, however it proved to be a *Dinah* and both 452 and 54 Squadrons were recalled; instead a section of four

457 Squadron Spitfires led by the CO, SqnLdr Ken 'Skeeter' James, climbed to intercept the intruder. James made the interception at 26,000 feet and despite experiencing some problems in jettisoning his slipper tank, he "...commenced closing in...to about 250 yards and fired a two second burst from line astern...I observed strikes...round the port engine...smoke issued from the port engine, and then from the starboard...the aircraft began to lose height...There was no evasive action...and he began to spin. When the aircraft was about 5,000 feet above the ground it blew up...after circling the area for about five minutes, I returned to base and landed at 1045 hrs."

Captain Shunji Sasaki, CO of the 70th DCS and his observer, Lt Akira Eguchi died when their Ki-46 *Dinah* was downed by the CO 457 Squadron, SqnLdr Ken James on 18 July 1943. Photo: Susumu Akasaka.

The crew of *Dinah*, manufacturer's number 2414, comprised the CO of the 70th DCS, Capt Shunji Sasaki, and his observer, Lt Akira Eguchi; both were buried in shallow graves at the crash site the following day by Intelligence personnel under the IntellO, FlgOff C. D. Pender. Apart from being the unit CO, Sasaki was apparently an important figure; a radio intercept of Japanese traffic reported that the *Dinah* carried a 'Takaki Commander [of a] famous Takaki unit.' An Intelligence Summary of 27 September confirmed the report. "He was a very excellent air officer and [had] flown many times over Australia" Shunji Sasaki's biographer, Ikuhiko Hata wrote, "It was natural that he was awarded a special citation and this reached the Emperor's ear (highest honour)."

Lieutenants Saburo Shinohara and Hideo Ura flew a mission over Darwin on 11 August and despite interception by FSgt E. Batchelor of 457 Squadron managed to escape; Batchelor claimed one *Lily* damaged. A further reconnaissance mission was flown on 17 August; this time in force, with five *Dinahs* departing Lautem to photograph the Darwin, Fenton and Coomalie areas; 2206, 2233 flown by Capt Sumi, 2250, 2237 and 2273. It proved disastrous for the Japanese, with four *Dinahs* shot down and the loss of eight crew members, two from Ku *202*.

The aircraft were picked up by radar at 1040 hours and 457 Squadron was scrambled at 1115 hours. FltLt Peter Watson DFC and FSgt E. Batchelor - who spotted *Dinah* 2250 heading west from Fenton, was unable to call Watson before attacking the aircraft over Emu Springs east of Fog Bay. After a brief burst his guns stopped. The aircraft disappeared into cloud and with his radio now serviceable Batchelor was able to warn Watson of the approaching *Dinah*. Watson intercepted the aircraft and "When at about 5000 feet the enemy aircraft disintegrated completely in the air after another explosion, and I saw a parachute silhouetted against the ground...but there was nothing in it." The aircraft crashed inland from Channel Point, taking the crew of Lts Kyuichi Yokamoto and Yasuro Yamamoto with it.

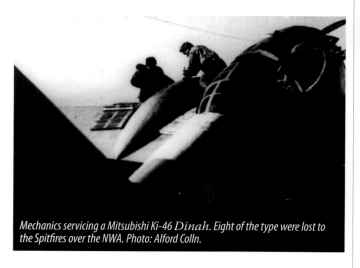

Mechanics servicing a Mitsubishi Ki-46 *Dinah*. Eight of the type were lost to the Spitfires over the NWA. Photo: Alford Colln.

At 1125 Hours SqnLdr Ken James intercepted *Dinah* 2237 at 30,500 feet over Fenton. In his combat report James recorded that as "...I followed him, I observed a fire start in the fuselage. He continued to turn to port and then began to dive. I fired two more short bursts, but the aeroplane was obviously out of control, and commenced to dive vertically...when he hit, he exploded." The intercept had been watched by personnel of the 380th Bomb. Gp, 319 Radar and 133 HAA Bty, whose War Diary recorded "OC major [sic] Townsend, OC 133 major [sic] Randle, HQ Sub Lt Osborne and Lieuts Jones and Nicholson visited crashed Jap plane and photographs taken. The remains of

the aircraft were scattered over an area of 100 yards & the only portions of the plane which had not been completely shattered were the two (2) motors. Nothing remained of the fuselage or wings." Nor of the crew of Lts Shin-ichi Matsu-Ura and Kyotoshi Shiraki. They were also carrying a ceramic doll provided by Shunji Sasaki's mother, which was to be thrown down over Fenton, the place where her son was thought to have been killed a month previously.

The remains of *Dinah* 2237 at Fenton after being downed by SqnLdr Ken James on 17 August 1943. The object at left appears to be a motorcycle sidecar made from an auxiliary fuel tank. Photo: Alford Colln.

Some 150 kilometres north of Fenton FSgts Rex Watson and J. R. Jenkins intercepted *Dinah* 2273 over the water south of Cape Gambier on Melville Island at 1150 hours. Ordered to orbit Cape Gambier at 30,000 feet they had waited 30 minutes before spotting the aircraft approaching; the Spitfires attacked the *Dinah* from astern and watched it crash north of the Bathurst Island Mission. The squadron's operations record recorded that "F/Sgts. R. Jenkins and R. Watson shared the third *Dinah* and sent it down in flames on BATHURST ISLAND, from which some wreckage and two bodies have already been recovered, including a new type compass." The crew of Lts Saburo Shinohara and Hideo Ura were buried near the crash site in a brief service overseen by Padre Roberts of the RAAF who was visiting the islands. Equipment recovered from the wreck included a range of documents, photographic plates, spools of film, a Rookua-Sha Tokyo Telehexar camera and a 7.7mm machine gun, number 3988.

Late that afternoon, Ku *202* sent over a *Dinah*, one of few operated by the navy. It was intercepted 16 km northwest of Darwin at 1625 hours by WgCdr Clive Caldwell and FSgt P. R. Padula. Locating the *Dinah* ahead of A-A fire,

A SHOW OF FORCE

Caldwell spotted the aircraft over Charles Point at 26,000 feet. An initial attack by Caldwell hit the aircraft, while Padula's attack was made too far out. Caldwell then made a further two attacks and the *Dinah* "...began losing height" Caldwell reported, "first gradually and then steeply until I was obliged to dive at 360 m.p.h. I.A.S. in order to retain my position abreast of the E/A...[which] appeared to...make an attempt to level out momentarily and hit the water at a point 20 miles due west of CAPE FOURCROY...flew at zero feet around the debris." With the *Dinah* went CPOs Tomihiko Tanaka and Shinji Kawahara.

Ground crews and administrative staff of the 70th DCS wave off the Dinahs from Lautem on 17 August 1943. Three of the unit's five aircraft failed to return. Photo: Susumu Akasaka.

Learning the lessons of the August mission, two *Dinahs* departed Lautem at 0710 hours on 7 September, this time under an escort of 36 *Zekes* of Ku *202*. The CO Kurayasu Ichikawa and his observer, Lt Togo Maki, acted as an independent aircraft whilst Lt Muramitsu Sasaki and his observer, Lt Muneo Kubo, were briefed to reconnoitre the airfields from Darwin to Batchelor. As they approached Bathurst Island Ichikawa's *Dinah* "scattered many pieces of tin foil at 100 km north from Darwin, to disturb the enemy's radar function" Muramitsu Sasaki wrote, "...At 0910 our formation passed over Bathurst Island. After a short time, at the north side of Darwin, more than 20 Spitfiers [*sic*] appeared from the left front side, and began an air battle between our Spitfiers [*sic*] and our indirect-escort Zero fighters... [the] two *Dinah*s continued flying south...but after a short time 6 Spitfiers [*sic*] came to attack...and a hot dog-fight occurred...[the] two *Dinah*s gave up the reconnaissance ...Lt. Sasaki's *Dinah* flew back...and Captain Ichikawa's *Dinah* left west at full speed independently. This operation ended in failure, but it remained as valuable experience for us, that plural number of reconnaissance plain [*sic*] performed these duties under the escort of many fighters."

A RAAF airman at the site of Dinah 2273, which crashed on Bathurst Island, 17 August 1943. Photo: Alford Colln.

Despite claims by the Japanese of destroying 18 Spitfires, three were lost during the engagement. SqnLdr Ron McDonald was hit and baled out, landing near Tumbling Waters where he was later "...picked up by a Tiger Moth from Doc Fenton's rescue squadron and flown back to Strauss. Later, after a few beers, was driven down to the hospital at Coomalie. Some burns and a bit of stuff in my leg." His log book entry for the day recorded "LZ884...scramble...Oh dear! 1 Recco plus 15-20 fighters (Zeros, Haps, Oscars, Tonys) Wing jumped. Squadron score one Tony destroyed, I Oscar probably, 2 *Oscar*s and 1 Zero damaged."

Flying Officer Paul Tully, also of 452 Squadron, baled out of his aircraft, BR549, after being hit and was rescued, while

Lieutenants Saburo Shinohara, Hideo Ura and Takebyashi take a break at their Lautem base. Both Shinohara and Ura were killed in Dinah 2273 on 17 August 1943. Photo: Susumu Akasaka.

A SHOW OF FORCE

FlgOff W. T. Hinds of 54 Squadron was killed when his aircraft, EF558, was hit and crashed near Pioneer Creek at Kangaroo Flats. The Japanese lost one *Zeke* flown by CPO Yoshio Terai.

All the Spitfire pilots reported radio problems before the interception; "Interference in the R/T resulted in the SPITFIRE squadrons meeting the enemy in [a] poor position" the 54 Squadron historian noted, "The ground control R/T was making a whistling noise, and could not be understood." The tin foil scattered by Ichikawa and Sasaki may have been more successful than they could have realised.

In the nine months of combat in the Darwin area, from 6 February to 12 November 1943, the three Spitfire squadrons of 1 Fighter Wing claimed 65 enemy aircraft destroyed for the loss of 62 Spitfires, 38 of these in or as a result of combat, and 21 pilots. The effectiveness of the Spitfires has been debated and despite the high number of 'kills' the Japanese lost far fewer aircraft than were claimed. What is known is that Japanese were also prone to exaggerating their claims. Over the same period they claimed 113 Spitfires destroyed and six probables, but they also had mechanical problems with their aircraft, suffered from pilot inexperience and endured difficult maintenance conditions as did 1 Fighter Wing.

Flying Officer Colin Duncan of 452 Squadron surveys the damage to his Spitfire following combat over Darwin on 7 September 1943. Photo: Paul Tully.

What was of concern to Cole, who had taken over from Bladin in July, and MajGen A. S. Allen, Commander Northern Territory Force, was not so much the ability of the pilots and their leaders, but the limited range of the Spitfires that had seen them forced to withdraw while the Japanese fighters were able to loiter over the combat area. Allen expressed the view that the RAAF lacked the aircraft to escort any anti-invasion bomber attack. In referring to both the Spitfire and Beaufighter, the available high altitude fighters lacked sufficient range whilst those with sufficient range lacked the necessary performance. In a 2 July report Allen stated that "Fighters of the P-38 (Lightning) type are required." Cole agreed and followed it up on the 23rd in correspondence to AVM Bostock that he couldn't "... guarantee the initial security of this area from an air point of view...the present equipment is scarcely sufficient deterrent in power to make enemy air raids uneconomical."

Bostock responded quickly, confirming the "...present insurmountable difficulty lies, not in the lack of appreciation of requirements, but in the physical ability to procure the necessary aircraft. On three specific occasions during the last six months I have forcibly represented to... General Kenney...the need for increased fighter strength in the [NWA] and, in particular...for the allocation of one or more P-38 squadrons...[Kenney] is fully aware of the situation but...has determined that priority of available fighter squadrons must be given to the [NEA] in the present situation" He also suggested that if required aircraft might be flown into NWA from the Fifth Air Force to deal with any emergency. And so, the *status quo* remained.

The Japanese failed to heed their own advice in not sending out unescorted reconnaissance sorties and paid the price on 12 June 1944 when a *Dinah* crewed by Lts Katsutoshi Tsutsui and Keisuke Shimazaki was intercepted and shot down over Point Blaze. Three 452 Squadron pilots, FlgOffs K. M. Gamble, C. F. O'Loughlin and PltOff M. 'Junior' Beaton along with nine other Spitfires had been scrambled from Sattler, and the three made contact soon after. O'Loughlin's engine failed following the intercept and he was forced to ditch A58-117 into the sea; he was subsequently rescued by a 43 Squadron Catalina and returned to his unit.

The incident effectively brought to a close any further intrusions by the Japanese over the Northern Territory. The Ki-46 *Dinahs* of the 70th DCS had flown some 157 missions over the Territory and lost seven aircraft and their crews

A SHOW OF FORCE

whilst *3 Ku/* Ku *202* had lost a C5M2 *Babs* and a *Dinah*. The one failing in these missions was the forewarning the flights gave to the Allies; usually a raid could be expected within one or two days of a *Dinah* sortie.

With the raids over, the battle for the Spitfire units now was with boredom, though entries in some earlier squadron records had already alluded to the problem. In his July 1943 report the 457 Squadron historian noted that the "...lack of action and the feeling that the Japanese are neglecting us is making the pilots restless. The general impression is that the Japanese are being so deeply involved in the Solomons...and having lost so many aircraft during the recent raids... [has] forced him to be a little more conservative in his long-range raids." Others state matter-of-factly that the "Dull routine, featureless surroundings, for months on end tend to impair the efficiency of the men..." or "It has been a dull month, relieved by only the one action and several false alarms" and "The first day of October passed without incident." The comments became more caustic through 1944 and 1945 as the fighter squadrons around Darwin languished.

When GpCapt Walters was posted south, WgCdr Caldwell took over the Wing, however his tenure was short; soon after Cole took over HQ NWA, 1 Fighter Wing was disbanded. While AVM Bostock considered it necessary to keep the three Spitfire units together, as they may have been required to provide fighter protection in different areas - the detachment at Milingimbi during May was possibly a part of this thinking - and he requested RAAF HQ to disband the wing accordingly. Headquarters agreed and directed that the fighter squadrons come under the administrative umbrella of NWA, whilst operational control of all fighter operations be vested in 5 Fighter Sector HQ. This was also intended to overcome confusion that had arisen on a number of occasions when the controller had tried to control the fighters, at times to Caldwell's frustration. Only the sector commander, in this case WgCdr T. Primrose AFC, could give orders to the wing leader and fighter squadrons in the air.

Some months later AVM Jones re-introduced the title No. 1 (Fighter) Wing, in that "The uncertainty concerning the wing organisation for the fighters in Darwin has occurred through the officer commanding the wing in the past not being fully qualified to control the fighters from the Operations Room. With the posting of WgCdr Jeffrey, this difficulty has been overcome." WgCdr Peter Jeffrey, a highly regarded veteran of the Middle East replaced Caldwell, who went on to command 80 Wing when it formed at Sattler.

Meanwhile the Beaufighters continued their strike missions as part of NWA's show of force, though on occasion they were beaten by the weather. On 6 August they were assigned to provide top cover for the vessel *Macumba* and her escort HMAS *Cootamundra* but bad weather prevented them locating her. However, two 934th *Ku* floatplanes found *Macumba* near Croker Island and attacked, one bomb exploding in the engine room. Taken in tow by *Cootamundra* she later sank, taking two crew members with her. Four days later two Spitfires flying out of Milingimbi intercepted a *Jake* and a *Rufe* 55 km north of the island. The *Jake* was shot down, taking the crew of PO3c Ishiwata, FCPO Nagano and the gunner PO2c Takagami with it, while the *Rufe*, manned by the 934th's newly promoted CO, Lt Toshiharu Ikeda, despite being damaged managed to escape due to the short range of the Spitfires.

Over the period 12 June to 17 August the Beaufighters flew 51 sorties against Taberfane, destroying ten floatplanes and damaging a further 11, while losing A19-118 and the crew of FlgOffs B. W. Gillespie and A. J. Cameron on 24 July. They had been part of a 12 aircraft attack on Taberfane when the Beaufighters were intercepted by *Rufes* flown by FCPO Kawaguchi, PO1c Ichikawa and PO3c Imada. Two other Beaufighters were damaged but made it back to Coomalie, despite the Japanese claiming two 'kills'.

A Ku 202 Zeke is caught on the strip as 31 Squadron Beaufighters attack Langgoer on 31 May 1943. The photo was taken by FSgt F. A. McMurchie in A19-63 flown by PltOff A. M. Shorter. Photo: James F. Lansdale.

A SHOW OF FORCE

Whilst the Beaufighters were highly successful in their low level high speed attacks there had been concerns raised over their vulnerability in not having top cover; 10 aircraft and 18 crew members had been lost to June 1943.

In correspondence from AVM Bostock to HQ NWA and 31 Squadron of 18 June, apparently in response to concerns at NWA HQ level and one that seemingly coincided with Cole's request for P-38s, he noted the "Beaufighter formations gained considerable success when attacking grounded aircraft. The surprise achieved...was no doubt due to the operations having been well thought out...It has been noted also that the losses of Beaufighter[s]...have been light to date. I appreciate the vulnerability of Beaufighters when strafing without proper cover, but believe there remain targets of opportunities for low level attacks of considerable value away from aerodromes heavily defended by Zeros...It is out of the question to provide a squadron of Lightning aircraft at this stage, but...be assured that the requirement for long range fighters...for top cover duties is well understood...I would suggest that unacceptable losses will be avoided if well thought out operations are planned against appropriate targets."

Despite any unease over the Beaufighters, they were continuing to inflict losses on the enemy. On 17 August nine Beaufighters led by FltLt J. D. Entwhistle departed Coomalie heading for Taberfane, though one aborted due to generator problems. The remainder made landfall 3 hours later at Maikoor inlet and turned south for Taberfane, arriving five minutes later and climbed to 600 ft for the run in on the floatplane base. In the 12 minutes they spent over the target four floatplanes including a *Rufe* attempting to take off were destroyed, killing the pilot, Flyer 1c Osamu Yoza.

Two other *Rufes* were in the air and attempted to intercept but were taken on by the Beaufighters. They were claimed downed by FltLt Taylor flying A19-51 *Snifter* and FSgt Kilpatrick as COO54 and were both confirmed independently. A *Pete* was claimed by FltLt Entwhistle and confirmed, while FltLt McCutcheon claimed a *Rufe* destroyed. There were no losses by the Beaufighters and the only damage recorded was a folded wingtip on the aircraft of FltLt 'Squizzy' Taylor, the result of a very tight turn to attack a *Rufe*.

Four days later seven Beaufighters hit Taberfane but lost two crews when A19-47 and '63 collided and crashed into the sea. Flight Lieutenant F. J. Gardner and FlgOff L. J. Lyne along with FlgOffs V. C. Leithead and R. S. Graves were listed as 'death presumed'. The Japanese lost Flyer 1c Toyu Inohara who was caught trying to take off to intercept the Beaufighters; he died of his injuries two days later.

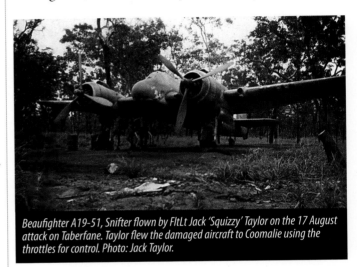

Beaufighter A19-51, Snifter flown by FltLt Jack 'Squizzy' Taylor on the 17 August attack on Taberfane. Taylor flew the damaged aircraft to Coomalie using the throttles for control. Photo: Jack Taylor.

Other raids followed; mainly on the floatplane bases in an attempt to eliminate the threat they posed, but also against airfields, barges and coastal vessels and infrastructure. Squadron Leader G. W. Savage, a veteran of over twenty missions with 31 Squadron described a typical sortie over Timor, wondering at first, "...if we will find plenty to hit. The first part of the journey is always the worst because we are travelling over water...as soon as I see land everything is different and life is pleasant...after crossing the [enemy] coast we fly over beautiful hills and valleys...When flying low there isn't time for thinking, because you're far too busy scraping over trees and dodging hillsides. My observer tells me when we are 3 or 4 miles from the target...everything happens very suddenly. I get my hand on the gunbutton, and get ready to pick out what I will try to hit...I must find it quickly. Then I dive the aircraft towards the target and press the gunbutton...we always seem to surprise the Japs and we see them running...Halfway across the target, A-A opens up. But it does not worry us much...where a target is well defended our attack only lasts for 20 seconds or so...we put on more speed as we leave the target... [and] sometimes Zeros are waiting for us at the coast...I put on more speed [and] race them out to sea. We fly very fast until we get well out to sea, then we settle down to a steady cruise home. We are very tired after flying more than 5 hours..."

A SHOW OF FORCE

Savage's matter-of-fact commentary contrasts sharply with the dramatic words penned by War Correspondent, Bill Moore, who reported 31 Squadron as the "'Buckjumpers of the Air', because they have the uncanny knack of bouncing off the enemy's palm trees, jumping over his hangars and installations, and generally kicking Tojo's treasures to smithereens."

The Mitchells of 18 NEI Squadron had also been busy over the latter months of 1943, working in concert with the Beaufighters and remaining Hudsons of 2 Squadron. They flew their first mission from the new base at Batchelor on 11 May, a reconnaissance of the Somniliquoy-Tanimbar Island and Laha-Ambon areas, while operations over Koepang harbour, Penfoie and Dili were also flown. The same day also saw LtCol J. J. Zomer arrive as the new CO.

The mixed Dutch-Australian crews were also mounting anti-shipping strikes at mast head heights which proved to be extremely hazardous with instances of premature detonation when delayed action fuses failed. Targets were many and varied; Dili, Manatuto, Selaru, the Kai Islands, Ambon, Laha, Penfoie, Lautem, Fuiloro, Langgoer, Koepang harbour and Tenau among others. They ranged from convoy and anti-submarine patrols to supply dropping, reconnaissance and shipping strikes to strafing enemy airfields and positions.

Gus Winckel (second left) and his crew in front of N5-131 Pulk at Batchelor, 1943. The aircraft remained in service from August 1942 to March 1948. Photo: Gus Winckel.

On 2 June they attacked a small fleet of ships midway between Timor and Wetar Island. Bombing and strafing the vessels, the B-25s came under concentrated A-A and machine gun fire from shore and from the vessels themselves, in one case shattering the pilot's window in N5-146. One aircraft, N5-150 attacked what appeared to be an "...M/V. of 2000 tons, but which proved to be a destroyer of 5000 tons..." Last seen by the crews of N5-146 and 151, N5-150 failed to return to base. The crew of SgtMaj H. van den Berg, Sgt Bouwman and three RAAF crew members, FSgts R. L. Morrison and T. E. W. Williams and Sgt F. G. Prichard were presumed killed.

On 6 July the Mitchells carried out a night strike on Selaru, bombing the main target and following up with strafing attacks on the villages of Cape Toewaoe, Werain, Eliase, Lingat and Foersoey, expending 3,320 rounds of .50" ammunition. A-A fire damaged N5-137, fouling the landing gear and necessitating a crash landing at Batchelor. Similarly, a raid on Laha and Ambon on 9 September saw N5-153 *Rene* damaged over the target, preventing the nose wheel leg from extending. The pilot landed at Batchelor and the crew escaped unharmed. Another, N5-145, *The Flying Dutchman*, which had been converted to the 'strafer' version, ran off the runway at Batchelor on 18 October and was badly damaged; again the crew were uninjured.

One crew member was not so fortunate. A flight mechanic, Sgt Keesmat, was killed when N5-156 crashed near Hughes airfield during a night bombing exercise on 21 October. Part of a four aircraft exercise with N5-155, '158 and '161, a flare ignited in the rear fuselage; Sgt Engels and his crew were able to bale out – Sgt Keesmat went down with the aircraft.

Some missions ended in frustration for the crews. An attack on enemy shipping, including a destroyer and troop transport, by Mitchells, Beaufighters, Liberators and Hudsons was planned, however they failed to locate the vessels and returned to base, some with bombs still aboard. Searches for Spitfire pilots missing in combat following the 30 June and 6 July raids on Fenton located only two pilots, whilst a search for a missing Beaufighter on 23 November failed to locate any sign of the aircraft or crew.

The Beaufighter was A19-145 which went missing during a flight from Milingimbi to Coomalie following a combined raid on Taberfane with six 18 Squadron Mitchells on 21 November. It was not until September 1944 that the wreckage was finally found by Aborigines and the remains of the observer, PltOff T. J. Jones recovered. Those of FSgt H. H. Gaunt have not been located.

A SHOW OF FORCE

Four 18 NEI Squadron B-25Ds, N5-218, N5-230, N5-188 and N5-226 over the Northern Territory coastline. Photo: Gus Winckel.

From September, 18 Squadron was boosted by the arrival of the new better equipped and heavily armed models, the B-25J series. Flown in by crews trained at the Jackson Mississippi joint Dutch Army-Navy facility, they were able to mount offensive operations at least on a par with the Beaufighters in terms of firepower, if not as fast. In all 18 Squadron received 46 of the new aircraft, though nine were later transferred to 2 Squadron RAAF.

October saw 18 Squadron engaged in the offensive against the enemy in the NEI in support of the New Guinea offensive by the Allies, making night attacks against Koepang, Lautem, Fuiloro and Langgoer. They flew a number of attacks with 2 Squadron and the Catalinas of 11, 20 and 43 Squadrons from Cairns and Karumba, bombing Ambon over October and November. During November and December the Mitchells extended their reach by staging through Merauke to bomb targets in Dutch New Guinea, mainly at Timoeka and Kaukenau in concert with 7 Squadron Beauforts and 84 Squadron P-40 Kittyhawks.

In the meantime those aircraft at Batchelor were engaged in strikes, on patrolling the Giraffe, Horse and Jackass lines, in practice bombing and gunnery missions, searches, and on shipping patrols. The last missions for 1943 were flown on 30 December; N5-146 flew a clockwise search of the Giraffe line and N5-138 an anti-clockwise search of the Jackass line.

In September the CO TAIU, Col Frank T. McCoy, had released Memorandum No. 2 listing Japanese aircraft wrecks located throughout the SWPA. In it were listed those aircraft located in the Northern Territory which he had inspected. They included *Zekes* 5349, 916 and 6540, *Bettys* 5414 and 3677, the Nakajima Ki-49 *Helen* 174, and *Dinahs* 2414 and 2273. The *Betty* on Cox Peninsula remained unidentified as did *Dinah* 2237 at Fenton; a total of twelve, counting *Val* 3304, which was erroneously listed at Yule Island in New Guinea. *Dinah* 2250 and a Sumitomo propeller from either a *Zeke* or *Betty* found in a fishing net can be added to the list, along with some others suspected of not returning to their bases; a far cry from the 135 plus Japanese aircraft claimed over the period 19 February 1942 to 12 June 1944.

While the raids over Darwin and its hinterland had finished, the Japanese no doubt needed to demonstrate the ability to strike at will, particularly in that their air strength in the region had been greatly reduced from July 1943. With little risk to themselves, they attacked the old Kalumburu Mission and 58 OBU at the nearby airfield (Drysdale) on 27 September, killing Father Thomas and five Aborigines sheltering in a trench. Four buildings marked with red crosses were destroyed along with an ammunition store at the airfield.

The combined force comprising over 20 Ki-48 II *Lilys* of the 75th *Sentai* and 21 *Zekes* of Ku 202 was picked up by 317 Radar Station at 0956 hours and thirty minutes later they struck, bombing and strafing the airfield and buildings and leaving some 86 bomb craters in the mission compound alone. With no fighter opposition they had a free hand and departed the target area unscathed. The raid was the last appearance of the *Zekes* over the NWA and the end of daylight raids on mainland Australia.

The latter half of 1943 also saw a further five airfields well underway. Sattler, at the 20-mile peg from Darwin, was initially commenced early in the year by the AWC and later 61 Works Wing and 9 ACS. The airfield was almost completed by June 1944 but for sealing the runway and taxiways, which was completed by 1 MWS. The first Spitfires of 452 Squadron arrived that month followed by 457 Squadron. A new staging base on Vansittart Bay north of Drysdale was also under construction by 14 MWS. Named Truscott this airfield became an important staging base for USAAF and RAAF B-24s, 2 and 18 Squadron Mitchells, and later the Mosquitos of 1 PRU; it became operational in July 1944 when four Beaufighters staged through for a raid on Maumere on the 16th.

A SHOW OF FORCE

In far north east Arnhem Land another airfield near Yirrkala was under construction by 3 and 8 MWS units, along with a flying boat base at nearby Melville Bay. Approval had been given for the new facilities on 13 August with the requirements for an all weather runway for medium bombers and an alighting area for flying boats, dispersal areas, 12 mooring buoys and a camp for 500 personnel; all at a cost of £100,000. By 30 August an advance party arrived and by the end of September 637 personnel and 13,000 tonnes of equipment had arrived aboard the *Wanaka* from Darwin. The first aircraft landed on 24 October, and the airfield was subsequently named Gove.

Immediately south of Batchelor another airfield was under construction, also by elements of GpCapt D. J. Rooney's 61 Works Wing. Named Gould, it was briefly occupied by the Beauforts of 1 Squadron from February 1944, and 18 Squadron. Transit aircraft also used its facilities when staging through Batchelor on occasion.

At Pell airfield the RSUs, 7 and 4, continued their largely unsung role in salvaging, repairing and servicing a range of aircraft types. Salvage crews roamed the countryside, travelling to remote crash sites to salvage aircraft wreckage and in some cases the remains of pilots and crewmen trapped in cockpits or fuselages. During 1943 the salvage parties travelled to some 71 locations, recovering the remains of a variety of types, predominately Spitfires by 7 RSU, but including P-40s, B-25s, Wirraways, de Havilland Dragons, and Beaufighters.

From February 1943 the number of units assigned to 4 RSU for technical support had increased with 31 Squadron assigned on 14 February. By month's end the unit was supporting 12 and 31 Squadrons, 1 PRU, 9 RC, 31, 38, 39, 105 and 132 Radar Stations, along with OBUs at Darwin, Groote Eylandt, Batchelor, Venn, and Drysdale.

By June 2 Squadron, 6 Comm. Unit and 2 AAU and the AOB on Bathurst Island were added, while 24 aircraft were either serviced, repaired or had scheduled inspections carried out. By year's end the number of units had reduced to 2 and 31 Squadrons, 1 PRU and 6 Comm. Unit under FltLt Clyde 'Doc' Fenton. Over the year 49 aircraft were salvaged.

Most were repaired at Pell and returned to service whilst those that were beyond repair were either sent to 14 ARD at Gorrie or 'converted to components' and written off.

Pilots of 452 Squadron RAAF at Sattler, 12 December 1944. Seated from left, SqnLdr Birch, GpCapt Clive Caldwell DFC DSO and SqnLdr Lou Spence CO 452 Squadron. Photo: Dr. J. H. Milne.

A SHOW OF FORCE

Gorrie had been constructed from late 1942 as a huge servicing and stores centre in support of the NWA operations, and occupied by 9 Stores Depot in December that year; 14 ARD followed in February 1943.

The personnel of 14 ARD carried out major servicings on all aircraft types and engines, whilst ground equipment and vehicles were serviced or repaired. Three mobile operations rooms were also produced and many replacement parts were manufactured in the machine shops.

On 18 October a mobile oxygen plant under FlgOff Miller was sent to 4 RSU from 14 ARD to produce breathing oxygen for flying and industrial oxygen for welding. The unit suffered two fatalities when an explosion occurred on 21 April 1944; LAC C D Hoffman was killed instantly and the detachment CO, FlgOff F W Miller, died shortly after admission to 1 MRS; the explosion was caused by a lethal combination of oxygen and grease.

Beaufighter A19-43 was one of three 31 Squadron aircraft which force landed on 16 September 1943. A19-70 and '43 were salvaged by 4 RSU personnel whilst A19-30 was written off. Photo: D. Strachan.

While 7 RSU had an enviable record in salvaging, servicing and repairing the Spitfires of 1 Fighter Wing, 4 RSU had "... the unique distinction, which no other RSU can claim, of servicing, repairing or inspecting every type of aircraft that has come into the North-Western Area with perhaps one exception, the B17 [sic]", wrote the unit CO in his report for August 1944.

By year's end, the war in the NWA had undergone a complete change. The Japanese air strength had rapidly decreased and they were unable to maintain any more than a few aircraft at their main bases and whilst they were able to intercept Allied raids they were forced to hold most of their aircraft beyond a 1,000 km range from Darwin. Losses in the Solomons and around Rabaul had also forced a redistribution of Japanese air strength, particularly that of the 23rd *Koku Sentai*, to the central Pacific. A much weakened 7th *Hikoshidan* was also withdrawn from Wewak to Ambon to assist in the defence of the Celebes area.

A B-25J Mitchell of 2 Squadron at 14 ARD Gorrie, January 1945. Personnel of 14 ARD carried out major servicings and overhauls of all RAAF aircraft in the NWA. Photo: Alford/AHSNT Colln.

The strategic role of the NWA had shifted also. Cole was now thinking more of an offensive policy, whereby Darwin's potential as a base for launching an invasion of the NEI was assured. He had commenced moving forward stores, repair and maintenance facilities and was awaiting the arrival of new aircraft and units - the B-24 Liberators of the RAAF's 82 Wing, B-25s of 2 Squadron and Venturas of 13 Squadron among them. The use of Darwin as a base for the Boeing B-29 Superfortresses was also mooted.

The mood was now one of increasing the pressure on the weakened Japanese forces to the north and a vital part of this was the role of the heavy bombers operating from their bases in the NWA.

CHAPTER 10

THE HEAVY BOMBERS
Striking afar and a circus arrives

With the arrival of the 90th Bomb. Gp's 319th Squadron and its detachment from Batchelor at Fenton on 3 February 1943, the requirement by General MacArthur for reconnaissance on his southern flank was to be fulfilled. The B-24s carried out the task efficiently despite not being equipped for the job; instead they relied on photographers from the RAAF's 1 PRU and crewmen hastily taught the fundamentals of photography. Handheld cameras were used in lieu of the specialised aircraft and equipment available in other theatres, the RAAF's troubled P-38 Lightning F-4s notwithstanding.

Despite the handicap, the missions were mostly successful and involved some of the "...longest bombing missions flown by any outfit in World War II up until that time...", commented Bill Hagerty, the 319th's Line Chief at Fenton. Of Fenton itself, he maintained that "...it was a desolate place in the out back country...Outback as they called it in Australia and the only thing around there was [sic] critters." The comment was mild compared to some that followed.

As had American units to the time, the 319th reported to AVM W. D. Bostock but came under Bladin's operational command at HQ NWA. Bladin was a diplomat, and had shown previously with the 49th Fighter Gp and other American units that to allow flexibility with mission planning, operational requirements and timing provided an atmosphere of mutual respect: in complete contrast to a number of quite false and seemingly self-serving comments critical of Australian control and the "rampant acrimonious feelings among the Americans" cited by American senior officers, MajGen R. Richardson among them.

Two days after arriving at Fenton the unit had commenced operations with an eight aircraft mission to Ambon. Four days later Capt Charles E. Jones led the squadron on a twelve hour mission, again to Ambon, and followed it up with further raids on the town on the 15th and 21st, though, "...This time the flak was fairly heavy..." Jones reported.

"Three Zeros came up to intercept us, and pulled a new stunt which I had not seen before" Charles Hesse also recalled, "They climbed above us and dropped bombs... which exploded in big white puffs...sending out many streamers of burning material, maybe phosphorous... fortunately none...came in contact with our planes...the Zeros [then] pressed their attacks...using their cannons and machine guns." Hesse's aircraft suffered a large hole in

the main spar of the port wing and the remaining aircraft returned unscathed.

On 2 March the squadron was alerted to a possible attack on Fenton and the aircraft were evacuated to Katherine overnight. One aircraft, 41-23753 *Lady Millie*, was assigned to carry out a reconnaissance mission, however its regular pilot Lt Clarence 'Bud' Eckert, after whose wife the aircraft was named, was replaced by Lt Anderson. It was fortuitous for Eckert, but a disaster for the 319th when the aircraft crashed shortly after take off, killing eight of the eleven crew members; only Anderson and two others, Sgts Clark and Stewart survived.

The B-24D 41-23753 Lady Millie, of Lt Clarence E. 'Bud' Eckert and crew at Fenton 1943. Named after Eckert's wife, the aircraft was lost in a fiery crash on 2 March. Photo: Clarence Eckert.

Capt Paul E. Johnson recorded in his diary that, "...we had a horrible accident - as Anderson was taking off ...on [a] recco, he had a power failure and crashed – the ship burned." Two days later he wrote of going "...to the funeral of the men on Lt. Anderson's crew...Afterwards we went by the hospital to see Andy. He is doing as well as could be expected."

The cause of the accident appeared to be "...as a consequence of failure to use auto-rich fuel mixture settings. Most of the pilots used the auto-lean settings for idling or taxiing but it was imperative to switch to auto-rich before take off," contended 'Bud' Eckert.

Six days later Hesse and his crew took off on an armed reconnaissance to the Celebes and across to Dili, however malfunctioning upper turret guns saw the secondary targets at Saumlaki in the Tanimbars and Babar Island attacked instead. "We dropped our six 500-pound

THE HEAVY BOMBERS

demolition bombs on Saumlaki and photographed it from 10,000 feet..." Hesse reported, "We made some good hits, then dropped propaganda leaflets... [then] proceeded to... Babar and dropped leaflets for the natives to read...Then we headed back to Fenton. The flight lasted eight hours."

On 16 March another armed reconnaissance was flown in search of Japanese shipping along the southern New Guinea coast, this time by four aircraft led by the CO Capt Charles E. Jones. Hesse and Lt John Wilson split from the others and bombed shipping before heading back to Fenton. On arrival they learned from Lt Hal Hevener that Jones' aircraft had blown up, probably as the result of a fuel leak, and plunged into the sea with no survivors. The aircraft 41-23731 *Dirty Gertie*, was "...one of the sentimentally favourite airplanes" Hesse wrote, "...What a tragic loss, ten good, talented men..." Among the crew was RAAF photographer, Cpl Darcy A. Sharland. To make matters worse, Jones was aware of the problem, and had ordered Hevener to "Get away from me!"

Captain Roy Olsen took over command of the 319th, though he lasted only a further three and a half months before being killed in a Japanese suicide attack.

Two days later another B-24 was lost, though this time with no fatalities. Aircraft, 41-11869 named *One Time* was flown on a single aircraft armed reconnaissance mission to Ambon under the command of Lt Alden H. Currie. Ten Japanese fighters intercepted the aircraft, wounding a waist gunner. The gunners aboard the aircraft claimed four Japanese fighters whilst a waist gunner was seriously injured. Badly damaged, the aircraft crash landed at RAAF Darwin and was written off as a result. Ray Jackson of the Bomb Disposal Unit recorded in his diary that a "... Liberator had crashed on the runway at Darwin RAFF [*sic*] after being shot to pieces by 8 Jap Zeros...up the Nightcliff end of the runway!! (All the crew survived)."

Currie and his crew were "...intercepted by ten Zeros..." Charles Hesse wrote, "In the ensuing battle, his gunners claimed that they had shot down four of the intruders. They limped back to Darwin on three engines and with six guns shot out of commission. One of his gunners had been shot in the hand. Lt. Currie had to crash land his airplane."

Jim Case, a crewman on the aircraft that day confirmed it was not their normal aircraft, *Roaring Rosie*, but that "We

were to fly the B-24 called *One Time* from Fenton to Darwin where we were to load six 500 lb bombs and top up our fuel tanks..." *One Time* was normally flown by Lt John Arrant, and had been renamed from *One Ball Riley*.

In a letter addressed to the 319th Squadron, AirCdre Blaidin congratulated the unit on shooting down four Japanese aircraft during the mission.

Despite setbacks the missions continued from Fenton. A six aircraft night raid on Ambon on 19 March was met with "... ack-ack fire [which] appeared more intense than...during daylight raids; I believe it was more of an optical illusion" Hesse recalled, "...As we started our bomb run it appeared that we would have to penetrate a solid wall of tracer. We made it through unscathed." So too the landing back at Fenton where "...we arrived...at about 5:00 AM...and I made my first night landing since leaving the States. It wasn't the smoothest...but the airplane held together and the crew walked away from it; so it was okay."

On 3 April Hesse and his crew sought a transfer from the 320th Squadron to the 319th. They felt that "...if we were flying with the 319th, why not join them, officially? Sgt. Gudmunsden was referring to us as the *Orphans of Asterperious*...because we belonged to the 320th which was doing nothing to take us back; asterperious was the adjective adopted by the 319th to describe how its personnel felt about themselves, *a superior attitude in an inferior environment*. Our crew didn't want to be a part of the inferior environment."

The transfer was arranged and Hesse and his crew became part of the 319th on 11 May. Two days later was the 90th's first birthday. "Flying had been canceled[*sic*]; there was a baseball game, extra food, ice cream and beer!" Asterperious became synonymous with the 319th thanks to a cartoon of a native drawn by former Walt Disney artist, Lt Ken Strong.

To date the 319th Squadron, along with the 'orphans' of the 320th, had flown some 75 missions, one a photo reconnaissance sortie of 4,000 kilometres to Surabaya, along with individual sorties. Forty eight of the missions were reconnaissance or armed reconnaissance with extra crewmen; in a number of cases Australians attached from 1PRU as photographers.

By the end of May the men of the 319th were expecting the first of the 380th Bomb. Gp personnel and aircraft to arrive in the area to relieve them, though they continued flying.

THE HEAVY BOMBERS

A six aircraft strike on Kendari was flown on 16 May, followed by another on Kaimana in western New Guinea six days later, sinking one ship. The unit's aircraft were all taken off combat readiness in an effort to have them fully serviceable for an all-out joint reconnaissance with the newly arrived 380th on the 27th.

B-24D 41-11866, The Nipper flown by Lt Sanxter and his crew of the 319th Squadron, 90th Bomb. Group, later named The Jolly Rogers. Photo: Alford/ AHSNT Colln.

There must have been some misapprehension on the part of the 319th veterans at Fenton. The 380th Bomb. Gp was untried in combat, after having formed at Davis-Monthan AFB outside Tucson Arizona on 21 November 1942. The new unit didn't get off to an auspicious start. "My God, these men are a flying circus..." commented Brigadier General Eugene L. Eubank, Director of Bombing, in describing the 380th Bomb. Gp at a parade on 30 March 1943. Eubank's comment went through the ranks quickly, but later the Group used the name "The Flying Circus" with some pride, adding the phrase "King of the Heavies" to denote its role in the heavy bombing offensive against the Japanese.

The 380th had begun arriving in the Darwin area in late April after seven B-24s each carrying a flight crew, key administrative and maintenance personnel along with Command Navigator set out from Hamilton AFB in California on the long haul across the Pacific. After almost 48 hours of flying they arrived at Amberley RAAF base outside Brisbane and were then sent to Charters Towers west of Townsville. Others arrived over the coming days, whilst some had nose turrets fitted at the Hawaii Air Depot in lieu of the glasshouse noses of the B-24Ds.

The ground crews and administrative staff travelled across country by rail before arriving at San Francisco and after some days at Camp Stoneman boarded the USS *Mt Vernon*, a converted passenger liner, on 5 May; it left San Francisco the following day and arrived in Sydney on the 22nd.

By 26 April most of the Group's aircraft were at Charters Towers being serviced or modified with the CO's aircraft LtCol Bill Miller's *Miss Mary* the first completed along with that of the 528th Squadron CO, Capt Zed Smith; they were to fly to Fenton to set up the base for the remaining units the 529th, 530th and 531st. The pair flew in on the 26th and met up with Bladin and Capt Roy Olsen of the 319th Squadron – who no doubt made them well aware of conditions at Fenton.

At Charters Towers crews were also being prepared for a detachment to the 5th Air Force at Port Moresby. On 27 April 14 aircraft and crews, mostly from the 530th and 531st Squadrons departed for combat operations in New Guinea whilst two crews flew across to Fenton to assist Capt Smith set up facilities. Eleven aircraft were to descend upon Fenton expecting facilities to be ready for them, whilst others remained receiving field modifications. At best the situation was confusing in that the squadrons were split up; at worst those who arrived at Fenton over the 3rd and 4th of May were stunned at their new 'home'.

"This place called Fenton Field gave new meaning to the adjectives 'remote' and 'primitive'..." the 380th Historian wrote, "...as the new arrivals discovered their tower lacked radio equipment and only one permanent building stood at the facility. This...was a corrugated, tin-roofed mess hall that served additionally as the briefing room and general hangout for off-duty personnel. Pyramid-style... tents provided the only other shelter...the field had been carved out of a dense forest that still harboured a variety of wild creatures...[the] runway was not level...[and] all maintenance was done outdoors...[with] no support buildings or shade...from the scorching sun." The 319th personnel must have wondered how they'd managed to survive all those months.

With the lack of facilities, Smith sent seven of the eleven aircraft to Batchelor as "...good dispersal [is] a real problem here" he signalled, "...will move aircraft from Batchelor as space becomes available." In time they adapted however, with the priority to get the Group into action. On 6 May Capt John Henschke the 528th Squadron Operations Officer

THE HEAVY BOMBERS

flew the first combat mission for the 380th as co-pilot to Capt Paul Johnson of the 319th. They flew to Manokwari and bombed an oil storage tank in a mission that lasted ten hours 45 minutes and covered some 2,575 km.

Three days later the first combat mission was flown by the 380th when Henschke took Capt Jack Banks and his crew back to Manokwari in a borrowed 319th Squadron aircraft. This trip saw Japanese fighters attempt to intercept the B-24, however they escaped by pushing the engines to the limit; so much so that the 319th mechanics sought a ban on 380th pilots using their aircraft and damaging valuable equipment. Capt Olsen complied.

One of a number of bush timber shelters used as workshops by the mechanics of the 319th Squadron during their time at Fenton. Photo: Wiley O. Woods.

By 14 May facilities at Fenton had been improved and the remaining 528th Squadron aircraft were flown back from Batchelor where they joined in operations with the 319th, a number of these from Corunna Downs in Western Australia's harsh outback. With the B-24s of the 319th Squadron and now the 380th Bomb. Gp proving their worth to Bladin in monitoring the enemy in the NEI and capability in striking distant targets, he decided to send the B-24s on missions as far as Java and Borneo.

One mission flown from Corunna Downs by Lt John Arrant on 13 March, a photographic sortie over Surabaya had proved the wisdom of using the site as it extended the range of Bladin's bomber and reconnaissance force considerably, allowing flexibility in planning missions.

Corunna Downs was a secret base scraped from the desert floor east of Port Hedland near Marble Bar – one of the consistently hottest places on earth. It boasted temperatures

ranging from 'cool' to 48.9° C, fuel was stored in 208 l drums in the open with attendant problems of condensation corrupting the fuel, and an oiled gravel runway. Conditions were at best appalling and the site was described as "...a God-forsaken spot...inhabited chiefly by flies."

The air traffic control facilities at Fenton included the tower, fire and ambulance services. Prior to the arrival of the 380th Bomb. Group only a poorly equipped tower was in existence. Photo: Bob Wynans.

Bladin ordered the first mission flown from Corunna Downs, but by no means the last by the 380th, a reconnaissance to Surabaya, on 29 May. Miller sent Capts Jack Banks and Bill Shek, however the mission was delayed for a day. At sunset on the 30th Banks, with Capt John Henschke as co-pilot in 42-40496, which became *Juarez Whistle*, and Shek with Capt Jack Kelly in 42-40495, *Dauntless Dottie*, took off on the long flight to Java.

Banks found the target clouded over so instead flew to Den Pasar airfield and dropped his single 45 kg bomb before heading back to Corunna Downs, where he found his aircraft adorned with tree branches collected during his take off the previous evening. For Shek and Kelly it was a different story, they returned with the first photos of the Wonokromo oil refinery and the important Japanese air base at Malang – then crowded with some 60 aircraft.

Shek had problems with one engine on the return flight and a replacement was destroyed when the RAAF Hudson transporting it, A16-217, crashed on landing; eventually a replacement was fitted and Shek returned to Fenton after some days idling away the hours at the remote base.

That first 380th mission from Corunna Downs was also significant in that it was the first flight of a B-24 fitted with RCM and was the first manned by a RAAF RCM operator,

THE HEAVY BOMBERS

Sgt Dick Dakeyne, one of a number of Section 22 members serving in the NWA. *Juarez Whistle* was the first of a number of 380th aircraft fitted with the RCM equipment, which could locate the Japanese radar, determine the frequencies it was using and plot its effective range.

A B-24 of the 530th Squadron 380th Bomb. Group waiting to head out on a mission from Corunna Downs. The aircraft in the background is from the 528th Squadron. Photo: Bob Wynans.

Dakeyene and Sgt Joe Holohan had been detached from the RAAF's 44 Radar Wing near Adelaide River to attend the RCM School in Sydney during February and were two of eight graduates. Four went to Catalinas operating out of Cairns, two to Darwin-based Hudson squadrons and both Dakeyne and Holohan were attached to the 319th Squadron at Fenton in April. There they met up with Sgts John Graham and Jack Hardacre also RCM operators, though without any RCM capable aircraft they had been flying as gunners with the 319th.

Founded by a Royal Navy officer and radar expert, Lt Hallett, Section 22 grew over time to include the CO, WgCdr Lyn McCann, SqnLdr Swan, PltOff Keith H. Bevan, Lt John Page of the Royal New Zealand Navy – one of two RNZN members - and Sgts Dakeyne, Holohan, Graham, Hardacre, Ray Hawkins and later, John Carroll. Unfortunately, the small group dwindled as operations with the 319th and 380th claimed them. Dakeyne and Holohan tossed a coin to see who went with Jack Banks on the Java mission; Dick Dakeyne won and on 11 June Holohan died with the Capt Jim Dienelt crew when 42-40500 *Careless* was shot down into the sea off Koepang by *Ku* 202 *Zekes* led by FCPO Mitsuomi Noda.

Twelve days later Sgt John Graham was killed along with the 319th CO, Capt Roy Olsen and his crew in *Pelly-can* and on

21 November PltOff Keith Bevan died with the Lt Maurice Beller crew when 42-40967 *Black Widow* disintegrated after being hit by A-A fire over Manokwari; a 60 per cent loss rate for those Section 22 members on operations. Dick Dakeyne went on to fly 41 missions over two tours with the 380th before flying with the 90th Bomb. Gp out of Biak and later with 24 Squadron RAAF to war's end.

On 31 May the last of 12 officers and 288 ground personnel had been airlifted to Fenton from Sydney to provide the maintenance and other facilities required to maintain the Group's combat capabilities. The remainder boarded the *Charles P. Steinmetz* on 8 June and sailed for Darwin; the same day as the 380th Bomb. Gp in the NWA was declared fully operational. As if to emphasise their new status, LtCol Miller and Capt Zed Smith went on an armed reconnaissance to Lautem, home base for the 70th DCS *Dinahs* and the 59th *Sentai* Ki-43 *Oscars*, and shipping in Vila Nova harbour on 2 May.

B-24D 42-40496, Juarez Whistle of the 530th Squadron was the first 380th Bomb. Group aircraft fitted with RCM equipment. Sergeant Dick Dakeyne RAAF is standing, second from right. Photo: Dick Dakeyne.

Miller took the Lt Maurice Beller crew in 42-40393 *Black Magic*, whilst Smith took the Capt Charles Sowa crew in 42-40486 *Dis-Gusted*. Over the target they met heavy A-A fire, damaging an engine, hitting bomb racks, puncturing fuel tanks and severing hydraulic lines in Miller's aircraft, whilst Smith was attacked by three 59th *Sentai Oscars* led by the 2nd *Chutai* leader, Capt Shigeo Nango. Both aircraft eventually made it back to Fenton though Smith was forced to belly land *Dis-Gusted* with two punctured main wheel tyres.

It was not a good start to operations by the 380th and the following day Capt Johnson recorded that whilst the 380th

THE HEAVY BOMBERS

wasted no time in commencing operations. "...2 ships of the 380th went out after the convoy this a.m. and got hell shot out of them by Zeros. One ship made [a] belly landing here...They missed the boats." None aboard the aircraft was hurt, though the two aircraft lasted only another seven weeks before they were destroyed in the Japanese raid of 30 June.

In the meantime aircraft and crews of the 529th and 531st Squadrons had moved from Batchelor to Manbulloo west of Katherine, where construction was advanced enough for the units to occupy whilst awaiting the construction of their permanent base at Long Field, east of Fenton. Despite quite primitive conditions Manbulloo did provide several important diversions. "It was located near the Katherine River" the Group's Historian wrote, "...and provided a respite from the heat...the swimming hole was complemented by an unexpected luxury, ICE...Manbulloo also had the distinction of being located near an Australian hospital, complete with female nurses... [who] would provide the men with hours of fanciful diversion."

A gathering at the 380th Bomb. Group camp during the period of operations from Manbulloo. The 529th and 531st Squadrons moved up to Long airfield in late 1943. Photo: Alford/AHSNT Colln.

One of the final missions by the 319th prior to flying jointly with the 380th was a two aircraft strike on a four ship convoy spotted near Timor. Led by Capt Paul Johnson, he and Lt Andrews "...found the convoy. We bombed at 6000' and scored a near miss" Johnson's 2 June diary entry reads, "...6 Zeros intercepted but no damage done. My no. 4 engine cut so we had to fly...back on 3 engines."

In acknowledgment of the importance attached to the floatplane patrols by the Japanese, and particularly in light of the losses to the Beaufighters, Bladin ordered an attack on their base at Taberfane on 22 June. Three B-24s of the 319th attacked the seaplane base at 1500 hours, followed at 1635 hours by nine 31 Squadron Beaufighters.

The 319th B-24s were intercepted by four *Rufes* flown by FCPO Kawaguchi, PO1c Ichikawa, PO3c Inohara and Flyer 1c Yoza and claimed a possible victory; the B-24s returned to Fenton safely though one had two engines damaged. "We [Hesse and Lts Hal Hevener and Alden Currie] arrived at the target just before dusk bombing from low level and strafing too" Hesse recalled, "...Four enemy planes made it into the air, and one was claimed shot down by Currie's crew. Another was destroyed while attempting to take off...Lt. Hevener had two of his engines shot out when he returned to make a second pass at the base. He did a remarkable job of flying...safely back to Darwin...and I made another rough [night] landing."

The Beaufighters claimed four aircraft damaged, two of these on the water, whilst one of the airborne *Petes* flying cover was forced to land. Four *Rufes*, flown by the same pilots, claimed a probable, though two Beaufighters force landed at Milingimbi whilst returning to base.

The following day the 380th personnel arrived in Darwin aboard the *Steinmetz* and after disembarking were transported to Fenton and Manbulloo. While they were being jolted along what was loosely called a highway, Capt Roy Olsen and his crew, including Joe Holohan, in 42-23688 *Pelly-can*, were in dire trouble over Macassar in the Celebes. They were part of a combined 17 aircraft mission covering over 3,540 km to bomb shipping there. Three aircraft including Olsen's, and Lts Sanxter and Wilson, were from the 319th on their last trip before departing Fenton to join the remainder of the 90th Bomb. Gp.

As the B-24s attacked Macassar an obsolescent Mitsubishi B5M1 *Kate 61* landed at nearby Mandai airfield. It was commandeered by Lt Yuji Kino, who with Flyer 2c Tsuro Manabe, took off to intercept the attacking force and on gaining altitude flew directly at Olsen's aircraft, ramming it and taking everyone with it. There were no survivors. But, the day wasn't over for the 319th. Landing back at Fenton, 41-23767, *Chosef* slewed off the runway with a flat tyre stopping opposite the tower with its tail protruding onto the runway. Despite the wreck being lit up, Lt Olan Fleming in 42-40516 *Robbie L* managed to hit *Chosef*, taking the

THE HEAVY BOMBERS

rear fuselage with him as he hurtled off the runway into trees at the side of the strip; two crewmen were injured and *Chosef* served as a source of spares for some time.

Mechanics examine the wreckage of B-24D, 41-23767 Chosef, the morning after Lt Olan Fleming had hit it during a night take off in Robbie L. Photo: Wiley O. Woods.

"Thirty eight tons of bombs, ranging from 2000 pounders to small incendiaries, were dropped in the town, the dock area and the harbour...fires were visible 70 miles away..." reported the 25 June edition of *Army News*. Despite having achieved excellent results over the target, including shipping and buildings it had been an expensive mission for the 319th, with one crew, that of their CO, and three aircraft lost.

On 24 June Hesse and his crew were sent to Sydney on leave. It was the last they saw of Fenton before rejoining the 90th Bomb. Gp at Iron Range. It may have been just as well, as six days later the Japanese raided Fenton destroying another 319th aircraft, 42-40346, *Nobody's Baby*. The Japanese raided Fenton again on 6 July and as it had on 30 June, PltOff John Reen's 319 Radar Station picked up the raiders. Sited north of the airfield overlooking Fenton Creek, the Radar unit proved its worth in picking up the force at 190 kilometres; the 3.7-inch guns of the 133rd HAA Bty sited around the airfield fired 88 rounds and claimed a *Betty* bomber, though only one was downed that day by the Spitfires of 1 Fighter Wing.

The following day the 319th departed Fenton for Iron Range and the 90th Bomb. Gp. In six months of operations in the NWA the unit had flown 238 sorties and claimed 45 enemy aircraft. Two B-24s had been lost on operations, whilst four others had been lost through a variety of causes including *One Time*, lost on its return from a mission.

While the 319th may have missed out on the campaign in the SWPA it had provided valuable service to Bladin and in turn, MacArthur, whilst ensuring the 380th became combat ready in only two months.

With the 319th Squadron gone, the four squadrons of the 380th continued operations from Fenton, Manbulloo and, from October 1943, Long airfield. They flew hundreds of missions against the Japanese in the islands to the north: Macassar, Surabaya, Pomelaa, Lombok, Laha, Langgoer and Ambon but a few and some as far as Balikpapan - a sixteen hour round trip facing A-A and fighter defences to bomb the oil storage facilities there.

The first was in August when the oil refinery was raided over two strikes by a total of 22 aircraft from the 13th; two further aircraft, 42-40489 *Miss Giving* and 42-40512 *She 'Asta* provided post strike photos on the 15th. The first strike involved eleven B-24s staging through Darwin to top up fuel and upload bombs for the long haul. Each aircraft carried 15,900 l of fuel and six 227 kg bombs with a gross take off weight in excess of 29,937 kg. Led by Capt Forrest Lee Brissey of the 531st Squadron in 42-40515 *Sooper Drooper*, the aircraft were assigned a variety of targets including the refinery, lubricating oil plant and shipping.

Two aircraft failed to bomb due to poor weather and another, 42-40369, *Shady Lady,* commanded by Lt Doug Craig was force landed on a salt pan near the old Pago Pago Mission near Drysdale when higher than normal fuel consumption was recorded following a running battle with Japanese fighters. The landing tore away the nose wheel and turret and it was some days before the crew was rescued. The aircraft was repaired and flown out in September; assigned to the Townsville depot it never returned to the 380th.

The success of the raid on the 13th was followed up by eleven aircraft on the 16th/17th though Maj Richard Craig in 42-40504 *Gus's Bus* aborted the mission with a fuel leak and Lt Dexter Baker in 42-40521 *The Golden Goose* was 'weathered out'. Lieutenant Bob Fleming, a 531st Squadron pilot in 42-40526 *Prince Valiant* earned a DFC for nursing his badly damaged aircraft back to Darwin: one engine failed soon after leaving the target and another over Timor whilst a fire burned out the nose area.

The B-24s were lucky. The raid on the 13th saw the 23rd *Koku Sentai* HQ quickly transfer elements of *Ku* 202 to

THE HEAVY BOMBERS

Manggar airfield near Balikpapan; the importance of the reaction to the raid was in sending veteran, LtCdr Minoru Suzuki, as the detachment commander. The move was not a success however; FCPO Takeshi Takahashi was lost whilst intercepting *Miss Giving* on the 15th. Flown by Capt Jack Banks and desperately short of fuel the aircraft just made it back to Fenton before an engine stopped during taxying; 16 hours and 25 minutes after take off. No B-24s were lost on the 16th/17th mission.

The Golden Goose, a B-24D 42-40521 served with the 528th Squadron. Normally flown by Lt Dexter Baker, it was transferred to Townsville after 34 missions. Photo: John Henschke.

The raids achieved their aim. The refinery and oil storage tanks had been damaged, the 12,000 tonne *Katori Maru* had been sunk and other facilities put out of action with no losses by the 380th. But more than the damage caused was the impact the 4,300 kilometre round trips had, not least in drawing fighters from other areas. "Previously 'safe', undefended areas would now have to be protected" the 380th Historian wrote, "...A/A defences and fighter units were [subsequently] pulled out of New Guinea to help protect these important targets. Some pressure had been taken off MacArthur's forces...Following the August raids the 380th noticed a marked change in shipping in the Flores Sea area. The Japanese no longer used large vessels...the [Flying] Circus was able to sink 30,000 tons of shipping with no loss to themselves..."

The strikes had been a remarkable feat and a Presidential Unit Citation was recommended by both MacArthur and Gen George C. Kenney. Congratulations by AVM Adrian 'King' Cole, who had taken over from Bladin in July, and under whose control the 380th fell, were also received. The Australian Governor General, Lord Gowrie, also praised the work of the military in the NWA during a visit in

August. "The Allied Air Forces have struck continually at the enemy wherever he could be reached" the 19 August edition of *Army News* reported, "By their aggressive action they have greatly delayed the consolidation of the enemy's gains and compelled him to keep many of his aircraft out of the vital battles now being waged..."

Officers of Ku 202 photographed in 1943. The unit CO, Cdr Motoharu Okamura is in white uniform whilst LtCdr Minoru Suzuki is seated fourth from right, second row. Photo: Alford Colln.

The 380th continued operations over the last half of 1943. Kendari, Penfoie, Babo and Surabaya were all struck with the aircraft staging through Corunna Downs for the longer missions. They were not without loss however. The 531st Squadron lost its new CO, Capt Howard Merkel, on 10 July when 59th *Sentai Oscars* downed 42-40507 *Esmeralda II* and the Lt Francis McDowell crew aboard 42-40292 *Miss Mary* disappeared somewhere on the long flight between Babo and Manbulloo the same day. They were never located.

Others effectively brought disaster upon themselves and took the lives of others with them. Lieutenant Hugh Parris was one. Shortly after its arrival at the 530th Squadron, 42-40509 *Nothing Sacred* was assigned as part of a combined nine aircraft 529th and 530th Squadron mission to attack the Japanese-held aerodrome at Langgoer in the Kai Islands on 21 September. *Nothing Sacred* under Lt Hugh Parris was assigned to fly on the mission commander, Maj A. J. Bratton's starboard wing; Parris was flying his first mission.

The aircraft reached the target area, but heavy cloud forced them to make a second bombing approach. They were intercepted by *Zekes* of *Ku* 202 and Parris had one engine shot out. Parris released his bomb load and rejoined the lead formation to support the following two flights. The

THE HEAVY BOMBERS

Japanese continued to attack the formation with the six *Zekes* and two Ki-45 *Nicks* of the 5th *Sentai* from Langgoer. One 530th aircraft, 42-40532, *Little Joe*, piloted by Lt Wilbur Morris was severely damaged and crash landed on a coral reef some eighteen kilometres from Langgoer. One crew member died as a result of the crash and the remainder spent the rest of the war as POWs.

The remaining eight aircraft headed for Australia. Bratton ordered any damaged aircraft to land at Darwin, whilst others were to return to Fenton. "Eight Liberators returned to Australia where another of their number crashed three miles short of the Fenton runway" the 380th Historian wrote, "The doomed plane was *Nothing Sacred*, flown by Hugh Parris' rookie crew. In his inexperience, Parris had elected not to land at Darwin, but to continue on to Fenton. The decision cost ten men their lives. Only the photographer, S/Sgt. Frank McGarry, survived, for he jumped just before impact. This desperate act cost him both his legs..." The wreckage of *Nothing Sacred* lies in the bed of a seasonal creek west of the former 530th Squadron camp.

Four crews were lost over the last months of 1943, three of them on operations: the Capt John A. Farrington crew off the Celebes on 26 October, with seven of the crew taken prisoner; the crew of Lt Fred Hinze in 42-40518 *Golden Gator* off Timor the same day, with four crew rescued; and the Lt Maurice Beller crew with RAAF RCM operator PltOff Keith Bevan aboard on 21 November.

The remains of B-24D 42-41242 the morning after the crash on 11 November 1943. The eleven man Lt Wilfred L. Grenfel crew died in the inferno. Photo: John Henschke.

The fourth took the Lt Wilfred L. Grenfel crew of eleven in a fiery crash north of Fenton on 11 November when their new B-24D-150-CO, 42-41242, slammed into the ground and exploded following an engine fire shortly after take off. Four others were killed when 42-24248 *Alley Oop* snagged a tree in a night landing at Fenton after dropping AVM Cole off at Batchelor. Colonel Edward F. Shepherd, Capt Samuel S. Poor of the Standard and Poor financial house and two crew members, Raymond E. Siple and T/Sgt Clifford D. Cater perished in the crash.

The 529th and 531st Squadrons moved from Manbulloo to their new permanent base at Long airfield in early October after advance parties had managed to provide facilities prior to the move. When the "...main echelons arrived... they found showers, mess halls, administrative buildings, tent sites and a veritable minimum of chaos", the historian noted. "Long was about as good as you could make it in the under-supplied, gruesome Australian northwest," he continued, "...otherwise it was just a routine base, paralleling...Fenton... [but] By the side of other bases, Long Strip was paradise..."

In December the 380th had a respite of sorts when 24 aircraft were detached to Dobodura to cover MacArthur's landings at Cape Gloucester, Arawe and Saidoor. Before making the long flight the Group was assigned a strike by Cole to maintain the pressure on the Japanese to tie up their resources in strengthening the NEI. With an eye on the gathering monsoon Cole selected Koepang in light of its relatively close proximity to Darwin, and, mindful of it's A-A defences and some 21 *Zekes* of *Ku* 202 based there, ordered a 27 aircraft strike for 3 December.

On the morning of the 3rd Capt Bill Shek flew a weather reconnaissance, however he developed engine trouble and aborted. Of the aircraft assigned the mission, three aborted whilst the remainder, each armed with five 227 kg bombs to improve manoeuvrability in the event of interception, along with extra ammunition, flew on. Poor weather over the target saw Penfoie also 'weathered in' and instead the force flew west to Soemba and bombed Waingapoe destroying most of the buildings and town around the jetty. All returned safely, but the mission emphasised the value of obtaining reliable weather information. Three days later the assigned aircraft departed for New Guinea.

Operations from Fenton and Long recommenced on 2 January 1944 with "...an uneventful strike on the nickel mines at Pomelaa, followed by missions to Waingapoe and Tenau over the following two days." Despite these

THE HEAVY BOMBERS

uneventful trips January proved the worst month for losses by the 380th for the war, with the loss of seven aircraft and 59 aircrew members, seven of them as POWs.

February was better, statistically at least. The Group completed 121 missions over 1,638 combat hours, losing two aircraft, one of them 42-73126 *Foil Proof Mary*, when it crash landed on Croker Island, and claiming one enemy fighter. The figures for May confirmed 246 missions over 3,065.35 combat hours. Some 232,920 kg of bombs were dropped and four enemy aircraft claimed for the loss of one B-24, 42-41117 and the Lt Roy Parker crew – including the RAAF co-pilot, FltLt N. T. Badger – on the 8th. During the period 9 May 1943 to 31 May 1944 the Group flew over 2,500 sorties against Japanese targets throughout the region.

A second Presidential Unit Citation was awarded to the 380th for sustained attacks against a range of targets including the air bases at Babo, Manokwari, Jefman on Dutch New Guinea and the Kamiri and Nambar airfields on Noemfoor Island. As a result the enemy's striking power was drastically curtailed and resistance at Wadke and Biak effectively reduced. The period detailed in the Citation was from 20 April to 17 May and the aircrew were quick to compliment the tireless ground crews and their efforts in maintaining the aircraft.

"Ask a pilot who the most important man on his crew is and don't be surprised if he tells you his crew chief, a ground man" the Group historian wrote, "With his crew of mechanics, this man keeps this airplane flying...No less diligent are the mechanics whose day [sic] depends on what needs to be done. Eight hours?...Sixteen sometimes... his life overseas is spent at the line. He gets back to camp to eat and usually to sleep. He might see a movie once every two weeks. Most of the time he's working." There were occasions though when the USO shows featuring well known actors and actresses, comedians and singers toured the bases to provide a brief moment of sanity for ground and air crews alike. Gary Cooper, Phyllis Brooks, John Wayne, Jerry Cologna and Bob Hope, among others, helped ease the boredom, routine and terror faced by the youngsters on an almost daily basis.

There were other compensations, particularly for the Americans and any Australians serving with them: the regular 'fat cat' supply flights to southern capitals to stock up on small luxuries – ice cream, foodstuffs, alcohol (including the brandy and whisky dispensed to aircrews returning from missions) and other necessities to sustain life. Even these flights were not without their dramas however.

Entertainment provided an important outlet for men serving in the Northern Territory. John Wayne and Phyllis Brooks (left) put on a show at Fenton, 8 January 1944. Photo: John Henschke.

Major Everett Ware flew 42-40491 *Poochie* south in July 1943 and laden with goods became lost on the return trip. Short of fuel he landed on the Daly River floodplains and with the necessities of life on hand he and his crew awaited rescue. It wasn't long coming and a flare was sent up, only to land in the grass, start a fire and burn out the aircraft. Ware was sent back to the USA, and the members of an Australian patrol enjoyed the task of salvaging and consuming the remaining luxuries. In August 1944 Lt Herb Woodward loaded up with groceries, soft drinks and alcohol in Adelaide, took off and pulled a tight turn over the suburbs, ejecting the lot. *Bomb-Bay Door Falls From American Plane, Bomber Drops Liquor & Eggs on Adelaide, Narrow Escapes* and *Eggs Near Fowlyard* the headlines of the of the 23 August edition of the *Advertiser* raged.

One of the 380th's 'fat cats' was a war weary B-25D, 41-30222, formerly *Hawgmouth* flown in New Guinea by Lt Raymond Geer of the 500th Squadron, the "Rough Raiders" of the 345th Bomb. Gp. Later 'acquired' by the 380th, she was flown to Adelaide by Capt Vince Morobito in January 1945 with Lt Jim Johnston as navigator and three crew members. On the return trip on the 25th they became lost north of Alice Springs, and short of fuel landed in the Tanami Desert after radioing their position.

It was a good landing and with 1,361 kg of stores including foodstuffs, beer and champagne aboard they would want

THE HEAVY BOMBERS

for nothing. They set up camp chairs, rigged a shelter and awaited whatever might come their way. It wasn't long coming; a 380th B-24 dropped supplies that evening and they were rescued the following morning. The aircraft remained in the Tanami until the 1970s when it was recovered and displayed in Darwin.

"They set up camp chairs... and awaited whatever might come their way." The crew of B-25 41-30222 await rescue following their forced landing in the Tanami Desert. Photo: Jim Johnston.

The one enduring mystery was that of 42-40387, *Beautiful Betsy* only a month after Vince Morobito's adventure. One of the original 380th aircraft to fly to Australia, 'Betsy' had flown 24 missions before being overstressed during a mission to Rabaul. Retired from combat as a result she was used in trials to insert 'Z' unit operatives behind enemy lines and following this *Betsy* was retained by the 528th Squadron as a 'fat cat' aircraft.

It was in this role that she took off under the command of Lt William McDaniel on 26 February 1945 and simply disappeared. Despite extensive searches no trace of the aircraft or crew were found. Aboard were McDaniel, Lts E. A. Kilcheski, J. W. Owen and H. E. Routt, TSgts R. L. Tucker and H. A. Lemons, along with two RAF pilots, FltLt T. J. D. Cook and FlgOff R. A. A. Cannon as passengers; Cannon was heading to Brisbane for his wedding.

Over the years, many supposed sightings were recorded, aircraft wreckage reported, personal effects jettisoned from other aircraft located and false leads followed up. All kept the mystery of *Beautiful Betsy* alive, until July 1994 when a Park Ranger, Mark Roe, found aircraft wreckage in the Kroombit Tops National Park in Queensland. *Beautiful Betsy* was a mystery no more. After 49 years the American authorities were able to confirm the fate of the aircraft and those on board. The families of those crew members at last knew the fate of their relatives; many still await some news of loved ones missing from the war years, swallowed by the bush or the sea.

Following successes in the Admiralty Islands and with signs of a weakening Japanese presence on western New Guinea MacArthur issued orders for landings at Hollandia and Aitape. It was a bold move questioned by some, but it was successful and with the April 1944 capture of Hollandia, landings at Aitape and the elimination of much of the Japanese air threat in New Guinea, the 380th concentrated on attacking distant targets including airfields and seaports.

In support of the operation, and under directions from General Kenney, the RAAF's focus remained on targets closer to home, though the Catalinas of 11, 20 and 43 Squadrons were utilised in long range attacks on shipping and mining enemy held harbours at Balikpapan, along with those at Manokwari, Kaimana and Sorong in Dutch New Guinea. All were carried out without any fighter protection in the face of renewed defensive measures by the Japanese; General Kenney's 5th Air Force fighters were well beyond their range.

The 380th's role also changed during March and April, when Australian crews began flying with the Group. With the RAAF gearing up for the introduction of its own heavy bomber force the intention was to have some 20 crews each of ten men fly with the 380th following flying time on B-24s with the 5th Air Force in New Guinea. It was a situation advantageous to both the Americans and Australians: on the one hand the 380th was receiving regular replacements whilst the RAAF crews were gaining valuable experience on type.

Among the first to fly a mission with the 380th were the crews of FltLts John Napier and Dick Overhue flying with the 529th Squadron: a raid on Kamiri airfield on Noemfoor Island on 24 April. The B-24s bombed from 12,000 ft with unobserved results and Capt Virgil Stevens of the 529th Squadron decided to take a closer look at 2,000 ft. This was followed up by low level strafing runs, during which a number of enemy aircraft were destroyed by the five aircraft in Stevens' flight. Napier was forced to fly home on three engines but all returned safely.

THE HEAVY BOMBERS

Whilst the Group Commander, LtCol Brissey, was most displeased with the risk in strafing at low level and made Stevens well aware of his ire, a visiting General had decorations handed out instead. Stevens received a DFC and Silver Star, Napier a DFC and Overhue a Bar to his; each of their crewmen was awarded a U.S. Air Medal. A signal from Cole the following day, Anzac Day for the Australians, read, "Heartiest congratulations to all concerned on your excellent operation yesterday. Your strafing activities, which would have done credit to a fighter squadron, are particularly meritorious. Well done indeed!"

The introduction of RAAF crews to the four squadrons of the 380th continued as they came from the 5th Air Force training centres and they integrated well into the American system. It wasn't to last more than a few months however as the RAAF was beginning to see the results of moves initiated as far back as December 1941 in gaining a heavy bomber force.

Beautiful Betsy was retired from operations and was later used in trials to insert Z Special Unit operatives behind enemy lines. Used as a 'Fat Cat', she disappeared on 26 February 1945. Photo: Alford Colln.

CHAPTER 11

LIBERATORS
The RAAF gets seven league boots

On 19 December 1941 the ACH Controller at Halong on Ambon, WgCdr E. D. Scott, had signalled RAAF HQ that it "...would be preferable if large aircraft of the B-17 type or preferably the B-24 could be acquired or borrowed by the RAAF for offensive action against the Japanese...at the moment absolutely nothing can be done in the Ambon area to interfere with the Japanese plans...for an offensive drive into the eastern portion of the Netherlands [East] Indies...it is urgently recommended that B-17 aircraft be placed under the control of ACH Ambon forthwith, and that as a subsequent consolidation of an offensive policy, steps should be taken to acquire long range (not less than 2,000 nautical miles) heavy bombers for employment by the RAAF."

Unfortunately Scott was forced to rely on the Hudsons for any offensive operations in those early days, with the European Theatre soaking up the available resources. It was a further fifteen months before Dr H. V. Evatt travelled to America to further discuss proposals he had communicated to President Roosevelt regarding the allocation of aircraft to the RAAF. None additional to those already allocated, some 475 of all types, were available from the 1943 production lines however. AM Sir Richard Williams was, however, able to obtain an undertaking by Roosevelt that he would give the matter his personal attention in early 1944.

Other political games were being played out at the time. General Kenney, no doubt with a keen eye on bolstering his own 5th Air Force command, supported an Australian proposal for seven squadrons of heavy bombers for the RAAF, however he apparently "...showed little inclination to assist...by providing A/C from his own increased resources", a January 1944 summary by the RAF reported.

Sir Charles Portal, the British CAS objected to the Australian proposal, stating that he would not release Australian aircrews or aircraft, and that they should fulfil their commitment to the European Theatre via the EATS. At the time Australian aircrews were contributing far in excess of expectations and with disproportionate losses, Portal's statement was at best ignorant of the situation in the Pacific - and this is doubtful - or at worst, self serving. In the event, AM Sir Richard Williams was able to arrange the release of RAAF crews to ferry any forthcoming Liberators from the USA to Australia.

Air Vice Marshal George Jones was also lobbying, but with a different approach, contending that the lack of heavy bombers was having an effect on morale within the RAAF. Most of the spectacular attacks were being made by the 5th Air Force and all the publicity was going their way, he commented. But, at a conference on 5 January he contended that in relation to the allocation of Liberators, "... great difficulty was experienced in obtaining any assurance that these would be provided. Both...Kenney and AM Sir William Walsh [RAF] were prepared to support our bid, but... [had] to make a strong case in support of their own requirements. It was finally agreed that we should receive 150 B-24s (Liberators) spread over the period July to December 1944, and in addition we should receive immediately 6 part-used Liberators from the 5th Air Force in Australia..."

A war weary B-24, 42-40512 She'Asta, flew 35 missions with the 530th Squadron 380th Bomb. Group before being assigned to the RAAF as A72-5. Photo: Alford/AHSNT Colln.

Thus through the intervention of Roosevelt, Williams, Evatt and Jones the RAAF received the Liberators; Jones' comment regarding the "...6 part-used Liberators...", saw the arrival of war weary aircraft straight from the bottom of Kenney's barrel. However it was a start and the RAAF eventually received 286 Liberators under the A72- serial range; 13 of them transferred from the 5th Air Force. The first batch to arrive was a mixed bag of veterans formerly flown by the 43rd, 90th or 380th Bomb. Gps. One, 42-40512, She 'Asta, had previously been flown by RAAF pilot, FlgOff Ed Crabtree, whilst serving with the 380th. One of the original Group aircraft, She 'Asta had flown 35 missions and the others had similar histories.

Ed Crabtree had been among the first four RAAF pilots to fly with the 380th. As early as August 1943 the Australians

LIBERATORS

had begun to fly as co-pilots on the B-24s and over nine months flew on operations to the Celebes, Ceram, Aru Islands and Balikpapan, before being posted south to 7 OTU at Tocumwal as instructors.

"Australians have been selected to fly Liberator bombers..." the 26 February 1944 edition of *Army News* reported, "...the men are on tip-toe with keen-ness to show what they can do in the Liberators...and are confident they will add to the outstanding record the RAAF has gained in other planes overseas and in Australia."

Whilst some Australians began training on Liberators at the huge base at Tocumwal in southern NSW, others were given instruction at the American CRTC at Nadzab or Port Moresby flying missions either with the 90th or 43rd Bomb. Gps there. Flying conditions were made to conform as closely as possible to combat situations; including the tropical weather patterns that could see cumulus and its inherent dangers as high as 35,000 ft and nil visibility though the mountainous terrain.

Flight Lieutenant 'Mick' Jacques, a highly experienced 22-year old RAAF pilot, recalled his instructor at CRTC was a "...brand new shave tail straight from the states, [*sic*] with... about 300 hours in his log book. I forget who was...more surprised when we discovered he was to teach me how to fly heavies. We...had loads of fun learning... [and] our crews all graduated with no casualties... We are all due to go south after doing about 15 missions each."

From the training centres, many RAAF crews were posted to the newly forming squadrons, of 82 Wing. Numbers 21, 23 and 24 Squadrons were to make up the Wing with their operational debuts projected as December 1944, March 1945 and August 1944 respectively. Number 24 Squadron was operational a month ahead of expectations, while 21 and 23 were a month behind. Numbers 12, 25, 99 and 102 Squadrons became operational between February and May 1945. Along with 200 and 201 Flights they formed 85 Wing, which formed in July that year.

A new B-24J of the RAAF's 7 OTU on a training flight from Tocumwal in southern NSW. Photo: Jack Fox.

LIBERATORS

More than forty crews completed their training with the USAAF, including WgCdr Derek Kingwell, who became the CO of 82 Wing, Arch Dunne an ex-Hudson pilot of 13 Squadron and WgCdr John 'Long John' Hampshire, who became CO 24 Squadron. Ground crews also received their training under the 5th Air Force Service Command and though they had experience with the Pratt and Whitney R-1830 engines, the weaponry, turrets, hydraulic, fuel and power systems, superchargers, control rigging and a host of intricate operations particular to the Liberators had to be learned.

Those Australians posted to the 380th were involved in flying combat missions virtually from the day they arrived. They flew as complete crews or as part of American crews to Dili, Java, Langgoer, and as far as Borneo. Then FltLt, Dick Overhue's crew included FSgt Les McDonald, a Flight Engineer; both flew with the 529th Squadron from Long airfield and McDonald's log book details more than 45 sorties together, ten of them strike missions. One, a 9 May strike on Langgoer by six aircraft was flown by Overhue in B-24J 42-73113, *Big Ass Bird*; McDonald succinctly recorded the events of the mission as "Bombs on dispersal area. Fired 300 rds. No interception. Heavy Ack Ack."

'Tommy' Thompson a 528th Squadron flight leader recalled flying with RAAF pilot he was to check out. "We did a couple of circuits and landings before I handed over to him...he 'greased' that B-24 onto the runway and just kept the nose up instead of lowering it on [to] the nose wheel...I couldn't understand it until the aircraft just slowed down on its own...without him even touching the brakes – then he put it down on the nose wheel. He just used the wing and flaps instead...and I was supposed to be checking this guy out! I was very impressed – and I learned something along the way."

The Australians fitted in well with the Americans and when they began to leave in late 1944 one unit historian wrote that during the time the Australians "...flew with us they achieved a personal popularity that was remarkable. Living...and flying together has made the military alliance between our countries...a very real and personal thing...We regretted losing the three crews but have already become fond of the three...that were sent to replace them."

In fact the 380th lost one Australian crew, that of FlgOff A. L. Harrison on 29 October 1944. Flying 42-110120, *Sleepy*

Time Gal, Harrison radioed that he was having fuel transfer problems and had lost one engine. A second call confirmed problems with a second engine north of Timor; nothing further was heard of aircraft or crew.

With Liberators reaching the RAAF in sufficient numbers, squadrons were advised of postings to the NWA. The first was 24 Squadron under WgCdr Hampshire, which flew its aircraft from Amberley to Manbulloo between 8 June and 6 July before moving to their new base at Fenton.

The 380th Bomb. Gp had been advised of a move a month earlier when the Fifth Bomber Command signalled that the Group was "...to move from Fenton to RAAF aerodrome Darwin earliest. As and when operational commitments permit. Attached RAAF personnel to move with squadrons concerned. Advise date move will commence..." Pending any move the Group was assigned a number of missions including Namlea and support of the invasion of Noemfoor. By June the New Guinea campaign was almost over and MacArthur was preparing for his much vaunted return to the Philippines. He planned to leave the 380th in the NWA to continue to harass the Japanese in the Timor-Ceram-Celebes-Amboina areas, and with the RAAF coming on line with its Liberators the Group was assigned to the RAAF Station in Darwin as part of his overall strategy.

The 530th departed Fenton in early July followed by HQ a week later. The 529th and 531st vacated Long in early August and the 528th joined them at the dustbowl camp on McMillans Road north of the airfield on the 22nd. After almost two years the four squadrons were operating as an entity for the first time since leaving America. One of their last jobs was that of a continuing threat posed by the large coastal defence guns on Lombok Island overlooking Lombok Strait.

The U.S. Navy had requested they be destroyed to protect its submarines and target photographs were obtained by a four aircraft element of the 530th Squadron under Capt Forrest 'Tommy' Thompson on 5 January. This was followed up by a 12 aircraft strike on the 7th, and of the ten aircraft that reached the target, their 454 kg bombs, caused only minimum damage. A follow up raid the next day put the guns out of commission and the navy sent a coded congratulatory message to the 380th: "Nice work making the pigs grunt at Hogcaller X. Please express the gratitude of all submariners to all concerned for their part in discouraging them from putting their snout in our trough."

LIBERATORS

A line up of 529th Squadron B-24s at RAAF Station shortly after the 380th Bomb. Group's move to Darwin. Aircraft 42-73134 "Milady" is at right. Photo: John Henschke.

The Group commenced a move further north, to the Philippines, in February 1945, after having dropped some 422 tonnes of bombs each month. The departure of the Group left the RAAF to maintain the heavy bombing role against the Japanese.

In all 53 aircraft were lost by the 380th Bomb. Gp during its service in the NWA, whilst 289 aircrew, some of them RAAF members, lost their lives in combat or accident. Twenty three 380th personnel were captured and served as Prisoners of War – four were interrogated, beaten and executed.

Not all losses were as a result of combat or operational accidents. In early 1945 combat operations were reduced pending their move to the Philippines, however training was maintained to provide crews with the skills they needed in combat. There were also pitfalls: training accidents were rare but when they struck they took valuable personnel with them.

On the morning of 17 January 1945 Lieutenant Bobby Neal and a crew of five climbed aboard 42-73134 "Milady" to

carry out a practice bombing mission over Quail Island southwest of Darwin. Less than two hours later they lay dead among the wreckage of the aircraft only minutes from Darwin. The circumstances of "Milady"'s crash remain conjecture. Some say it was due to the blast effect of the bombs and others maintain that Lt Neal was 'buzzing' the coast at low level when he became disoriented and crashed.

"Milady" had flown over 50 missions with the 531st Squadron. Lieutenant William Zagrobski and his crew flew her regularly during her early days and it was on a mission over Ambon on 19 January 1944 that ""Milady"'s" waist gunner, Staff Sergeant Peter Parlo, shot down a 934th *Ku Rex* flown by FCPO Sadayoshi Yokata. In a long running battle with the Japanese fighters including Ki-45 *Nick* aircraft of the 5th *Sentai*, two other 380th Bomb. Gp B-24s were shot down.

Four members of Lt Harold Van Wormer's crew in 42-73187 *Paper Doll* were killed and seven taken prisoner after crashing into the sea following an attack by a *Nick* flown by Lt Totaro Ito. They were interned at the notorious

LIBERATORS

Tan Toey POW camp on Ambon. Lieutenant Gorman Smith ditched his aircraft, 42-73117, *Doodlebug*, near Seroea Island, losing six crew members - the remaining five were rescued by a RAAF Catalina, A24-32 of 43 Squadron. Staff Sergeant William G. Benshoff was among those killed: he was flying his last mission before returning home. Almost exactly twelve months later, on 17 January 1945, "*Milady*" crashed, taking her crew of Lt Bobby Neal. The wreckage remains on Cox Peninsula west of Darwin.

The wreckage of 42-73134 "Milady" on Cox Peninsula. Photo: Eric Lundberg.

Allied pilots also came to grief during training. Flying Officer A. K. Kelly of 452 Squadron was flying practice intercepts in A58-435 when he miscalculated his closing speed and collided with No. 1 engine of 42-73116, *Heavenly Body*, flown by Lt John DiDomenico on 18 September 1944. The impact sheared off the propeller of the B-24 and the port wing of Kelly's aircraft. Kelly had no chance of getting out and the Spitfire went into the sea about one mile west of Cape Van Diemen. A pilots' knee pad, reportedly belonging to a Spitfire, was all that was recovered.

The 380th Bomb. Gp continued flying missions from Darwin and still with RAAF crews, flying 260 sorties to year's end, though a number were aborted and some aircraft returned their bombs to base. One mission, on 9 September, was described in the Bombing Evaluation Report as "...one of the most successful this Group has had for some time...a total of 230 x 500# [lb bombs] were carried...and expended as follows:
528 - 60 x 500# on Target...LETEKER AIRDROME
529 – 50 x 500# on Target...TOEAL TOWN
530 – 60 x 500# on Target...LANGGOER AIRDROME

531 – 60 x 500# on Target...FAAN AIRDROME
230 x 500#..."

The Group began its move to Murtha Field on Luzon early in the New Year and by 6 March 1945 they were gone, bringing an end to 22 months of combat operations in the NWA and New Guinea campaigns.

Those Australians who had remained with the Group were transferred to the RAAF units, which had moved into Fenton and Long airfields. The aircraft and personnel of 24 Squadron had moved up to Fenton on 1 September 1944 taking up residence in the former 528th Squadron camp; 82 Wing HQ was sited on the hilltop along with the quarters of the Group CO, GpCapt Kingwell, though the unit was placed under the control of the 380th Bomb. Gp.

The squadron flew its first operational mission from the new base on the 9th though the first combat mission by a RAAF B-24 squadron had been flown a month earlier when FltLt M. D. Frecker and his crew in A72-41 carried out a sortie to the Banda Islands where bombing and strafing runs were made against a Japanese vessel. The vessel returned fire, killing the rear gunner and Lancaster veteran, FlgOff B. J. Middleton; he was buried at Adelaide River the following day, 7 August. On 24 August FltLt J. A. Carrigan and his crew were on a search mission when they sighted a five vessel convoy. Climbing to 10,000 ft they dropped eight bombs, scoring direct hit on the largest, a 6,000 ton vessel, leaving it smoking.

In September 24 Squadron joined the 380th Bomb. Gp on missions with a substantial number of aircraft flown by RAAF personnel; one combined operation saw 14 of 21 aircraft manned by Australians.

The first aircraft lost by the squadron was A72-39 on 7 September, when FltLt C. E. Parsons lost control of the aircraft after a tyre burst shortly after landing at Fenton. Hitting a ditch opposite the control tower the port undercarriage collapsed and the aircraft was damaged beyond repair; none of the crew was injured.

The squadron and RAAF Liberator force lost its first crew on operations when PltOff K. H. Richards and his crew in A72-70 were downed by the accurate A-A fire of the Cape Chater Bty on 23 January 1945. The loss was particularly unfortunate: Richards had only recently been promoted

LIBERATORS

in order to receive the DFC and was due to fly south on a week's leave for the investiture.

The second of the RAAF B-24 squadrons to arrive in the NWA was 21 Squadron, also assigned to the control of the 380th Bomb. Gp, which arrived from Leyburn in Queensland in three elements. An advance party under WgCdr Peter Parker arrived at Fenton on 27 October and by 23 December the last of the ground parties arrived at their camp in the former 530th area east of the 24 Squadron site. It was not until 3 January 1945 that the aircraft arrived under SqnLdr Ivor Black and one week later he led the squadron's first mission, a bombing raid on Laga in Portuguese Timor in A72-53, during which FltLt T. Duigan took A72-55 down to low level and strafed a radio station on Moena Island.

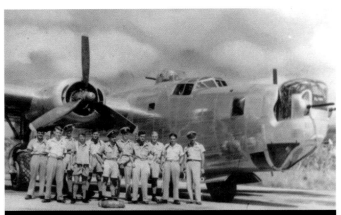

The FltLt Roger Court crew in front of B-24 A72-84 Cock O'The North at Fenton, January 1945. Court is fourth from right, whilst the bomb aimer, PltOff Russ Brooks is at right. Photo: Russ Brooks.

Number 82 Wing was declared operational on 11 January, though it was a further three months before 23 Squadron joined the Wing, at Long airfield in April. The following day, FltLt Roger Court of 24 Squadron, flying his third mission, scored the first 'victory' for the Wing in strafing a 110 tonne vessel and setting it on fire. After battling a tropical storm and flying at 1,000 ft, there "...was a 'sugar dog', a Japanese vessel...camouflaged with netting and coconut fronds. Our bomb aimer Rus [sic] Brooks tried to set up his equipment... but each time we made a bombing run the ship would quickly change course...I told him to forget the bombing, and...diving to line up with the ship at 100 ft, I instructed the gunners to fire when ready. At that height I could see that they were loaded with drums of fuel and supplies and the crew [were] diving for cover... We left the ship well alight. Total [flying] time was 12 hours 30 minutes..."

Three weeks later the vagaries of the monsoon season struck as veteran ex-Hudson pilot, FltLt Arthur Cambridge, was returning to Fenton from a shipping strike in near cyclonic conditions on 3 February. He missed the flarepath in poor visibility and attempted another circuit, however fuel pressure on engines 1 and 3 dropped to Zero. Power was increased on No. 4 to maintain height, however the aircraft, A72-88, crashed through trees west of the airfield. The impact ruptured the APU fuel tank and the aircraft nose area caught fire, trapping FltLt J. R. Parkinson and FlgOff J. M. Pitt. They had no chance of escape and were killed whilst the remaining crew members, one seriously injured, managed to exit the wreckage. Pitt and Parkinson were buried at Adelaide River the following day.

The wreckage of B-24 Liberator A72-88 of 24 Squadron following its crash west of Fenton on 3 February. Photo: AHSNT Colln.

Only a fortnight earlier FltLt Court and his crew including bomb aimer PltOff Russ Brooks had flown low level practice bombing sorties in the same aircraft over the period 21-25 January in rehearsing for a very low level strike on a target they had yet to briefed on: the Siman and Mendalan power houses at Kali Konto on Java. Other crews involved in the planned mission to destroy the facilities were those of WgCdr R. E. Bell, SqnLdr A. W. Nichols and FltLts W. W. Kirkwood, R. Court and E. V. Ford.

Mosquito aircraft of 87 (PR) Squadron flew reconnaissance missions over the area as part of the planning for the mission, though weather conditions precluded any reliable photographs. The strike went ahead and five aircraft flew from Fenton to Truscott on 26 January, where "...our 5 crews were surprised that [GpCapt] Kingwell was there before us..." one crewman commented. The following day the six aircraft departed Truscott in "Formation low level – 6 x 500lb M.C.

LIBERATORS

[bombs]", PltOff E. C. R. Russ Brooks' log book recorded, "... Ceiling zero ft. at target – bombs jettisoned at sea..."

The two aircraft of Kingwell and Kirkwood had taken off earlier and made it through to the target; though damaged in the attack the power houses were still operational. That did not deter the media who made much of this first raid. The 15 May 1945 edition of *Wings* described the attack in detail, "...Climbing as they neared the target area the two Liberators...quickly picked up their targets. Twenty minutes later South East Java's electric light and power supply had been blacked out by 21 members of the RAAF..."

An attempt to complete the job was made by Bell, Nichols, Court and Ford on 5 February. Flying A72-84 *Cock O'The North*, Court recalled flying in "...loose formation to conserve our energy and eventually reached the point where we had to reduce our height to get under their radar. Now at 10 ft above sea level...we closed in to a tighter formation... the weather was in our favour [and] as we approached the coast...we broke formation and proceeded to the target independently, some 50 ft above sea level..."

Arriving over the target at 1,200 ft Court identified the power house and could "...see billowing smoke from the bombs dropped by the aircraft ahead of me..." After bombing he pulled into a tight climbing turn and could "... see that our bombs had gone right through the target and onto the penstocks with [a] large fountain of water gushing out." After evading an enemy aircraft which dropped a phosphorous bomb, Court and the others made it safely back to Truscott.

Three days later they again flew to Java and the power houses. This time the destruction was complete and it was recognised as the most successful of the three missions. The Siman power station was hit by the Bell and Ford crews while Nichols and Court, again in A72-84, attacked the Mendalan facility. "Bombing at 1200' – 6 x 500lb bombs..." Russ Brooks' log book reads, "Destroyed transformers and workshop – intercepted by 2 *Oscar*s – 2 phosphorous bombs dropped by *Oscar* – 3 C. of P. attacks made – Nil damage." The destruction at Siman also put that facility out of action. The crews had proved the capability of the Liberator in low level bombing and had the satisfaction of a job very well done; and that's all they got. "I was always disappointed that the 4 successful skippers...and their Bombardiers [*sic*] were not decorated for the destruction of Siman and Mendalin [*sic*]," one 24 Squadron crewman commented.

The final mission against the Mendalan and Siman power stations on 8 February 1945 put them both out of action. The B-24's capability in low level attacks was proven as a result. Photo: Russ Brooks.

The raids had also proved the usefulness of a new navigational aid, **Lo**ng **Ra**nge **N**avigation, or Loran. Developed by American scientists in collaboration with the UK and the forerunner of Australia's CSIRO (CSIR), the system relied on pulse transmissions from ground stations with the time intervals between transmission and reception measured and converted to distances to give an aircraft's position.

In December 1943 MacArthur had directed, via his staff, that three triangulating ground stations be established in the NWA. After surveys had been completed the proposed sites were Sir Graham Moore Island north of Truscott airfield, Champagny Island northwest of Broome and Bathurst Island north of Darwin. From January 1944 work on planning and establishment of the stations progressed quickly and the Bathurst Island facility at Point Fawcett (Wiyapurali) was completed in October that year and manned by American communications personnel. The others were also completed and each was provided a 'key' or station number – Bathurst Island was assigned 160, Sir Graham Moore 161 and Champagny Island 162. A monitoring station at Drysdale Mission was assigned key number 163.

RAAF navigators on B-24s at Fenton and 7 OTU Tocumwal, were receiving instruction on the new system and whilst AN/APN-4 Loran sets were fitted to a number of aircraft the stations had to be completed before it could be used. Some didn't bother using them even when they became operational, relying instead on the tried and true 'dead reckoning' method; surprisingly, the 380th Bomb. Gp knew only of its existence. "We never used LORAN and none of our aircraft were equipped with a set..." one 380th navigator, Ted Williams, recalled, "I remember that there were lectures given...concerning LORAN with the promise that we would have it soon...some of the later navigators [said] that they never used celestial [navigation]...because LORAN was so much easier."

Flying Officer Harry Seymour, the navigator on FltLt Roger Court's crew, remembered that Loran was of "...great use on trips to Java and the Celebes. The raids on the power stations at Siman and Mendalan were able to use LORAN to maintain track to East Java before turning and diving below radar at Medan to the target at low level... [LORAN] was nice to have around...as I can vouch for having it there even then was a great help keeping us away from storms while turning to be identified..." The crew's bomb aimer and later squadron bombing leader, Russ Brooks, remembered LORAN as nothing more than "...bloody great charts with curves representing the time differences all over them!"

February 1945 saw the aircraft of 82 Wing involved in further shipping strikes as the Japanese attempted to extract its ground forces from the islands for redeployment. As the shipping increased however, so did the A-A defences employed by the *Sugar Charlie* (300 to 1,000 gross tonnes with two hatches) and *Sugar Dog* vessels (150 to 300 gross tonnes with a single hatch), along with larger ships. A number of Liberators learned the hard way, bringing back damaged aircraft as a result.

B-24 Liberators of 82 Wing depart the target, leaving the port and oil storage facilities at Balikpapan alight. Photo: Alford/AHSNT Colln.

The Japanese air forces, whilst badly depleted, also continued to prove they were not completely out of the picture in the NWA. GpCapt Kingwell and two crew members were slightly wounded when his aircraft, A72-59, was intercepted by Japanese aircraft identified as a *Zeke* and an *Oscar* during an attack on two *Sugar Dogs* at Bima, Sumbawa Island on 22 March. Over a forty minute period the Liberator was subjected to gun fire, the dropping of small unidentified cylinders and a length of chain, which hit the nose and turret, port tailplane and vertical fin. Damaged, the B-24 limped home and despite an undercarriage leg not locking, landed safely. Kingwell was awarded a DSO.

The following day SqnLdr N. H. 'Fanny' Straus and his 24 Squadron crew perished when their aircraft, A72-80, crashed into Vansittart Bay after taking off from Truscott on a shipping sweep. Unable to gain height, Straus remained in contact with Truscott tower for 23 minutes before crashing. Straus, his co-pilot FltLt C. D. Parry-Okeden and FSgt W. A. J. Rodgers were recovered and buried at Truscott some days later; they were reburied at Adelaide River on 7 November. The other crew members, including Cpl D. W. Madden of 42 Squadron were posted 'missing presumed killed'. Pilot Officer Russ Brooks was made the Adjusting Officer for Straus' personal belongings, commenting that it "...was a bloody tough job as everybody knew everyone and [I] had built friendships with them."

Truscott was being used extensively by the Liberators of 82 Wing, 87 PR Squadron Mosquitos, Spitfire detachments, and the B-25, PV-1 Ventura and Beaufighters of 79 Wing. There the aircraft staged overnight utilising the refuelling and other facilities before setting off on long range missions. Dave Sieber, a RAAF gunner flew with the 380th Bomb. Gp's 531st Squadron and later 23 Squadron from Long. He recalled Truscott as eminently forgettable, "It left no lasting impression on anyone...I don't remember much about [it]...It was a place we went to top up with fuel for a long trip to [the] N.E.I." Despite the best efforts of the flying Padre, Vic Pederson, in providing movies, tea and biscuits and entertainment, the remote airfield was never a popular base. A Salvation Army Captain, Pederson also flew his Tiger Moth to the remote radar and other sites pioneering the Salvation Army's Flying Service in northern Australia.

April 6 was a black day for 82 Wing: two 24 Squadron aircraft and crews were lost, with only three survivors of 22 crew members making it back. Two days previously the Japanese Natori-class 5,800 tonne cruiser, *Isuzu* and four vessels were reported by submarine as located in the Flores Sea heading southeast for Timor. The convoy was to pick up troops and equipment from Timor in what was an open challenge to the Allied air strength in the NWA. The 7th *Hikoshidan* was to provide fighter cover for the convoy from what bases it had remaining in the islands.

Salvation Army Padre, Capt Vic Pederson was instrumental in maintaining morale at the remote Truscott base. Rare moments of relaxation supplemented the mundane military rations. Photo: Vic Pederson.

At the time the convoy was reported, 19 Mitchells of 2 and 18 Squadrons were attacking Tanimbar, thus precluding any attack on the convoy. Air Commodore A. M. Charlesworth, who had taken over from Cole, took up the challenge and ordered a strike early on the 6th when the convoy was expected to be heading out from Koepang. All available 82 and 79 Wing aircraft were to make the attack. Two Mosquitos made photographic runs from 21,000 ft before heading for Koepang and back to Coomalie via Truscott, while three 43 Squadron Catalinas shadowed the vessels over the night of the 5th.

On the 6th ten Mitchells each from 2 and 18 Squadrons took off to attack the convoy, along with nine Liberators, four from 21 Squadron and five from 24; each of the Liberators was laden with 11,735 l of fuel, extra ammunition and eight 227 kg bombs. The Mitchells were first to reach the convoy and with the Liberators running late, were forced to attack due to their limited range. Over two separate attacks from 10,000 ft the Mitchells claimed two hits and a number of near misses though the convoy remained intact. Japanese fighters engaged them and whilst no damage was reported, A-A fire from the convoy was described as accurate but trailed the attacking aircraft.

Twenty minutes later the Liberators arrived. Led by GpCapt Peter Parker, they bombed at 12,000 ft and encountered very accurate A-A fire. The enemy fighters also intercepted, one closing to within 20 ft of FltLt Court's aircraft, whilst another attacked FltLt S. L. McDonald's aircraft, A72-81, from 20 m. Cannon fire started a fire in the nose area and McDonald ordered the crew to bale out. The aircraft dived vertically before pulling out, only to stall in a climb before diving again and exploding as it headed towards the *Isuzu*.

Then Parker led the remaining Liberators on a second run, something Kingwell was adamant should not be done. "You only make one pass at a target like that – you never come back a second time…and he did it because they missed…" he related to author Alan Powell, "…By this time the cruiser had got its altitude and its speed and the fighters were there and they lost an aircraft." The aircraft was A72-77, flown by FltLt E. V. Ford, also of 24 Squadron. With one engine and the area around the nose wheel on fire, Ford ordered the crew to bale out. Five managed to get out while Ford held the aircraft level; then it rolled on its back and exploded on impact with the water.

Roger Court recalled the Japanese fighters as he commenced his final bombing run. "They sorted our formation out. I saw them out ahead executing aerobatics; slow rolls, rolls off the tops [sic], loops, just waiting their turn…I noticed the insignia painted on their rudders, a

LIBERATORS

streak of lightening [*sic*]...One of them closed in on us... at the 11 o'clock position...his tracer...racing by the nose of our aircraft...if he held his present course he would pass between my port wing and the...aircraft on our port side..." With every chance of a collision with Court's and another Liberator the Japanese pilot banked and squeezed through a narrow gap between them: and was gone.

Court then "...ordered the remaining aircraft to get down to sea level to try and sight any of the downed airmen. We saw a number of them floating with their Mae-West inflated...[the Liberators] also carried a spare eight man dinghy ... [and] I instructed them to...throw these out to them, together with a smoke bomb...making it easier for the air-sea rescue Catalina to locate [them]."

Warrant Officer Keith Shilling was the sole survivor of the FltLt S. L. McDonald crew killed during the 6 April attacks against the Japanese cruiser, Isuzu. Photo: Bob Piper.

One was WOff Keith Shilling, who had parachuted from McDonald's aircraft, and was the sole survivor of that crew. He spent a most uncomfortable next few hours both in and out of the water. After the cruiser had tried to machine gun he and another survivor, a vessel tried to run him over but was too fast and the bow wave pushed Shilling aside. Some 25 minutes later a 112 ASRF Catalina, A24-54, landed and picked up three of the survivors, Shilling, WOff C. G. Vickers and Sgt Sayer. The 'Cat' was in turn attacked by a Japanese fighter, caught fire and sank. Shilling was sprayed by burning fuel, suffering severe burns to his back before escaping the blazing aircraft with assistance from the pilot, FltLt C. R. Bulman and FSgt Scholes.

They were picked up by a second Catalina, A24-58, flown by FltLt R. M. Corrie, some time later and "...as the last survivor clambered aboard [six from Bulman's Catalina and three from the Liberators] an *Irving* was sighted making for us. The enemy made his first attack as we were taking off and scored hits..." Shilling recalled, "Our return fire did no visible damage. A running fight ensued for about twenty minutes. The attacks ceased and we headed for Darwin, reaching there about 2230 hours."

The *Irving*, one of a handful operated by Fighter *Hikotai* 902 based at Koepang to assist in the evacuation, was thwarted from its attack by a 21 Squadron Liberator, A72-72, flown by Flt Lt Eldin Moore, who had taken off from Fenton in response to an air-sea rescue alert. He arrived to see Corrie's Catalina under attack and placed the Liberator between it and the *Irving*. With his gunners firing at extreme range it was enough to deter the Japanese; Moore received the DFC for his action. Despite searches no further survivors of the day's events were found. The *Isuzu* was sunk north of Sumbawa by two American submarines the following day. Fighter *Hikotai* 902 was transferred to home defence shortly afterwards.

Armed reconnaissance and anti-shipping missions were flown by 82 Wing aircraft over the following months to July 1945. In April, fifteen aircraft along with ground crews of both 21 and 24 Squadrons were deployed to Morotai, though small detachments were maintained at Darwin. Led by Gp Capts Kingwell and Parker the detachment was to bomb a range of targets including the oil production facilities on Tarakan off Borneo before the Allies landed there in May as part of the 'OBOE' series of operations intended to rid the NEI of the Japanese and reinstate the Dutch "...to establish a firm base of operations for subsequent consolidation", as MacArthur put it.

In May four aircraft of 12 Squadron, newly arrived in the NWA, were attached to 21 Squadron at Fenton. From 20 to 23 May the unit conducted anti-submarine patrols though no sightings were reported. Number 23 Squadron, which had arrived in the NWA on 6 April carried out a number of sorties, mainly armed reconnaissance. Dave Sieber a member of SqnLdr J. 'Mickey' Finlayson's crew recorded two of the missions in A72-103, one on 8 May, an "...Armed Recco Bombed Kaliangat. Demos [demolition bombs] carried. Concentration of barges." The second was a "...Strike on Saoebi [sic] Float Plane Base. 9 x 500 lb demos dropped. 1 Float plane seen taxing [sic]. 1 Oscar seen at Soembawa-Basar. 10.45 hours."

On the 28th a HQ NWA Warning Order detailed instructions to the squadrons to prepare for movement with 82 Wing. The destination was not disclosed for security reasons though with the detachment at Morotai it took no genius to work out their next location.

The move, to Morotai as it was later revealed, and no doubt reacted to with complete surprise, commenced on 3 June and by the 17th all remaining personnel of 82 Wing had been transported to Darwin, where they boarded the liberty ship, *Louis Arguello*. The vessel sailed at 2100 hours that evening, leaving 12 Squadron as the sole heavy bomber unit in the Darwin area. After re-equipping from its Vengeances to the Liberators, the squadron had arrived in the NWA as part of 85 Wing on 1 May under WgCdr N. G. Hemsworth and took up residence at the former 380th camp area on McMillans Road. The four aircraft previously attached to the Wing at Fenton joined them at the RAAF Station.

The arrival of the squadron was marred when A72-160 crashed in a pre-dawn take off from Truscott on 20 May. Armed with depth charges, the aircraft dug a wing in on

The crew of FltLt Keith Johnston at the RAAF Station Darwin following 12 Squadron's arrival with B-24s in May 1945. Photo: Keith Johnston.

LIBERATORS

the edge of the runway and crashed. The aircraft erupted, killing the pilot, FlgOff Frank L. Sismey, a pre-war test cricketer, and his crew. The wreckage remains in the scrub at the end of the remote airfield; a long way from home for Sismey and his ten crew members.

A part of the April deployment from Darwin, 24 Squadron B-24, A72-49 GR-E, is seen flying formation off Morotai during June 1945. Photo: Rod McDonald.

The unit flew its first mission on 24 May and two days later three Japanese vessels were strafed. Other targets included the Kalabahi, Toenwawan, Ambesia and Kendari airfields and a Japanese rest camp on Flores, continually keeping the pressure on the remnant Japanese forces. Koepang was also attacked to cover the Allied landings there. The squadron's last mission was a raid on Kendari on 10 August and from then it fought a 'paper war', consigned to dropping leaflets informing the inhabitants of the NEI of the Japanese surrender.

Though arriving late in the war 12 Squadron was still able to "...take a very active part in the war against the Japanese, but their opportunity was to last them just a little under three months" the unit historian wrote, "In that time it was able to mount numerous attacks against Japanese outposts and shipping in the Timor, Bunda [*sic*] and Arafura Seas." At war's end 12 Squadron joined other units in the huge operation of evacuating POWS to Darwin and southern states, dropping food and medical supplies and generally assisting the NEI inhabitants.

From August the squadron remained at Darwin in company with 'Doc' Fenton's 6 Comm. Unit and the RAF Spitfire squadrons at the Civil 'Drome, and 112 ASRF at Doctors Gully. They were in effect the only flying units in the Darwin area, which, only 18 months earlier had boasted over a dozen operational squadrons, with a further three to come, along with a vast range of support units.

THE OFFENSIVE ROLLS ON
Moving north and boredom the enemy

By the end of 1943 heavy aircraft losses by the Japanese navy over Rabaul and the northern Solomons, along with losses in the NWA had seen a dramatic redeployment of units in the region with most of their fighters based beyond a 1000 km range. The army's 7th *Hikoshidan*, along with its fighter, medium and heavy bomber units, had been transferred to New Guinea in July, whilst the 6th *Hikoshidan* became part of the 7th and moved to Ambon with a mix of Ki-43 *Oscars* and Ki-45 *Nicks*.

The navy's *Ku* 202 had moved to the Aru Islands in September to intercept the B-24s of the 380th Bomb. Gp and other Allied aircraft, and had divided into *Ku* 202, and Fighter *Hikotai* 301 and 603, each with 48 A6M *Zekes* based at Langgoer and on Sumatra. *Kokutai* 202 had maintained detachments at Koepang, Ambon, Macassar and Balikpapan throughout 1943, whilst the latter months also saw them at Surabaya, Kendari and Sorong. In March 1944 *Ku* 202 was posted to the 22nd *Koku Sentai* and later the 1st *Koku Kantai* before being sent to the central Pacific. The 934th *Ku* had transferred to Manokwari during December and maintained a number of small detachments in the islands including *Jakes* at Macassar.

By March 1944 the Japanese were still able to maintain a number of units in the region, despite being badly depleted. The army had elements of the 5th *Sentai* in detachments on Timor and Ambon and at Sorong in western New Guinea with an available strength of 20 *Nicks*, 5 HQ aircraft and six heavy bombers. The 6th *Hikoshidan* was based on Ambon with a mix of *Oscars* and *Nicks*, whilst a further *Oscar* unit, the 24th *Sentai*, arrived in the area from Japan in May. The 13th *Sentai* and its *Oscars* and *Nicks* under Major Hisao Machida relocated from the Halmaheras to Manokwari in April and later Ambon and Kendari.

A further navy unit, *Ku* 153 was based at Babo with the latest model A6M5 *Zekes*, whilst *Ku* 381 was at Balikpapan, also equipped with the A6M5. The 934th *Ku* had also begun to re-equip, bringing on strength Kawanishi N1K1 *Rex* floatplanes to replace the *Rufes*, which were phased out by March.

At the same time, Cole had 13 operational squadrons at his disposal in the NWA, and whilst only four of these, including the Boomerangs of 83 Squadron, were fighter units, his offensive capacity was the priority in order to keep the Japanese tied up in the islands:

1 Squadron with Beauforts at Gould;
2 Squadron with Beauforts at Hughes;
18 NEI Squadron with Mitchells at Batchelor;
31 Squadron with Beaufighters at Coomalie;
43 Squadron with Catalinas at Doctors Gully;
83 Squadron with Boomerangs at Gove;
452 Squadron with Spitfires at Strauss;
457 Squadron with Spitfires at Livingstone
54 (RAF) Squadron with Spitfires at Darwin RAAF;
528th Squadron with B-24s at Fenton;
529th Squadron with B-24s at Long;
530th Squadron with B-24s at Fenton; and
531st Squadron with B-24s at Long.

Squadron leader Roy Goon (seated, centre) and 83 Squadron pilots at Gove in remote Arnhem Land, 1944. Photo: Peter Callaghan.

Even with these movements and the end of enemy raids the previous November, Darwin it seems, "...had a quiet spell in 1944..." one correspondent wrote, "War correspondents delved into the past for copy... [and] reported on inter-unit football matches." They need not have. Despite a number of units, notably the Spitfire squadrons, languishing in a lack of action, the RAAF and USAAF were still very active in the NWA.

Cole's strength had increased in January when 83 Squadron and its Australian designed and produced CAC Boomerang fighters moved into the newly completed Gove airfield in north east Arnhem Land on the 19th. Formed at Strathpine in Queensland in early 1943 the first elements of the squadron, FltLt R. Holt's 'B' Flight, had preceded the main party, flying instead to Milingimbi during November the previous year. 'A' Flight remained at Gove, though the aircraft were rotated between them. Over the months to August 1944 the unit flew constant shipping patrols,

THE OFFENSIVE ROLLS ON

covering convoys and the sea route from Horn Island to Darwin.

The squadron was ably led by SqnLdr Roy Goon, an Australian born Chinese, and former CFI with the Victorian Aero Club in the mid-1930s. Despite the entrenched racism in the military – a 1940 RAAF publication decreed that for EATS "...all candidates must be British subjects of pure European descent and also sons of parents both of whom are...British subjects" - Roy overcame the obstacles and became a highly respected pilot and leader. He was awarded a MID, the citation for which read, "...these shipping patrols were particularly arduous. They necessitated long flights over the sea in single-engined aircraft in all weathers." As squadron CO he was responsible for 24 aircraft and 350 squadron personnel along with the Gove Fighter Sector, the chain of radar stations on the north coast and a communications and control centre, the construction of which he supervised.

Armourers of 83 Squadron cleaning the 20mm Hispano cannon of an Australian designed and produced CA-12 Boomerang during a deployment to Milingimbi. Photo: Alford/AHSNT Colln.

In between these duties he also managed to fly. "We had some scrambles against suspected Japanese..." he recalled, "but we never caught up with them...I was in one scramble against a couple of *Betty* bombers which got far away before we reached 20,000 ft." The unit lost no aircraft due to combat, however some demonstrated the Boomerang's tendency to swing on landing, putting them into the bush off the runway. The only fatality was that of FlgOff R. E. Ayre, whose engine caught fire at low altitude during a gunnery exercise on 22 May. The aircraft, A46-173, crashed near Cape Shields; Ayre was buried on site before later being reburied at Adelaide River.

All in all, 83 Squadron's stay in the NWA was not spectacular despite the vital role the Boomerangs played. The war was moving rapidly north and 13 Squadron with its longer range Lockheed PV-1 Venturas were due in the area. September 1944 saw 83 Squadron withdrawn to Camden in NSW.

In the Darwin area the Spitfire squadrons were cooling their heels, with boredom the enemy since the last of the raids the previous November. If tedium had been a concern in July 1943, the weeks and months following the last raid saw it become a major problem for the services in the NWA for the remaining war years. "Morale is a very big factor up here these days with the war a long way off and no prospect of action from day to day..." the 452 Squadron historian wrote, "All we do is pray for the time to come when we will be told to get packing and see some war."

Recreation became an important part of unit routine, despite the usual flying and abortive scrambles to intercept what more often than not were returning RAAF or USAAF aircraft. Swimming at Berry Springs, boxing tournaments, movie shows and concerts, football and cricket, and indoor games all helped relieve the boredom, but not the desire to see action.

While training flights were the norm, new equipment was also arriving in the Mk VIII Spitfires. The first, A58-304 (JF822), was delivered to 452 Squadron from 1 AD on 11 January. "The long awaited arrival of the Spitfire Mk VIII aircraft was heralded with great joy. Five of the aircraft arrived safely and five of Spitfire Mk VC aircraft are to be taken south..." the unit historian recorded. The Mk VIIIs arrived at regular intervals over the next few months though they suffered coolant pipe problems and flying was restricted. It was not until April that 22 of the type were recorded as being on strength.

The Mk Vcs of 457 Squadron and 54 Squadron were to soldier on for some time however; 54 Squadron re-equipped in May and 457 received its first Mk VIII when it moved to Sattler the following month.

February saw the loss of a popular figure in 31 Squadron, when SqnLdr R. 'Butch' Gordon was killed on the 27th. On 4 January he had led eight Beaufighters as cover for an attack on shipping near Koepang by six 18 Squadron B-25s. Gordon downed a *Betty* near Cape Mali, his 5th aerial victory and seventh overall. Over the five month period

THE OFFENSIVE ROLLS ON

from 11 August 1943 he had destroyed two *Rufes*, a *Pete*, three *Nicks* and the *Betty*, a *Rufe* and the *Pete* on the water. He, and no doubt other aircrews, were well due for a rest and Gordon and his observer, FlgOff Ron Jordan, were put on reduced flying by the CO, WgCdr Bill Mann. With no flying planned on the 27th, Jordan took a group swimming.

Spitfire Mk Vcs of 452 Squadron taxiing at Sattler prior to the arrival of the new Mk VIIIs. Photo: Malcolm Beaton.

Gordon decided to carry out a test flight to check the feathering propellers on A19-165 taking FSgt Keith Smith as observer. The aircraft circled Coomalie twice at low level and was then seen with the starboard propeller feathered and the port 'windmilling' as it went behind hills at 200 ft. The aircraft crashed opposite 1 MRS at the Batchelor Road junction "...at about 1730 hours" the hospital's history records relate, "...An ambulance was immediately despatched to the scene in charge of F/Lt. C. H. ANDERSON. At...1800 hours the ambulance returned with a survivor...S/Ldr R. L. GORDON, in a badly burned and shocked condition. S/Ldr Gordon died 2½ hours later." Gordon died the day he was awarded a Bar to his DFC.

The following day the offensive operations by the Beaufighters and Mitchells were strengthened with the arrival of the Bristol Beauforts of 1 Squadron under SqnLdr D. W. I. Campbell. Arriving at the newly completed Gould airfield immediately south of the main runway at Batchelor, the unit commenced operations with 31 and 18 NEI Squadrons on 20 March. The Beauforts had also been arriving at 2 Squadron from January under SqnLdr L. A. Ingram and in March the unit joined 31 and 18 NEI Squadrons in the formation of 79 Wing under that old Territory hand, GpCapt Charles Eaton. Headquartered at Batchelor since the previous November, the Wing commenced operations as a cohesive force in mid-March.

Number 1 Squadron joined the Wing later that month.

GpCapt Charles Eaton returned to the NWA in early 1944 as OC 79 Wing. Photo: Alford Colln.

In early March the reported arrival of a Japanese naval force at Singapore and its departure on 4 March caused a major dislocation of units in the NWA. With further submarine sightings of the force north of Lombok it was suspected that Fremantle might be the target. A hurriedly convened conference at Allied Air Headquarters in Brisbane on the 8th saw Gen Kenney order AVM Bostock to take charge of Western Australia's air defences and oversee the rapid deployment of units from the Darwin area. At the same time he ordered the 380th Bomb. Gp detachment to return from New Guinea, with the proviso that if the threat developed it would move to Cunderdin or Geraldton in Western Australia.

Fourteen 31 Squadron Beaufighters departed Coomalie on 9 March flying through to 'Potshot', an airfield on Exmouth Gulf - later called Learmonth - whilst nine C-47 aircraft transported 124 squadron personnel and equipment. The Mitchells of 18 Squadron also deployed to Potshot: 16 Mitchells and eight C-47s flew men and equipment enough "...for a fortnight's operations" to the remote airfield.

Another Dutch unit, 120 NEI Squadron equipped with P-40N Kittyhawks was hastily moved across the continent, whilst the P-40s of 84 Squadron from Horn Island moved to Strauss to replace the RAAF Spitfire units; only 54 (RAF) Squadron remained in the Darwin area.

The RAAF Spitfire squadrons, 452 and 457, were deployed to Guildford near Perth in a 3,000 km flight in poor weather, staging through airfields that had few ground facilities and

THE OFFENSIVE ROLLS ON

A Mk VIII Spitfire of 452 Squadron is run up by a Fitter IIE at Sattler, 1944. Photo: M. Brown

that left pilots and groundcrews alike tired and frustrated. The weather also played havoc at Potshot when "...cyclone storms [*sic*] struck the area and converted the airfield and camps into a swamp..."

Searches by the Beaufighters and Mitchells over the next few days were little more than training flights in comparison to operations in the Darwin area. Sergeant Doug Crosbie, a gunner with 18 Squadron recorded his flights in N5-171 over the period; flying with the Lt Deknatel crew his log book entries read "OPERATIONS – Nil Rds Fired. GUN TESTING – Nil Rds Fired. DEFECTIVE FIRING PIN...SEARCH – NIL RDS FIRED."

The entire emergency operation proved abortive, though it did provide experience in deployment for the transport units. The interlude ended on 20 March when Kenney signalled Bostock confirming the threat had passed and ordering the return of the squadrons to their bases.

The Spitfire units had been more fortunate in being able to at least partially enjoy their stay in Perth. Following their eventful flight south and the failure of the enemy to appear,

the units returned to their northern bases on the 25th. The Spitfire groundcrews "...returned to the area in the same trusty aircraft they had left it in and brought with them a plentiful supply of very welcome eggs, ham, grapes, apples, and bacon."

In contrast, the 380th had arrived back from New Guinea to find the wet season had left creeks and roads flooded, taxiways washed out or breaking up and supplies held up. Aircraft broke through the soft taxiways, camps were flooded, roads cut and supplies had to be ferried in via aircraft liferafts. Fortunately they weren't required for the deployment; conditions would no doubt have prevented a rapid response in any event.

As it transpired there had been no plan to attack either Western Australia or anywhere else. The Japanese fleet had departed Truk in fear of being destroyed by American carrier aircraft had it remained, particularly in a lack of any air support there.

Operations continued for the Beaufighters, Mitchells and later, the Beauforts on returning from Potshot, with 18 NEI Squadron receiving newer models of the B-25

THE OFFENSIVE ROLLS ON

with tail turrets. Soon after larger raids were commenced against Timor. Ten Mitchells accompanied by 1 Squadron Beauforts raided Koepang on 16 April and three days later twelve of the newly arrived B-25D-30 and -35 models attacked Soe village in company with eight Beaufighters and 16 Beauforts of 1 and 2 Squadrons.

Beaufighters of 31 Squadron in hastily prepared revetments during the March 1944 deployment to 'Potshot', an airfield at Exmouth Gulf in Western Australia. Photo: Murray Weste.

Whilst 31 Squadron operated under 79 Wing, a number of missions independent of the other units were also flown. Raids on Roti Island, Tenau harbour and Semau Island over the period 28 to 31 March saw five prahus, a 500 tonne vessel and a number of smaller vessels destroyed. The operations were not without loss however. Flight Lieutenant K. A. Fitton and his observer, FSgt R. C. Foyle, were killed instantly in the Roti Island raid of 28 March when they flew so low that their aircraft, A19-182, hit the mast of a beached prahu, crashed and exploded. A further strike on Senau Island was carried out on 6 April, during which a 30 m oil barge was set afire and a number of buildings damaged. Accurate A-A fire damaged A19-156 flown by FlgOff D. Strachan and his observer, FSgt J. Brassil, forcing Strachan to make a forced landing on Cartier Island at Ashmore Reef. They were rescued shortly afterwards by FlgOff R. J. Marr of 43 Squadron in Catalina A24-44.

Over the month 31 Squadron flew over 70 sorties against targets on Timor, Senoea and the Tanimbar Islands along with strikes on a number of villages, Lautem and Soe in particular. The unit lost two aircraft, that of Strachan and Brassil, and A19-178 flown by FSgts H. S. Ashbolt and E. J. Hiskins, both of whom were killed when the aircraft crashed into the sea off Timor on the 15th.

The Beaufighters also flew operationally with the Spitfires for the first time on 17 April, with 54 (RAF) Squadron employed on its first offensive operation in the NWA. Orders were received that each Spitfire squadron was to provide three aircraft to attack a Japanese radio station and its surrounding buildings on Babar and Wetan Islands in the Banda Sea. They were to accompany two Beaufighters from 31 Squadron, all under the command of GpCapt Peter Jeffrey DFC, DFM, and WgCdr Dick Cresswell DFC

FlgOff D. Strachan's aircraft A19-156 is seen pulling away at upper left after setting an oil barge alight in Pelican Bay Semau Island. Photo: David Strachan.

Staging through Bathurst Island the force flew at 50 ft before reaching Babar Island in mid-morning on the 18th. The Beaufighters attacked the radio station followed by the Spitfires which strafed a number of targets of opportunity including barges and buildings. The developed camera gun film indicated that the target was practically destroyed and *RAAF Saga* reported that "...a combined force of Spitfires and Beaufighters attacked enemy installations in the Babar Islands, 300 miles north of Darwin...the Spitfires and Beaufighters made several strafing runs ... [attacking] huts, machine gun posts and barge hide-outs, and destroyed a wireless station." Any hint of the boredom being relieved for the Spitfire units as a result is not recorded.

The aircraft and crew of 79 Wing were kept busy throughout April and May with missions against a range of targets from Manatuto on Timor's north coast to the Aru Islands - those in April in support of the Hollandia and Aitape landings planned for the 22nd. Eaton also planned to conduct a large raid three days prior to the landings, involving 1, 18 NEI and 31 Squadrons.

THE OFFENSIVE ROLLS ON

On the 19th 15 Beauforts, 12 Mitchells and 8 Beaufighters took off in the early morning to attack Soe town and the Japanese barracks. The force rendezvoused at 10,000 ft an hour after take off and nearer the target dropped to 8,000 ft and picked up speed. With the Beaufighters providing top cover, the Beauforts dropped high explosive and incendiary bombs and reported large fires in buildings, tents and a dump site. At the same time 18 NEI Squadron carried out its bombing run with all the bombs landing in the town area. On the day of the landings 31 and 18 NEI Squadrons raided Dili whilst the B-24s of the 380th Bomb. Gp bombed Noemfoor Island. Catalinas of 11, 20 and 43 Squadrons also mined harbours and sea lanes at Balikpapan, Manokwari, Sorong and Kaimana to close off shipping during the Hollandia-Aitape operation.

The Wing lost four aircraft during May, one during a training exercise, when the crew of Lt R. Bousche of N5-176, including RAAF gunner, Sgt Doug Crosbie, perished during a practice bombing mission over Quail Island on the 30th. Operations took the other three. A second Mitchell of 18 NEI Squadron was lost on the 18th when the Lt J. H. Geerke crew in N5-177 was shot down during a raid on the Tanimbar Islands. The aircraft was one of four including N5-170, '172 and '188 sent to attack Japanese installations as part of mission NEI 7.

Three weeks later 18 NEI Squadron lost its CO when N5-162 was hit by A-A fire and crashed into the sea during an attack on Timor on 23 June. Part of a four aircraft strike mission, the aircraft was flown by Lt Jansen with LtCol Te Roller flying as second pilot. None of the crew survived the explosion and subsequent crash. The remaining aircraft, N5-163, '180 and N5-185 returned safely to Batchelor. Lieutenant Colonel D. L. Asjes took over as the new CO on 1 July and he was in turn replaced by LtCol M. Van Haselen on 7 October.

Two crews of 1 Squadron were lost over Penfoie during an attack on army barracks by six aircraft on 8 May. A-A fire was observed bursting close to the formation and the Beauforts of SqnLdr G. B. D. Roxburgh, A9-541, and FSgt T. Wallace, A9-477, failed to return to base. The Beauforts had "...travelled to DRYSDALE Airborne from DRYSDALE to strike PENFOIE military barracks. Task completed Duties 3 and 8 failed to return...Task carried out", the unit historian recorded matter-of-factly. Squadron Leader Roxburgh, FlgOff Kerr, WOff Lomas, and FSgt Jamieson, along with

FSgts Wallace, Hich, Hodges and Sandwell were never recovered. The squadron was over Penfoie striking the same target three days later in an eight aircraft mission; all returned safely.

The arrival of the first of the de Havilland Mosquito reconnaissance aircraft, A52-2, in the NWA, 26 May 1944. Photo: Bill Preston.

From 26 May the NWA finally had a dedicated photographic reconnaissance capability with the departure from the de Havilland facility at Bankstown of the first Mosquito bound for Coomalie. The aircraft, A52-2, the first of the type modified for the photo reconnaissance role, was flown by FlgOff Ken Boss-Walker and PltOff Jeff Love and landed at Coomalie later that day.

Fitted with two F24 split vertical cameras in the nose and a third, an F52 model, installed in the rear fuselage, the Mosquito also carried an extra 820 l of fuel, bringing its total to over 4,000 l. Increased oil capacity and extra oxygen bottles were also installed.

The arrival of the new aircraft took the responsibility from the 380th Bomb. Gp which in turn had taken the task over from the 319th Squadron and the problem plagued aircraft of 1 PRU. Importantly, it allowed Cole to free up the B-24s; it had been necessary to send six of the bombers to carry out the mission a single Mosquito could undertake relying on its speed and high altitude flying. During June A52-2 flew nine operations, including sorties over Flores and Soemba Islands, Tiworo Strait, Ceram, Nanda, Kendari, and on the 25th, Surabaya. The remaining Lightning flew four sorties during the month, the last before it crashed at Coomalie on 1 September.

During May both RAAF Spitfire squadrons had moved up from their bases at Livingstone and Strauss to Sattler, 33

THE OFFENSIVE ROLLS ON

kilometres from Darwin; the move was made in preparation for the arrival of a further two RAF Spitfire squadrons. On arrival at Sattler 452 and 457 Squadrons settled in at either end of the airfield; 452 Squadron operated from the northern dispersal and taxiway areas and take offs were said to be interesting should the two squadrons 'scramble' at the same time. On 15 June the first of the RAAF's Mk VIIIS arrived at 452 Squadron in what was deemed by the unit historian as "...a "Red Letter" day...as it was marked by the arrival of the first five of the new Mk VIIIs. Great joy was shown by all the pilots...and hopes are held for the speedy fitting out...with this new mark of Spitfire."

Fire crews were quickly on the scene when Lightning A55-1 crashed at Coomalie on 1 September 1944. It was the last of the trouble plagued aircraft on RAAF strength. Photo: Bill Preston.

Number 54 (RAF) Squadron moved from Darwin to Livingstone on 9 June though it maintained small detachments at Truscott, whilst the 80 Fighter Wing HQ moved to Sattler.

June also saw the end of the brief association with Beauforts by 2 Squadron with the arrival of the unit's B-25D Mitchells, most of which were transferred from 18 NEI Squadron including A47-1 to A47-35 and A47-37 to A47-39 following a directive of 19 April. By the end of June the squadron had 17 of an establishment of 20 Mitchells on strength, 12 of which were serviceable, along with 72 officers and 369 ORs. A year later 11 B-25J models, A47-40 to '50 were allocated to the squadron between April and August 1945, however only A47-41 and '43 made it to the unit.

The first operation was flown on the 27th following three weeks of training sorties on the type. Joe Gleeson, a WOff second pilot recorded 13 sorties involving splash gunnery at Lee Point, high level bombing at 7,000 ft and masthead

bombing over the training period, flying a range of Mitchells including A47-5, '6, '10, '13. '15 and A47-16; all with FSgt Dinsdale at the controls.

Bristol Beaufort A9-560 KO-V of 2 Squadron following a landing accident at Hughes on 18 May 1944. It was later repaired by 4 RSU and sold off in 1953. Photo: Malcolm Long.

The mission of the 27th was a nine aircraft "Strike [on] LAUTEM WEST STRIP. No contact. Intense A/A 7 x 500 MC [seven x 227 kg Medium Capacity high explosive bombs] U/I [unidentified] Jap A/C sighted airborne." Gleeson's log book recorded. It was the first of many missions 2 Squadron flew with GpCapt Eaton's 79 Wing over the following months, a number of them in concert with 18 NEI and 31 Squadrons.

On 4 July a shipping strike in the Kai Islands saw A47-3, '7 and '13 sight and attack a "...Sugar Charlie...in succession the formation bombed the ship while two aircraft strafed it. 12 x 500 M/C bombs...dropped. Many near misses scored but no direct hits" the unit records relate, "The stern of the vessel was seen to lift from water...smoke was rising from superstructure and steering appeared damaged, possible 20 MM [fire] from stern gun platform silenced after strafing." A second vessel was attacked on the way home to Hughes where the aircraft arrived safely.

Three days later three aircraft carried out a shipping strike around Dili and while no shipping was sighted the airfield was bombed through cloud from 10,000 ft. A47-16 returned its bombs to Hughes after they failed to release.

The Mitchells and Beaufighters attacked enemy barges between Timor, Babar, Sermata and Leti Islands during July and on the 29th Penfoie was attacked at sunset by a mixed force of 18 Mitchells, nine each from 2 and 18 NEI

THE OFFENSIVE ROLLS ON

Squadrons. By the end of July 2 Squadron had flown a total of 89 sorties of an overall total by 79 Wing of 354. Number 1 Squadron flew 82 sorties for the month, 18 NEI Squadron 107, and 31 Squadron 76. A majority of the 2 Squadron sorties were searches along the Gull, Heron and Jackass search lanes.

A B-25D Mitchell KO-U of 2 Squadron over Timor in mid-July 1944. Photo: Joe Gleeson.

A mix of camouflaged and natural metal B-25 Mitchells of 2 Squadron preparing to take off from Hughes on their first operation, 27 June 1944. Photo: Malcolm Long.

The following months saw 2 Squadron fly the search lanes, carry out shipping sweeps including masthead attacks on enemy vessels and strikes on airfields and other Japanese infrastructure. Between the two Mitchell squadrons, 54 vessels were sunk or damaged during October and on 6 November a combined force attacked Waingapoe on Sumba Island, where motor vessels had been reported in the harbour. Four Mitchells from 2 Squadron were to carry out a mast head attack on the vessels – based on the discretion of the leader, SqnLdr P. J. Norriss - while 12 from 18 NEI Squadron were to bomb A-A positions around the town. Staging through Truscott the aircraft carried out their allotted tasks. Norriss' four aircraft straddled the vessel and it was reported as 'severely damaged'. The vessel, *Special Submarine Chaser No. 118*, was later confirmed as sunk in Japanese records.

Accidents claimed a number of aircraft. A47-13 crashed on the Adelaide River bombing range after its bombs exploded under the aircraft on 22 April, while A47-17 swung into its revetment during an engine run on 9 May, badly damaging the port wing and nose area. On 2 September A47-6 crashed into the sea off Peron Island while searching for A47-12 which had force landed on the beach. Chaplain FltLt H. C. Easton and an Armourer, WOff G. S. King, were killed in the crash. A47-8 taxied into trees at Hughes on 19

February 1945, damaging a wing and no doubt the pilot's pride.

The squadron lost three aircraft during December. A47-11 *Petunia* came to grief on the 5th when it was damaged during a shipping strike around Wetar Island and the north coast of Timor. Hit by 20mm A-A fire whilst attacking a barge the fuel feed system to the starboard engine was damaged. Failure of the port generator prevented fuel transfer and over Bathurst Island the port engine failed. The pilot, FltLt Norris, force landed the aircraft on a mangrove flat north of the Mission. The crew were uninjured but the aircraft was written off.

A47-33 disappeared during a shipping patrol around the Tanimbar and Kai Island groups on 20 December 1944. Plotters at 105 FCU reported it 64 km from Cape Hotham on course for Hughes. No further plots were received. Despite intensive searches over the following days no trace of the aircraft was found and the crew of FltLt W. F. E. Thompson, FlgOff L. T. Forsyth, WOffs J. E. S. Thompson and F. H. Mathews and FSgts J. A. Rolfe and T. H. Rowlands were posted 'missing presumed killed'.

The third loss was on Boxing Day 1944 when A47-9 crashed on take off from Hughes airfield. Flying at No. 3 in a four aircraft formation briefed to attack enemy shipping in the Lucipara Islands, the fate of the aircraft was probably determined as the first two "...took abnormally long runs before becoming airborne and in one case the pilot...only cleared the trees...by a narrow margin..." The pilot of A47-9, FltLt R. L. Avery was in a similar situation and was "... forced to decide quickly and since it appeared improbable...

THE OFFENSIVE ROLLS ON

[he would] clear the trees at the south end of the strip – he crash landed straight ahead into the clearing." The aircraft caught fire and the bombs exploded however the crew were unhurt. Joe Gleeson, flying as second pilot in the last aircraft recalled flying over the burning aircraft before hearing and feeling the explosions as the bombs detonated.

Three days later, A47-2 *Stormbird* was severely damaged returning from a shipping strike. The aircraft was 15 minutes ahead of its ETA and was over Hughes when a message was sent for the flight to divert due to an approaching storm. The pilot, FltLt Ekert, was close to landing when the aircraft was hit by a severe squall and heavy rain, reducing visibility to 5 or 10 yds. Committed to landing Ekert put the aircraft down, crashing at the end of the strip but avoiding any injuries to the crew.

Another shot of B-25D KO-U of 2 Squadron, this time preparing to take off from Hughes. Photo: Malcolm Long.

The New Year saw the squadron anticipating a move north to the islands. Both 2 and 18 NEI Squadrons had been advised of a move north as 79 Wing vide Circular No. 232 of 11 December and Operation Instructions for the move to Jacquinot Bay were issued on the 31st. While advance parties, including 60 personnel of 2 Squadron and some of 79 Wing HQ had departed by Martin Mariner aircraft on 28 February, others including 83 OBU, 28 Air Stores Park, 27 Medical Clearing Station and 18 RSU went by sea aboard the *William H. Seward*. No sooner had the move begun than it was found that the Jacquinot Bay airstrip would not be completed before March 1945. To further compound the situation the Dutch had made representations to General HQ that they should be deployed to Dutch territory – presuming their continued control over the NEI. On 9 May AVM Bostock cancelled the order and instead assigned 79

Wing to the 1st TAF for operations in Borneo.

The Mitchell squadrons were resigned to waiting for the move, whilst continuing their searches, shipping sweeps and strikes on airfields, ground targets and Japanese infrastructure throughout the NEI. The Japanese had moved their forces further north and north west and in doing so restricted operations, particularly by the Beaufighters which were forced to hit targets at extreme range. "Probably the greatest obstacle...to the squadron at this time was the flying distance...On 16 August [1944] for example, when the squadron attacked Maumere, on landing it was found that the aircraft had only sufficient fuel for a few minutes flying time..." the unit historian noted.

For the Mitchells the situation wasn't so dire, despite their medium range. John Marks, a RAAF gunner with 18 NEI Squadron, recorded nine sorties in his log book for the month. A shipping strike saw him flying with Lt Van Veelan in N5-218 "...around Tanimbar and Timor Island[s]. 2 large (1500 TNS) merchant ships (JAP) sighted at Timor. Bombed at 3,000ft around Tanimbar Islands. Landed at Darwin due to engine trouble in both engines. Bombs and all ammo jettisoned to prepare for ditching. Made Darwin on one motor." Flight time for the mission was six hours 30 minutes. Marks' tour included eight reconnaissance, 12 day and 10 night sorties, 18 shipping strikes, one low level attack and three photographic sorties.

Simply captioned 'spare parts plane' this photo shows one of 18 NEI Squadron's B-25 Mitchells stripped down to the bare essentials. Its eventual fate is unknown. Photo: Arthur Ashworth.

Despite being on reduced flying the Mitchell squadrons continued their operations fully expecting to be moved at any time, however it was not until mid-year that any advice was received. In the meantime a number of awards had

THE OFFENSIVE ROLLS ON

been gazetted to airmen in 2 Squadron. On 20 May it was announced that FltLts Greenway and Simpson had been awarded DFCs, FSgt B. Hocking a DFM, FltLts J. P. Squires and P. T. Sanders, along with FlgOffs K. E. Coughlan and A. B. Weston were all awarded MIDs. All but Sanders' MID were for operational flying during 1944.

By July 1945 18 NEI Squadron was finally on the move to Balikpapan, with a total of 512 personnel involved from the 15th; 13 officers and 253 ORs of the RAAF and 52 officers and 194 ORs of the RNEIAF. The Mitchells flew into their new base two days later, leaving behind a country they had called home for over two years. The 23 December 1944 edition of the Melbourne *Argus* newspaper had lauded the squadron – *They have fought homeless for two years,* the headline read, *Netherlands Fliers Operating From Australia Overcame Many Difficulties,* ran the sub-heading.

"The Dutch manned and RAAF controlled Mitchell squadron based in north-west Australia has just celebrated its second anniversary of aggression against Japanese-infested territory 500 to 600 miles beyond Australia's northern and north-western coastline. In that time the Dutchmen have joined with RAAF and American units in a ferociously maintained offensive, which has driven the enemy so far back that medium bombers based in the north-west have now to fly mostly at extreme range to hit him. Burnt out trucks and tanks on Timor, shattered docks and anti-aircraft posts in the Flores, wreckage strewn and pitted airfields in the Kai and Tanimbar Islands, rusting hulks in scores of island bays, and thousands of graves tell their own story of the huge area ravaged by these homeless men. In round figures [they] have sunk or damaged 30,000 tons of Japanese shipping...dropped 2,000 tons of bombs...and fired one million rounds of ammunition in some 4,000 sorties...These flying Dutchmen have experience, ability, tenacity and courage. The Japanese occupying their country have every reason to fear them in their pursuit of justice and freedom."

Number 2 Squadron wasn't far behind in moving. A month later on the 14th six Mitchells and 60 personnel took off from Hughes bound for Balikpapan. One, A47-37, disappeared during the flight with the FltLt Slater crew listed as 'missing presumed killed'. The war ended the following day, further compounding the tragedy. Despite intensive searches over the next few days no trace of the aircraft or crew was found.

Squadron HQ moved to Balikpapan on the 22nd and the following day four Mitchells and 50 personnel flew from Hughes. By the end of August all 72 officers and 300 ORs along with 20 Mitchells had been moved to their new base, though 12 aircraft were unserviceable. After waiting almost nine months to move, the squadron now found itself involved in peacetime activities. It returned to its birthplace, RAAF Laverton, in December.

'One bottle per man, per week, per-haps'. RAAF personnel of 18 NEI Squadron enjoying their weekly beer ration, Batchelor, 1944. Photo: Alford/AHSNT Colln.

For 31 Squadron the move had been much easier. The squadron was advised of an impending move during November 1944 and sorties were governed by the availability of aircraft as servicings were carried out and preparations for the move continued. A part of these preparations included the fitting of rocket rails to the Beaufighters. Previously modified to carry bomb racks under the wings

THE OFFENSIVE ROLLS ON

the aircraft had enjoyed considerable success in bombing targets. The new weapons added to their firepower and the squadron was the first RAAF unit to use them in the SWPA, though not without a cost: FlgOffs R. J. Ingle and A. S. Way were killed during a rocket training exercise south of Coomalie on 6 October when A19-203 crashed on the range. A number of strikes were carried out with the rockets including one on Celestina de Silva in Timor on 16 November. It was followed up five days later by a strike on Bacau. In all 72 of the 3-inch rockets, each with a 27 kg high explosive warhead were used in the strike.

Eric Coleman joined 31 Squadron as a FlgOff navigator in September 1944, with his first operational sortie with FlgOff T. W. Ellis on 19 October ending prematurely when, "...on our way to attack targets at Dilli [*sic*] Timor, the rear entrance hatch flew open and I was unable to close it so we had to return to base, very embarrassed and annoyed! Pilot was not impressed." His second trip, from the squadron's new base at Noemfoor on 12 December was much more interesting, as Eric recalled, "...whilst flying in the Celebes area we destroyed an enemy bomber parked along the edge of the Langgoer airstrip on our second run over the airfield. Target went up in flames but our aircraft A8-8 was hit in the starboard wing and 2 feet blown off the wing tip." The aircraft made it home without further incident.

Flying Officer Harry Moo also flew in the Australian produced Beaufighters A8-10, '14 and '16 with FltLt J. Gibbings on seven sorties including a six hour 35 minute trip via Truscott to Dili and return on 18 November. Operations by the squadron ended with the mission to Bacau on the 21st however training continued as aircraft became available. The air movement of squadron personnel from Coomalie began on the 29th.

Malcolm Philps, a wireless fitter recalled the previous day when, "We finished packing...at the wireless hut in the morning and personal packing in the afternoon...We were briefed at 1900 [hours] that evening, and were awakened by blaring music...at 0135...finished packing and had breakfast at 0400 of fried steak and egg...That would have been an

One of 31 Squadron's regular targets was Selaru Island. Here a Kawasaki Ki-48 Lily is left burning after a raid on 22 July 1944. Photo: Murray Weste.

exceptionally good meal as given to a condemned man. Roll call at 0430 – 48 men to travel in two DC3's [*sic*] at 0545...we flew along the coast to Millingimbi [*sic*]..." On 1 December the 21 Beaufighters "...packed with extra gear and each carrying four passengers departed Coomalie...arriving at Noemfoor, where it came under...First Tactical Air Force." The squadron left in its wake a scoreboard of 22 enemy aircraft shot down and 61 destroyed on the ground; 58 vessels destroyed and a further 90 damaged; extensive destruction of Japanese infrastructure and an estimated 782 Japanese killed. It also left behind many members, all friends and fellow airmen.

Over the months from the 21 August 1943 raid on Taberfane and the loss of the Gardner and Leithead crews, 31 Squadron lost a further 13 aircraft and 26 crew; 14 lives were lost on or as a result of operations over the Aru Islands and Timor. Others were lost in accidents or went missing, including three airmen who remain unaccounted for. While it took 49 years to solve the mystery of the B-24, *Beautiful Betsy's* disappearance, there is one that may never be solved: the disappearance of three 31 Squadron airmen in 1944.

On 24 September 1944 two Beaufighters, A19-192 crewed by PltOff L. F. Ritchie and WOff G. R. Warner and '208 with SqnLdr W. L. Wackett and PltOff K. W. Noble were returning to Coomalie after completing escort duty for a Catalina north of Timor. Crossing the coast well east of Darwin and in visibility restricted by pitch darkness and grass fire haze, both aircraft turned east instead of west, looking for the railway and north-south road. A19-192 ran short of fuel and both Ritchie and Warner baled out near Brocks Creek. Only Warner walked out next day; Ritchie was never found.

Meanwhile Wackett had turned east again, circling the South Alligator River area and obviously realising his predicament he switched on the aircraft's IFF; it was still signalling 12 minutes after Fenton radar lost the aircraft from its screen. Intensive day and night searches were mounted however no traces of aircraft or crew were found. Thirteen months later a prospector found the wreckage of A19-208 in a small creek, but there was no trace of the crew. In mid-1946 Mounted Constable Ted Morey, a renowned Territory policeman, and two Aboriginal trackers found the remains of a camp site on a small ridge overlooking the wreckage; a parachute and rations tins confirmed someone

had been there, but who will probably never be known.

What is known is that Wackett was experienced in survival, after having walked out of the New Guinea jungle a week after his 75 Squadron P-40 was downed in 1942. What is also known is that the aircraft came down, probably under some control, and one or both crew members survived for a time before the bush took them - and all the while, whoever it was, only had to travel a short distance to the main Oenpelli Track and 12 km south to Goodparla Homestead. The Sir Lawrence Wackett family had a memorial to the lost flyers erected and dedicated at the site in 1980.

The wreckage of A19-208 after being found some months after its disappearance. Both SqnLdr Wilbur Wackett and FlgOff K. W. Noble remain missing. Photo: Sir Lawrence Wackett family

As the units in 79 Wing were awaiting word to move north, they were joined by the only operational squadron to have formed in Darwin when eight of 13 Squadron's Lockheed PV-1 Ventura and 96 airmen arrived at Gove airfield on Melville Bay on 16 August 1944. After re-equipping at Queanbeyan near Canberra the unit had been based at Cooktown in Queensland from May. Following a detachment to Merauke in early August, the unit was advised of its move to Gove.

The unit had re-equipped in accordance with RAAF Organisational Memorandum No. 404 of 17 December 1943 which had outlined its future in operating "...9 Venturas (type B34) as they become available...No. 13 Squadron will then consist of one flight of 9 type PV1...and one flight of 9 B34 Venturas."

In its first month of operations the squadron flew 76 sorties, all convoy patrols, increasing to 87 during October, at times refuelling at Merauke, Darwin or Higgins Field on Cape

THE OFFENSIVE ROLLS ON

York. In November 86 sorties were flown and whilst patrols were the norm, offensive shipping sweeps were also flown in the Kai, Tanimbar and Aru Islands area. Targets were also hit at Dobo, Taberfane, Tafermeer, Cape Derchi, Cape Oelar and Tami Island, whilst propaganda leaflets were also dropped over occupied areas. In the absence of Japanese shipping, shore installations were also struck. Buildings and the main jetty at Elat Baju were destroyed in one mission. Aircraft staged through Darwin and Truscott on occasion to strike targets further afield but their work was generally confined to the area around east Arnhem Land and waters to the north.

A total of 84 sorties were flown during December including a New Year's Eve armed reconnaissance of the squadron's old haunt at Ambon by the CO, WgCdr W. J. Keenan in A59-71. "One almost wonders if the ghosts of past comrades sent up a silent cheer", the unit historian mused.

The crew of a Lockheed PV-1 Ventura of 13 Squadron prepares to depart Gove on a mission over the NEI, 1944. Photo: Peter Callaghan.

One hundred and thirteen sorties were flown from December to the end of March 1945 when the squadron was advised of an imminent move as part of 79 Wing's push north. Operational activity ceased from 1 April and the month was spent preparing for a move to Labuan. An advance party of 100 personnel departed by C-47 on 16 May and on 3 June the *William H. Seward* docked at Melville Bay to begin loading stores and personnel. The vessel sailed at 0630 hours on the 6th, bound for Darwin to pick up the remaining 79 Wing personnel and equipment.

The squadron's return to the Territory had been brief and in the main, monotonous, however the Venturas and their crews had provided vital convoy patrols, sea searches and

offensive strikes, the latter further depleting the Japanese infrastructure on the islands to the north. But, as with all the squadrons serving in the NWA their stay was not without loss.

In its short stay in the NWA 13 Squadron lost two aircraft. A59-70 crashed near Bremer Island southeast of Gove during a gunnery exercise on 27 January 1945, killing three crew members, Flight Lieutenant E. Calder, WOff Peacock and FSgt L. Ames. The pilot, FlgOff P. Clarkson, and WOffs Cathro and Murdoch were rescued by a 42 Squadron Catalina. A second aircraft and its crew were lost the same day when A59-84 slammed into a hill on finals into Batchelor. The crew of FltLt G. Anderson, FlgOffs B. Poole and C. Watts, PltOff N. Chowns, WOff J. Kay and LAC J. Pugh were all killed.

Wireless Air Gunner Nerdan A. Chowns' last log book entry was completed by the unit Adjusting Officer, "26.1.45 [sic] A59-84 F/O Anderson. Ops travel GOVE-BATCHELOR 2.30 [flight time]." "You realise that Don is with us no longer because the job must be done..." the CO wrote to Chowns' brother, "...and we must go on doing it until it is over...Don... has helped us hasten this conclusion of a weary time for all of us."

With 79 Wing gone there were only a handful of RAAF operational squadrons remaining in the Darwin area by mid 1945. The Catalina squadrons made up the bulk of these units with 112 ASRF and 76 Wing operating from Doctors Gully and East Arm, the Mosquitoes of 87 PR Squadron were at Coomalie and 'Doc' Fenton's 6 Comm. Unit was operating from Batchelor.

At the Darwin Civil 'Drome the RAF Spitfire units were attempting to overcome the boredom of waiting on the word to move south before returning home. On 15 June 1944, 54 Squadron was joined in the NWA by 548 (RAF) Squadron and its Spitfire Mk VIIIs under SqnLdr W. H. A. Wright when they flew in to Gorrie Airfield. There they were refuelled by 14 ARD personnel before flying on to Livingstone. The following day 549 (RAF) Squadron and its Mk VIIIs under SqnLdr E. P. W. Bocock arrived at Strauss. Both units had formed at Lawnton in Queensland on 15 December 1943 and both were the result of further requests by Dr. H. V. 'Doc' Evatt during his second visit to London. Whilst there he had requested an additional Spitfire squadron, another of Lancasters and a third of Sunderland flying boats.

THE OFFENSIVE ROLLS ON

Spitfire Mk VIII aircraft of 549 (RAF) Squadron being serviced at Livingstone strip. Both 548 and 549 Squadrons joined 54 Squadron in Darwin but saw very little action. Photo: Walter Venn.

Again, AM Sir Charles Portal rejected a request by the Australians to enhance their defensive and offensive capabilities and again he was overruled by Churchill, who contended that "It is of high importance for the future of the British Commonwealth and Empire that we should be represented in the defence of Australia...the single squadron...we have sent has played a part out of all proportion to the size of the unit." Obviously Churchill had not been informed of the lack of action by his single RAF squadron, or that of the RAAF Spitfire units in Darwin.

In the event Evatt's request was whittled down to two further Spitfire squadrons, manned by British pilots and predominantly RAAF ground crews. Both units became operational in early July but their stay in Darwin was one of continuous boredom interrupted by an occasional 'scramble' usually found to be an incoming RAAF or USAAF aircraft, and some morale boosting strikes on ground targets in the NEI. In September 548 Squadron strafed Lingat while 549 Squadron escorted the Mitchells of 2 Squadron on a raid against a radar station on Selaroe Island, strafing the target prior to the bombing. October saw a low level sweep on the 11th and an escort for Mitchells on the 16th.

Once in the Darwin area the units settled into a routine of squadron readiness, scrambles, patrols, night flying, practice scrambles and deployments to Truscott. Both were declared operational in July 1944, and in September both flew a 'rhubarb', with 549 Squadron escorting 18 NEI Squadron Mitchells on a raid on the Japanese radar installation on Selaroe Island. The Spitfires of 548 Squadron joined the action in an attack on Lingat.

A further mission was undertaken on 27 November following the discovery of radar aerials on Timor. A chance photograph taken by a returning B-25 testing a new camera revealed the installation and plans for an attack were drawn up. The joint Wing Leader and WgCdr Operations, WgCdr R. C. Wilkinson RAF, conferred with the RAAF Wing Leader, GpCapt. Brian 'Blackjack' Walker, agreeing that 549 Squadron would provide ten Spitfires - four Mitchells, two 1 Fighter Wing Spitfires (spares flown by Walker and Wilkinson) and a Catalina flying boat would make up the force.

In the event seven Spitfires staged through Austin airstrip on Bathurst Island to fly what was the longest Spitfire raid of the war; four hours and fifty minutes in total, requiring additional wing and jettisonable belly tanks. Leading the attack was GpCapt B. R. Walker DSO, OC 1 Fighter Wing, along with WgCdr R. C. Wilkinson OBE DFM and Bar, 1 Fighter Wing, SqnLdr E. P. W. Bocock DFC, CO 549 Squadron, FltLts W. B. Wedd and L. F. Webster and WOffs A. N. Franks and J. Beaton, all of 549 Squadron.

Importantly, the raid was a morale booster to the RAF squadrons in particular, whose morale was at "..an all time low...personnel were terribly worried how their families were faring against the bombings by the German V1 and V2 rockets".

GpCapt Clive Caldwell, OC 80 Fighter Wing, 'pre-flights' his Spitfire Mk VIII prior to departure from Sattler to Morotai, 16 December 1944. Photo: Alford/AHSNT Colln.

In late 1944 it was found that the coolant pipes in the new Spitfires were corroding, when FlgOff Carter's aircraft lost its coolant during a flight to Truscott and he was forced to ditch in the sea. An inspection revealed corrosion to most aircraft, the result of an incompatibility between the

THE OFFENSIVE ROLLS ON

American inhibitor and British coolant. The ground crews worked long hours repairing the engines as the modification kits arrived from 14 ARD at Gorrie. Number 549 Squadron reluctantly handed its aircraft over to 54 (RAF) Squadron, who had moved to Parap on 20 December, whilst its aircraft were modified. Most of the aircraft sat on the ground well into 1945.

The lack of any operational activity but for these desultory actions and the usual practice flights had a debilitating effect on the newly arrived RAF squadrons in particular. A visit to the Darwin units by AirCdre Richard Grice, the British senior officer in Australia, to congratulate the officers and airmen on their achievements was well received by the men; no doubt the 60 dozen eggs and Christmas cheer he brought with him also helped.

The following month the first of the RAAF units, 452 and 457 Squadrons began a long awaited move to Morotai. The move had been expected for some time and the 452 history records show that there had been "...more than a hint that we should soon throw the dust of the Territory off our heels." The move commenced on 16 December when GpCapt Caldwell, CO 80 Fighter Wing, led a mix of 24 Spitfires of both units to Morotai via Gove and Merauke under an escort of three Mitchells, losing FltLt J. R. Sturm who was killed when his Spitfire crashed on landing at Merauke. Four more 452 Squadron aircraft followed on the 28th and the final flight of 24 aircraft was made to Morotai, again under Caldwell and a Mitchell escort, on 6 February. Squadron personnel commenced moving in mid-January via the transport ship *Nicholas J. Winnott*, whilst a number of 452 Squadron ground crew personnel had flown to Morotai by air on the first ferry flight. Others went by air on 4 February.

The departure of the RAAF squadrons left the three British units in Darwin, posing questions by a Ministry of Supply official as to "Why should these fine squadrons be left to languish there?...Surely...they have outlived their usefulness in Australia?"

The questions persisted and in one case the bitter comments by the 548 Squadron CO, SqnLdr E. D. Glaser, in his April 1945 report were returned for rewriting. "As month after month draws to a close the ridiculous situation out here becomes more and more apparent" he wrote, "The squadron has been in Australia since...January 1944,

and has spent at least three quarters of [that] either with no aircraft, or aircraft that are completely grounded. Not a very enterprising outlook for men who are supposed to be fighter pilots...much time is spent sailing and swimming... to...overcome the boredom and uselessness of being a fighter squadron defending an area which is so much to the rear of the war that the word Jap is fast becoming a myth." Glaser's report stood.

The RAF units continued their detachments at Truscott. One RAAF ground crew member, Sgt W. A. Nash recalled his time there as having "...been at Truscott since the 19th March...we left Darwin in a Douglas D.C. 3 [sic] at 6.15... we hit heavy weather in the latter half [of the trip] which made things very unpleasant. It has been a big holiday... since I arrived as we only do the dailies and then we play cards, read or sleep. Some of the boys go fishing but it is hard work." For the pilots however, it was a different story. "I have never experienced...such an atmosphere of gloom, despondency, frustration and couldn't care less attitude than [that] which now exists in these squadrons" the RAF Medical Officer wrote.

Squadron leader E. D. Glaser, CO 548(RAF) Squadron in his Spitfire Mk VIII at the Darwin Civil 'Drome, 1945. The RAF units saw little action and boredom became the enemy. Photo: Marjorie Nash.

The personnel of 548 Squadron had some relief from the boredom on 3 June, when they flew "...a 'morale boosting' level attack on Cape Chater. The raid, ordered by Group, caused the Wing Leader to wash his hands of the operation. S/Ldr Glaser was ordered to lead and rendezvous with six B-24s at Jaco Isle, east of Timor, to bomb and strafe...Japanese aircraft on the Cape Chater strip. Operational orders were to strafe after the bombing...hence the wing leader's non-involvement. The dust from the bombing covered all... [and] on his way out the squadron leader almost collided with a tree..."

THE OFFENSIVE ROLLS ON

Fortunately for the British pilots, however, their time in the north was nearing an end, but for a brief deployment to Truscott in July, and a scramble on the 26th with no result. The following month the Japanese surrendered, on 14 August, and personnel began preparing for repatriation home.

On 21 August 1945 *Wings* magazine had featured an article, "RAF Spitfires still with us", highlighting the RAF squadrons' service in the Darwin area, along with the score of 24½ planes claimed destroyed in combat, eight probably destroyed and sixteen damaged - all were attributable to 54 (RAF) Squadron, and were "...achieved during raids on Darwin...It is twelve months since they had even a taste of aerial combat - a Jap recce went down in flames near Drysdale Mission on July, 20 1944."

Despite the frustrations of its fellow RAF squadrons, 54 Squadron had enjoyed a measure of success during a detachment to Truscott in July 1944.

An intruder was picked up by an early warning station on Cape Leveque west of Truscott at 0855 hours on 20 July and the information passed on to 154 Radar at Truscott, where the Sgt operator, Keith Blackshall, recalled that the equipment was "was relatively new... [with] an effective range of only 50 miles...the operation was handled by two radar operators with a pilot as Flight Controller...we received a 'Tally Ho' from the Spitfires...and we went outside...to watch...It was a very shortlived affair, and the *Dinah* was soon in flames and diving earthwards...the pilots of the Spitfires visited the Radar camp that day..."

A58-329. The intercept was made at 25,000 ft but not before the type identified as a *Dinah* had released fragmentation bombs over them; they exploded harmlessly and Gossland fired. "He crossed my sights at 300' range, 10° angle off. I gave a short burst and saw strikes on the port engine, along the fuselage and the starboard engine. The *Dinah*...went into a very steep dive, smoke pouring from both engines, right in front of Red 1 who followed him down firing...I saw strikes... on the port wing which went up in a sheet of flame and shortly after fell off outboard of the port engine... [and] settled on the sea about half a mile from the main crash..."

The Japanese crew of Lts Kyoshi Iizuka and Hisao Ito of the 70th DCS at Lautem perished in the crash and were later recovered and buried on a remote beach. The 54 Squadron pilots returned to Darwin and a week later Meakin died when his aircraft, A58-390, disintegrated after clipping a tree during combat practice. He was three weeks short of completing his tour and returning home to England.

The downing of the *Dinah* was the first interception over Western Australia and the last in the NWA before the war ended.

Following war's end 548 Squadron moved up to the Civil 'Drome at Parap on 23 October 1945 to join 54 and 549 Squadrons. A number of Spitfires had been ferried to Brisbane and Oakey near Toowoomba from as early as March 1945 and by September there were regular ferry flights from the Civil 'Drome. The last of the Spitfires were flown to Oakey and eventual destruction on 31 October 1945.

The remains of the Mitsubishi Ki-46 *Dinah* shot down on 20 July 1944 were barged to Truscott for investigation. The aircraft is believed to be a Ki-46II model, manufacturer's number 1059. Photo: Alford Colln.

Those pilots were FltLts D. M. Gossland and F. 'Freddie' Meakin in Spitfires A58-312 and '390 and FSgt A. E. Knapp in

Squadron Leader E. D. Glaser, CO 548 (RAF) Squadron and ground crew at the Civil 'Drome Darwin, 1945. Photo: Marjorie Nash.

CHAPTER 13

GAME OVER
The unsung strength, victory at last and Darwin today

They fly through the air with a nonchalant air
With the Zero's they play like the tortoise and hare
So the word gets around for the Japs to beware
For the Cat boats are flying tonight.

They hang on the bomb racks a dozen or more
While 20lb frags simply litter the floor
So start up the donks and we're off to the war
For the Cat boats are flying tonight...

Comes a break in the clouds and a light down below
The skipper has had it so [yells] "Let 'em go"
And mixed bombs and beer bottles rain on the foe
For the Cat boats are flying tonight.

They head her for home and the skipper retires
To dream of the headlines next day that fires
Were visible 90 miles distant The Liars!
Oh the Cat boats are flying tonight...

Though dicing with death most nights of our lives
We still have some time for our sweethearts and wives
Whacko when the 240 hourly arrives
This Cat boat will <u>Not</u> fly that night.

(Sung to the tune of, and apologies to, the *Man on the Flying Trapeze*)

In those units remaining in the NWA from mid-1945 arguably lay the real strength of air operations and the ability of the RAAF to provide the vital support needed to maintain attack missions. Photographic reconnaissance, the rescue of downed aircrews, the mining of enemy bases and the bottling up of enemy shipping along with the re-supply of remote radar and other bases saw these low profile units afforded little publicity.

Of all the operational aircraft used by the RAAF during the war years, perhaps the least publicised is the Consolidated PBY-5 Catalina flying boat. They carried out many of their missions at night, operating from remote bases and were out of the public spotlight, which provided for some much dramatised media attention. While the fighters and bombers, predominately the P-40s and Spitfires, Hudsons, Mitchells and Liberators were constant reminders of air operations in the NWA, the Catalinas flew out for anything up to 24 hours at a time.

Their missions, be they rescue, minelaying ('courting') or bombing were hazardous in the extreme. The 'Cats' were slow, lacked proper defences and were vulnerable, however they sank shipping, and bottled up the Japanese with precision mine-laying as far north as the Philippines, Hong Kong and Taiwan. Thirty three Cats were lost in air operations throughout the war years, taking with them 173 airmen.

Darwin's association with the type went back to late 1941, though these were the aircraft of the U.S. Navy's Patrol Wings 10 and 22. While Darwin had been the pre-war base for the large C Class flying boats of Qantas, any RAAF Catalinas were only random visitors during the early war years. The squadrons equipped with the type were based mainly at Port Moresby, Cairns and Bowen.

A Consolidated PBY Catalina of the US Navy's Patwing 10 on Darwin Harbour in late 1941. Four of the type were destroyed during the 19 February 1942 raids. Photo: Alford Colln.

The first of the RAAF's Catalinas, A24-1, arrived in Australia on 14 February 1941 and was allocated to 11 Squadron. Flown by one of Australia's true aviation pioneers, Scotty Allen, the aircraft had left San Diego under Qantas registration VH-AFB on 25 January. Allen had flown with the RAF in the Middle East, with Charles Kingsford Smith and Charles Ulm, with fledgling airlines and later with Qantas. When he joined the RAAF in 1939 he had some 10,000 flying hours to his credit. His wartime career included time as CO RAAF Rathmines, home to the RAAF's Catalina maintenance and overhaul facilities. There he ran a very tight ship, not always in accordance with RAAF policy, but productivity and professionalism were the legacies of his skills.

GAME OVER

The number of Catalinas staging through Darwin increased in 1942 and 1943, however it was not until 25 August 1943 that four aircraft, A24-32, '40, '50 and '48 under WgCdr Green staged through Darwin where mines were loaded and the aircraft refuelled before setting out for Surabaya. Eight mines were successfully released and the aircraft staged though 'Heron Haven' in Exmouth Gulf, Western Australia, where the American seaplane tender *William B. Preston* refuelled them. The flying time for the mission was 20 hours. Two further missions were flown from Darwin during the year when the harbour approaches at Batu Kelat and Pomelaa were mined on 26 and 29 September.

On 25 November A24-45 FJ-D under FlgOff R. F. Honan, with FSgts Mutch and Bennett as second pilots, flew to Darwin from 11 Squadron's base at Cairns to join a combined mine laying operation in Surabaya harbour. Crews from 11, 20 and 43 Squadrons were briefed on the mission, code named 'Virago', "...that afternoon...by S/L Keith Bolitho, meteorology forecasters, and intelligence officers..." Bob Honan recalled, "...We took off at 1800 hours on Friday 26th November...and headed for a point south of Timor...We were concerned that we would be passing close to Koepang...so we flew low over the water to avoid radar detection. The weather deteriorated rapidly, which removed the threat of enemy fighters, but caused problems surviving the elements...The rain poured down so heavily... [that] the aircraft was hard to control, and the slow airspeed, caused by the two mines, made the flight dangerous....We pushed on, possibly foolishly..."

Missing the datum on the first run over Surabaya harbour, Honan was forced to make a second run "...at extremely low altitude...whilst expecting any minute to be shot out of the sky...There was relief with the mines gone. The aircraft became responsive and manoeuvrable and I applied maximum climbing power." With daylight approaching and the threat of enemy fighters should they head for Darwin, the aircraft flew instead to 'Heron Haven.' The flight had taken 19 hours and 25 minutes.

Three weeks later A24-45 was again caught in severe weather during the flight to attack Kavieng, and again the sturdy aircraft under FltLt Brooks made it back to base. Bombs including four 113 kg high explosive and 20 13.5 kg incendiaries were dropped across the runway dispersal areas and a dump.

Early 1944 saw eight Catalinas fly to Darwin in preparation for a raid on Kaoe Bay in the Halmaheras on 14 January. Two aircraft became unserviceable and another, A24-65 under FltLt 'Chick' Chinnick, developed an oil leak and was forced to return to Darwin two hours into the flight. The aircraft, a 43 Squadron machine, struck a 52 OBU RAAF launch, O15-16 *Whyalla*, shortly after landing in the dark and was badly damaged.

The second pilot, Bob Honan, recalled that "...very soon... [after] we touched down...an object appeared out of the dark...and crash...our starboard wing was nearly broken off, just outside the mine, which was still hanging there." A Court of Enquiry the following day "...found that the flare path had been laid too close to the shore and in future a pilot should supervise the laying and control of flare paths." And that is what he did for some days when "...the only jobs I did were to supervise a flare path and taxi two aircraft to the dispersal area in East Arm..." In the meantime the damaged aircraft was towed into the newly-developed Doctors Gully flying boat base on Darwin's foreshore, crated up and despatched to Rathmines, where it was repaired and returned to service a year later.

The seven remaining aircraft were attached to Darwin until 22 January and flew a further three mine laying missions against Kaoe Bay on the nights of the 16th, 18th and 20th. One aircraft, A24-46, caught fire during refuelling at Melville Bay, burning away the fabric on the wing trailing edge and ailerons; it was towed the 320 km to Darwin by HMAS *Mercedes*.

On 20 February six Catalinas arrived at 'Heron Haven' in preparation for the first minelaying mission over Balikpapan. The six successfully mined the port on the 22nd, noting the presence of four and possibly a further two tankers. Slight opposition was encountered over the target but it was more intense for SqnLdr Keith Bolitho and his crew in A24-62 early next morning when they were attacked by two *Rufes* of the 934th *Ku* detached to Timor. Led by FCPO Naoyuki Yonezawa, they failed to down the Catalina, though it suffered 14 hits. After 18 minutes the Japanese flew off and Bolitho flew the aircraft on to Darwin and a second mission to Balikpapan two days later.

A week later the *Rufe* component of the 934th *Ku* was disbanded and the pilots flew their aircraft to Surabaya, following which they converted to *Zekes*. The remaining

GAME OVER

elements of the 934th *Ku* were redeployed to Ambon and Macassar before disbandment on 1 October. For the loss of five pilots killed and 33 to 40 aircraft, mostly to the Beaufighters, the unit had claimed 10 air victories.

Darwin became a permanent Catalina base during April when it was occupied by the personnel and aircraft of 43 Squadron under SqnLdr P. J. McMahon on the 10th. Previously based at Karumba on the Gulf of Carpentaria, the unit had moved overland and by air over the previous few days. From Darwin the unit was tasked to undertake fulltime minelaying duties. Two missions against Balikpapan were mounted by the squadron on 24 and 27 April, operating from 'Shecat' an advance support base in Yampi Sound north of Derby in Western Australia. Following these visits it was reported that "...Japanese shipping notices showed that the [Balikpapan] harbour was closed between 20 and 29 April and for an undetermined period thereafter. A delayed action mine...sank the Japanese destroyer *Amagiri*...on 23 April." Further operations were conducted throughout May.

Strikes against Halong, a convoy off Vesuvius Bay and Balikpapan were undertaken on the 4th, 11th and 18th whilst Balikpapan was again visited on the 22nd and 26th, with the Catalinas staging through 'Shecat'.

On 1 June 1944 42 Squadron joined 43 Squadron at Darwin when aircraft and personnel moved in to the East Arm flying boat base adjacent to the covert Lugger Maintenance Section of 'Z' Special Unit. Commanded by WgCdr J. P. Costello, 42 Squadron commenced operations, however the unit's stay in Darwin was shortlived. The unit moved to the newly completed Melville Bay and Drimmie Head camp area in east Arnhem Land during July though it maintained a permanent detachment at East Arm.

A proposed move to Melville Island by 11 Squadron was also shortlived. The unit had commenced a move to a new site at Snake Bay on the island's north coast and 60 personnel were in the process of setting up administration and other facilities when RAAF Operations Instruction No. 68 directed the squadron to move instead to Rathmines.

Catalina FJ-K of 11 Squadron on the ramp at Doctors Gully Flying Boat Base in 1944. Photo: Alford/AHSNT Colln.

GAME OVER

By September 1944 the effectiveness of the Catalinas at minelaying was telling and as a result AVM Bostock assigned 20, 42 and 43 Squadrons to undertake the task.

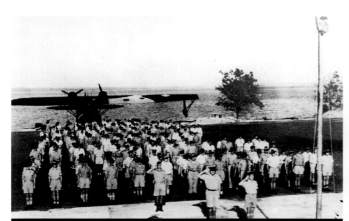

Personnel of 42 Squadron on parade at their new base at Melville Bay in east Arnhem Land. The unit arrived in Darwin during June 1944 only to be transferred a month later. Photo: Peter Callaghan.

With each squadron capable of 830 flying hours per month and with each mission under 24 hours in duration Bostock calculated that the squadrons could undertake 100 missions per month in comparison to the 20 flown during the first six months of operations.

Bostock also directed that 76 Wing HQ at Cairns transfer to Darwin and take control of the three units. By October the Wing was established at Doctors Gully under the command of WgCdr R. E. 'Reg' Burrage. Also based at Doctors Gully was 52 OBU Marine Section with its launches, including the ill-fated *Whyalla*.

To September six Catalinas had been lost with two crews rescued, whilst 25 Japanese ships had been claimed as sunk or damaged. One of those lost was A24-45, which had undertaken a number of missions, initially with 11 Squadron before being transferred to 43 Squadron. Assigned to attack shipping in Namlea harbour on 20 July two aircraft, A24-45 under FlgOff D. Temperly and A24-82 under FlgOff A. Etienne departed Darwin that evening.

Striking very bad weather and unable to locate the target Etienne returned to Darwin. Temperly and his crew, FlgOffs R. M. Harsley and L. J. Blackwell, along with WOff J. Storer, FSgts H. L. Coggin and G. I. H. Neate and Sgts R. J. Robinson, A. Thompson and R. S. K. Wheatland failed to return and were listed as 'missing presumed killed'. Postwar searches failed to locate the aircraft and it was not until

December 1993 that woodcutters found aircraft wreckage on a mountain on the Indonesian island of Buru. A RAAF investigation team confirmed the wreckage as that of A24-45 and on 7 October 1994 the crew was laid to rest at the Australian War Cemetery on Ambon; the crew was buried in a single coffin symbolising the way they had flown and died – together.

Catalina OX-V of 43 Squadron at Doctors Gully. Bob Honan was surprised to find the Salvation Army "...at the top of the cliffs..." handing out tea and biscuits after a mission. Photo: Marjorie Nash.

Doctors Gully also provided a welcome service to crews returning from the long tiring missions. "...at the top of the cliffs, which surround the bay, we were surprised to find the Salvation Army, with cups of tea and biscuits even though it was after midnight" Bob Honan recalled, "...it was the only time that I can remember a welfare organization [*sic*] meeting us after an operation..." The attention was no doubt welcomed as the missions lasted anything up to 20 or more hours; and following that were the debriefings before finally trying to fall asleep.

Sergeant H. D. Davis, a Flight Engineer on the WOff Spaulding crew recorded a flight from Darwin to Panaroekan and return over a total of 24 hours on 25 September. Over six missions during October he flew a total of 79 hours 50 minutes, 67 hours 35 minutes of these at night. In November it was no better:
'13.11.44...A24-68 W/O Spaulding Mine Laying – Enemy Waters – Maccassar'
Flying times - 6.50 hours day 12.00 hours night.
'21.11.44...A24- 57 W/O Spaulding Darwin-West Bay... Mine Laying - Cape Seletan'
Flying times 3.30 hours, 5.30 hours day 12.00 hours night.
Over the month 53 hours, 29 of these day flights were flown. In March 1945 Davis was involved in a number of missions

GAME OVER

from the Philippines, dropping mines around Amoy and Hong Kong. By the time he had completed his operational tour he had flown a total of 592.25 hours, 284.20 of them at night.

September 1944 had seen the capture of Morotai and with it another stepping stone for MacArthur's much vaunted return to the Philippines. The seaplane tender *Tangier* moored off Morotai and by October mining missions against Balikpapan, Brunei Bay, Sandakan, Tarakan, Cape Seletan, and Balabac Strait were conducted staging through the new facility. The 2,400 tonne *Seeto Maru* and 3,000 tonne *Kokko Maru* were sunk at Balikpapan in October and 12 ships were reported bottled up in Brunei Bay – all as a result of visits by the 'Cats' of 20, 42 and 43 Squadrons.

Crew 72 of 43 Squadron. Rear L-R, PltOff Thompson, Flt Mitchell, FlgOff Gray (Capt), Sgt Higginson and FSgt Quinn. Front L-R, Sgt Worthington, Sgt Campbell, Sgt Hay and Sgt Thomas. Photo: Alford/AHSNT Colln.

On 7 December six aircraft of 11 Squadron were ordered to Darwin under HQ Eastern Area Operations Order No. 9, which directed that the unit was to proceed to East Arm Darwin where they would join up with 20 and 43 Squadrons to conduct an operation. It was to be the largest single RAAF minelaying operation of the war. Servicing and loading operations were carried out over two days and 12 aircraft of 11 and 43 Squadrons flew out on the 11th. They were followed the next day by seven, including a spare, from 42 Squadron from both Darwin and Melville Bay.

Staging through Woendi Island the aircraft flew into San Pedro Bay at Leyte, a developing American base but apart from refuelling facilities, WgCdr Bolitho reported, the base "...proved somewhat unsatisfactory from several points of view...the squadrons...were tended by USS Heron...quite inadequate for the job. The Seventh Fleet and USAAF were unable to provide...intelligence which it hoped would be available..."

Over the next two days 76 Wing officers trudged through the Leyte mud trying to obtain information on the target they were to risk their lives minelaying. Unsuccessful, they "...took off with very little reliable information as to the defences of Manila or the amount (and) disposition of shipping in the harbour." Despite their failings at San Pedro Bay the Americans assisted the operation with counter-measures and harassing raids on enemy aerodromes and the mission took place as planned on 14 December.

Whilst the mission was successful, two aircraft failed to locate the datum and jettisoned their mines, whilst one 11 Squadron aircraft had a mine hang up. One aircraft was lost on the operation; A24-64, OX-D was assumed to have flown into a hill and the nine members of FlgOff R. Broadstreet's crew were presumed killed. Each of 11 Squadron's aircraft used in the Manila Bay operation returned to Rathmines with 5590 km flown; it had also been the longest wartime operation carried out by the RAAF.

A further Catalina unit was formed at Darwin on 10 December 1944 with the establishment of 112 ASRF by SqnLdr K. Crisp and his crew from 20 Squadron. The unit's first mission was flown on the 27th when Crisp flew A24-77, on loan from 20 Squadron, to Seroea and Nila Islands to rescue an Allied meteorological party. The unit remained without its own dedicated aircraft, though it stood its first ASR standby on 5 and 7 January; its first aircraft, A24-54, arrived on the 26th.

The New Year saw the 'Cats' continue their long range missions though the northwest monsoons hampered operations during January. The squadrons under 76 Wing were also operating detachments to Jinamoc in the Philippines from February, during which mines were dropped in the South China Sea; 67 successful missions were flown during the month.

Sorties were also flown against China, Hong Kong and Taiwan, utilising refuelling facilities at Lingayen Gulf. Sergeant H. D. Davis' log book entries recorded some of the missions flown against these targets during March;
"11-3-45 1730 A24-82 P/O Spaulding Darwin – Jinamoc - Ops. Travel 3-45 12-00"
"13-3-45 1145 A24-82 P/O Spaulding Jinamoc - Lingayen

GAME OVER

Gulf 5-15"

"13-3-45 1830 A24-82 P/O Spaulding Lingayen Gulf – Hong Kong – Mine Drop 3-10 12-00"

"19-3-45 1000 A24-82 P/O Spaulding Jinamoc – Lingayen Gulf 5-05"

"19-3-45 1650 A24-82 P/O Spaulding Lingayen Gulf – Amoy – Mine Drop 4-40 12-00"

"21-3-45 1815 A24-82 P/O Spaulding Jinamoc – Darwin – Ops Travel 2-25 12-00"

A Catalina of 112 ASR Flight at the Doctors Gully base, 1945. The unit provided valuable search and rescue missions following war's end and was disbanded in late 1947. Photo: AHSNT Colln.

The missions from Jinamoc and Lingayen accounted for 96 hours 30 minutes of his 100 hours 20 minutes flying time for the month.

On 2 May 1945 SqnLdr M. Seymour assumed command of 43 Squadron and he was appropriately involved in one of the last minelaying operations by 76 Wing. "The most difficult part being the take off from Labuan which was carried out in slick, calm conditions" he commented. Number 42 Squadron also underwent a change in command when SqnLdr G. Miedecke took over from SqnLdr 'Bluey' Costello.

The last minelaying mission flown by the RAAF was carried out on 30 July when three aircraft, A24-202, '205 and '307 flown by FltLts H. Healey and K. Hammer and SqnLdr A. Emslie flew out from Labuan. All returned safely to Darwin. The last weeks of the war were spent harassing the retreating enemy whenever and wherever possible. Secondary aerodromes were bombed whilst the major bases at Mandai and Kendari were also attacked. 112 ASRF continued its activities after covering the Liberators

of 82 Wing and losing A24-54 following the attack on the *Isuzu* and its escorts. In July the unit provided A24-112 as a standby aircraft at 'Potshot' in the event the newly introduced Qantas Lancastrians were forced to ditch, while Catalinas also provided support for the operations of 200 Flight, a B-24 Liberator unit formed for use by the Allied Intelligence Bureau and its 'Z' Special Unit operatives.

August 15 saw the cessation of hostilities in the Pacific. The Catalinas were tasked with the transportation of supplies to the NEI and the repatriation of POWs, with ground and air crews working tirelessly to keep the aircraft flying. A24-99 was the first aircraft to arrive into Singapore, on 9 September; aboard were AIF and RAAF officers assigned to witness the surrender of the Japanese forces on the 12th.

The first group of Catalinas tasked to undertake the repatriation flights left Rathmines on 28 August, flying to Darwin before heading to Labuan to evacuate the POWs there. It was hoped the first two 'Cats' in RAAF service, A24-1 and A24-2, would lead the operation to repatriate POWs from Changi. The aircraft arrived at Darwin on 14 September and next morning after an aborted take off due to an oil leak and following repairs, a further attempt was made by A24-1 on the 15th.

Fate intervened and A24-1 crashed on take off in East Arm. Harry Kirkhouse was the flight engineer to the pilot, WgCdr Keith Bolitho, and recalled that "A24-1 was due for a 240 hourly or even a complete overhaul. The engines were gutless and the hull was not in the best shape, however it was decided to utilize [sic] A24-1 to bring back POWs from Changi and on completion [it] was to be placed in the National Museum as...it was the first Catalina we received. It had lasted the war and it's [sic] crowning glory would have been the bringing home of the prisoners."

"All was fixed for...take off at 1415 hours..." Kirkhouse continued, "[and] after a number of attempts we became airborne but the engines started to lose power...there was a mud island just ahead of us [and] Keith had no option but to pull the throttles...the A/C stalled back onto the water and broke its back...we had a crash boat in attendance [so] we were not in the water long...A24-1 was towed to its last resting place..." His log book records succinctly, "Darwin to Labuan crashed on take off A/C sank 1½ minutes."

GAME OVER

After their success in 'courting,' bombing and rescue duties the Catalina units remained in Darwin only briefly once the POWs had been repatriated. 42 Squadron was disbanded on 30 November and both 20 and 43 Squadrons were advised of their move to Rathmines. Effectively 76 Wing was also disbanded, though 112 ASRF remained in Darwin until 1947, performing a number of search and rescue flights prior to disbandment on 1 October.

The Doctors Gully Flying Boat Base remained operational until late 1947 when it went into private ownership. The site is now a popular tourist attraction. Photo: AHSNT Colln.

Perhaps the success of the Catalinas flying out of Darwin was best summed up by Rear Admiral Akira Matsuzaki the Chief of Staff of the Second Expeditionary Force at Surabaya from 1943 to 1945 who confirmed that "...By the end of 1943 mines became of serious consequence...A radar warning net was established as well as...[using] watchers. By tracking planes with radar an effort was made to establish the dropping point. Night fighters were employed but proved quite ineffective. Beginning in 1944, mining had a considerable effect on the exploitation of the vast resources of the [NEI]. Not only were ships and cargoes destroyed but convoys were delayed and unloading areas were jammed at Soerabaya and Balikpapan pending sweeping operations. The destruction of tankers and the delay in oil shipments were particularly serious....about 40% of all vessels over 1,000 tons...were either sunk or damaged by mines. In many cases ships were salvaged only to be sunk a second time...After February 1945 no attempt was made to sail large ships and only smaller vessels, schooners and wooden barges were employed."

Another of the unsung units in the NWA was 6 Comm. Unit, which was formed at Manbulloo on 15 December 1942 as No. 6 Comm. Flight. Equipped initially with a

"...very small fleet of Tiger Moths and Dragons, [it] was working continuously carrying mail, cargo and personnel to outlying bases", the unit records read. The unit moved north to Batchelor and closer to the operational area in February 1943 and its mixed fleet was increased with the arrival of three Supermarine Walrus amphibians seconded from 9 Squadron at Bowen in Queensland.

By October 1943 the unit strength was five DH 84 Dragons, seven DH 82 Tiger Moths, two Walrus and one Avro Anson. By December 1944 the number had swelled to seven DH 84s, eight DH 82s, 12 Ansons, two Walrus, three Vultee Vengeances, one Hudson and a Catalina; an adaptation of the Beaufort, the 'Beaufreighter,' was added in 1945.

Commanded by FltLt Clyde C. Fenton the unit was in good, if not a little unpredictable, hands. Fenton had completed medical school in England and served briefly with the RAF before migrating to Australia and passing through Darwin, where he maintained the Government Medical Officer, Dr. Cecil Cook, had 'press ganged' him. He started his own medical service, flying to remote stations and settlements and destroying a number of aircraft along the way.

Known as 'Doc' Fenton, the 'larrikin flying doctor' and a number of less complimentary but respectful titles, he served the Territory for a number of years and knew it like the back of his hand. He was the ideal choice to command 6 Comm. Unit, but, his independence and dislike of authority saw him fall foul of the bureaucrats and senior RAAF officers on a number of occasions.

Squadron Leader Clyde Fenton (right) was a popular commander whose pre-war antics were legendary. His dislike of formality kept 'the Brass' at HQ on their toes. Photo: Courtesy Katherine Historical Society.

Fenton "...knew the Top End so well he never needed a map and had spent years flying a Tiger Moth to visit his patients"

GAME OVER

Gavin McEwin, a controller at Batchelor recalled, "He had complete and utter disregard of the rules of aerodrome control and of the top brass commanding N.W.A. Nobody ever seemed to know where he was, or if they did, when he was leaving, [or] where he was going next...He was...the cause of a number of air raid alerts and even a number of scrambles – 16 or more fighters would scramble in a hurry only to...locate Doc Fenton stooging along about tree top level. His sole guiding rule was – 'If some one out there is sick, then that's where I will be.'"

The unit carried out a wide range of activities throughout the Top End of the Northern Territory. A Tiger Moth "... daily mail service from HUGHES to GORRIE has been in operation for over 12 months, official inter-unit mail and "Army News" is carried. Personal and official mail is always carried...and in...June, 1944, a mobile cinema organisation was set up for showing at remote bases...Five outposts... get one pre-release picture a week.", the unit historian recorded.

Perhaps one of the more important aspects of unit operations and certainly one of the least publicised, was the rescue of pilots downed over the hostile environment of the Territory. The unit's Operations Record Book entries are succinct:
"Anson DJ322, Pilot F/Lt. FENTON conducted search for Spitfire Pilots around PERON ISLAND areas." Further entries record "4 Jul [1943] Anson DJ322, Pilot F/Lt. FENTON conducted search around ADELAIDE RIVER for missing Spitfire Pilots.", and "6 JUL. X9520 (Walrus). Pilot F/O Lobwein proceeded to PERON ISLAND and picked up Spitfire Pilot, F/O HINDS."

Over 30 pilots and air crew were located and rescued whilst the unit maintained its daily mail, ration, stores and medical flights to outlying bases. Flying Officer Lobwein was also involved in a search for any survivors of the Japanese *Helen* that was shot down into Adam Bay during the 20 June raid on Darwin. Locating a fuel slick Lobwein put the Walrus down and salvaged a Mae West containing a Japanese flag, a strip of red cloth, name tags, a note book and some papers. A fuel tank was found floating nearby but there was no trace of Lt Kenjiro Matsuhara or the six crew members.

At Christmas 1943 Spitfire A58-51 of 54 (RAF) Squadron overflew Drysdale and its pilot, FlgOff Derek Gray, force landed in shallow waters at St George's Basin on the remote Kimberley coastline. Located initially by a Hudson, 6 Comm. Unit was called on and a DH 84 flown by FlgOff G. Jenkins dropped a message to Gray before flying on to nearby Kunmunya Mission.

A Supermarine Walrus of the type used by 6 Comm. Unit and flown by FlgOff Lobwein. A2-17 flew with 12 Squadron and was later destroyed in action in the Mediterranean. Photo: Les Collings.

Jenkins was forced to dodge anthills on the 'runway' and, probably in ignorance of the complete isolation there, asked the Missionary if many aircraft used the runway. "Oh, yes!" he replied, "Quite a few. I have been here five years and four have landed in that time." The anthills were cleared and supply drops to Gray continued until the arrival of FlgOff Lobwein in the trusty Walrus. Gray was rescued, though his aircraft remained in the mangrove mud guarded by crocodiles until salvaged by the RAAF 45 years later.

At the time preparations were underway for Christmas dinner and as the unit historian recorded, "...it had been a hard year...everyone was 'home' except George [Jenkins] and 'Lobby' [Lobwein]...imagine our surprise and pleasure when at 1830 hours the 'Duck' [Walrus] and 'Horror Box' [DH 84] flew in formation over the camp." Fenton, now a Squadron Leader, presided over the dinner declaring that, "...it was a fitting climax to the year's activities that, following on a year's hard work, yet another rescue should be added to the many that have been effected by the unit..."

Not all flights carried out by the unit were so straight forward, and most had an element of risk if not outright danger. Fenton conveyed freight to the Wessel Islands in far East Arnhem Land in Anson DJ322, however the strip there was "...small and finishes on [the] edge of [a] cliff. Aircraft becomes airborne by going over [the] cliff and diving towards [the] sea..." he recorded, "...continuance will depend on availability of ANSON aircraft."

GAME OVER

An Avro Anson of 6 Comm. Unit under cover at Batchelor, 1945. The aircraft is a Mk I, EF921, one of many that retained its RAF serial. Photo: G. Mould.

By May 1944 the unit had a strength of 24 officers and 205 ORs whilst the aircraft strength had also increased to 11 DH 84s, six DH 82s, two Ansons, three Walrus, four Vengeances and a Hudson. A total of 982 hours were flown over the month, conveying 125 passengers and some 36,200 kg of stores. By July 1945 the figures varied little, testimony to the wide range of activities undertaken even as the war had moved away from the NWA.

August 1945 saw the cessation of hostilities though following a rumour of a peace offer by Japan, "...some enthusiasts held a 'dummy run' in preparation..." the unit historian noted on 11 August. On the 12th he noted that the camp was "...strewn with corpses in various stages of disintegration. Those able to move formed "hair of the dog" parties and started afresh." The words are undoubtedly those of Fenton.

When peace did come, Fenton was at the Loran site at Cape Fawcett on Bathurst Island and was informed by the Americans there. He then "...returned to base...called a general parade, announced the news, congratulated all ranks...and thanked them...declared a general stand-down until further notice and broke the news regarding the special beer issue of two bottles per man, which had been cooling down for some days in anticipation [and] then repaired to the Officer Mess to deal with the A.O.C. [AirCdre Charlesworth] who, aided by a thirsty bodyguard, had just arrived to see for himself how the bar was standing the strain..." The following day he wrote, "Camp very silent and subdued."

At the Loran site on Bathurst Island the personnel were also subdued but for a different reason. The surrender "...

had not made too much difference here as [the] operation continues on a 24-hour basis...the 16th and 17th saw us celebrating V-J Day with a precious product...known as eggs, fresh, not powdered. Supplementing our regular ration of beer was an extra 2 bottles issued to all the Allied forces in the Northern Territory."

'Fenton's Flying Freighters' as 6 Comm. Unit had become known, continued their supply runs to the Loran station and radar stations dotted along the northern coast. They also flew personnel to various locations, and it was during a travel flight that Vengeance A27-527 was lost on 11 September.

Flown by FlgOff Morgan, the aircraft had flown to Broome to pick up WgCdr J. P. Ryan the CO of RAAF Station Darwin. As the aircraft neared Port Keats, Ryan mentioned he could smell petrol and Morgan decided to land. He flew over Port Keats before commencing his approach and at about 800 ft he lowered the flaps. It was then that the aircraft caught fire with flames completely enveloping the rear cockpit. Ryan made no attempt to bale out and Morgan was thrown clear as the aircraft went into a dive; he remembered nothing before waking up hanging from his parachute in a tree. Ryan was killed, though it was suspected he had been overcome by fumes before the fire and subsequent crash.

On 7 October the unit moved to the Darwin Civil 'Drome where it remained in support of the outlying areas until disbandment on 19 March 1946. The unit had performed an unsung but vital role in the NWA and had lost very few aircraft; two Vengeances A27-422 and '527, along with two DH 84s, A34-52 and '63. Others had been involved in accidents, including one involving Fenton himself, but most were repaired and returned to service. Vengeance A27-422 had been force landed by WOff F. L. Ellis at Hughes on 16 February 1945 when the fuel system failed. The aircraft was written off as a result.

While 'Fenton's Flying Freighters' were operating from Batchelor, 1 PRU was involved in a number of missions from nearby Coomalie. The first operational flight for the Mosquitoes was carried out on 1 June by A52-2, only three days after its arrival in the NWA when FlgOff K. Boss-Walker and PltOff J. Love flew to Ambon and return whilst the first of the long range missions was flown by the same crew in the same aircraft to Surabaya on 25 June; the port

GAME OVER

engine failed over the target and Boss-Walker flew it back 1,450 km to Broome, a 10 hour 25 minute trip.

On 15 July A52-2 was flown to Biak from where it was to photograph the Davao Gulf area however poor weather prevented any photographs being taken and the aircraft returned to Coomalie on the 19th. Eleven days later the aircraft flew via Truscott to Balikpapan and return. Flown by FlgOff J. D. 'Pop' Bowden, the trip of some "...2,235 statute miles [was] the longest flight yet made by the unit." A52-2 was airborne an hour and a quarter after its return to Coomalie, bound for Ambon under SqnLdr R. Green and PltOff J. Love.

A de Havilland Mosquito of 87 (PR) Squadron being refueled and serviced between sorties. The unit was renamed from 1 PRU in September 1944. Photo: AHSNT Colln.

A52-2 was relieved to an extent when A52-4 was received in August however its 'rest' wasn't to last. The wing leading edges were badly delaminated flying through a typhoon and hail during a flight to Leyte on the 9th. Green diverted to Noemfoor where "We stuffed the leading edge area with rags and doped fabric over the rags...and set off for Darwin and then Bankstown so that de Havillands could examine the aircraft and work [out] a modification for tropical service. The mod consisted of doping rubberised fabric over the leading edges."

Intelligence and photographic information was still required as to the strength of the Japanese naval forces in Leyte Gulf as part of MacArthur's lead up to invasion on 20 October. A52-4 flew to Noemfoor on 22 August however bad weather prevented any operational flying until the 30th. The crew of SqnLdr S. Hermes and PltOff A. L. Kirley tried again on 4 September however they were forced to ditch in Geelvink Bay due to fuel exhaustion as a result of the poor weather. They were rescued by a US Navy Catalina.

By September 1944 the unit was down to three aircraft following the crash of Lightning A55-2 on the 1st. The hard worked Mosquito A52-2 was unserviceable and only two Wirraways, A20-178 and '605, were available. The unit was also redesignated on the 10th, reforming as No. 87 (PR) Squadron, while a further three crews arrived along with the third Mosquito, A52-6. A further aircraft, A52-7 was received during November, allowing a total of 25 sorties, 21 of them considered successful, over targets in the NEI, the Halmaheras, the Celebes, East Java, Bali and the Kangean Islands. In the period September to December, 21 aircrew members arrived at the unit and on the 20th SqnLdr H. 'Herb' Gamble took over as CO.

The long range flights staged through Truscott and one take off there could have ended in disaster. Jim Thompson, a pilot with the 4th Photographic Charting Squadron USAAF's B-24 F-7 type recalled "...an RAAF De Haviland [sic] Mosquito taking off early one morning going one way on the Airstrip while we were waiting to take off going the other way – I was very impressed!"

On 2 March A52-26 was written off when it swung on landing at Coomalie, bringing the available aircraft down to three – A52-2, '6 and '9. A balance of sorts was struck four days later when A52-600, the first of the Mk XVIs arrived, and this was followed by A52-601 which flew its first operational flight to Flores over a five hour 20 minute flight on the 23rd. A52-600 flew to Timor and return the same day. Between 29 April and 22 May four more Mk XVIs were brought on strength when A52-606, '608, '609 and '604 arrived at Coomalie.

Whilst the new Mk XVIs were faster and performed better at altitude, their "...fuel consumption rate...is higher...so that the maximum range is less than the Mk 40 aircraft. So far the use of these Mk XVI aircraft is restricted to the shorter range operations...", the unit historian wrote.

During June, 33 missions were briefed, though five were cancelled. One mission, a detachment of three aircraft to Cocos Island from the 10th was to photograph Singapore for the Supreme Commander SEA Command, Admiral the Lord Louis Mountbatten. Staging through Learmonth poor weather saw the aircraft disoriented and unable to locate Cocos despite the best attempts by personnel there, including the hasty setting up of the still-crated equipment for a Direction Finding station. Two, A52-604 and A52-6

GAME OVER

made it down after being guided in by RAF Spitfires however A52-606, a new Mk XVI aircraft remained missing. With fuel exhausted the aircraft was ditched on North Island near the main Cocos Island group; the crew of FltLt R. Langsford and FlgOff T. Tozer were rescued by launch next morning.

The continued bad weather saw only one mission flown during the detachment, and this was to Christmas Island instead of Singapore. A more successful mission had been flown by FltLt N. G. Johnston and FlgOff L. Williamson on 2 June when they confirmed the previously reported existence of Japanese medium bombers on Cape Chater airfield. The following day four Liberators of 23 Squadron bombed the airfield destroying four aircraft, whilst Spitfires of 548 (RAF) Squadron destroyed another in strafing attacks.

Cec Wright, an LAC Fitter with 1 PRU and a friend in the camp area at Coomalie, 1944. Photo: Cec Wright.

Despite the ditching of A52-606 incidents were few; only four Mosquitoes were lost prior to the cessation of hostilities. The first was A52-7 flown by SqnLdr K. J. Gray and FlgOff W. Sudlow during a planned flight to East Java and Bali, the unit's 85th sortie, on 28 February 1945. Staging through Broome the aircraft was five hours into the flight when Gray reported engine trouble. Despite deteriorating weather and tropical storms the aircraft made it back to the Australian coast where Gray ditched it in King Sound near Disaster Bay, Western Australia. They eventually reached the shore in their dinghies and after a three day walk they met an Aborigine who led them to the Lombardina Mission. In such inhospitable country they were fortunate to have survived.

On 18 June a takeoff crash at Coomalie saw A52-611 written off though the crew were unhurt. Whilst the aircraft was written off the fuselage was retained and later used as part of the VJ Day celebrations. Despite the losses of A52-606 and '611, June was a successful month for the unit. A record number of photographic prints were produced, some 10,488 in all, through the combined efforts of the aircrews and ground crews, along with the hard pressed personnel at photographic section who worked under adverse conditions to develop the films ready for the photographic interpreters as the aircraft returned from their missions.

Personnel of 1 PRU Photographic Section hard at it. Despite the horseplay, they worked under adverse conditions in an effort to develop film for the Allied intelligence units. Photo: Collis via Alford.

The first fatality for 87 Squadron was recorded only a fortnight before the war ended. Squadron Leader J. Gillespie was to lead a detachment of two aircraft, A52-605 and '600, to Labuan in accordance with a HQNWA Operations Order No. 1 of 2 August 1945. The following morning Gillespie commenced his takeoff run in A52-605 at 0713 hours however the aircraft swung off the runway, hit a drain and spun around. It burst into flames and though badly burned, FlgOff F. Haymes, the navigator escaped. "... the cockpit was well alight when the aircraft came to a rest" Haymes related, "Just before the aircraft came to rest I opened the escape hatch and leapt out...my clothing was alight at this time." Gillespie was able to exit the cockpit but was in a bad way and was rushed to 1 MRS via the Station Sick Quarters; after 48 hours he deteriorated rapidly and died on 5 August. He was buried at Adelaide River the following day.

"It is saddening to know that this month, bringing as it does the final victory, should also include our first Squadron

GAME OVER

casualty." the unit historian wrote. Haymes recovered and went on to fly with the post war Survey Flight.

Flight Lieutenant G. Lundberg and FlgOff J. Kercher in A52-604 replaced Gillespie and Haymes and the detachment operated from Labuan without incident over the period 6 to 22 August flying a total of 11 missions.

They flew out in war and came back in peace. A52-609, a Mk XVI Mosquito preparing to take off on the last mission of World War II from the NWA. Photo: Richard Luxton.

Four successful sorties were flown during August, whilst a further eleven were recorded by the two aircraft operating from Labuan. July had seen the unit's longest most successful mission flown; on the 23rd FltLt J. Kearney and PltOff J. Hardwick flew A52-9 some 4,000 km to Semerang in East Java and return over a nine hour trip. The last wartime mission was flown from Coomalie on 15 August, despite an announcement over the radio of the Japanese surrender. At least that was the plan.

A52-609 set off as planned, based upon having received no advice to the contrary. The crew, FltLt Bill Maitland and FlgOff Bill Reedy, took off and with "...great fanfare the crew set off on what everyone knew would be the last wartime mission." The aircraft was recalled an hour into the flight to the Timor target and on arrival back at Coomalie, Maitland made a fast low level pass down the runway before landing. Celebrations for VJ Day included the torching of the remains of A52-611, the fuselage suitably daubed with 'Gamble's Folly'.

Following war's end 87 (PR) Squadron remained at Coomalie before moving to Parkes in NSW on 10 October, though aircraft were also operating from Labuan. The squadron was disbanded on 24 July 1946, albeit temporarily; a Survey Flight was formed soon after and served until 1953.

Ground staff of 87 Squadron ponder the future of A52-611 after its take off accident on 18 June 1945. As 'Gamble's Folly' it was burned as part of the VJ Day celebrations at Coomalie. Photo: Richard Luxton.

The war was brought to an abrupt end with the dropping of the atomic bombs on Hiroshima and Nagasaki. Japan surrendered unconditionally on 14 August 1945 and the following day was declared VP (Victory in the Pacific) and VJ (Victory over Japan) Day.

No doubt everyone in the NWA remembered the events that followed, notwithstanding the extra beer ration. Austin Asche, a RAAF LAC based at 38 Radar Station on Bathurst Island recalled that "On VP Day I was on Bathurst Island serving in the RAAF as a Radar Operator on Cape Fourcroy...We celebrated VP Day on Bathurst with as much beer as we could decently (or indecently) handle. Here we were helped by the kindness of a few chaps who didn't drink, and generously let us have their ration. We still manned the radar equipment ('the doover') and I was on duty that night and made myself very unpopular with our radio operator. He had imbibed freely and dossed down on the floor and went soundly to sleep. At about 2.00am I spotted an incoming plane. With great difficulty I awoke the operator and insisted that he signal this to base. He was ropable, pointing out, with some forceful language, that the war was over. But I had heard of the incident on 19 February 1942, when an observer at Bathurst Island had spotted a large fleet of aircraft heading to Darwin and had reported this to base and been ignored; and this had turned out to be the first Japanese raid on the Australian mainland. My reasoning was simple. The supposed surrender might have been a fiendish Japanese trick to lull us into a false sense of security; and this unknown plane (without identification) may have been proceeding to Darwin with the Japanese

GAME OVER

equivalent of the atomic bomb. I was blowed if I was going to go down in history as the radar operator who let it through. With much grumbling (and some regrettable reflections on my sanity and legitimacy), the wireless operator sent the message. Although I pointed out to him that I had possibly saved us both from a court martial and, probably, a firing squad, he didn't seem the least bit grateful. Of course, nothing came of it and the chaps at Base were probably in the same condition as the radio operator. In case anyone thinks that I am trying to depict my behaviour on that night as that of an excessively virtuous and responsible LAC, I hasten to dispel the illusion. I was not in much better condition than the radio bloke. But I could still recognise a bloody blip when I saw it. My theory about the plane...was that it was some Flying Officer type who...in his exuberance, had forgotten to switch on his identifying mechanism. This often happened when the pilots were sober. After VP Day we didn't have much to do until orders came to dismantle the doover...Some months later we were sent down South to be discharged. Everyone else was delighted. I wasn't. As an old Territory boy, I could have stayed on Bathurst indefinitely."

Further north at the Loran Station at Wiyapurali, the American crews celebrated with fresh eggs and their extra beer ration, but were no wiser as to their eventual fate as the unit historian wrote. "Naturally, as all over the world, time was taken for celebration, but not to the extent that one would expect. Most of the celebrating here was done in the form of bull sessions and in the minds of the men were such questions existing as when we should leave, will the station fold...and thousands of others..." The last of the Americans left in December, leaving the station in the hands of the RAAF.

On 2 September 1945 General Douglas MacArthur accepted the Japanese surrender aboard the USS *Missouri* in Tokyo Bay, whilst Australians, among others including the Dutch, accepted the surrenders of the Japanese in the islands to the north. Australian representatives were also aboard the *Missouri* for the signing of the surrender and whilst MacArthur had praised the Australians in a speech on 17 August, the British dampened the affair by proposing the presence of an Australian at the Japanese surrender ceremony - but only as an appendage to the British delegation - contending that Australia was a part of 'Empire' and thus was not required to be represented.

The arrival of LtGen Berada, GOC Japanese Forces British North Borneo, and his party for the formal surrender to Australian and Allied forces on 30 October 1945. Photo: Flo Stewart.

This prompted Evatt to counter the British attitude with an attack that, whilst aimed at the British, was no doubt also intended for the Americans who had quite deliberately shouldered Australia aside during the war years despite a vow of equality by MacArthur. "...for years" Evatt fired, "... the United States and Australia fought alone in the South-West Pacific, yet despite fine speeches by British leaders and protests from Canberra, there was [a] deplorable tendency to relegate Australia to a subordinate state and either not consult it at all or consult it in a perfunctory way and not on the footing of equality". The Australians attended the ceremony, but not as a part of the British delegation.

To those servicemen and women remaining in the Territory, and the Top End and Darwin in particular, little changed with a number of army and navy units remaining, more to fulfill garrison duties. For the RAAF it was a matter of 'hurry up and wait' for the remaining RAF Spitfire units, 6 Comm. Unit, 12 Squadron, 112 ASRF and a host of support units all awaiting word on demobilization. They were more fortunate however, in that they were at least employed on a number of rescue and supply missions, though even these dwindled over time.

The airfields and airstrips south of Darwin were abandoned and the caretaker units moved to Darwin and the RAAF Station which had enjoyed a resurgence of sorts over the months leading up to war's end. The AWC had commenced a rebuilding program of the facilities destroyed or damaged in the Japanese raids of 1942 and '43, whilst in 1944 the Americans had sponsored the construction of a series of huge timber framed igloo hangars, taxiways and revetted

GAME OVER

inserts to accommodate the expected B-29 Superfortresses. Instead the B-29s were assigned to Pacific bases from which they attacked the Japanese home islands, culminating in the dropping of the atomic bombs over Hiroshima and Nagasaki.

The B-24s of the 380th Bomb. Gp, 4th Air Charting Squadron USAAF and the RAAF Liberators utilised the new facilities instead. Later they were used by a number of RAAF units until Cyclone Tracy destroyed them in December 1974; one was used for fire trials and burned to the ground.

The rapid advances in aircraft technology and dramatic increases in aircraft size, weights and performances saw the pre-war Darwin Civil 'Drome closed down, whilst the RAAF Station became a joint military and civilian facility. The development of Darwin was slow however. Civilians evacuated as early as 1941 returned to the Territory though bureaucratic delays meant they stayed in small townships awaiting approval to return to their shattered homes and businesses to start anew. When they were permitted to return they came to what was still a military town, predominately navy, which retained control over much of

Darwin as HMAS *Melville* until the 1960s.

Former military camps, particularly those at Stuart Park and Nightcliff became home to many families whilst the infrastructure at camps and wartime sites throughout the Territory was surveyed in readiness for the postwar disposals. Territory wide, buildings and equipment at the camps, airfields and bases were disposed of through tender and removed for utilisation in the construction of outstations, businesses and homes in outlying 'suburbs' of Darwin.

But even as the military reduced its strength and planned for postwar security, Darwin remained an important link in the repatriation of Prisoners of War returning home from the prison camps of Ambon, Singapore, Malaya, Thailand, Borneo and beyond. For many, Darwin was the first glimpse of Australia and an important part of their repatriation in the long journey back to normalcy.

The Japanese were also present - this time as alleged war criminals held prisoner at Emery Point on the Larrakeyah army base awaiting trial. It was a bitter irony at the end of a bitter conflict that had cost so many lives.

Repatriated POWs receiving packages from an Australian Comforts Fund unit, September 1945. Darwin was the first Australian port of call for many POWs from the NEI. Photo: Jean Johnson.

GAME OVER

But, from the war came the benefits of reliable permanent power and water supplies, infrastructure and sealed roads, setting the Territory up as an emerging economy and no longer seen as the 'white elephant' of the South Australian and early Commonwealth eras.

In time the RAAF all but disappeared, retaining a skeleton staff at 9 Stores Depot at Winnellie and at the RAAF Station. By the early 1950s however, the RAAF base was hosting units engaged in annual exercises; the P-51 Mustangs of 21 (City of Adelaide) Squadron used the base and Leanyer Air Weapons Range facilities regularly. Later the de Havilland Vampires, GAF Canberras and CA-27 Sabres deployed to Darwin for the annual Air Defence Exercises and in the 1960s the Mirage III fighters of 2 (F) OCU, 75, 76 and 77 Squadrons along with Canberras of 1 (B) OCU, 1 and 6 Squadrons followed. The former wartime airfield south of Katherine, 'Kit Carson', was redeveloped by 5 ACS, 'The Flying Shovels' and, as Tindal, became the north's second forward air base.

Since the 1970s the realisation of the north's military potential has been confirmed with the development of extensive facilities in communications, radar and early warning facilities, a naval patrol boat base, the huge Robertson army barracks and extensive redevelopment of the RAAF Base and its facilities. The RAAF's F/A-18 Hornet force is concentrated in the Top End whilst both the army and navy continue to increase their role in the region.

Darwin has suffered the vagaries of climate and human folly over much of its history. Destructive cyclones in 1897, 1937 and 1974 saw the town all but destroyed, whilst the Japanese raids, ably assisted by the military in many instances, added to the score. In their wake however a vibrant cosmopolitan city has emerged, with modern development tempered to an extent by the tangible reminders of a rich heritage. Today, the Territory is a bustling, rapidly developing force in the Australian economy with its natural beauty a magnet for tourists - who also contribute to its largest income earner. It is also the repository for thousands of wartime sites.

These sites are no longer bustling camps, airfields, warehouses, gun sites or headquarters, but remain as concrete slabs, discarded equipment and personal effects - tangible reminders of the thousands of personnel who provided Australia's northern defences in those perilous years from 1941 and who, for a short time, called the Territory home -

and a lot of other things besides. They remain as testimony to the brief span of intense activities during the period 1941 to 1945.

Many lost their lives over Darwin and the Top End and in the waters and jungles to our north, whilst others endured the harsh climate and primitive conditions in maintaining the operational effectiveness required to prosecute the enemy. Their efforts were not in vain and all are remembered for their vital roles in Darwin's Air War.

Only the scant remains of aircraft wreckage, rusted personal effects and military sites that played host to thousands of servicemen and women during the war years remain in the Territory. Photo: Bob Livingstone.

PILOT PROFILE

CLYDE H. BARNETT JR.

Born at West Palm Beach Florida on 23 June 1916, Clyde H. Barnett Junior worked his way through a Degree in Engineering at the University of Florida and after gaining his Bachelor's Degree joined the U. S. Army Air Corps as a flying cadet in 1941. He graduated from flight school as a rated pilot and Second Lieutenant and married Janet Williams of Orlando on 12 December 1941. He was then assigned to the 8th Squadron of the 49th Pursuit Gp at West Palm Beach.

Lieutenant Clyde Barnett and his ground crew following the 25 April 1942 combat. Photo: Clyde Barnett.

The Japanese attack on Pearl Harbor saw the Group assigned to Australia and after a trans-continental train journey to San Francisco, personnel sailed aboard the USAT *Mariposa* on 12 January 1942. Arriving in Melbourne on 2 February, they paraded through the city to Royal Park and a welcoming ceremony before travelling on by train to Bacchus Marsh (or 'Backward March') and nearby Camp Darley, "...an extremely barren looking place."

They remained there until 15 February, when they were transported by rail to their assigned training bases: the 7th Squadron went to Bankstown, the 8th to Fairbairn and the 9th to Williamtown near Newcastle. There they trained on RAAF Wirraways whilst awaiting the delivery of their Curtiss P-40Es from the Brisbane and Melbourne assembly depots.

From these bases the squadrons were posted to Darwin to provide for its aerial defences. The 8th Squadron arrived on the 17th only to find their permanent base still under construction; instead they were assigned to a small airstrip on the outskirts of Adelaide River. Some training flights were undertaken, however most of the pilots had barely 20 hours experience on type; Barnett made only one short familiarisation flight over Adelaide River itself before he and the squadron were called on to fly in combat with the remainder of the Group when *Betty* bombers of the Japanese Takao *Ku* raided Darwin on Anzac Day 1942.

This was the first occasion on which the 49th Pursuit Gp flew as a complete unit. Clyde Barnett was on standby from before dawn and at 1330 hours was still on 'alert'. Fifteen minutes later he was 'scrambled' as one of four aircraft under Lt 'Eck' Sims, with Lts Morse and Martin making up the flight.

Clyde's diary entry for the day records his first 'kill', a *Betty* bomber, and in it he recalls that even as he sprinted for his aircraft his throat went "...as dry as a bone and I couldn't swallow...my stomach heaved and I could taste sour bile...it was not until I was at 5000 feet that I settled down...I heard Morehead's voice very calm and distinct...'Enemy bombers three o'clock high'..."

"As we let down into the bombers...the Zeros dropped their belly tanks and dove on us...I immediately turned towards them...both...passed right across my nose...and I fired a long burst through each of them. As I was climbing, turning and shooting I stalled and flipped over on my back...When I recovered I was alone...except one bomber below and to my right."

"I manoeuvred into position...and...I went into my dive and started firing from a pretty good way back...I swept the whole fuselage from tail to nose and across the right engine. That engine burst into flame and also along the wing between the engine and the fuselage burned...I noticed a long stream of orange flame coming out of the tail blister."

"I pulled away from him and watched him burn and crash into the sea...I remember...after pulling up from a pass. I heard a 'Thud, thud, thud', and imagined I felt the plane jump."

After eventually landing at Adelaide River, with "...about 15 gallons of gas" remaining, Clyde's post flight inspection revealed a bullet hole on each wing and one in the port elevator – little damage indeed for a young pilot in his first combat and with his first 'kill'.

Clyde Barnett remained with the 8th Squadron, flying from Strauss Field until departing with the unit for New Guinea on 1 October 1942. By then he had added another enemy aircraft to his score, bringing his claims over Darwin to two. In New Guinea he claimed a further two *Zekes*.

Following war's end Clyde remained in the air force before retiring from the USAF with the rank of Lieutenant Colonel after 20 years service. He then worked for the Itek Corporation where he was mainly involved in designing and building specialised reconnaissance cameras for the air force. Clyde and his wife Janet retired and took up residence in Leesburg Virginia and later spent holiday and family times at a cabin on Bustin's Island in Maine.

PILOT PROFILE

JACK 'SQUIZZY' TAYLOR.

Jack Taylor was born at Gawler, South Australia on 19 October 1912 and attended local schools before commencing a Diploma of Dairying at Hawkesbury Agricultural College NSW in 1933. He became assistant manager of the Gawler Butter Factory whilst also learning to fly with the Royal Aero Club of South Australia.

After gaining his 'A' Licence on 21 December 1939 Jack joined the RAAF in early 1940 and completed 6 EATS Course. Continuing with 1 EFTS and 1 SFTS he graduated Dux of his course and was posted to 22 Squadron on 7 May 1941 as a Pilot Officer flying CAC Wirraways.

A year later Jack was posted to the American Ferry Pursuit Unit where he flew a wide range of USAAF fighter aircraft from assembly depots to the operational and other squadrons. In early September 1942 he was posted to 12 Squadron then located at Pell. Arriving on 7 September he commenced duties on Wirraways and in December was made 'A' Flight Commander at Batchelor.

The obsolescent Wirraways soldiered on in a variety of roles including shipping patrols, search and rescue and army cooperation. One involved flying at "zero ft to see if there were any boats or footprints on the sand indicating a landing overnight." Bread and mail were also delivered to the remote camps of the army, NAOU and radar sites, while mail was also picked up for delivery to HQ.

One Wirraway was modified with a six foot long hook under fuselage to allow the aircraft to retrieve the mail from a line between two poles on the beach. 'Squizzy' recalled one sortie where his observer, Warrant Officer Mitchell, informed him on landing that "...he did not bother to lower the hook – but we still picked up the mail."

Jack recalled the days at Batchelor fondly; yabbying or swimming in the Adelaide or Finniss Rivers, "...with several hand grenades plus a .303 in case we had underwater visitors."

From 12 Squadron 'Squizzy' was posted to 31 Squadron at nearby Coomalie Creek and following an eight week Beaufighter conversion course at 5 OTU joined his new unit on 22 June 1943. Though he maintains his Beaufighter tour was "...more or less uneventful..." the 17 August strike on the floatplane base at Taberfane was far from mundane.

Staging through Milingimbi nine Beaufighters made the long flight; six made the attack from very low level whilst the remaining three provided top cover. In his combat report for the day, Flight Lieutenant Jack Taylor recorded that he "...approached from west at dot feet and attacked Rufe just taking off. Pulled up to 2000 feet and opened fire at 70 yards...

hits scored along fuselage. Observer saw aircraft going down and smoke coming from the engine. Classed a probably destroyed...Climbed to 3000 feet taking evasive action from light...A/A...and turned in to attack a Rufe...closing to 50 yards. In making tight turn starboard wingtip folded up. I broke off and returned...to COOMALIE."

Despite his matter-of-fact report 'Squizzy' had three feet of his wing folded vertically with a loss of aileron control. He was forced to use the throttles for control throughout the return journey before landing safely at Coomalie Creek.

A month later 'Squizzy' was made 'A' Flight Commander and on 4 December was posted to 5 OTU Tocumwal as a Beaufighter Instructor where he served until a posting to 37 Squadron as a VIP pilot on Lockheed Lodestars.

Flying Officer Jack Taylor (left) and his observer prepare to set out on a patrol in their 12 Squadron Wirraway. Photo: Jack Taylor

Jack was 'Manpowered' from the RAAF on 16 January 1945 and returned to his peace time occupation as assistant manager in a butter factory. Jack and his wife Freda settled in Gawler on Adelaide's outskirts and after retirement took up travelling Australia, mostly the Northern Territory, in their unique self-designed and home-built caravan.

PILOT PROFILE

ROBERT DALKIN

Born in England on 21 February 1914, Robert Nixon Dalkin came to Australia in 1929 where he worked at odd jobs in country areas. He joined the CMF and in 1936 went to Salamaua in New Guinea, commencing his flying career there in 1937.

After two unsuccessful attempts at joining the RAAF in the early 1930s he was accepted in December 1939. On 8 January 1940 he was inducted into the RAAF and by March had completed a refresher flying course at Newcastle Aero Club and Service Flying Training on Hawker Demons at RAAF Station Richmond. Commissioned on 4 May 1940, he started a Navigation and Reconnaissance course at Point Cook and was then posted to 2 Squadron at nearby Laverton for conversion to the Lockheed Hudson.

In 14 months he completed over 50 anti-submarine and convoy escort sorties. After completing a specialist navigation course Bob spent a few weeks at the navigation school at Mount Gambier and six weeks instructing on Hudsons back at Laverton with 7 Squadron before being posted to Darwin as Flight Commander 'B' Flight 13 Squadron in March 1942.

Bob started his operational tour immediately. "We learned our trade as we went along in the ensuing weeks and months...the need was to learn quickly and, probably more importantly, to be lucky." He was involved in the first attack on Ambon from Darwin in conjunction with a formation from 2 Squadron led by SqnLdr 'Tich' McFarlane. Ambon was at the extreme range of the fully loaded Hudson and Bob recalled closing up "... at water level before the coast and it was quite a sight to see McFarlane's flight pull up over the hills with the palm trees and jungle swirling and parting with the blast of the engines."

"Up, over and down into the bay at high speed...and all the aircraft fanned out to select their targets. The bombs of one of the 2 Squadron flight ahead and on my right hit a ship, and aircraft and ship exploded. This was John Venn and his crew. Our three aircraft attacked ships tied up at the wharf and gained some hits. We were very low and I knew my aircraft had been hit, although there was no apparent damage...We turned southward...McFarlane's scattered flight was well ahead and was attempting to reform. I was at high power and wanted to catch up...but one of my...aircraft was in sight behind me and was clearly trying to join up...The problems of joining up solved themselves suddenly...first the left engine, followed immediately by the right engine, stopped."

"The second pilot was onto the hand operated 'wobble pump' in a flash. I had quickly changed tanks, and had sufficient speed to pull up to about 200 feet. Then, on the way down towards the water the engines burst into action one after the other. The problem then was, did we have sufficient fuel...? In the event we landed at Darwin with nearly empty tanks, petrol still streaming from a ruptured tank...Pieces of bomb were still lodged in the wing tank."

On 8 July 1942 Bob Dalkin RAAF was awarded the DFC by General George C. Brett U. S. Commanding General at an awards ceremony at Livingstone Airstrip; he was the sole RAAF member awarded at the presentation of U. S. air medals.

Bob remained with 13 Squadron and was appointed Operations Officer at HQ NWA until posted south as an Instructor at 1 OTU in 1943 and later Chief Instructor and acting CO of the General Reconnaissance School at Bairnsdale in Victoria. In October 1944 he was posted to liaison duties in England with RAF Bomber Command, where he flew operations to assess RAF techniques that could be developed for use by the RAAF in the Pacific.

Bob returned to Australia at war's end and following demobilisation was a founding member of Trans Australia Airlines before re-joining the RAAF after only a few months as a civilian. Returning to the RAAF with a permanent commission he flew a wide variety of aircraft until 1968 when he was appointed as Administrator of Norfolk Island. He served with distinction in the post until 1972 when he became an aviation consultant in Canberra.

In retirement Bob Dalkin DFC, AE, Air Commodore (Ret) devoted his time to serve as Patron of the proud RAAF Hudson Squadrons Association, joining in reunions to former battlegrounds, serving charities and writing of his many exploits in both war and peace.

"I MADE A PASS . . ."

By R. Hodgkins

Flight Lieutenant Bob Dalkin listens intently as Lt Andrew Reynolds discusses the finer points of fighter tactics. Photo: via Sid Grantham.

PILOT PROFILE

DAVID M. WHEELER

The son of the Rector of Bulwell, David Wheeler was born in Mansfield Nottinghamshire on 28 February 1922. After attending a number of schools including a public school for Clergys' sons, he commenced service with the Royal Air Force on 15 March 1941. Soon after, David was posted to Canada, where he commenced flying training with 32 EFTS on 28 June. After graduating from DH82c Tiger Moths to Harvards and with 94 hours on type he received his wings on 21 November.

From Canada he was posted to 55 OTU before joining 54 Squadron under FltLt Bob Foster, his flight commander from the OTU. Based near Scapa Flow David converted to the Spitfire Vb, an aircraft that was "...easy to fly, very forgiving but very poor visibility landing and taxying...Faster then the Hurricane but not so manoeuvrable [sic]." In late June the unit was moved south but remained unaware of the future for security reasons.

The squadron sailed aboard the *Stirling Castle* as part of "...a huge convoy", eventually landing in Melbourne where they were billeted under a grandstand at the Melbourne Cricket Ground. From Melbourne the unit moved to RAAF Richmond to await delivery of the Spitfire Mk Vc aircraft; David's first flight on the type was on 20 September 1942.

On 14 January 1943 the unit deployed to Darwin flying overland, and for the first time David and no doubt others realised "...what a huge country Australia is. The biggest hop was 3 ½ hours from Mildura to Oodnadata [sic]." He learned too that apart from heat, dust and flies, the voracious white ants considered canvas duffel bags a delicacy!

In Darwin 54 Squadron joined 452 and 457 Squadrons RAAF as part of 1 Fighter Wing. Number 54 drew first blood when FltLt Bob Foster downed a *Dinah* reconnaissance aircraft on 6 February 1943.

From that date David flew 28 hours on operations to 20 June when a force of Japanese army *Helen* heavy bombers, *Oscar* fighters and *Lily* light bombers of the 7th *Hikoshidan* raided Darwin. David remembered the date, recalling that "My big day came...I got one bomber which was a *Betty* [sic] confirmed but my aircraft had plenty of Jap bullets but managed to return to base...glad we could out dive the fighters." David had collected the bullets when he overflew a *Helen* during the intercept and the bomber's gunner had fired into him; he heard the rounds striking his armour plate. Returning to his base at Darwin a number of 7.9mm projectiles were recovered from the aircraft fuselage.

Celebrating in the Sergeants' Mess that evening and "...rather under the influence of drink...stood on the table and quoted:

the bands of marriage..." This, along with his background earned him the title 'The Flying Bishop'.

David's first tour finished five months later on 18 November and he was posted to Ferry Flight at 2 Aircraft Park at Bankstown where he had the "...most interesting 6 months of my RAF career...", flying to over 57 airfields as far north as New Guinea and the Admiralties. He returned to 54 Squadron at Livingstone airstrip on 8 September 1944 and to the Mk VIII Spitfire. Shortly afterwards the unit moved to the old Civil 'Drome at Fannie Bay.

David's second tour saw little other than training sorties conducted over Darwin and on 28 January 1945 his tour finished. He returned to England via New Zealand and following promotion to FltLt flew Hawker Typhoons and P-51 Mustangs till war's end.

Flying Mustang IV aircraft, David recalled escorting Lord Portal to the Potsdam Conference, a low level wing formation flight over Europe to observe the devastation caused by Allied bombing, and the first Battle of Britain flypast on 15 September 1945 as part of a 250 aircraft formation led by GpCapts Robert Stanford Tuck and Douglas Bader.

A group of 54 (RAF) pilots, Darwin 1943. David Wheeler is third from left. Photo: Alford Colln.

On 7 March 1946 David was posted to 19 Squadron and Mk XVI Spitfires before joining 100 Personnel Demobilisation Centre at Uxbridge two months later. Following demobilisation David Mortimer Wheeler joined a manufacturing company and became the Area Manager for London. He and his wife later retired to Hertfordshire to enjoy a family of three children and seven grand children.

Born of Dutch parents on Banka Island on 3 November 1912, Willem Frederik Auguste 'Gus' Winckel was partly raised and educated on Java, later studying at the Nautical College at Delfzijl in Holland. After serving at the Torpedo Research Depot for two years he successfully applied for pilot training in 1936, learning on the Avro 504K type. He gained further experience on a number of aircraft types, including the Fokker FVII and Lockheed Lodestars.

Following the entry of Japan into World War II Gus found himself flying over 200 hours a month during the period to 8 March 1942 when "...the last free day on Java dawned." From February however, Gus and his fellow pilots flew the Bandoeng to Broome evacuation flights; flying at night and in radio silence to avoid interception by the Japanese.

Many of the evacuees were at Broome on 3 March 1942 when nine *Zekes* struck at 0920 hours. Gus Winckel was at the airfield and on spotting the *Zekes*, "...ran to [the] Lodestar, pulled a 7.9 machine gun from its mounting, and made a stand behind a sawn-off tree...", shooting one down. Whilst firing at the attackers his hands and arm were severely burned by the red hot barrel; he was later awarded the Bronze Star for his bravery.

Despite the number of deaths and the devastation of the raid, the evacuation flights continued. Gus was able to evacuate a number of women and children, including members of his own family, from Bandoeng during one 24-hour operation, but was forced to leave his girlfriend, Yvonne, behind.

From Western Australia Gus joined the NEIAF and a newly forming unit, 18 NEI Squadron at Fairbairn on 1 April 1942. The mixed Dutch-Australian unit was in the early stages of equipping with the B-25 Mitchell medium bombers. On 4 June Gus was on patrol off the NSW coast when a submarine was sighted; he immediately attacked with "...six bombs of 300 pounds...from...400ft...just ahead of the foampath in front of the sub", he recalled. "...suddenly the bow came up... and remained like that for a few moments before settling... vertically into the depths."

Gus was recommended for the DFC however Dutch officialdom refused the award and it fell on the Australian Prime Minister and media to acknowledge the action.

After attaining operational strength 18 NEI Squadron was ordered north to McDonald Airfield near Pine Creek on 23 November 1942. Gus completed 41 missions in his first tour, with two *Zekes* credited to his crew. In October 1943 he was transferred to a desk job in Canberra until June 1944.

In April 1945 Gus commenced a second tour with 18 NEI Squadron as part of 79 Wing under GpCapt Charles Eaton.

Flying the new 'strafer' version of the B-25 he flew against ground targets in the NEI, destroyed a number of barges and flew armed reconnaissance missions to war's end. Gus recalled proudly that he failed to carry out only one mission during his tours with 18 Squadron; a kangaroo ran into his right engine during a night take off. "...the right engine became really rough. I had to carefully drop the bombs into the sea and slowly did a left hand circuit to land again. The prop was badly bent."

A youthful Gus Winckel. Photo: Gus Winckel

Following the war Gus returned to the NEI (Indonesia), dropping food and medical supplies to POW camps on Java before becoming CO of 18 NEI Squadron in late 1946. He was also able to locate Yvonne, whom he feared had become a victim of the Japanese and they married shortly after. From 1948 he was test pilot at the Bandoeng Repair Base until he was forced to evacuate an independent Indonesia on Christmas Day 1949.

Gus later turned his considerable flying experience to crop dusting in New Zealand and then became an instructor and charter pilot; a promising career as an airline pilot with NAC was cut short as a result of industrial action and he retired from flying. Gus and his family then returned to Australia and Queensland, where he and Yvonne later retired on the state's Gold Coast, before moving back to New Zealand.

PILOT PROFILE

MURAMITSU SASAKI

Born in the Ehime Prefecture of Japan in 1915, Muramitsu Sasaki graduated from the Academy of the Japanese Army Air Force in 1940 and was assigned as a Lieutenant in the 10th *Hikodaitai* (Flying Battalion) in June that year.

In July the following year Muramitsu was assigned to the 70th *Dokuritsu Dai Shijugo Chutai* DCS, a reconnaissance unit of the 3rd *Hikoshidan* and equipped with the Mitsubishi Ki-15 Type 97 Command aircraft, or *Babs*. In August 1941 he was promoted to Lieutenant and at the outbreak of war in the Pacific assigned to operations in the Burma campaign.

From Burma the 70th DCS was ordered to Java where it flew missions to provide information for the Japanese planners. The unit was also converting to the Mitsubishi Ki-46 II Type 100 Command aircraft, or *Dinah*, and was active from late 1942 flying missions over the NWA. Muramitsu recalled that from October 1942 "...the Squadron commenced the reconnaissance flight in the field, from Darwin to Fenton, to scout the disposition and movements of [the] enemy's air forces, facilities and warships, especially in Port Darwin...We used to take photographs of them at the high altitude. We flew two or three times every week over the field."

Lieutenant Sasaki was active in these operations from February 1943, flying from the squadron's base at Lautem on the northeast coast of Timor. He recalled a mission he undertook on 7 September 1943 as "...the most special event..." and remembered that on that day "Two *Dinah*s took off [from] Lautem airfield at 07:10, and flew to Darwin under the escort of 36 Zero fighters. Lt. Sasaki's *Dinah* (Observer/Lt. Muneo Kubo) had the duty to scout...the airfields from Darwin to Batcheler [*sic*] under the direct escort of 6 Zero fighters. And, 30 Zero-fighters followed his plain [*sic*] to escort indirectly."

In company with another *Dinah* flown by Capt Kurayasu Ichikawa, Sasaki followed the *Dinah* from which Capt Ichikawa's observer, Lt Takebayashi, was scattering tin foil to disrupt the RAAF radar; the first recorded mission by the Japanese employing such counter measures over the NWA. The formation passed over Bathurst Island at 0910 hours and was intercepted north of Darwin by Spitfires of 1 Fighter Wing RAAF.

A large air battle developed as the two *Dinah*s continued south until they too were attacked. Despite the direct escort *Zekes* protecting the pair Muramitsu recalled that they "... gave up the reconnaissance operation. Lt. Sasaki's *Dinah* flew back east under escort...and Capt. Ichikawa's *Dinah* left west at full speed independently."

Despite his contention that the operation "...ended in failure... it [also] remained as a valuable experience for us..." the mission was successful in one important aspect. A review of the combat reports submitted by the Spitfire pilots and the Fighter Sector revealed that a majority of them experienced considerable difficulties in radio communications, in all probability as a result of the 'window' dropped by Lt Takebayashi.

Muramitsu Sasaki was promoted to Captain in December 1943 and remained with the 70th DCS until he was assigned to China with the 28th *Hikodaitai* and its Ki-46 *Dinah* aircraft in August 1944. He later returned to Japan where he took part in the air defence of the Japanese mainland.

At war's end Muramitsu was demobilised in September 1945 and nine years later enlisted in the Japanese Self Defence Forces. Promoted to Battalion Leader in 1962, he remained on active service until retiring, under the age limit, in 1965.

Following a successful career in business Muramitsu Sasaki retired with his family in Yokohama.

Muramitsu Sasaki in uniform during his training days. Photo: Muramitsu Sasaki.

PILOT PROFILE
FORREST E. 'TOMMY' THOMPSON

A native of Kentucky, Forrest E. 'Tommy' Thompson was born in Paducah on 3 April 1920 and attended the town's grade and high schools before entering the U. S. Army in 1937. He served in the Panama Canal Zone before returning to Jackson Tennessee, his parents' new hometown, and then joining the National Guard in 1940. 'Tommy' then completed two years of college before being accepted for pilot training in late 1941.

Following pilot training at a number of bases, 'Tommy' graduated as a 2nd Lt on 20 March 1943 and was assigned to B-24 phase training in Idaho and Wyoming, before test flying the Ultra Top Secret 'Ferret' anti-Radar system at Eglin AFB in Florida.

Promoted to 1st Lt in late 1943 'Tommy' arrived in the SWPA and the 5th Air Force, where he flew 12 anti-radar missions with the 43rd Bomb. Gp over targets including Bougainville, Rabaul and Kavieng. In February 1944 he joined the 380th Bomb. Gp's 530th Squadron at Fenton Airfield under Capt Joe Cesario, his former pilot at phase training.

From February 1944 to early 1945 'Tommy' flew 530th Squadron B-24s, mostly *Sleepy Time Gal*, on a large number of bombing missions and shipping strikes over the NEI before it was lost with a RAAF crew on 30 October 1944. Targets including Balikpapan, Babo, Amboina, Laha, Kendari, Surabaya, Lombok and Lautem were struck from Fenton, whilst Corunna Downs was used twice to stage through on missions against Java.

In June 1944 'Tommy' won a local competition for the design of a Group emblem; his sketch of a lion sitting atop the world striking at Japan and with the logo 'King of the Heavies' remains the Group's proud emblem.

The following month 'Tommy' was promoted to Captain and Flight Commander, and in October volunteered to continue operations following the completion of his first tour of combat duty. Later that year he moved with the Group to the Darwin RAAF Station continuing operations before assisting with the move to Mindoro in the Philippines during early 1945.

In April 'Tommy' returned to the USA with a total of 48 combat missions over 444.5 hours of combat flying of his total of 615 hours flown in the SWPA. Following home leave he was involved in ferrying aircraft to storage depots and closing down a number of bases before returning to the Philippines in 1946 to become Squadron Commander of the 24th Squadron, 6th Bomb. Gp, equipped with B-29s.

He was later assigned to the 22nd Troop Carriers, flying Douglas C-54s over the Pacific before returning home in late 1948. A number of assignments followed until he was again called overseas, to Korea, where he served from 1951 to 1952.

With over 23 years of continuous service under his belt 'Tommy' Thompson retired from the USAF in 1964, however his association with the service was far from over: in 1981 he was instrumental in forming the 380th Bomb. Gp Association and in the following year was elected President for Life.

'Tommy' and his wife Helen took up residence in Arkansas and later, Tennessee, where the Association's affairs kept them from even semi-retirement. Their eldest son, an Air Force Academy graduate, flew F-15s with the 49th Tactical Fighter Wing at Holloman AFB – the same group that flew the Curtiss P-40E Warhawks in Darwin's defence during 1942.

Lieutenant 'Tommy' Thompson in typical flying rig, Fenton 1944. Photo: Forrest E. Thompson.

Acknowledgements

A book such as this requires valuable input from a large number of people and organisations, and in this respect we have been most fortunate.

Much of the information incorporated into the original and this updated and expanded edition has been drawn from correspondence and material provided over many years of research into the Northern Territory's involvement in the major activities during the period of the air war from 1941 to 1945.

Many people, predominately those veterans who served in the Territory, have written to relate their experiences, answering what must have seemed irrelevant questions and in turn themselves asking questions on a specific subject – the answers to which often triggered further research. To those direct and indirect contributors, our thanks are extended.

Hundreds of photographs have also been provided over the years and to those who donated or loaned their valued collections we thank you. The combination of both documentary and photographic material has served to increase our knowledge of the wartime activities over the NT beyond what in many cases has become conventional wisdom.

Many organisations including ex-service associations, Australian and international, have also assisted over many years, either through direct contact or through their regular newsletters. These in time have also become a very important source of information.

The 13 Squadron Association, 18 NEI-RAAF Association, 19th Bomb. Gp USAAF, 22nd Bomb. Gp USAAF, 49th Fighter Gp USAAF, 90th Bomb. Gp USAAF, 380th Bomb. Gp USAAF, 70th *Dokoritsu Dai Shijugo Chutai* in Japan, Australian War Memorial, B-24 Liberator Squadrons of Australia Association, Darwin Defenders Association, Hudson Squadrons Association, the RAAF Museum and the Spitfire Association are just a few of those who have provided their newsletters and whose input has helped make this book possible.

But, to name the many hundreds of contributors over the past 25 years or more would require more space than is available. However, in an effort to at least partially convey our thanks to them we have included their names in the text where possible and in the citations to those photographs selected for publication.

To those contributors who remain unnamed or whose contributions appear not to have been used, you are not forgotten. But, any oversight is solely the responsibility of the author and apologies are extended accordingly.

There are also those whose more recent research activities and generous sharing of the results of painstaking research has provided much new material that has assisted immeasurably in the preparation of this edition of *Darwin's Air War*. Among the many are:

In Australia; AHSNT, Ian Baker, Gordon Birkett, Peter Dunn, Darryl Ford, John Haslett, Shane Johnston, Bob Livingstone, Bob Piper, Owen Veal, David Vincent and the Heritage Conservation Unit of the Northern Territory Government.

In America; Ed De Kiep, Rick Dunn, Greg V. Hill, Glenn Horton, Jim Lansdale, Jim Long, Edward Rogers, Osamu Tagaya, Ryan Toews and Ted Williams.

In Japan; Susumu Akasaka and Muramitsu Sasaki.

In France; Bernard Baeza.

In Holland; Jacob Terlouw.

APPENDICES
APPENDIX 1. JAPANESE AIR OPERATIONS OVER THE NT, 1942-1944

Air Raids by the Japanese against Darwin and the Top End of the Northern Territory have been widely accepted as 64 in total, 46 of these against Darwin and the immediate area.

However, the Japanese flew many missions other than these, including reconnaissance, strafing and nuisance raids. These have not previously been reported as part of the Japanese air operations over the Northern Territory and indeed, the attacks against Milingimbi during May 1943 were not recorded despite the damage and losses caused.

The following table has been prepared based on official reports and documents from both Allied and Japanese sources, research, unit records, personal recollections and published works. It also includes missions mounted by the Japanese and not previously classified as raids.

The 'Own losses' column details only aircraft lost or damaged and does not quantify damage to buildings and infrastructure, whilst 'Enemy losses' refers only to enemy aircraft claimed as destroyed and those confirmed by Japanese records.

Mission Number	Date & Time	Enemy Aircraft	Target	Defenders	Own losses	Enemy Losses claimed
1	10.2.42 1335hrs	1 Recce C5M	Reconnaissance of Port Darwin	Nil	Nil	Nil
2	19.2.42 0958hrs	36 SSF 71 D/B 81 L/B	Harbour, wharf, town area, Civil 'Drome and RAAF Station. At least 252 deaths in both 19.2.42 raids	10 USAAF P-40s	11 P-40s, 4 PBY-5, 1 LB30, 1 C-53, 2 C-45s, 5 Hudsons 1 A-24 & 1 civil a/c	5 claimed dest. 1 D/B, 1 SSF Confirmed *
3	19.2.42 1158hrs	54 H/B	RAAF Station	Nil	See above	Nil
4	4.3.42 1400hrs	9 SSF, 1 Recce C5M	RAAF Station	Nil	1 Hudson	Nil
5	16.3.42 1330hrs	14 H/B 6 SSF	RAAF Station and A-A Bty Bagot	Nil	1 Hudson damaged	Nil
6	19.3.42 1140hrs	7 H/B	Darwin, Myilly Pt, Larrakeyah	Nil	Nil	Nil
7	22.3.42 1051hrs	9 H/B	Katherine	Nil	Nil	Nil
8	22.3.42	1 Recce C5M, 3 SSF	Darwin, Port Patterson areas	12 USAAF P-40s	Nil	1 Recce a/c claimed dest. 1 confirmed *
9	28.3.42 1213hrs	7 H/B	RAAF Station	16 USAAF P-40s	Wirraway damaged.	3 claimed dest. 1 H/B confirmed *
10	30.3.42 1532hrs	7 H/B 12 SSF	RAAF Station	8 USAAF P-40s	1 P-40	Nil
11	31.3.42 1350hrs	7 H/B 9 SSF	RAAF Station	8 USAAF P-40s	Nil	1 H/B, 1 SSF claimed dest. Nil confirmed *
12	31.3.42 2249hrs	3 H/B	RAAF Station	1 USAAF P-40	Nil	1 SSF claimed. Nil SSF on raid
13	2.4.42 1600hrs	7 H/B, 7 SSF	Darwin and oil tanks	16 USAAF P-40s	Nil	Nil

Mission Number	Date & Time	Enemy Aircraft	Target	Defenders	Own losses	Enemy Losses claimed
14	4.4.42 1348hrs	6 H/B, 6 SSF	RAAF Station, Civil 'Drome	14 USAAF P-40s	3 P-40s, 1 fatal.	6 H/B, 2 SSF claimed dest. 3 H/B confirmed * (*)
15	5.4.42 1259hrs	7 H/B, 9 SSF	RAAF Station	12 USAAF P-40s	Nil	Nil
16	15.4.42	4 SSF, 1 Recce C5M	Reconnaissance, Darwin and RAAF	Nil	Nil	Nil. No Allied report
17	22.4.42	4 SSF, 1 Recce C5M	Reconnaissance, RAAF Station	Nil	Nil	Nil. No Allied report
18	25.4.42 1430hrs	27 H/B 14 SSF 1 Recce C5M	RAAF Station	50 USAAF P-40s	2 P-40s damaged	10 H/B, 2 SSF claimed dest. 4 H/B, 1 SSF confirmed *
19	27.4.42 1237hrs	17 H/B, 21 SSF, 1 Recce C5M	RAAF Station	USAAF P-40s	4 P-40s, 2 fatal 3 injured.	3 H/B, 4 SSF claimed dest. 1 H/B confirmed *
20	13.6.42 1222hrs	27 H/B, 12 SSF	RAAF Station	36 USAAF P-40s	3 P-40s, 1 P-40 dam, 1 Hudson on ground	1 SSF claimed dest. Nil confirmed *
21	14.6.42 1330hrs	27 SSF	Darwin town.	USAAF P-40s	1 P-40	4 SSF claimed dest. Nil confirmed *
22	15.6.42 1250hrs	27 H/B, 21 SSF 2 x Recce C5M, 2x 3 SSF escort	Larrakeyah to oil tanks (OFI) at Stokes Hill area.	28 USAAF P-40s	2 P-40s (1 missing), 1 dam.	6 SSF claimed dest. Nil confirmed *
23	16.6.42 1231hrs	27 H/B, 27 SSF	Darwin town and OFI at Stokes Hill	12 USAAF P-40s	3 P-40s (1 missing), & 3 dam.	1 H/B, 1 SSF claimed dest. Nil confirmed *
24	25.7.42 2120hrs	Two flights of 3 H/B	RAAF Station, Civil 'drome	Nil	Nil	Nil
25	26.7.42 2209 and 2324hrs	Two flights of 3 H/B	Darwin town and Vesteys	Nil	Nil	Nil
26	27.7.42 2227hrs	3 H/B	RAAF Station and Knuckeys Lagoon	Nil	Nil	Nil
27	28.7.42 0152hrs	3 H/B	RAAF Station	1 USAAF P-40	Nil	Nil
28	29.7.42 0539hrs	3 H/B	Darwin town and Knuckeys Lagoon	Nil	Nil	Nil
29	30.7.42 0450hrs	3 H/B	Darwin and RAAF Station	Nil	Nil	Nil
30	30.7.42 1405hrs	29 H/B, 27 SSF	RAAF Station	27 USAAF P-40s	1 P-40 & 1 Hudson dam.	3 H/B and 6 SSF claimed dest. 1 SSF confirmed *
31	23.8.42 1242hrs	27 H/B, 27 SSF	Hughes airfield	24 USAAF P-40s	1 P-40, 1 Wirraway, 1 Buffalo damaged	7 H/B, 8 SSF claimed dest. 1 H/B, 4 SSF confirmed *
32	24.8.42 2154hrs	3 H/B	RAAF Station	Nil	Nil	Nil
33	24.8.42 2222hrs	3 H/B	Noonamah, Firdan	Nil	Nil	Nil
34	25.8.42 0005hrs	Two flights of 3 H/B	Darwin, Parap	Nil	Nil	Nil

Mission Number	Date & Time	Enemy Aircraft	Target	Defenders	Own losses	Enemy Losses claimed
35	27.8.42 0447 and 0520hrs	Two flights of 3 H/B	Cox Peninsula and Darwin area	Nil	Nil	Nil
36	28.8.42 0429hrs	3 H/B	Darwin and Port Patterson	Nil	Nil	Nil
37	30.8.42 0239hrs	3 H/B	Darwin town area and oil tanks	Nil	Nil	Nil
38	31.8.42 0514hrs - 0529hrs	3 H/B	Darwin town and Cox Peninsula	Nil	Nil	Nil
39	25.9.42 0341hrs	3 H/B	Darwin and Knuckeys Lagoon	1 RAAF P-40	Nil	Nil
40	25.9.42 0548hrs	3 H/B	Darwin and Livingstone 'strip		Nil	Nil
41	26.9.42 0522hrs	3 H/B	Livingstone 'strip	3 RAAF P-40	Nil	Nil
42	27.9.42 0435hrs	3 H/B	Bynoe Harbour area	2 RAAF P-40s	Nil	Nil
43	27.9.42 0544hrs	3 H/B	Darwin town and Frances Bay areas	1 RAAF P-40	Nil	Nil
44	24.10.42 0442hrs	3 H/B	Batchelor and airfield	2 RAAF P-40s	Nil	1 H/B reported crashed into sea. Nil confirmed *
45	24.10.42 0452hrs	3 H/B	Pell airfield	2 RAAF P-40s	Nil	Nil
46	24.10.42 0457hrs	3 H/B	Cox Peninsula	2 RAAF P-40s	Nil	Nil
47	24.10.42 0512hrs	3 H/B	RAAF Station	2 RAAF P-40s	Nil	Nil
48	25.10.42 0530hrs	2 Flights of 3 H/B	Darwin and RAAF Station	4 RAAF P-40s	Nil	Nil
49	26.10.42 0454hrs	3 H/B	Darwin and RAAF Station	Nil	Nil	Nil. (Japanese records state 9 H/B night of 26-27.10.42)
50	27.10.42 0220hrs	6 H/B	Darwin and RAAF Station	1 RAAF P-40	Nil	Nil. (Allied records state 4 flights of 3 H/B)
51	21.11.42	1 Recce C5M	Darwin area – weather recce	Nil	Nil	Nil. No Allied report
52	22.11.42	1 Recce C5M, 2 SSF	Darwin area	Nil	Nil	Nil. No Allied report
53	23.11.42 0300 and 0439hrs	5 flights of 3 H/B	Darwin and RAAF Station	1 RAAF P-40	Nil	1 H/B claimed. 1 H/B confirmed *
54	24.11.42	1 Recce C5M	Darwin area – weather recce	Nil	Nil	Nil. No Allied report
55	25.11.42	1 Recce C5M, 2 SSF	Darwin area	Nil	Nil	Nil. No Allied report
56	25.11.42	8 H/B	Darwin, Batchelor and Southport	Nil	Nil	Nil
57	26.11.42	1 Recce C5M, 3 SSF	Darwin area	Nil	Nil	Nil. No Allied report
58	26.11.42 0320hrs	6 H/B	Darwin, Strauss and Hughes	1 RAAF P-40	3 Hudsons dam.	Nil
59	27.11.42	1 Recce C5M, 3 SSF	Darwin area	Nil	Nil	Nil. No Allied report
60	27.11.42 0356 and 0446hrs	4 flights of 3 H/B	Hughes, Coomalie and Strauss	1 RAAF P-40	Nil	Nil. No raid reported in Japanese docs.

Mission Number	Date & Time	Enemy Aircraft	Target	Defenders	Own losses	Enemy Losses claimed
61	29.11.42	1 Recce C5M, 3 SSF	Darwin area	Nil	Nil	Nil. No Allied report
62	3.12.42	1 Recce C5M, 3 SSF	Darwin area	Nil	Nil	Nil. No Allied report
63	20.1.43 2244 and 0015hrs	2 H/B	AWC camp and AASL Ironstone	4 RAAF P-40s	Nil	1 H/B claimed possible. Nil confirmed *
64	21.1.43 2154hrs	2 H/B	Darwin and Frances Bay areas	4 RAAF P-40s	Nil	Nil. RTB (weather)
65	24.1.43	2 H/B	Darwin area	Nil	Nil	Nil. No Allied report
66	6.2.43 1250hrs	1 Recce Ki-46	Darwin area	2 RAF Spitfires	Nil	1 Recce confirmed *
67	7.2.43	1 Recce Ki-46	Darwin area	Nil	Nil	Nil – no reports by A-A
68	2.3.43 1334	21 SSF	Coomalie airfield	26 Spitfires	1 Beau' destroyed, 1 dam.	2 SSF, 1 H/B claimed dest. Nil confirmed *
69	11.3.43	1 Recce C5M	Darwin area – weather recce	Nil	Nil	Nil. No Allied report
70	12.3.43	1 Recce C5M	Darwin area - weather recce	Nil	Nil	Nil. No Allied report
71	13.3.43	1 Recce C5M	Darwin area – weather recce	Nil	Nil	Nil. No Allied report
72	14.3.43	1 Recce C5M	Darwin area – weather recce	Nil	Nil	Nil. No Allied report
73	14.3.43	25 H/B	RAAF Station	Nil	Nil	Nil. No Allied report of raid. RTB (weather)
74	15.3.43 1120hrs	22 H/B, 27 SSF	Darwin town and OFI	27 Spitfires	4 dest, 12 dam, 3 fatal	2 H/B, 6 SSF claimed dest. 2 SSF confirmed *
75	2.5.43 1015hrs	18 H/B 27 SSF	RAAF Station and Darwin town	49 Spitfires	12 dest. 2 dam, 2 fatals	4 SSF claimed. Nil confirmed *
76	9.5.43	7 H/B	Milingimbi (Stuart in Japanese records)	Nil	Nil	Nil
77	10.5.43	9 SSF	Milingimbi	5 Spitfires	1 Spitfire	2 SSF claimed dest. 2 SSF confirmed *
78	23.5.43	1 Recce Ki-46	Darwin area	1 Spitfire	Nil	Nil
79	28.5.43	9 H/B	Milingimbi	6 Spitfires	2 Spitfires 2 fatals	3 H/B claimed. 4 confirmed *
80	17.6.43	1 Recce Ki-46	RAAF Station, Winnellie	42 Spitfires	Nil	Nil.
81	20.6.43 1043hrs	18 H/B 9 Lt/B 22 SSF JIAAF	RAAF Station and Winnellie (High and Low level bombing and strafing attacks)	46 Spitfires	2 dest. 2 fatals	9 H/B, 1 Lt/B, 5 SSF claimed. 2 H/B, 1 SSF confirmed *
82	22.6.43	22 SSF JIAAF	Darwin area	Nil	Nil	1 reported lost.
83	27.6.43	1 Recce Ki-46	Fenton and Brocks Creek area	Nil	Nil	Nil
84	28.6.43 1107hrs	9 H/B 27 SSF	Vesteys	42 Spitfires	3 dest.	4 SSF claimed. Nil confirmed *

Mission Number	Date & Time	Enemy Aircraft	Target	Defenders	Own losses	Enemy Losses claimed
85	30.6.43 1230hrs	23 H/B 27 SSF	Fenton airfield (Brocks Creek in Japanese records)	38 Spitfires	6 dest. 2 fatals. 3 B-24, 1 CW-21 dest. on ground	6 H/B, 3 SSF claimed dest. Nil confirmed *
86	3.7.43	1 Recce Ki-46	Fenton and Brocks Creek area	Nil	Nil	Nil
87	5.7.43	1 Recce Ki-46	Fenton and Brocks Creek area	Nil	Nil	Nil
88	6.7.43 1202hrs	27 H/B, 21 SSF reported	Fenton airfield	33 Spitfires	7 Spitfires dest. 3 fatals. 1 B-24 on ground	10 H/B, 2 SSF claimed. 1 H/B confirmed *
89	18.7.43 1005hrs	1 Recce Ki-46	Fenton and Coomalie	1 Spitfire	Nil	1 claimed. 1 confirmed *
90	11.8.43	1 Recce Ki-46	Darwin area	1 of 8 Spitfires	Nil	Nil claimed.
91	13.8.43 2145hrs	5 H/B	Fenton airfield	7 Spitfires	Nil	Nil
92	13.8.43 2312hrs	7 H/B	Fenton, Coomalie and Batchelor	10 Spitfires	Nil	Nil
93	17.8.43	5 Recce Ki-46	Darwin to Fenton areas	4 Spitfires	Nil	3 claimed. 3 confirmed *
94	17.8.43 1550hrs	1 Recce Ki-46 JNAF	Darwin area	2 Spitfires	Nil	1 claimed. 1 confirmed *
95	21.8.43 0307hrs	12 H/B	Batchelor, Pell, Coomalie, Fenton	10 Spitfires	1 Seagull on ground	Nil
96	7.9.43 0910hrs	2 Recce Ki-46, 36 SSF	Darwin area. Use of 'window' reported by Japanese crew.	48 Spitfires	3 dest. 1 fatal.	1 SSF claimed. 1 SSF confirmed *
97	15.9.43 0025hrs	7 H/B	Fenton and Long airfields	Nil	Nil	Nil
98	18.9.43 0350hrs	7 H/B	Fenton and Long airfields	Nil	Nil	Nil
99	6.11.43	1 Recce Ki-46	Darwin area	Nil	Nil	Nil
100	12.11.43	7 H/B	Parap, Adelaide River, Batchelor	11 Spitfires	Nil	2 H/B claimed. 1 confirmed *
101	11.1.44	1 Recce Ki-46	Darwin area	Nil	Nil	Nil
102	20.4.44	1 Recce Ki-46	Fenton, Long & Brocks Ck area	Nil	Nil	Nil
103	16.5.44	1 Recce Ki-46	Darwin, Fenton areas	Nil	Nil	Nil
104	2.6.44	1 Recce Ki-46	Darwin area	Nil	Nil	Nil
105	12.6.44	1 Recce Ki-46	Fenton, Long & Brocks Ck areas	8 Spitfires	1 – engine failure	1 confirmed

Designations used in the table
Japanese aircraft:

H/B Heavy bomber	Mitsubishi G4M *Betty*, Mitsubishi G3M *Nell* (noon raid 19-2-42 only) and Nakajima Ki-49 *Helen* (20-6-43 raid only)
SSF Single seat fighter	Mitsubishi A6M2 *Zeke*, A6M3 *Hamp* and Nakajima Ki-43 *Oscar* (20-6-43 and 22-6-43 raids only)
D/B	Dive bomber - Aichi D3A *Val*
L/B	Level bomber - Nakajima B5N *Kate*
Lt/B	Light bomber - Kawasaki Ki-48 *Lily* (20-6-43 raid only)
Recce	Reconnaissance - Mitsubishi C5M *Babs* to 14-3-43 and Mitsubishi Ki-46 *Dinah* from 24-10-42 and 1943-44. The Ki-46 downed at 94 above was on strength to *Ku* 202 JNAF.

Allied aircraft:

PBY-5	Consolidated Catalina flying boat
P-40	Curtiss P-40E Warhawk/Kittyhawk of USAAF 49th Fighter Gp, 76 and 77 Squadrons RAAF
Hudson	Lockheed Hudson medium bomber
Wirraway	Australian built CAC Wirraway communications aircraft
Buffalo	Brewster Buffalo fighter adapted for RAAF reconnaissance
LB-30	RAF version of the B-24 Liberator
Spitfire	Supermarine Mk Vc Spitfire of 452 and 457 Squadrons RAAF and 54 (RAF) Sqn.
Beaufighter	Beau' in text. Beaufighter strike aircraft of 31 Sqn RAAF.
B-24	Consolidated B-24 Liberator of the 319th Squadron 90th Bomb. Gp, 380th Bomb. Gp USAAF
CW-21	Curtiss CW-21 Falcon utility aircraft ex NEIAF stock
Seagull	Supermarine Seagull (Walrus) flying boat – air sea rescue and communications

Note: The numbers and types of enemy losses contained in the above table reflect the numbers claimed by Allied forces and do not reflect the actual numbers lost in many cases. Those marked with an asterisk * denote figures made available through research and official records in recent years at a variety of repositories and requiring further research in confirming actual losses.

The notation (*) against Mission No. 14 denotes confirmation that three H/B were written off in crash landings at their base on return.

RTB (weather) - Returned to base due to weather.

Correction

An incursion was reported on 5 December 1942 when four 76 Squadron P-40s attempted to intercept what was later identified as a *Dinah* north of Darwin. The *Dinah* had the edge and 'went into a very slight dive and drew away...' the P-40 pilots reported.
(See National Archives of Australia. File 4/4/INTEL. *Attempted Interception of Enemy Aircraft. Interrogation of Pilots.* Copy courtesy Edward Rogers USA)

One reconnaissance mission by a 70th DCS *Dinah* inadvertently omitted was that of 7 March 1943. The *Dinah* was intercepted by four Spitfires of 457 Squadron RAAF and downed by FltLt McLean and FSgt McDowell. See also page 98.

These two incidents would therefore bring the total to 107 missions.

APPENDIX 2
MAJOR OPERATIONAL UNITS, NWA 1941-1945

Unit	Code	Service	Aircraft type	Major location/s
1 PRU (later 87 (PR) Sqn)	QK	RAAF	Buffalo, Lancer, Lightning, Wirraway, Mosquito	Hughes, Coomalie Creek
1 Sqn	US, NA	RAAF	Beaufort	Gould
2 Sqn	KO	RAAF	Hudson, Mitchell Batchelor, Hughes	RAAF Darwin, Daly Waters,
6 Comm. Unit	XJ	RAAF	Tiger Moth, Dragon, Walrus, Beaufort, Vengeance, Anson	Manbulloo, Batchelor
12 Sqn	NH	RAAF	Wirraway, Vengeance, Liberator	Civil 'Drome, Batchelor, Pell, RAAF Darwin
13 Sqn	SF	RAAF	Hudson, Beaufort, Ventura	RAAF Darwin, Daly Waters, Hughes, Gove
18 NEI Sqn	RNEIAF		Mitchell	McDonald, Batchelor
20 Sqn	RB	RAAF	Catalina	Doctors Gully, East Arm
21 Sqn	GA, MJ	RAAF	Liberator	Fenton, RAAF Darwin
23 Sqn	NV	RAAF	Liberator	Long
24 Sqn	GR	RAAF	Liberator	Fenton
31 Sqn	EH	RAAF	Beaufighter	Coomalie Creek
42 Sqn	RK	RAAF	Catalina	East Arm, Melville Bay
43 Sqn	OX	RAAF	Catalina	Doctors Gully
54 (RAF) Sqn	DL	RAF	Spitfire	RAAF Darwin, Livingstone, Civil 'Drome
76 Sqn	SV	RAAF	Kittyhawk	Strauss
77 Sqn	AM	RAAF	Kittyhawk	Livingstone
83 Sqn	MH	RAAF	Boomerang	Gove, Milingimbi
112 ASRF	LJ	RAAF	Catalina	Doctors Gully
452 Sqn	QY	RAAF	Spitfire	Strauss, Sattler
457 Sqn	XB, ZP	RAAF	Spitfire	Livingstone, Sattler
548 (RAF) Sqn	TS	RAF	Spitfire	Livingstone, Civil 'Drome
549 (RAF) Sqn	ZF	RAF	Spitfire	Strauss, Civil 'Drome
49th Fighter Gp		USAAF		HQ at 35-Mile
7th Sqn			P-40E Warhawk	Batchelor
8th Sqn			P-40E Warhawk	Adelaide River, Strauss
9th Sqn			P-40E Warhawk	Batchelor, Livingstone
19th Bomb. Gp		USAAF	B-17C & D Fortress	Batchelor
90th Bomb. Gp		USAAF		HQ at Iron Range Qld
319th Bomb. Sqn			B-24 Liberator	Fenton
380th Bomb. Gp		USAAF		HQ at Fenton
528th Bomb. Sqn			B-24 Liberator	Fenton, RAAF Darwin
529th Bomb. Sqn			B-24 Liberator	Manbulloo, Long, RAAF Darwin
530th Bomb. Sqn			B-24 Liberator	Fenton, RAAF Darwin
531st Bomb. Sqn			B-24 Liberator	Manbulloo, Long, RAAF Darwin
3 *Ku*	X-	JNAF	A6M2 *Zeke*	Timor, Ambon
Ku 202	X2-	JNAF	A6M2 and A6M3 *Hamp*	Timor, Ambon
Takao *Ku*	T-	JNAF	G4M1 *Betty*	Timor, Celebes
753 *Ku*	X1-	JNAF	G4M1 *Betty*	Timor, Celebes
70th DCS	*	JAAF	Ki-46 *Dinah*	Timor
934 *Ku*	P6 & 34	JNAF	Floatplanes – *Rufe*, *Jake*, *Pete* and *Rex*	Ambon, Aru Islands

Note: 3 *Ku*, Tokao *Ku* and 36 *Ku* were redesignated as *Ku* 202, 753 *Ku* and 934 *Ku* respectively from November 1942. The 934 *Ku* retained P6-xxx tail codes to September 1943.
 * 70th DCS tail marking was a reversed elongated 'S' extending from the leading edge of the fin to the trailing edge of the rudder.

APPENDIX 3
MAJOR OPERATIONAL AIRCRAFT, NWA 1941-1945

The following aircraft types have been included based upon their respective roles during air operations in, and in order of their appearance over, the NWA.

Fighter
Curtiss P-40E Warhawk/Kittyhawk
Length: 31ft 8 in (19.46m)
Wingspan: 37ft 4 in (11.38m)
Empty weight: 6,350lb (2,880kg)
Max take off weight: 8,810lb (4,000kg)
Powerplant: Allison V1710-39 V12 liquid cooled engine.
Max speed: 360mph (435km/h)
Range: 650 miles (1,100km)
Service ceiling: 29,000ft
Armament: 6 x .50" calibre Browning M2 machine guns.
Survivors in Australia: One flying at Temora Aviation Museum, one on display at AWM and RAAF Museum. A number of others are under restoration to either flying or static condition. Some relics on display at AAHC, Darwin.

Mitsubishi A6M2 Model 21 *Zeke*
Length: 29ft 8in (9.06m)
Wingspan: 39ft 4in (12m)
Empty weight: 3,704lb (1,680kg)
Max take off weight: 6,164lb (2,796kg)
Powerplant: Nakajima Sakae Model 12 14 cylinder air cooled supercharged radial engine.
Max speed: 331mph (533km/h)
Range: 1,930 miles (3105km)
Service ceiling: 32,810ft
Armament: 2 x Dianippon Oerlikon type 99 20mm cannon, 2 x 7.7mm type 97 machine guns.
Survivors in Australia: One on display at AWM. Remains of Manufacturer's number 5349 downed Darwin 19 February 1942 and A6M2 916 on display at AAHC, Darwin.

Supermarine Mk Vc Spitfire
Length: 29ft 11in (9.12m)
Wingspan: 36ft 10in (11.23m)
Empty weight: 5,090lb (2,309kg)
Max take off weight: 6,770lb (3,071kg)
Powerplant: Rolls Royce Merlin 45 supercharged V12 liquid cooled engine.
Max speed: 378mph (605km/h)
Combat radius: 470 miles (760km)
Service ceiling: 35,000ft
Armament: 2 x Hispano 20mm cannon, 4 x .303" Browning machine guns.
Survivors in Australia: One Mk Vc in private hands per Langdon Badger of Adelaide, one flying Mk VIII and one flying Mk XVI at Temora Aviation Museum. One Mk IIA on display at AWM. Some relics on display at AAHC, Darwin.

Bomber
Lockheed Hudson
Crew: Six
Length: 44ft 4in (13.51m)
Wingspan: 65ft 6in (19.96m)
Empty weight: 12,000lb (5,400kg)
Max take off weight: 18,500lb (8,390kg)
Powerplants: 2 x Wright Cyclone R-1820 9 cylinder air cooled supercharged radial engines.
Max speed: 246mph (397km/h)
Range: 1,960 miles (3,150km)
Service ceiling: 24,500ft
Armament: 4 x .303" Browning machine guns (2 in dorsal turret and 2 fixed in nose)
Load: 750lb (340kg) of bombs.
Survivors in Australia: One flying at Temora Aviation Museum, one on display at AWM.

Mitsubishi G4M1 *Betty*
Crew: Seven
Length: 65ft 6in (19.97m)
Wingspan: 81ft 7in (24.89m)
Empty weight: 14,860lb (6,741kg)
Max take off weight: 28,350lb (12,860kg)
Powerplants: 2 x Mitsubishi Kasei Model 11 14 cylinder supercharged radial engines.
Max speed: 265mph (428km/h)
Cruise speed: 196mph (315km/h)
Range: 3,132 miles (5,040km) overloaded.
Service ceiling: 27,890ft
Armament: 1 x Dianippon Oerlikon type 99 20mm cannon, 4 x 7.7mm type 92 machine guns.
Load: 1,764lb (800kg)
Survivors in Australia: None. One example is under restoration/display in Japan and one in USA. A number of salvaged relics are awaiting further conservation/restoration in USA. Some relics (G4M1 T-361) on display at AAHC, Darwin.

Consolidated B-24J Liberator
Crew: Ten
Length: 67ft 8in (20.6m)
Wingspan: 110ft (33.5m)
Empty weight: 36,500lb (16,590kg)
Max take off weight: 65,000lb (29,500kg)
Powerplants: 4 x Pratt and Whitney R-1830 14 cylinder turbo supercharged air cooled radial engines.
Max speed: 290mph (470km/h)
Cruise speed: 215mph (346km/h)
Combat radius: 2,100 miles (3,400km)
Service ceiling: 28,000ft
Armament: 10 x .50" Browning M2 machine guns in four turrets and two waist positions.
Load: Up to 8,000lb (3600kg) depending on range.
Survivors in Australia: One under restoration by volunteers of the B-24 Restoration Group at Werribee Victoria. Others flying or on display in USA and UK. Some relics on display at AAHC, Darwin.

Strike, Reconnaissance
PBY-5A Catalina
Crew: Eight
Length: 63ft 10in (19.46m)
Wingspan: 104ft (31.7m)
Empty weight: 20,910lb (9,486kg)
Max take off weight: 35,420lb (16,066kg)
Powerplants: 2 x Pratt and Whitney R-1830-92 Twin Wasp air cooled radial engines.
Max speed: 196mph (314km/h)
Cruise speed: 125mph (201km/h)
Service ceiling: 15,800ft
Armament: 3 x .303" Browning machine guns (later .50" Browning M2 machine guns)
Load: 4,000lb (1,814kg) bombs, mines or depth charges.
Survivors in Australia: Various examples on display at Powerhouse Museum Sydney, RAAF Museum, Lake Boga Flying Boat Museum, WA Aviation Heritage Museum, HARS Bankstown, Rathmines Museum and Qantas Founders Museum.

Bristol Beaufighter Mk VIc
Crew: Two
Length: 41ft 8in (12.7m)
Wingspan: 57ft 10in (17.65m)
Empty weight: 14,600lb (6,622kg)
Max take off weight: 21,600lb (9,797kg)
Powerplants: 2 x Bristol Hercules 14 cylinder sleeve valve air cooled radial engines.
Max speed: 315mph (507km/h)
Range: 1,480 miles (2,382km)
Service ceiling: 26,500ft
Armament: 4 x Hispano 20mm cannon, 6 x .303" Browning machine guns and 1 .303" GO gun.
Survivors in Australia: One (DAP 21) on display at ANAM Moorabin Airport and one at Camden in NSW. One under restoration at HARS Bankstown NSW. Some relics on display at AAHC, Darwin.

Mitsubishi Ki-46 II Type 100 *Dinah*
Crew: Two
Length: 36ft 1in (11m)
Wingspan: 48ft 3in (14.7m)
Empty weight: 7,194lb (3,263kg)
Max take off weight: 12,787lb (5,800kg)
Powerplants: 2 x Mitsubishi Ha-102 14 cylinder supercharged air cooled radial engines.
Max speed: 375mph (604km/h)
Range: 1,537 miles (2,474km)
Service ceiling: 35,170ft
Armament: 1 x rearward firing 7.7mm type 89 machine gun.
Survivors in Australia: None. One Ki-46 III on display at Cosford, Shropshire UK. Some relics on display at Australian Aviation Heritage Centre Darwin (Ki-46 II Nos. 2414 and 2250) and at Aviation Heritage Museum, W.A.

APPENDIX 4
COMPOSITION OF JAPANESE AIR FORCES

Background

Unlike the Allies, and the RAAF and RAF in particular, there was no independent Japanese air force during the China and World War II periods, with the Japanese Navy and Japanese Army each having their own air units. The USAAF on the other hand was a branch of the United States Army until it formed an independent arm, the United States Air Force, in 1946.

Whilst seemingly complex in their organisation the air arms of both the Japanese navy and army were similar in their hierarchy to those of the Allied air forces.

Imperial Japanese Navy air unit designations

There were about 90 different Air Groups in the Japanese Naval Air Force and these were based on a hierarchical order with the Allied equivalents as follows:

Koku Kantai – Air Fleet

Koku Sentai – Air Flotilla – a numbered air force

Kokutai (*Ku*) – Air Group – Wing

Hikotai – Flying echelon – Squadron. Also used to denote a smaller Air Group unit than a *Kokutai*

Chutai – Flight of nine aircraft i.e. three *Shotai*

Shotai – Section of three aircraft

Buntai – administrative designation (see below)

Koku Sentais were assigned either names or numbers. The Takao *Ku* (later 753 *Ku*) was a part of the 23rd *Koku Sentai* and thence the 11th *Koku Kantai*.

The named naval *Ku*s were linked to either a particular air command or home air base in Japan or occupied countries, including China and Formosa. When the Air Groups left Japan they were usually issued with an Air Group number. e.g. the *Kanoya* Air Group became the 253rd Air Group.

Kokutai were the main air units and these were further split into *Hikotai*, which themselves were fully integrated units. A *Shotai* comprised three aircraft and normally three *Shotai* formed a *Chutai* and in turn two *Chutai* formed a *Hikotai*.

On occasion the word *Buntai* is also used in the context of flying units, and is often interchanged with *Chutai*; however a *Buntai* was generally considered to be the number of personnel required to service and maintain a *Chutai* - that is, nine aircraft with a reserve of three aircraft.

On the eve of the Pacific War those IJNAF forces that were involved in the raids on northern Australia were equipped as follows;

Carriers of the 1ˢᵗ *Koku Kantai*

1ˢᵗ *Koku Sentai* the *Akagi* and *Kaga*. 18 A6M2 *Zekes*, 18 D3A1 *Vals*, 27 B5N2 *Kates*

2ⁿᵈ *Koku Sentai* the *Hiryu* and *Soryu*. 18 A6M2, 18 D3A1 and 18 B5N2.

Land based forces of the 23ʳᵈ *Koku Sentai*

Takao *Ku* – 72 Mitsubishi G3M1 *Nell* (converted to 54 G4M1 prior to the NEI campaign). Designated 753ʳᵈ *Ku* from November 1942

3 *Ku* – 92 A6M2 6 C5M2 and 12 A5M4 (later converted to 92 A6M2 and 12 C5M2 prior to the NEI campaign). Designated Air Group (*Kokutai*) *Ku* 202 from November 1942.

Imperial Japanese Army air unit designations

In light of only one recorded raid being mounted against Darwin by the army, that of 20 June 1943 (a second raid was abandoned on 22 June), the following designations are brief, notwithstanding the 18 month period of reconnaissance missions by the *Dinahs* of the 70th *Dokuritsu Dai Shijugo Chutai* (DCS), or Independent Command Squadron.

The Japanese Army Air Force referred to their air groups as *Hiko Sentai* and were normally numbered. They in turn were under a numbered *Hikodan* and then a *Hikoshidan*. Thus the units that attacked Darwin on 20 June 1943 were the 59th, 61st and 75th *Hiko Sentai* of the 7th *Hikodan*, 2nd *Hikoshidan*.

The army's air units were similar in organisation to those of the navy, with flights, squadrons, wings and numbered commands, however the titles were different. The hierarchy was as follows, with the Allied equivalents provided:

Kokugun - Flying Army - Theatre or Allied air force (strategic or tactical)
Hikoshugan – designation as at December 1941 but upgraded to *Hikoshidan* in June 1942
Hikoshidan - Flying Division - numbered air force, e.g. 1st Tactical Air Force
Hikodan - Flying Brigade - Wing
Hiko Sentai - Flying Regiment – Group (shortened to *Sentai*)
Hiko Chutai - Flying Company – Squadron (shortened to *Chutai*)
Hentai - Flying Section - Flight

At times a *Hikodaitai* was used to describe a Flying Battalion.

On the eve of the Pacific War those IJAAF forces of the 3rd and 5th *Hikoshugan* had some 700 aircraft dispersed over five *Hikodan*, three *Dokuritsu Hikotai* two *Sentai* and one *Chutai*. Included in the 3rd *Hikoshugan* (*Hikoshidan* from June 1942) were the 59th and 75th *Sentai* that were involved in the 20 June 1943 raid on Darwin. They later formed part of the 7th *Hikoshidan* along with the 61st *Sentai*. They were equipped as follows;

59th - Nakajima Ki-43 *Hayabusa, Oscar*
61st - Nakajima Ki-49 *Donryu, Helen*
75th - Kawanishi Ki-48 *Type 99, Lily*

APPENDIX 5
JAPANESE AIRCRAFT DESIGNATIONS AND ALLIED CODE NAMES

Background

In the early months of the war in the Pacific, the recognition and descriptions of Japanese aircraft encountered by the Allies was at best confusing. Despite some knowledge of the types and designations of Japanese aircraft and poorly distributed and studied recognition manuals describing them, the Allies knew very little of the Japanese system of designating their aircraft by type and name and their knowledge of aircraft and equipment was lacking.

The air war over Darwin and its hinterland highlighted the problem. American pilots and intelligence officers offered a range of descriptions, despite having wooden models, annotated photographs of them and silhouettes providing type numbers including Type 1 H/B and Type O SSF 'Zero'. Australian descriptions were no better, recording them variously as ssf, H/B, fighters, dive bombers, bombers, and 'recce', with no apparent attempt at classification beyond these vague descriptions.

Historical records, including combat reports, of the 49th Pursuit (later Fighter) Gp reveal a number of descriptions, ranging from 'Zero' to 'O' fighter' and 'fighter', 'bombers', 'heavy bombers' and 'twin engine bombers' without the use of type designations. In some cases attempts were made to identify the Japanese aircraft by type numbers with even more confusing results.

Among those descriptions used by 49th FG pilots in combat reports are 'Nakajima bombers type 96 and 97', 'type 96 fighters', 'Type 96 serial #3' and 'Nakajima type 97 reconnaissance'. In fact the use of these type numbers described, in some cases, aircraft that were not in service over the Northern Territory during the period of 49th FG operations.

The type 96 fighter referred to the Mitsubishi A5M *Claude*, an obsolete fighter not seen over the NWA, whilst Nakajima type 97 reconnaissance referred to the Nakajima B5N *Kate* used only in the 19 February 1942 morning raid on Darwin. The type 96 bomber referred to the Mitsubishi G3M *Nell*, which was used only in the noon raid on 19 February. The type 97 bomber referred to the Mitsubishi Ki-21 *Sally* – a type not seen over the NWA.

Obviously there had to be a better way of describing enemy aircraft.

Japanese designations

The Japanese method of designation was a 'layered' system, particularly for naval aircraft. Type numbers were applied to both naval and army aircraft, which may have led to their early use by the Allies, albeit wrongly in most cases, whilst the navy also used a system of short designations and later in the war, names.

The Japanese type numbers along with their Japanese pronunciations were assigned as follows and relate to those aircraft which flew over Darwin and the northern Territory.

Japanese Naval Air Force

Carrier fighters
Type 0 Carrier Fighter – Mitsubishi A6M2 *0 Shiki Kanjoh Sento-ki* Abbrev. *0-sen* (also referred to as *Rei-sen*)

Carrier bombers
Type 99 Carrier Bomber – Aichi D3A1 *99 Shiki Kanjoh Bakugeki-ki* Abrrev. *99 Kanbaku*

Carrier attack aircraft
Type 97 Carrier Attack aircraft – Nakajima B5N *97 Shiki Kanjoh Kohgeki-ki Abbrev. 97 Kankoh*

JAPANESE AIRCRAFT DESIGNATIONS AND ALLIED CODE NAMES

Land based attack aircraft
Type 96 Land Based Attack Bomber – Mitsubishi G3M *96 Shiki Rikujoh Kohgeki-ki* Abbrev. *96 Rikkoh*
Type 1 Land Based Attack Bomber – Mitsubishi G4M1 *1 Shiki Rikujoh Kohgeki-ki* Abbrev. *1 Shiki Rikkoh*

Land based reconnaissance aircraft
Type 99 Land Based Reconnaissance aircraft – Mitsubishi C5M *98 Shiki Rikujoh Teisatsu-ki* Abbrev. *98 Riku-tei*

Japanese Army Air Force
Fighters
Type 1 Fighter – Nakajima Ki-43 *1 Shiki Sentoh-ki* Abbreviated to *1 Shiki sen*

Heavy bombers
Type 1 Heavy Bomber - Nakajima Ki-49 *100 Shiki Juh Bakugeki-ki* Abbrev. *100 Shiki Juh-biku*

Light bombers
Type 99 Light Bomber - Kawasaki Ki-48 *99 Shiki Soh-hatsu Kei Bakugeki-ki* Abbrev. *99 Soh-ki*

Reconnaissance
Type 100 Command Reconnaissance aircraft – Mitsubishi Ki-46 100 *Shiki Shireibu Teisatsu-ki Abbrev. 100 Shiki Shi-tei.* A number of the type were also used by the JNAF, including *Ku 202.*

The Americans adopted a simple system of aircraft designation in which the role and series number of the particular type was allocated. For example, P-40 denoted Pursuit number 40, B-24 denoted Bomber number 24, A-20 denoted Attack number 20 and C-47 Cargo (transport) number 47. These designators were followed by a common name, for example the B-24 Liberator, P-40 Warhawk, C-36 Commando, etc., though in some cases these were applied by the British, the C-47 Dakota just one example.

The British named their aircraft for the Manufacturing Company followed by a common name. For example the Supermarine Spitfire, Avro Lancaster, Hawker Hurricane and Fairey Battle, though even these had a sequence relating to locations, weather phenomena, fauna, and a range of seemingly random applications.

In providing short designations to their aircraft Japanese naval authorities adopted a series of alpha and numerical designators relevant to their use, specification, manufacturer and model number from the 1920s. From 1932 the military authorities allocated a Kitai number to all powered aircraft designed or built to a specification or directive as to its operational requirements.

In 1931 the navy also introduced a system based upon the year of the reign of His Majesty Emperor Hirohito, or Showa, where the type was known as Shi. Thus, an aircraft designed in 1940 was designated Experimental 15-Shi, denoting the 15th year of Showa. Different projects were classified according to their purpose to avoid duplication, thus the 1937 designed Mitsubishi A6M design was allocated the designation Navy Experimental 12-Shi Carrier Fighter, whilst another design of the same year would have been designated, for example, Navy Experimental 12-Shi Reconnaissance Floatplane – the Aichi E13A *Jake.*

However, once the design for naval aircraft reached the stage whereby detailed drawings were submitted, a short designation was applied. This in effect became the 'surname' of every aircraft built to either that design or one closely related to it. These short designations were applied as follows:

1.   Letters denoting the function of the aircraft were;

A	Carrier borne fighter
B	Carrier borne attack bomber
C	Reconnaissance aircraft with wheeled undercarriage
D	Carrier borne bomber or dive bomber
E	Reconnaissance seaplane
F	Observation seaplane
G	Land based attack bomber
H	Flying boat
J	Land based fighter
K	Trainer
L	Transport or communications aircraft
M	Special seaplane
MX	Special purpose aircraft either powered or unpowered
N	Fighter seaplane
P	Bomber (general purpose)
Q	Patrol aircraft
R	Land based reconnaissance aircraft
S	Night fighter.

2. The letter denoting the function of the aircraft was then followed by a numeral, which identified the sequence number of the aircraft of that function or operational requirement.

3. The letter and number denoting the function and sequence of the aircraft were then followed by a letter which identified the manufacturer, some of which were foreign companies supplying aircraft to the navy as follows;

A	Aichi
B	Boeing Aircraft Co.
C	Consolidated Aircraft Corp.
D	Douglas Aircraft Co.
G	Hitachi Kokuki K.K. (Grumman Aircraft Engineering Corp.)
H	Hiro Dai-Juichi Kaigun Kokosho (Hiro Naval Arsenal). (Hawker Aircraft Ltd.)
He	Ernst Heinkel Fluzeugwerk A.G.
J	Nihon Kogata Hikoki K.K. (Junkers Fluzeug und Motorenwerke A.G.)
K	Kawanishi Kokuki Kukogyu K.K. (Kinner Airplane and Motor Corp.)
M	Mitsubishi Kukogyo K.K.
N	Nakajima Hikoki K.K.
P	Nihon Hikoki K.K.
S	Sasebo Dai-Nijuichi Kaigun Kukosho.
Si	Showa Hikoki K.K.
V	Vought Sikorsky Division of United Aircraft Corp.
W	K. K. Watanabe Tekkosho. (later Kyushu Hikoki K.K.)
Y	Dai-Ichi Kaigun Koku Gijitsusho (First Naval Air Technical Arsenal at Yukosaka).
Z	Mizuno Guraida Seisakusho.

4. In the case where two or more versions of the design were produced, a numeral distinguishing the particular version, was appended to the previous identification code. In the case of a Mitsubishi G4M1 bomber, it would be identified as;

G   Land based attack bomber
4   Fourth land based attack bomber produced
M   Manufactured by Mitsubishi Kukogyo K.K.
1   The first version of the type; the second version was designated G4M2.

A number of types were also allocated model numbers indicating modifications to the original. For instance the Mitsubishi A6M2 followed the A6M1 and was allotted MK I, and the A6M3 Mk II, though these changed to Model 21 and Model 32 in January 1943.

Type numbers were also introduced by the navy in 1929 and were based on the army system initiated two years previously in denoting the year of manufacture. For example the A6M2 was allocated the designation 'Type 0' indicating 1940, though the army designation was Type 100 as applied to the Mitsubishi Ki-46 Type 100 Command Reconnaissance aircraft later allocated the code name *Dinah* by the Allies.

Names were also allocated, with different types allotted names associated with meteorological phenomena, trees, the seas, and constellations among others used from 1943.

The Japanese army on the other hand retained the Kitai type numbers, Ki-43 (Type 1 Fighter), Ki-46 (Type 100 Command Reconnaissance aircraft), Ki-48 (Type 99 Light Bomber), Ki-49 (Type 100 Heavy Bomber), etc., in identifying its aircraft, followed by a name, such as the Ki-43 *Hayabusa* – Peregrine Falcon and Ki-49 *Donryu* – Storm Dragon. The navy followed suit in 1944.

Each new design was allocated a Kitai or body/fuselage number to identify the design through its various developmental stages. For instance the army's Type 1 fighter produced by Nakajima retained its Kitai or Ki number 43 throughout its life and was identified as the Nakajima Ki-43 followed by the various model numbers as modifications and improvements were incorporated. Whilst naval aircraft were also allocated a Kitai number, for example the identification plate found on Aichi Type 99 No. 3304 shot down over Darwin on 19 February 1942 was translated as "(Kitai Bango) 1 – Body Number: Aichi No. 3304.", its aircraft were assigned the alpha/numeric system described above – i.e. D3A1.

Thus when identifying navy or army aircraft used over the NWA, D3A1, G4M1, C5M2, A6M2 denote naval aircraft while Ki-43, Ki-49 and Ki-48 denote those army aircraft involved in the 20 June 1943 raid and Ki-46 denotes the *Dinahs* used for reconnaissance.

Allied code names
With the confusion in identifying Japanese aircraft, a simple classification system was needed, which would provide aircrew and intelligence staff with a system that was easy and effective in identifying individual Japanese types more accurately.

Around July 1942 the Director of Intelligence at HQ Allied Air Forces SWPA, Air Commodore James E. Hewitt RAAF, assigned USAAF Captain Frank McCoy, with what was considered a 'daunting task' at the time, that of classifying Japanese aircraft and codifying the names given to them for use by the Allies.

McCoy then commanded TAIU which had formed at Victoria Barracks in Melbourne in mid-1942, before later moving to MacArthur's HQ in Brisbane. TAIU became a vital part of Allied intelligence gathering in relation to identifying, classifying, assessing and reporting on Japanese aircraft and equipment through a range of manuals and memoranda.

An informal system of identification was in limited use at the time, with *Abdul* assigned the Nakajima Ki-27 (later named *Nate*) and *Jim* to the Nakajima Ki-43 (later named *Oscar*), however McCoy decided to start anew and with his two assistants, TSgt Francis Williams and Cpl Joseph Gratton, came up with 75 names in the first month. McCoy selected most of the names and many reflected his Tennessee background in relating to the Ozarks and other southern parts of America. *Rufe, Nate, Zeke, Jake, Irving, Myrt* and *Gus* were just a few. One that was not named by TAIU was *Tojo*, the Nakajima Ki-44 *Shoki*, which was named by HQ China Burma India (CBI) Theatre.

Other names were selected at random, but conformed to a system whereby bombers and floatplanes were assigned female names, fighters given male names, transport planes 'T' names, trainers were named after trees and reconnaissance and flying boats were also assigned female names.

Many were named by Williams. For instance, *Sally* was named for the wife of McCoy's Group Commander, *Joyce* for a WAAAF who worked in his section, and *Betty* after "...a well endowed nurse." The new version of the 'Zero', the A6M3 Mk II, was named *Hap*, however it is said the General 'Hap' Arnold didn't see the humour and it was changed to *Hamp*, another name common in the southern states.

Australian and American TAIU staff under LtGen George Brett at Allied HQ had been collecting information and photographs of Japanese aircraft, armament and air organization for some time and in order to disseminate the detailed information they had collected, a comprehensive manual was proposed. The lack of uniformity in the designations of Japanese aircraft was noted by McCoy and he urged that the new codenames be included.

The manual, *Intelligence Information Memorandum No. 12, Japanese Air Services and Japanese Aircraft,* was published in September 1942 by the Directorate of Intelligence, HQ Allied Air Forces SWPA and released under the aegis of General George C. Kenny, Brett's successor. The information it contained was state of the art and is informative even today.

The introduction to the manual explained the need for a system of code names, using the example of possible confusion caused by multiple 'Zeros', the name coined to describe almost any Japanese fighter encountered at the time. The *Zero* was assigned the code name *Zeke*.

Each section describing an aircraft was headed by its code name and official designation in smaller print. The second page was titled *JAPANESE AIRCRAFT* and included a *LIST OF IDENTIFYING NAMES (Replacing Serial Numbers),* in which code names were awarded to Japanese aircraft that had never been encountered in the S.W.P.A. Those first pages of the manual were virtually a sales tool for the code name system, which became known as the 'MacArthur Southwest Pacific Code Name System.'

Whilst the names took time to come into common usage, they eventually became part of the language in describing the Japanese aircraft and remain current today. Very few, for instance, would relate to the Mitsubishi A6M2 Mk I or A6M2 Model 21, however, the term *Zeke* evokes immediate recognition among aviation enthusiasts and researchers. But, even this had its problems, as the term *Zero* remained throughout the war and indeed remains in wide use.

JAPANESE AIRCRAFT DESIGNATIONS AND ALLIED CODE NAMES

In all, TAIU allocated 121 names to Japanese aircraft, though not all were operational types and some were either fictional or erroneously believed to have been in production. The Allied code names to those types used over the NWA or included in the text are as follows:

Babs   Mitsubishi C5M Navy Type 98 reconnaissance aircraft
        Mitsubishi Ki-15 Army Type 97 command reconnaissance aircraft
Betty   Mitsubishi G4M1 Navy Type 1 attack bomber *Rikko*
Dave   Nakajima E8N Navy Type 95 reconnaissance seaplane
Dinah   Mitsubishi Ki-46 Army Type 100 command reconnaissance aircraft
Emily   Kawanishi H8K Navy Type 2 flying boat
Hamp   Mitsubishi A6M3 Navy Type 0 carrier fighter model 32 – *Zeke* and *Hap* also used
Helen   Nakajima Ki-49 Army Type 100 heavy bomber *Donryu*
Irving   Nakajima J1N1-C and R Navy Type 2 reconnaissance aircraft
        Nakajima J1N1-S Navy night fighter *Gekko*
Jake   Aichi E13A Navy Type 0 reconnaissance seaplane
Kate   Nakajima B5N Navy Type 97 carrier attack bomber
Lily   Kawasaki Ki-48 Army Type 99 twin-engined light bomber
Mavis   Kawanishi H6K Navy Type 97 flying boat
Nell   Mitsubishi G3M Navy Type 96 attack bomber
Nick   Kawasaki Ki-45 Army type 2, two-seat fighter
Oscar   Nakajima Ki-43 Army Type 1 fighter *Hayabusa*
Pete   Mitsubishi F1M Navy Type 0 observation seaplane
Rex   Kawanishi N1K1 Navy Type 11 fighter seaplane *Kyofu*
Rufe   Nakajima A6M2-N Navy Type 2 fighter seaplane
Topsy   Mitsubishi Ki-57 Army Type 100 transport
Val   Aichi D3A Navy Type 99 carrier bomber
Zeke   Mitsubishi A6M2 Navy Type 0 carrier fighter – Mk I (later Model 21), but A6M3 Mk II (later Model 32) *Hamp* and A6M5 Model 52 were also known as *Zeke*.

A flight or Shotai of Takao Ku G4M1 Bettys, with tail number T-313 nearest the camera. Note the wartime censor has erased the other aircraft tail numbers. Photo: Bernard Baeza.

NOTES

CHAPTER 1 THE DEFENCE BUILD-UP: A military town, a RAAF presence and a war close to home.

Page 10.   'In 1883 the first of many Japanese...' For Wade's comments see Hammond Moore, John. *Over sexed, Over paid & Over here. Americans in Australia 1941-1945*. University of Queensland Press. 1981. Page 1. See also 'The Great White Fleet' in *The Evening News* of 20 August 1908.

'Jellicoe's report was some years behind...' For this part of Kitchener's report see Field Marshal Viscount Kitchener of Khartoum, G.C.B., O.M., G.C.S.L., G.C.M.G., Etc. *Memorandum of the Fixed Defences of Australia*. (Hand annotated date, 1909). Page 2. National Archives of Australia. Series A5954. Item 1082/7.

11.   'A further assessment of defence...' A more detailed summary of Salmond's visit and his recommendations is provided at page 21 of Powell, Alan. *The Shadow's Edge*. Melbourne University Press. 1988.

'A worsening international situation...' For information on the results of the inspection and recommendations regarding Darwin's defences see Lavarack, MajGen John D. C.B., C.M.G., D.S.O., C.G.S. Chief of General Staff in his report, *Darwin Defences. C.G.S. Report on Inspection – 1936*. Held National Archives of Australia as Series A816 Item 14/301/14.

12.   'Eaton was a well known figure...' For a biography on Charles Eaton see Farram, Steve. *Charles "Moth" Eaton Aviation Pioneer of the Northern Territory*. Charles Darwin University Press. 2007. See also file AL/EAT/1 held AHSNT/Alford Colln.

13.   'Six days later the squadron's main party...' For this and other recollections, see Fisher, Cec. *Through the eyes of a young Airman*. 1987. Manuscript held in AHSNT/Alford Colln. The document also provides a description of life in pre-war Darwin and was published in *The Territory at War*. Australia Remembers NT Committee. 1995.

14.   'The Hudsons had evolved...' Ron Barker's comments on the handling characteristics of the Hudson are quoted in Powell, page 34 and in conversation with the author, 1992.

15.   'None were considered suitable for operations...' Powell, page 35. See also *Royal Australian Air Force: North Western Area Campaign: Revised Brief*. AWM File 84/4/153 and specifically pages 8-9.

"Dear Mum, We had a sham fight..." The crash of Hudson A16-8 is described in 'Darwin Air Crash KILLS FOUR'. *Northern Standard*. 20 August 1941. Held on microfilm Northern Territory Library.

16.   'As late as February 1941...' Information on the American policy regarding the defence of the Philippines is generally in: Gillison, Douglas. *Royal Australian Air Force 1939-1942*. AWM. 1962. Pages 178-183; Matalof and Snell. *U.S. Army in World War II Strategic Planning for Coalition Warfare*. War Department. 1953. Pages 69-70; and Powell, pages 58-59.

'Shortly after, the B-17s began flying...' Information relating to the B-17 deployments is in: Gillison, page 181; Mitchell, John. *On Wings We Conquer*. G.E.M. Publishers. 1990. Pages 18 and 178 (listing the aircraft involved); and Powell, pages 58-59.

See also Rorrison, James. *Nor the years Contemn*. Palomar. 1992. Page 31.

17.   'The Americans too, were making attempts...' For information on the role and activities of General Brereton see Brereton, General Lewis H. *Brereton Diaries*. Morrow New York. 1946. Pages 24-25.

'Brereton went on to Port Moresby...' For information on the Brereton Route see Claringbould, M. J. 'Darwin Defenders'. *Flightpath* magazine. January 2002. See also *Brereton Route through Australia during WW2* on *Ozatwar* web site, http://www.ozatwar.com/airfields/breretonroute.htm

18.   'In Darwin from late November...' The activities of No. 13 Squadron RAAF are detailed in Grantham, Sid. *The 13 Squadron Story*. 13 Squadron Story Book Fund. 1991. Grantham is described as the 13 Squadron historian unless noted otherwise. For his description of the "...sense of something about to happen..." see page 31.

'The only positive note...' The widely accepted comment by Admiral Isoroku Yamamoto as '...having woken a sleeping tiger...' has been disproved as having been scripted for the movie 'Tora, Tora, Tora'. His comment was as related here. See Aiken, David. Director Pearl Harbor History Associates. *Things he did say*. In correspondence of 8 September 2005. Copy held by the author.

NOTES

CHAPTER 2 DESPERATE TIMES: The RAAF in the NEI, ABDACOM and withdrawal.

Page 19.   'The units began operations immediately...' Arch Dunne's recollections of early Hudson operations are quoted in Powell, pages 60-62 and in Grantham, pages 35, 36 and 59.

'Arch Dunne took over the lead...' Ron Cornfoot's recollections are contained in a series of papers (henceforth, the Cornfoot Papers) quoted in: Grantham, page 34; andPowell, page 64.

See also Gillison, pages 375-376 and the Cornfoot Papers including correspondence, Cornfoot to author, held AHSNT/Alford Colln.

20.   'Ron Cornfoot was involved...' Some question remains over the type of aircraft used to intercept the Hudsons on 12 January 1942. In his 1998 manuscript, Murray Moore (Moore, Murray. *The 80% Loss Raid*. 1998. Page 25. Copy held by the author) writes that the Hudsons were intercepted by *Zekes*, *Babs* and *Dave* floatplanes. In the Australian War Memorial's *Wartime* magazine Issue 11, Spring 2000, pages 24-27, he writes that '...the Japanese defence was more than ready for them, with 24 Type O "Zekes" and "Babs" aircraft patrolling...These aircraft belonged to the...3rd Naval Air Group, which had only arrived in the area the day before...' In this he cites the work of noted Japanese researcher, Teruaki Kawano and 3 *Ku* records, however the presence of *Babs* reconnaissance aircraft and the *Dave* floatplanes remains unclear. 'January 12 had been a black day...'   The recollections of Bob Dalkin are contained in Dalkin, Robert N. *Flying Fifty Years Ago and Other Experiences*. 1991. Henceforth called 'The Dalkin Papers', they are held in the AHSNT/Alford Colln.'It was a matter of getting back and refuelling...' Powell, page 62

'From 20 to 31 January...' Lloyd Edwards' experiences are related in 'My Thirteen Squadron RAAF Story.' *Darwin Defenders*. June 2007. Page 12.

22.   "Our base must be Australia..." Eisenhower, Dwight D. *Crusade in Europe*. Doubleday. 1948. Page 22 and in Matalof and Snell, page 87. Eisenhower's report took three hours to prepare for Gen George C. Marshall and was formally approved by him on 17 December 1941. See also Dwight D. Eisenhower Memorial Commission. *Ike Sets Wartime Pacific Strategy – In Three Hours*. http://www.eisenhowermemorial. org.stories/Ike-sets-strategy.htm

22.   "Part of the response..." Rorrison, page 30.

24.   "...Americans responsible should be subject to trial for criminal negligence." See letter from Davies dated September 1942 entitled 'To the surviving officers and men of the 27th Bomb Group.' In Dow, Wayne G. *Unit History – 27th Bomb Group (L)*. Transcription of microfilm. 2007. Page 24.

'The other two squadrons...' For a description of the incident see Clarke, Hugh V. *The Long Arm*. Roebuck Society. 1974. Page 67.

25.   'The first of the new Provisional Squadrons...' See 17th Pursuit Squadron (Provisional) Diary. Anon. Transcribed by Gordon Birkett. 2005. Further information on the formation and deployment of the provisional squadrons can be found in: Birkett, Gordon. *Early USAAF P-40E/E-1 Operations in Australia*. Parts 3, 4 and 5. Manuscript. 2005; Gillison, page 381; and Powell, pages 68-69.

27.   "...a typical army *snafu*," John Glover in conversation with the author, February 1989.

CHAPTER 3 19 FEBRUARY 1942: The first raids – Australia under attack.

Page 29.   'Takahara recalled the mission...' For a detailed summary of the action see: Piper, Bob. 'Flying into the flames of the Rising Sun.' *The Canberra Times*. 19 February 1992, and in correspondence, Sissons, David of The Australian National University to Piper dated 21 February 1984. Copies held by the author.

30.   'The flight crews and their aircraft were ready.' Rayner, Robert. *The Army and the Defence of Fortress Darwin*. Rudder Press. 1995. Pages 187-189; and Shores, Christopher and Cull, Brian with Izawa Yasuho. *Bloody Shambles Volume Two: The Defence of Sumatra to the Fall of Burma*. Grub Street. 1993. Page 176. See also Kawano, Teruaki. Captain. *The Japanese Navy's air-raid against Australia during the World War Two*. Military History Department of the National Institute for Defence Studies. August 29, 1997 and Alford files held by the author as *Japanese Air Forces over the NWA 1942-1945*.

31.   'At much the same time a land based bomber force...' There has been some conjecture over the composition of the force that conducted the noon raid, with various publications stating it was made up

NOTES

of 54 G4M1 (*Betty*) and a mixed force of G4M1 and G3M1 (*Nell*), whilst Kawano, states on page 4 that the force comprised 28 G3M2 of Kanoya *Ku* and 27 G3M2 of the 1st *Ku*. Osamu Tagaya (Tagaya, Osamu. *Mitsubishi Type 1* Rikko *'Betty' Units of World War 2*. Osprey. 2001. Page 34) states a mixed force of 27 Type 1 (*Betty*) of Kanoya *Ku* and 27 Type 96 (*Nell*) of the 1 *Ku* were used, whilst Douglas Lockwood (Lockwood, Douglas. *Australia Under Attack. The Bombing of Darwin – 1942*. New Holland. 2005. Page 206.), cites documents provided by Hitoshi Tsunoda, Deputy Director of Naval War History in Tokyo, confirming this. These latter references and Japanese film footage held by AWM have been used here to relate the types involved.

31.   'The first casualty that day was a PBY-5 Catalina...' For accounts of the action and subsequent events see: Moorer, Lt. Thomas H. *Account of action engaged in by the crew of PBY-5 number 18 during period 19 to 23 February*. 23 February 1942. Copy held AHSNT/Alford Colln. See also: LeBaron, Allan G. *Interview with Admiral Thomas H. Moorer, USN (Rtd) 27 January 1978*. Copy held AHSNT/Alford Colln; Lockwood, Appendix III, pages 204-205; Mason, John T. Jr. *The Pacific War Remembered. An Oral History Collection*. Annapolis Naval Institute Press. Chapter entitled 'A PBY Meets With Destiny. Admiral Thomas H. Moorer.' c. 1976. Copy held AHSNT/Alford Colln; Messimer, Dwight R. *In the Hands of Fate*. Naval Institute Press. 1985. Page 255; and Shores *et al*, pages 174-184.
'They were too late.' Curnock's message is quoted in Rayner, page 190.

32.   'The only viable defence over Darwin...' and 'Bob McMahon had parked three bays...' Robert F. McMahon's recollections of the 19 February raids are contained in correspondence of 4 July 1990. Copy held by the author.
'Perry was the first airman downed...' The sighting by members of the 2/14th is quoted in Newsletter of the 2/14th Australian Field Regiment of 1991 held in AHSNT/Alford Colln and referred to in Lockwood, page 24 and in Rayner, page 181.

33.   'After searching they found...' Messimer, pages 33-34. McMahon's combat and rescue is also related in Lockwood, pages 33-34.
'Glover and McMahon identified Pell's body...' See: Alford typed, hand annotated notes *Interview with Colonel Robert F. McMahon ex-33rd Pursuit Squadron (Provisional) USAAF Darwin 19.2.42. Interview conducted 12 May 1992*; and Alford File Note *Death of Major Floyd Pell*, 30 August 2001, in which McMahon states he and Glover identified Pell's body when it was taken to 119 AGH. Copies held in file AL/33PS/1. AHSNT/Alford Colln.
'Oestreicher reported that...' Oestreicher's claim of two aircraft downed is provided in his report, *Activities of 33rd Pursuit Squadron Provisional – Feb 15, 1942 to Feb 19, 1942* dated 12 July 1942 and in his report *C-E-R-T-I-F-I-C-A-T-E* dated 1 September 1942; in research notes of the events of 19 February 1942 by Bernard Baeza, author of *Soleil Levant sur L'Australie* (Avions-Bateux. 2008), who accessed the official Japanese records (Sentô Kodoshôchô) confirming the losses over Darwin of one Mitsubishi A6M2 *Zeke* from the carrier *Hiryu* and one Aichi D3A1 *Val* from the *Kaga*. A further *Zeke* and a *Val* were ditched on return to the carriers and the crews rescued. Baeza states that the "...[ditched] D3A1 had been the victim of 1/Lt...Oestreicher's fire...", though there is no citation to the passage. (In correspondence, Baeza to author of 15 May 2009); in correspondence, Sadao Seno to Bob Piper, 11 July 1989, in which extracts of the *Japanese Official War History Naval Attack Operations Against East Indies and Bay of Bengal*, pages 350-351 are quoted Sadao writes that one *Zeke* from the *Hiryu* and one *Val* from the *Kaga* were 'self destruction' i.e. shot down; and in Cranston, Frank. 'Ten Men Alone.' *The Canberra Times Midweek Magazine*. 19 February 1992, in which McMahon is quoted at length and a number of inconsistencies in Oestreicher's report highlighted. Cranston also writes that "...McMahon's recollections, though they may agree with the official histories in many areas, are much more reliable when it comes to the initial encounter..." Copies of these documents held by the author and in AHSNT/Alford Colln. For a personal perspective on Oestreicher see McEwin, Gavin. *Commentary on Darwin's Air War*. Comments providing additional personal recollections on *Darwin's Air War* publication. 1992. Page 13. Copy held AHSNT/Alford Colln. Further information is provided in: Gillison, page 431; Kawano, page

NOTES

4; Lockwood, page 206; and Powell, page 93.

34.   'The Japanese crews were intent on their mission...' The recollections are quoted in:
        Maeda - 'Japanese flyer recalls bombing raids on Darwin and Pearl Harbor.' *Northern Territory News.* 7
        December 1991;
        Morinaga – 'Bomber asks us to forgive him.' The *Sunday Territorian.* 9 February 1992; and Yamamoto –
        'The morning I bombed Darwin.' *The Sunday Age.* 16 February 1992, and reprinted in 18 Squadron NEI
        Newsletter No. 38, July 1992.
        'Bruce Beales, an observer with 12 Squadron...' In correspondence to the author, 30 June 1991. Held
        AHSNT/Alford Colln.
        'Gunner Peter Roberts was at East Point...' Oral History tape recorded in an interview 4 April 1987. Item
        held AHSNT/Alford Colln.

34-35. 'At the Civil 'Drome, Aeradio operator...' *Personal Papers of Bruce Ackland Diary Darwin Air Raids,*
        held National Archives of Australia in Series M431, Item 1. Copies held NT Archives Service as part of
        Dermoudy Colln and in AHSNT/Alford Colln.

35.   'Flying Officer C. Saxton...' See AWM file AWM54 Series, Item 812/3/16 *Report on Bombing in Darwin.*
        Copy held AHSNT/Alford Colln. See also National Archives of Australia. Series A9695 Item 469.
        'Murry Lawson was a young Fitter...' In correspondence and notes on his service career and recollections
        in response to the author's questionnaire 'Can You Help?' Undated. 1991. Item held AHSNT/Alford Colln.

36.   'When the Japanese struck, AL521 was parked...' See Glenn, Bob B. Lt. *Brigadier Patrick J. Hurley's
        Mission to Expedite Blockade Runner Ships to the Philippines.* Diary extracts. February 1942. Entry for
        20 February 1942. Item held AHSNT/Alford Colln.
        'To add to the Hudson losses...' Edwards, page 13.
        'Other Hudsons evacuated ground crews...' Quoted in Bennett, John. *Highest Traditions. The History of
        No 2 Squadron RAAF.* Australian Government Publishing Service. 1995. Page 151.

36-37. 'Japanese losses incurred in the raids...' Information on the Japanese losses is provided as notes to page 33.

37.   'As they landed back on the carriers...' Correspondence Sadao Seno to Bob Piper, 11 July 1989.
        'Of the two aircraft confirmed as lost...' See the following: Appleton, William. *Rikai means
        Understanding. A Guide to the Japanese War Cemetery Cowra NSW.* 1998. Page13; Appleton in
        correspondence to author 17 August 1998; correspondence via Bob Piper, 4 March 2003; Piper, Bob.
        Japanese War Graves - Cowra N.S.W. January 2005 (Copyright invoked by R. K. Piper 2005); and photo
        of the Airmen's grave courtesy Ron Wattus. Copies held AHSNT/Alford Colln.

37-38. 'Des Lambert, a gunner with 2 HAA Bty...' In correspondence to the author, 10 December 2005 and in
        telephone conversation, Des Lambert and author, 11 December 2005. For further information on the
        crash and subsequent research see Alford, Bob. *Aviation Archaeology - relics of Australia's northern
        air war, 1941-1945. Case studies in identification.* Chapter 13. A Mystery 'Val.' (In draft 2009).

38.   'The other aircraft lost and perhaps the most publicised...' The story of Toyoshima's forced landing, his
        capture and eventual fate are covered in detail in: Piper, Bob. 'Epitaph for a Darwin Raider.' *The Canberra
        Times.* 12 February 1983; Piper. *Japanese War graves – Cowra N.S.W.*; and Sissons, David. 'Where Japs
        got the third degree...bizarre interrogations at a stately Melbourne mansion.' *Australasian Post.* 17 July
        1986. Pages 2-4. See also Lockwood, *Australia under attack.* Page 170.
        'As the Japanese landed back on the carriers...' The statement by Mitsuo Fuchida to Nagumo is quoted
        in a number of sources including: Bell, Morgan. *World War II Database* http://ww2db.com/battle_spec.
        php?battle_id=22; http://ww2db.com/person_bio.php?person_id=98; Lockwood, Douglas. *Australia's
        Pearl Harbor.* Rigby. 1975. Page 5; and Prange, Gordon W. Goldstein, Douglas M. and Dillon, Katherine V.
        God's Samuari: lead pilot at Pearl Harbour. Brasseys. 1990. Page 56. See also Alford, Bob. *The Bombing
        of Darwin. A historic Association.* Presentation paper to RAAF and American representative to the U.S.
        Ambassador 19 February 2006. Copy held by the author.

NOTES

CHAPTER 4 AFTERMATH: Initial defences, airfields and Australia reinforced.

Page 40.   'On the day following the Darwin raids...' *The Courier Mail.* 20 February 1942. Coverage of the Darwin raids was featured in interstate newspapers under a range of headlines and most included excerpts of Curtin's speech.

'There was confusion in Darwin itself...' See Powell. Alan. "The Darwin 'Panic', 1942". *Journal of the Australian War Memorial.* Issue 3. October 1983. Pages 3-9. Powell also deals in part with the so-called 'Darwin Panic' in *The Shadow's Edge*, page 92. In these passages Powell provides a balanced approach to the aftermath of the 19 February 1942 bombings and in doing so dispels much of the sensationalist writings of a number of authors.

'For many years also the debate over Japanese plans...' See Stanley, Dr. Peter. 'The invasion that wasn't'. In *Wartime. Official magazine of the Australian War Memorial.* Issue 19. Pages 6-9. See also Powell, page 99, and Tanaka, Hiromi. 'The Japanese Navy's operations against Australia in the Second World War'. *Journal of the Australian War Memorial.* Issue 30, April 1997.

40-41.   'On 20 February the surviving...' McMahon correspondence, and in Cranston.

41.   'Gen Barnes also reported the action...' See Signal 42-2-21 D-1393 *Operations: Java Campaign.* Barnes to AGWAR of 21 February 1942. Copy held by the author via Gordon Birkett. Despite his reporting seven P-40s landing in contrast to the confirmed five, Barnes' report is one of very few records of the USAAF action, apart from that of Lt Robert G. Oestreicher. Compiled some months later, Oestreicher's report has been heavily relied upon by many authors however a number of areas in it have been disproved in recent years.

41-42.   'One of the A-24s remained...' In correspondence Brian Walker to author, 22 March 1990. Copy held AHSNT/Alford Colln. See also: Alford, Bob. 'The Douglas A-24 in Australia – 1942'. *Flightpath* magazine. September 1990. Pages 57-60; McEwin, Gavin. *Commentary on Darwin's Air War.* 10 October 1995. (Attachment entitled 'A tribute to Brian Reginald Walker' - personal recollections of Brian 'Blackjack' Walker). Copy held AHSNT/Alford Colln; and Underwood, Anthony. ''Blackjack' Walker marks 50 years in aviation'. *RAAF News.* April 1986. Page 7.

42.   'From 20 February work at the RAAF station...' In Jackson, Ray. No. 52 OBU UXB team. Oral History tape recorded in an interview March 1987 and in correspondence. Items held AHSNT/Alford Colln. For background information see 6 Bomb Disposal Unit in Australia during WW2 at http://www.sandgate.net/dunn/raaf/6bdu.htm

43.   'As early as 23 January 1942...' For the draft prepared by the Chiefs of Staff see National Archives of Australia Series A1196, Item 1/501/431. *Interceptor Aircraft from USA and UK – Allotment to Australia for Fighter Squadrons.* Pages 77-78. See also pages 9-10 for Churchill's chiding of Curtin in 'Immediate Secret' correspondence 1.10186 of 14 March 1942.

'In order to disperse what aircraft...' For further information regarding the survey, selection and development of the airfields, see Yeaman, J. *Notes on Aerodrome Selection Programme in North Western Area as from 1st January 1942* and *Aerodrome Development in the Northern Territory pre 1943.* B/511. From official RAAF records. Copy held NT Archives Service as part of Dermoudy Colln. See also Casey, Hugh J. Major General. Chief Engineer. *Airfield and Base Development. Reports of Operations United States Army Forces Southwest Pacific Area.* Office of the Chief Engineer General Headquarters, Army Forces Pacific. 1951. Pages 16-20. Copies held AHSNT/Alford Colln.

44.   'Tom Skillman was with...' In correspondence, Tom Skillman to author, 1991. See also Brauns, John W. Col. U.S.Army. Retired. *History of the 43rd Engineers in the South-West Pacific.* 43rd Engineer Regiment. 1976. 'Eventually elements of the 808th...' In Correspondence, Harry Geary to author, 12 June 1998, with accompanying photo of arrival of train and American vehicles and troops. For further information on the 808th Battalion see Glover, Lt Colonel Ralph C. *The History of the 808th Engineer Aviation Battalion.* Typewritten historical record held National Archives, Washington, D.C. USA. Copy courtesy Professor Alan Powell, Dean of History, Northern Territory University.

45.   'Syd James was an LAC...' See Bower, Coleen. *No. 1 Mobile Works Squadron. February 26th - October 6th 1942. An Oral History as Recalled by Frank Beale and Syd James.* January 1993. Copy held AHSNT/Alford Colln. For further information on airfield development by RAAF units see Wilson, David.

NOTES

Always First. The RAAF Airfield Construction Squadrons 1942-1974. Air Power Studies Centre. 1998. See also correspondence from Harry Evans of 23 October 1996 to Museum & Art Gallery of the Northern Territory. Copy held AHSNT/Alford Colln.

'By year's end a dozen operational airfields...' Casey, page 16.

'Initially the new unit also provided...' For Peaslee's comments on the fighter sector and the vectoring of aircraft to intercept enemy raids see Peaslee, Jesse. *Activities of the Ninth Pursuit Squadron.* 1942. Chapter 1, pages 4-5. See also Cyril Holyoake in correspondence to the author, 11 May 1986. Copy held AHSNT/Alford Coll.

45.   'Bill Woodnutt, a LAC wireless operator...' For a commentary on Woodnutt's establishment of the '8X2' watch station and activities see: Alford, Bob. *A Heritage Assessment of the proposed ADF facility at Point Fawcett, Bathurst Island.* For URS. 2002. Copy held NTG Heritage Conservation Branch; correspondence Woodnutt to author, 2 January 1992; correspondence Alan Stubbs to author, 1987 (AHSNT/Alford Colln. file AL/STU/1); and Simmonds, Ed. *The RAAF on Bathurst Island in 1942.* Manuscript. 1987.

45-46.   'It was a lonely existence but the airmen...' The correspondence from Wurtsmith is in Woodnutt. Copy held AHSNT/Alford Colln.

46.   'On 29 December a Beaufighter crew...' Woodnutt. See also *Northern Territory News* of 26 and 29 May 2000 and *Weekend Australian* of 27-28 May 2000 for articles relating to the Beaufighter wreckage.

46-47.   'At that time 'B' Flight of 13 Squadron...' 'The Dalkin Papers'.

'Two days earlier Gen Douglas MacArthur...' Mitchell, John H. *On Wings We Conquer.* G.E.M. Publishers. 1990. 106-107. Mitchell provides a historical record of the activities of the 19th Bomb. Group USAAF and particularly its role in Java and at Batchelor.

47.   'Gavin McEwin, an Aerodrome Control Officer...' McEwin, page 12.

'A week after the Group's arrival...' In correspondence S.A.S. 1572 of 9 February 1942 from AirCdre Bladin entitled 'Allotment of U.S. Air Corps Fighter Squadrons to R.A.A.F.' This followed Signal NR252 of 5 February from Gen Adams in Washington to USAFIA confirming that the Group was to come under 'the command of the Chief of the RAAF.' HQUSAFIA followed it up in correspondence 452.1/3 of 11 February 1942.

48.   'The accidents became such a concern...' See Signal ACS-3 KSE, JP of 5 March 1942 from Brett to AGWAR (Adjutant General, War Department, Washington).

49.   'Far to the northwest at Daly Waters...' See hand written notes of a telephone interview, Ron Buckingham with the author, 20 July 1991. Copy held AHSNT/Alford Colln.

'Others fell victim to the weather and terrain...' In Piper, Bob. 'Four Flew Out.' *Wings* magazine Winter 1997. Pages 19-20. See also *Form A50 Operations Record Book.* RAAF Station Fairbairn. Entry for 28 March 1942.

CHAPTER 5 INTO COMBAT: The enemy exposed, radar and a learning curve.

Page 50.   'On 28 March 1942, the 49th Pursuit Gp...' See Cypher Message HQUSAFIA 2342 of 28 March 1942 to CO US Forces Bankstown, Williamtown and Canberra. Extract of file 3/215/AIR. Copy held by author courtesy Gordon Birkett.

'On 14 March the Japanese sent...' For a commentary on the events of the 14 March 1942 raid on Horn Island, see: Boniece, Robert J and Scott, Louis T. *Historical Record 49th Fighter Group USAAF.* AAF Historical Office. Historical Records Division. Maxwell AFB. 18 November 1946. Pages 18-22; correspondence RJRH/FH. Headquarters Thursday Island Sector. R. J. R. Hurst, Fortress Commander to HQ Northern Command of 17 March 1942 entitled *Thursday Island Sector – Enemy Air Raid No. 1.*; and Kawano, page 14. Copies held by the author. See also a chronology of the raid translated from Japanese sources entitled *Deals with the activities of 3 squadrons, two squadrons' activities on the 14 March 1942, and one squadron's activities on the 18th March 1942.* Copy held by the author.

51.   '...there were six men working out the front...' See Ann Cox interview notes taken by Penny Cook, 1 July 1991 and entitled Mrs Anne Cox (nee Fogarty). For the National Trust (NT). Bert Nixon's recollections featured in 'Katherine was bombed!' *The Katherine Times.* 22 March 1985. See also Department of the

NOTES

Navy Correspondence 478/54 of 23 March 1942. *5th Air Raid Darwin – 1st Air Raid Katherine*. Copy held by the author.

'At the aerodrome the 808th Engineers...' Glover, pages 58-61. See also Dod, Karl C. *U.S. Army in World War II (The Technical Services) The Corp of Engineers: The War Against Japan*. Center of Military History U.S. Army. 1966.

'While the P-40s of the 9th Squadron...' For John Scott's recollections see Simmonds, Ed. (Ed.) 'Radar Yarns, 31RS at Dripstone Caves, Darwin, NT.' *Darwin Defenders*. September 2006. Pages 16-17. For further reading on the development of radar in the Northern Territory during WWII see also: Hall, Bon. *A Saga of Achievement*. Bonall. 1978; and Simmonds, Ed. *Radar Yarns* and *More Radar Yarns*. Both E.W. and E. Simmonds. 1992.

52.   'The effectiveness of the RDF set...' Peaslee, pages 4-5.

'Even then the American pilots...' Barnett, Clyde H. Jr. Correspondence to the author, 25 November 1984.

'Number 31 RDF Station was the forerunner...' Porter, Flt Lt Hal. *Adventures in Radar*. Self published. 1945. (Reprint 1991). Page 28.

52-53.   'The 102nd AA Bn had arrived...' See generally, Brace, Richard, *et al. World War II History of the 102nd Antiaircraft Battalion* (AW), New York National Guard of Buffalo, New York. Buffalo, NY (Buffalo and Erie County Historical Society 1961/1983), and correspondence Edward Rogers USA to author, 5 June 2009. Copy held by the author. Russell Tapp's award was announced in *The Canberra Times* Saturday 12 June 1943.

53.   'Four *Bettys* and one *Zeke* were claimed...' See Signal from NW Area Darwin to Commanding Officer USAAC of 29 March 1942.

'The *Bettys* were from Takao *Ku*'s...' In correspondence, Hickey, Larry of International Research & Publishing to author, 16 July 1988, citing translations of the Japanese records by Osamu Tagaya. See also: Alford, Bob. *'Betty' Bomber, Cox Peninsula Heritage Assessment Report*. For Heritage Conservation Services. 2006. Page 8. Copy held Heritage Conservation Branch; and Tagaya, page 43.

54.   'Lieutenant Cyril Molyneux...' In correspondence to author, 30 August 1987. Copy held AHSNT/Alford Colln.

'Despite having at least two aircraft...' Australian War Memorial. Item No. 423/2/51. *Methods of Recording Data on Makers' Plates from Crashed Enemy Aircraft*. Directorate of Intelligence. Allied Air Forces. South West Pacific Area. 8 May 1943.

'At the 34-Mile airstrip the 9th Squadron...' For James Selman's recollections of the Lt Livingstone incident see correspondence and hand annotated site plan to the author, 7 December 1987. Copy held AHSNT/ Alford Colln.

54-55.   'The losses of the aircraft...' In hand annotated note, "P-40s which flew across the aerodrome with wheels down shot at by own Ack-Ack." In *Report on Air Raid – Darwin 4th April 1942*. Folio 12A of a file held by RAAF Historical Section. 1988. Copy held AHSNT/Alford Colln.

55.   'Livingstone was buried...' Anon. *Log of Events Since Leaving Williamtown*. Diary of 9th Squadron activities. 6 April 1942 entry. Page 5. Copy held AHSNT/Alford Colln. See also 14 April entry, page 5 and personal comment (hereafter pers comm.). Edward Rogers to author 28 March 2009.

'Despite extensive searches...' See entries in *Pine Creek Police Day Journal* for 22, 24 and 25 June 1942. Held NTAS under file NTRS 2119. Reports into the incident are covered in detail in National Archives of Australia, Series A705 Item 32/18/122, A8325 Items 21/4/1942 PART 1 and PART 2, and A11093 Item 373/8. See also file AL/ADY/1 held AHSNT/Alford Colln.

56.   'The lull in raids by the Japanese...' *Forms A50 Operations Record Book*. No. 12 Squadron. April 1942. Copy held AHSNT/Alford Colln.

'The unit was also involved...' Jack 'Squizzy' Taylor's recollections are included in undated biographical notes, in conversation with the author, 1989-90, and in files AL/TAY/1 and AL/12SQN/1 held AHSNT/ Alford Coll.

57.   '*Zeke* pilot PO1c Shiro Murakami...' For Hennon's combat report see Boniece and Scott, pages 35-36.

'Morehead also narrowly missed...' In Morehead, James. *Additions to the history of the 49th Fighter Group, Darwin Australia, 1942*. Correspondence to the author, 16 June 1986. Copy held AHSNT/Alford Colln.

NOTES

'Lieutenant Martin landed...' For the reports of Lt Martin and Lt Barnett see Boniece and Scott, pages 36-37. For Morehead's account of his landing see page 2 of correspondence cited above.

57-58. 'Despite the Japanese claims...' For the report by observers at Emery Point see report entitled Report *on P/40 Crashes, 27.4.42*. From Intelligence Officer 5 Fighter Sector to Staff Officer Intelligence, H.Q. North Western Area. 29 April 1942. Copy held AHSNT/Alford Colln.

58. 'Lieutenant Fish was observed...' Ibid.

'Lieutenant Stephen Andrew...' Boniece and Scott. For Lt Andrew's experience see pages 39-44, and for Lt Martin, see pages 44-45.

'Finding his radio was still working...' Ibid. Page 45. Turtle's report is provided at pages 45-46.

58-59. 'An unannounced visit...' See the following relating to the Gen George incident: Ind, Allison. *Bataan: The Judgement Seat*. MacMillan London. 1944. Pages 374-389; McEwin, page 14; and National Archives of Australia Series A11093 Item 000/093A; *Headquarters Allied Air Force - South West Pacific Area - Investigation - Aircraft accident to C40 number 519 and P40 aircraft at Batchelor on 29/4/1942*. See also File AL/GEO/1 held AHSNT/Alford Colln.

59. 'After the losses of 25 and 27 April...' For the move to Strauss by the 8th Squadron see Boniece and Scott, page 51.

'As they occupied the new strip...' See Morehead, James B. *In My Sights. The Memoirs of a P-40 Ace*. Presidio. 1998. Pages 96-101.

'The dust also played havoc with engines...' *Log of Events...*, page 8.

59-60. 'Similar conditions were encountered...' The *Hammond Times*.1943. Quoted in Alford, Bob. *Darwin's Air War*. AHSNT. 1992. Page 27. Copy of original article held AHSNT/Alford Colln.

60. 'The 43rd AMS had arrived...' Rorrison, pages 352-254, provides an overview of the arrival and establishment of the 43rd AMS at Adelaide River. See also *Lt. Col. Manual Burke Von Wald* on http://home.st.au/dunn/usaaf/burkevonwald.htm and *43rd Service Squadron Formerly Known as the 43rd Materiel Squadron in Australia During WW2* on http://home.st.net.au/dunn/43rdservice.htm in Ozatwar.

'Five days later Lt William Payne died...' In correspondence, Bob Oestreicher to Payne family, 15 June 1942. Copy courtesy Gordon Birkett.

61. 'The P-40E 41-5513 of HQ Squadron pilot...' In Gribble John H. *Search for P-40 relics on Melville Island by Mr. John H. Gribble, in charge of natives*. Undated report. See also Van Auken, Capt Robert D. *Combat Report of Capt. R. D. Van Auken*. Undated. Copies of both documents held AHSNT/Alford Colln.

'Another pilot reported being strafed...' For Kingsley's report see Boniece and Scott, page 58. See also a further report by Kingsley in folio entitled *105 F.C.U. Headquarters Combat and Attack Reports 20.6.42. Subject - Enemy Shooting at Parachute* in NWA Interviews Book 1, held RAAF Historical Section. Copy held AHSNT/Alford Colln.

62. 'On the 14th the raiders were detected...' For Stan Goodwill's recollections of the Lt Brown incident and of visiting the site of Val 3304 downed on 19 February 1942, see correspondence to the author, 10 April 1986. Copy held AHSNT/Alford Colln. See also photo caption on image provided by Ron Wattus and held by the author.

1-63. 'Lt Clarence Johnson wasn't so lucky...' For Lt Johnson's report and subsequent recommendations following his experiences see Boniece and Scott, pages 60-63. Jack Mulberry's report is on page 63.

63. 'Lieutenant Chester Namola...' See Lt Randall Keator's report in Boniece and Scott, page 69.

'Lieutenant James Martin...' Gribble report '*Search for P-40 relics...*' See also Barnett, Clyde H. Jr. *War Memories 1941-1945*. c. 1992. Copy held AHSNT/Alford Colln.

63-64. 'In the meantime a de Havilland Tiger Moth...' For the report by 'Smiler' Fejo see *"Smiler" Fejo's Report of Search for Lt. Harris in Fog Bay Area* of 11 July 1942. Reported to PltOff J. F. Mahoney Unit Intelligence Officer 5 Fighter Sector. In folio 16B of uncited RAAF Historical Section file. Copy held AHSNT/Alford Colln.

Darwin's Air War 213

NOTES

CHAPTER 6 CHANGES IN THE AIR: Reorganisation, Americans depart and the RAAF takes over.

Page 65.   'The day following Lt Harris' rescue...' For the full story of the experiences of Sgt Frank Smallhorn, Cpl Philip Bronk and AC1 George Booth, see, Booth, George. *33 Days*. Greenhouse. 1988. Specifically pages 9, 12, 15-18. See also McEwin, pages 16-19, in which he provides a detailed commentary on the possible reasons for the aircraft becoming lost and quotes Smallhorn at length. Copy held AHSNT/Alford Colln.

66.   'By mid year also, 5 Fighter Sector...' Anon. *History of the Forty-Ninth Fighter Control Squadron (Sep) Book II*. Page 8. Copy courtesy LtCol Horace Levy USAF (Retd) and held AHSNT/Alford Colln.
'With a lull in the air raids...' The medals parade at Livingstone is described in Boniece and Scott, page 73. A listing of medal recipients is proved on pages 73-73, but fails to mention Bob Dalkin's award.

66-67.   'During the flight the aircraft...' In correspondence, I. B. Jack Donalson to author, 6 February 1987. For further information on the incident see also: Boniece and Scott, page 74;
Hubbard, Lucien. *Air Force: The Magazine for Pilots, November, '42*. (In a dramatised and inaccurate account entitled the 'Fighters at Humpty Doo'); Noah, Joe, and Sox, Samuel L. Jr. *George Preddy: Top Mustang Ace*. Motorbooks. 1991. Pages 46-47. (Noah and Sox tend to rely on Hubbard's highly dramatised and inaccurate version above); and Ward, Susan. *The Story of World War II Flying Ace George Preddy Jr*. Stardust Studios. 2002.

67.   'On 30 July three *Bettys* took off...' Boniece and Scott, page 79.
'The USAAF almost lost another P-40...' Morehead, *Additions...* Attachment *Unscheduled Mission of 30 July, 1942, Darwin Australia*.

68.   'After the claims of the 23rd...' MacArthur's message is quoted in Powell, page 113. For Wurtsmith's congratulations see Signal 1103 of 25 August 1942. Copy held AHSNT/Alford Colln.
'Number 1 PRU had arrived from Laverton...' Bladin's comments on the Brewster Buffalos allotted to 1 PRU are quoted in Vincent, David. *Mosquito Monograph*. Self published. 1982. Page 132. Information on the acquisition of the type and concerns over their capabilities is contained in National Archives of Australia Series A5954 Item 230/12. *Brewster Buffalo Aircraft*.

69.   'The first of the 49th Fighter Gp...' See *Diary of Ralph L. Boyce, 7th Squadron, 49th Pursuit Group, USAAC*. Entry for 9 September 1942. Original Diary transcribed by author, 1988 and held AHSNT/Alford Colln.

69-70.   'As the 8th Squadron at Strauss was preparing...' Boniece and Scott, page 94.

70.   'That day also saw the 49th FG issued...' Ibid. Pages 94-95.
'Two weeks later on 25 September...' See Diary of Clyde H. Barnett jr. Copy of handwritten diary held AHSNT/Alford Colln.
'The 9th Squadron was not far behind...' *Log of Events...* Entries for 28 September 1942 and Peaslee, page 9.

71.   'Three weeks passed before the next raid...' For details of the raid of 23 November 1942 see: Cresswell, R. SqnLdr. *Form 105 (A). Combat (Fighter) Report*. 23 November 1942; Department of Veterans Affairs. *Australians at War Film Archives*. Archive No. 0582. Interview with Richard Cresswell. Copies held by the author; and Kawano, page 8.

72.   'A more poignant find...' See Australian War Memorial file AWM54 Item 423/4/92 *Intelligence Reports of Japanese Aircraft*. Copy held by the author. See also Headquarters Allied Air Forces Directorate of Intelligence Report No. 120 of 5 January 1943. Courtesy Jim Long USA. Copy held by the author.

CHAPTER 7 STRIKING BACK: Hudsons take the lead – and pay the price.

Page 74.   'The remoteness of the airfield...' For the comments by Murry Lawson, Lt George Preddy and FltLt Bob Foster, see: Foster, R. W. Wing Commander DFC AE, with Franks, Norman. *Tally-ho! From the Battle of Britain to the Defence of Darwin*. Grub Street. 2008. Pages 109-110; Lawson, Response to questionnaire; and Noah and Sox, page 27.
'On the 20th A16-100 force landed...' 'The Dalkin Papers.'

74-75.   'On the 30th Bob Dalkin led...' Ibid. See also Bennett, page 151.

75.   'WAG, Lloyd Edwards had joined...' Edwards, page 14.

76.   'Omsby somehow survived...' See *RAAF Index of Missing Aircraft*. Report on Hudson A16-196. Copy

NOTES

held AHSNT/Alford Colln. See also Bennett, pages 160-161.

'South of Birdum the 19th Bomb. Gp...' For details on the crash of *Gazelle* at Daly Waters see Rogers, Edward. In correspondence of 12-13 June 2009, in which he cites the diary entries of Lts Alfred and James Mangan and *5th Bomber Command Journal* of 14 March 1942. Copy held by the author.

77.   'Another B-17, 40-3067, had been lost...' Len De Grussa's recollections are held in correspondence to the author of 31 August 1983, though he writes that the incident was in May 1942. Research has confirmed the incident as occurring on 28 January. The details regarding McAllister's death are contained in extracts of American records. Copy held by the author. See also Dermoudy, Peter. *Americans in the N.T.* Report for Museums and Art Galleries Board of the N.T. 1983.

'During June a detachment...' *History of the Forty-Ninth Fighter Control Squadron...* Page 11.

77-78. 'Another B-17 unit, the 64th Bomb. Squadron...' For a historical overview of the activities of the 64th Bomb. Squadron in the Northern Territory see *64th Bombardment Squadron (H) Diary 1942-1944.* Extract from File SQ-64-BOMB-HI. Maxwell AFB Historical Research Centre USA. Entries 15 July – 3 October 1942. Copy held AHSNT/Alford Colln.

78.   'A new unit the Technical Air Intelligence Unit...' For information on the formation and activities of TAIU see: Clayton, Mark. 'The north Australian air war, 1942-44.' *Journal of the Australian War Memorial* (undated). Pages 39-40; Collier, Basil. *Japanese Aircraft of World War II.* Mayflower. 1979. Pages 50-51; Dunn, Richard L. *Japanese Codenames in Perspective.* 2005. Copy held by the author; Francillon, Rene. *Japanese Aircraft of the Pacific War.* Naval Institute Press. 1988. Pages 46-59; Gwynn-Jones. 'Zeros Over Brisbane.' *Flightpath* magazine (undated) Pages 59-62; Mikesh, Robert C. *Japanese Aircraft Code Names and Designations.* Schiffer. 1993; and Piper, Bob. 'Technical Air Intelligence Unit Souvenirs From Japan.' *AOPA* magazine. June 1995. Pages 97-101.

79.   'In September 1943, then Major McCoy...' Australian War Memorial file AWM54 series, item 423/2/13. *S.W.P.A. Technical References to Inspected Enemy Airplanes.* A.T.I.U. Memorandum No. 2 of 27 September 1943. See page 5 for a listing of aircraft in the Northern Territory by report number and known serial numbers. Copy held by the author.

80.   'On 18 August three Hudsons...' Grantham. Page 71.

'In some cases crews were flying...' Extracts of *Flying Log Book.* Richard Overhue, and biographical notes attached. Copy held AHSNT/Alford Colln.

'The first loss for the second half of the year...' Powell, page 117. See also correspondence Bernard Baeza to the author 20 June 2009 in which he states "Hudson A16-234 was on armed reconnaissance...when it met the Jake manned by Ens Sasaki (pil), PO/2 Takemura (nav) and NAP Uehara (gun) which patrolled the area...F/O Meucke's crew had no time to send an SOS and perished."

81.   'Meanwhile one of the remaining Hudsons...' Bennett, page 169.

'Missions continued throughout October...' Grantham, page 72.

82.   'The Marauders were in four aircraft elements...' For a summary of the activities of the 22nd Bomb. Group deployment to Batchelor, Sgt Tom Roberts' involvement and the loss of B-26 #41-17593 see: Hitchcock, Charles I. Captain, 2nd BS, 22nd BG. Report entitled *B-26B (#41-17593) water landing of Nov. 3, 1942 in the Timor Sea.* Dated 3 May 1943. Copy held AHSNT/Alford Colln; Mrozek, Donald J, Higham, Robert and Newell, and Allen, Jeanne Louise. (Eds) *The Martin Marauder and the Franklin Allens.* Air Force Historical Foundation. 1980. Captain Franklin Allen diary entries for the period 1 to 5 November 1942; National Records Centre USA. *Combat Mission Report, Darwin No. 2. November 3, 1942.* Copy held AHSNT/Alford Colln; Roberts, A. G. Sgt. RAAF. Extract of *Flying Log Book.* Entries for 2-5 November 1942. Copy held AHSNT/Alford Colln; and Wray, Christopher. *Timor 1942.* Hutchinson Australia. 1987. Page 153.

82-83. 'Captain Franklin Allen summed up...' Mrozek *et al*, page 345.

84.   'Adams went further...' Melbourne's *The Argus* newspaper. Undated. Copy held AHSNT/Alford Colln.

85.   'On 2 December 31 Squadron...' McDonald, Kenneth Neal DFC. *Commando Charlie's Commandos.* Banner Books. 1996 Pages 22-23.

'After a dawn takeoff...' Ibid. Page 24.

86.   'A week later a *Sun* War Correspondent...' See *Commandos of the Air in Dawn Strike* in the Melbourne *Sun News-Pictorial*, 12 December 1942.

86.   'A further squadron was added...' Powell, pages 155-156.

CHAPTER 8 CHANGING FORTUNES: The Spitfires arrive and the enemy under pressure.

Page 92.   'The request was refused...' Churchill's comment on the symbolism of sending the Spitfires to Australia is quoted in Powell, page 180.

93.   'The 76 Squadron CO...' Extract of *Form A50. Operations Record Book*, No. 76 Squadron.

At least one *Betty* was badly damaged...' Bullard, Steve. 'Flying with Eagles.' *Wartime. Official magazine of the Australian War Memorial*. Issue 26. Page 43.

'The action on the night...' Southall, Ivan. *Bluey Truscott. Squadron Leader Keith William Truscott, R.A.A.F., D.F.C. and Bar.* Angus and Robertson. 1958. Page 198.

94.   'The personnel and equipment...' Extract of *Form A50 Operations Record Book*. No. 7 RSU. Copy held AHSNT/Alford Colln.

'The Spitfire squadrons remained...' For the move from Batchelor to Livingstone see Extract of *Form A50 Operations Record Book*. No. 457 Squadron. Copy held AHSNT.

'The aircraft and personnel of 54 (RAF) Squadron...' Foster, "We had been a long time coming". Page 112.

94.   'Despite his misgivings...' Ibid. Pages 120-123. Foster's *Form 105 (A).Combat (Fighter) Report* is presented in full.

95.   'The squadron record confirmed it...' Extract of *Form A50 Operations record Book*. No. 54 RAF Squadron.

'After a five hour trip and a camera run...' Hesse, Charles. *World War II Report of Charles Hesse While a Member of the 90th Bombardment Group*. c. 1991. Entry for 25 January 1943. Pages 2-3.

96.   'The Nakajima Ki-43 *Oscars*...' For information on the various Japanese army and naval air forces in the NWA see generally: Baeza, Bernard. Correspondence relating to the activities of the 36/934 *Ku* and Japanese aircraft types; Dunn, Richard L. *Air Combat Australia – 1943*. Manuscript. 2006. Chapters XI Japanese Army Raid and XVIII Fading Presence August – September 1943; Gillison, Douglas. *Royal Australian Air Force 1939-42*. AWM. 1962; Hata, Ikochito and Izawa, Yasuho. *Japanese Naval Aces and Fighter Units in World War II*. Airlife. 1989; Hata, Ikochito, Izawa, Yasuho and Shores, Christopher. *Japanese Army Air Force Fighter Units and Their Aces 1931-1945*. Grub Street. 2002; Horton, Glenn. *The Best in the Southwest*. Mosie Publications. 1995; and Odgers, George. *Air War Against Japan*. AWM. 1957.

96.   'The 934th *Ku* was also involved...' The story of Rev. Len Kentish is related in Powell, pages 139-140.

96-97.   'On 31 January a dawn raid...' Extract of *Flying Log Book*, FlgOff Jack Taylor, No. 12 Squadron. Entry for 31 January 1943.

'A third aircraft landed...' Meredith, Bob. '39 R.D.F. Port Keats. Memories of Radar WW2. Royal Australian Air Force 1942-1943.' *Darwin Defenders*. September 2008. Pages 12-14.

97.   'The warning had come from...' For an account of the activities of the Australian SigInt organisation see Ballard, Geoffrey. *On Ultra Active Service. The Story of Australia's Signals Intelligence Operations during WWII*. Spectrum 1991. The intercept of the signal confirming Yamamoto's itinerary is detailed on Page 189, however, whilst Ballard fails to attribute the intercept directly to 51 Wireless Section further research confirms it was one of a number of stations to intercept the message, including one at Dutch Harbor in the Aleutians. In correspondence of 26 January 2010, Don Kehn Jr refers to Smith, Michael. *The Emperor's Codes*. Penguin. 2000. Pages 182-183, and to Holmes, W. J. *Double-Edged Secrets*. Naval Institute Press. 1979. In the former he states that "...as the message filtered down to the lower Japanese echelons it was later intercepted (in lower level systems) by FRUMEL *and* 51Special Wireless Section in Darwin..."

98.   'Ed Simmonds, an LAC radar operator...' For Ed Simmonds' recollections of the raid see *Darwin*

NOTES

Defenders. December 2007. Page 10. Geoff Wisby's recollections were related on page 8 of the September 2007 issue in '112th Light Ack Ack Regiment'.

'It was too late...' McDonald. Chapter 8. 'Demise of a Friend <u>A19-31</u>'. Page 59.

'While Churchill expressed satisfaction...' Powell, page 183.

99.   'The combat raged so close over Darwin...' In correspondence, Cliff Taylor to author. 1990. Held in file AL/A-A/2. AHSNT/Alford Colln.

'What is also known is that the RAAF...' McEwin, page 25.

'Two weeks after the raid...' Extract of *Form A50 Operations Record Book* in Woodgate, Fred. *Lion and Swans.* Self published. 1992. Page 133.

101.   'On 17 December 1943...' Grantham, page 78.

'A16-230 was shot down...' *RAAF Index of Missing Aircraft.*

103.   'One Hudson, A16-217...' An extract of the article on FltLt J. S. 'Bunny' Austin is related in Bennett, page 189.

104.   'The same day had seen...' McEwin, page 24.

'For the Spitfire squadrons meanwhile...' Odgers, pages 45-46.

104-105.   'After having flown in from Kendari...' The events of 2 May 1943 have been covered at length in numerous publications. A brief list of sources covering a range of aspects is provided as follows: Claringbould, Michael J. 'Spitfire Sunday'. *Flightpath* magazine. March 2008; Foster., pages 140-149; Grant, Jim. *Spitfires Over Darwin 1943.* Techwrite Solutions. 2003. Pages 67-81; Odgers, pages 47-50; and Powell, pages 183-184. See also File AL/A58/6 containing research notes on the 2 May 1943 combat held AHSNT/Alford Colln.

105.   'By the time the Spitfires had assembled...' Grant, page 78.

'BR239 was damaged in combat...' Bill Hardwick's adventure is related in Grant, pages 162-167 and in a slightly varied form in *Flightpath* magazine. June 1987. 'Pranged by the *!#?* navy!'.

106.   'BR547 suffered CSU problems...' Ross Stagg's experiences are related in 'The man who cheated the swamp of death'. *The Sunday Mail.* 26 February 1972. Page 119. See also Stagg, Ross Smith. *Caterpillar Club Survivor. Lost in the Top End, 1943.* C. Stagg. 2007.

'For WgCdr Clive Caldwell...' General Kenney's comments are related in Powell, page 184.

106.   'The newspapers picked up...' Grant, pages 68-69.

107.   'Indeed it had and Prime Minister Curtin...' Foster, page 140.

'Probably the most contentious comments...' Claringbould, page 49.

'Inexperience would certainly have been a factor...' Caldwell's report on the 2 May 1943 raid is quoted in full in Foster, pages 143-148.

'Caldwell was awarded a DSO...' Grant, page 81.

CHAPTER 9 A SHOW OF FORCE: The Japanese a fading threat?

Page 108.   'Charles Hesse was leading...' Hesse. Entry for 4 May 1943. Page 10.

'The Beaufighter strike on Taberfane...' No. 31 Squadron Report on Operation COO 4 of 6 May '43. Copy held AHSNT/Alford Colln.

'Shortly after the two Beaufighters...' Pers comm. Phil Biven to author, 31 Squadron reunion, Darwin, November 1988 and written on reverse of photo A19-72 wreckage.

109.   'One of the Spitfire pilots...' Piper, Bob. *Great Air Escapes.* Pagemaker. 1991. Pages 71-75. Combat reports and gun camera photos relating to the raid are held National Archives of Australia. Series A11095 Item 319/12K and A11231 Items 5/79 INT and 5/80 INT.

109-110.   'By early March 12 Squadron...' McPherson, Cyril. In correspondence to the author, 22 September 1995; "So we took out some gelignite and...blew the bastard up!" *RAAF News.* August 1987; *Form A50 Operations Record Book.* (Extract) No. 12 Squadron; and Meggs, Keith. 'Vengeance!', in which McPherson is quoted at length. *Flightpath* magazine. April 2002. Pages 76-80.

110.   'On 18 March the CO...' *Form A50.* See also Odgers, page 58.

110-111.   'The mission set a landmark...' McPherson correspondence.

111.   'A further directive from Kenney...' Powell, page 150. For Scherger's comment see Rayner, Harry. *Scherger: a biography of Air Chief Marshal Sir Frederick Scherger.* AWM. 1984. Page 68.

NOTES

'Instead of the usual dawn strike...' McDonald, page 86.

111-112.   'Flying at 20 ft above the water...' Ibid. Page 91.

112.   'The lack of facilities encountered...' For the developmental proposals for Groote Eylandt, Arnhem Bay, Milingimbi Cape Fourcroy and Drysdale, see correspondence entitled *Aerodrome Requirements in Western and Northwestern Parts of Australia*. 5 June 1943. Item held National Archives of Australia Series A705 Item 711/1655. Copy held AHSNT/Alford Colln.

  'The Japanese conducted five major raids...' The Japanese units involved in the 20 June 1943 raid are detailed in: Dunn. *The Army Raid* (copy held by the author); Foster, page 154; and Odgers, pages 59-60.

112-113   'RAAF Sgt, Dick Dakeyne...' The incident of 20 June 1943 is described in: Dakeyne correspondence to the author and included in Horton, pages 27, 32 and 36; extract of *Flying Log Book*; including news clipping (Newspaper and date unknown) entitled *F/SGT Dakeyne. The story of a Flight Sergeant who has made a name in the North by sheer guts*. Copies held AHSNT/Alford Colln.; and Horton, pages 36-37.

113.   'In the ensuing combat...' Caldwell's comment is in Grant, page 81.

  'While the Japanese fighters...' Keith Colyer's comments are an extract of his *Flying Log Book* entry for 20 June 1943. Copy held AHSNT/Alford Colln.

  'Despite the number of enemy aircraft...' The Intelligence report on the downed Ki-49 *Helen*, manufacturer's number 174, and reference to the Adam Bay relics is held in the National Archives of Australia, Series A5164 Item 1/4/2/INTEL. A report on the raid is held under Series A9696 Item 207.

114.   'Lieutenant Kenjiro Matsuhara...' Ben Walker's recollections on the 20 June 1943 raid, the 20 June 1944 shooting down of the Ki-46 at Truscott and No. 1 MWS were related in interviews with the author, 29 June - 2 July 1987. Copy held in file AL/WAL/1 AHSNT/Alford Colln.

  'Six days later the Japanese...' SqnLdr Gibb's comments are related in Grant, pages 114-115.

115.   'One constant in the enemy's intrusions...' The downing of Ki-46 2414 by SqnLdr Ken James is described in James' *Combat Report* of 18 July 1943 and in correspondence to the author of 22 May 1989. Copies held AHSNT/Alford Colln.

  'The crew of *Dinah*, manufacturer's number 2414...' The comments regarding Sasaki's status revealed in the radio intercept are quoted in Ken James' correspondence above. The observations by Sasaki's biographer are contained in correspondence Ikuhiko Hata to Bob Piper of 23 November 1979. Copy held by the author.

116.   'The aircraft were picked up...' Extract of *Form 105 (A).Combat (Fighter) Report*, FltLt Peter Watson DFC of 18 August 1943 and in Piper, Bob. 'Darwin's War of the Sky Spies'. *Australasian Post*. 27 February 1988. Pages 8-9.

  'At 1125 Hours SqnLdr Ken James...' In James' *Form 105 (A) Combat (Fighter) Report* of 17 August 1943 and in *Form A50 Operations Record Book*. No. 457 Squadron. The activities of the 133rd HAA Battery personnel are contained in extracts of the unit's *War Diary* provided to the author by a former gunner with the unit, Keith Pearce. See correspondence to author of 2 February 1989 and Pearce, 'Handwritten extract of War Diary' held as *4/16/45, 133 Heavy Anti-aircraft Battery June to August 1943 and August [1943] to September 1944*. In correspondence to the author. November 1989. Copies held file AL/PEA/1 and in aircraft crash files, AHSNT/Alford Colln.

  'Some 150 kilometres north...' *Form A50 Operations Record Book*. No. 457 Squadron. The recovered equipment is detailed in: *Report on enemy aeroplane shot down at Bathurst Island on 17th. August, 1943*. Flying Officer C. D. Pender, IntellO, 5 Fighter Sector. 21 August 1943; and *Allied Translator and Interpreter Section SWPA. Bulletin No. 315*. 'Document from DINAH crashed Bathurst Island – 17 Aug 1943'. Copies held by the author.

116-117.   'Late that afternoon, *Ku* 202 sent over a *Dinah*...' Extract of *Form 105 (A) Combat (Fighter) Report*. See also Grant, pages 134-135 and Odgers, page 110.

117.   'Learning the lessons of the August mission...' Muramitsu Sasaki's recollections are in documents entitled *War Service over Darwin* and *Personal History*. 1991. Copies held AHSNT/Alford Colln.

  'Despite claims by the Japanese...' In correspondence to the author, 1987 and in extract of *Flying Log Book*. Copies held AHSNT/Alford Colln.

NOTES

118.   'All the Spitfire pilots reported...' Woodgate, pages 129-130.
        'What was of concern to Cole...' See Odgers, page 104. For BrigGen Allen's comment see correspondence of 2 July 1943 entitled 'Appreciation of the Situation by Commander, Northern Territory Force'. In it Allen writes that "...There are no fighters to give high cover to bombers beyond a radius of 150 miles...Fighters of the P-38 (Lightning) type are required. B-25 medium bombers, modified for mast-head attacks, are also required..." *AWM data base collection. Australian Army War Diaries; WW2; HQ Units; divisions and forces; 12 Division (NT Force) G Branch; Jun-Jul 43.* Frame 71. Copy courtesy Rick Dunn USA.
        'Bostock responded quickly...' Odgers, page 105.

119.   'With the raids over...' *Form A50. Operations Record Book.* No. 457 Squadron. 31 July 1943.
        'Some months later AVM Jones...' Odgers, page 106. See also footnote to item.

120.   'Whilst the Beaufighters...' In correspondence Bostock to HQ NWA and No. 31 Squadron dated 18 June 1943. National Archives of Australia. Series A11312 Item 6/10/AIR.
        'Squadron Leader G. W. Savage...' *Wings – The Official magazine of the RAAF.* Vol. 1, No. 3. 11th May, 1943. 'The Beaufighter Strikes in the North'. Page 6. Both this and the article by Bill Moore describing the squadron as the 'buckjumpers of the air' are held in file AL/31SQN/1-2 AHSNT/Alford Colln.

121.   'On 2 June they attacked...' Extract of *Operations Record Book.* 18 NEI Squadron. 2 June 1943.

122.   'In September the CO TAIU...' McCoy Memorandum. Further information on Japanese aircraft wrecks is held AHSNT/Alford Colln, in *Aviation Archaeology* ('Japanese Losses -Rubbery figures?' in draft) and in the author's collection.
        'While the raids over Darwin...' For a description of the raid of 27 September see Perez, Father Eugene OSB. *Kalumburu War Diary.* Artlook. 1981. Pages 129-135. See also Dunn, *Fading Presence.* Page 3, and Odgers, pages 112-113.

124.   'While 7 RSU had an enviable record...' Extract of *Form A50* in Venn, Walter. *Restore to Service.* Australian Military History Publications. 1999. Page 55.

CHAPTER 10 THE HEAVY BOMBERS: Striking afar and a circus arrives.

Page 125.   'Despite the handicap...' Correspondence, Bill Hagerty to author, 1988. Held in file AL/90th BG/1, AHSNT/Alford Colln. See also Alcorn, John S. *The Jolly Rogers. History of the 90th Bomb Group during World War II.* Historical Aviation Album Publication. 1981. Page 45 for descriptions of Fenton on the arrival of the 319th Squadron.
        'As had American units to the time...' The comments by MajGen Richardson are summarised in Powell, pages 103 and 111. Gillison makes mention of the relationship on pages 452, 540 and 572, whilst Powell also contrasts the attitude of Richardson with the situation in the 380th Bomb. Group. Page 165.
        'Two days after arriving...' Capt Charles E. Jones report on mission of 25 January 1943. Copy held AHSNT/Alford Colln.
        'Three Zeros came up...' Hesse, page 6.
        'Capt Paul E. Johnson recorded...'. *Excerpts from Diary of Paul E. Johnson Pilot 319th Squadron 90th Bomb Group From Feb 2, 1943 to Jul 9, 1943.* 1943. Entries for 2 and 4 March 1943. Copy held AHSNT/Alford Colln.
        'The cause of the accident...' Eckert, Clarence 'Bud'. In correspondence to the author, 18 November 1990. Held in file AL/ECK/1, AHSNT/Alford Colln. See also Livingstone, Bob. *Under the Southern Cross.* Turner Publishing. 1998. Page 59.

126.   'Six days later Hesse and his crew...' Hesse, page 7.
        'On 16 March another armed reconnaissance...' Ibid. Pages 7-8. See also Livingstone, page 59 for the warning by Jones to Lt Hevener to "...get away from me!"
        'Two days later another B-24...'. Jackson. Interview and correspondence.
        'Currie and his crew...' Hesse, page 8.
        'Jim Case, a crewman...' Case, Jim. In correspondence to the author of 20 November 1994 detailing the 18 March 1943 mission in B-24, *One Time.*
        'Despite setbacks the missions...'. Hesse, page 8.

NOTES

'On 3 April Hesse and his crew...' Ibid. Page 9.

'The transfer was arranged...' Ibid. Page 11.

127.   'There must have been some misapprehension...' Horton, page 7.

'"This place called Fenton Field..." Ibid. Page 17.

'With the lack of facilities...' Ibid. Page 21.

128.   'Corunna Downs was a secret base...' Powell, page 163. See also: Horton, page 26; Nelms, Michael. *From Tocumwal to Tarakan*. Banner Books. 1994. Pages 56-57; and Odgers, page 66.

128-129.   'That first 380th mission...' Horton, page 26. See also: Dakeyne correspondence; Nelms, page 54; and National Archives of Australia. Series A11093 Item 320/3J5 relating to the establishment of Section 22.

129-130.   'It was not a good start...' Johnson. Entry for 2 May 1943.

130.   'In the meantime aircraft and crews...' For the description of Manbulloo and its attractions see: Horton, Glenn and Gary. *King of the Heavies. 380ᵗʰ Bomb. Group 1942-1945*. Self published. 1983. Page 18; Horton, Glenn, page 35; and Powell, pages 162-163.

'One of the final missions...' Johnson. Entry for 2 June 1943.

'The 319th B-24s were intercepted...' Hesse, page 13.

132.   'The raids achieved their aim...' Horton and Horton, page 42; Horton, page 26; and Powell, pages 163-164.

133.   'The remaining eight aircraft...' Horton, page 100-101. A commentary of the raid is provided at pages 98-102. See also Alford, Bob. *A Heritage Assessment of the remains of B-24* Nothing Sacred. For Heritage Conservation Branch. 2004.

'The 529ᵗʰ and 531ˢᵗ Squadrons...' Horton and Horton. Page 45.

'Operations from Fenton and Long...' Horton and Horton, page 47.

134.   '"Ask a pilot who the most important man..." Ibid. Fain, James (Ed-in-Chief). *The Flying Circus, 380ᵗʰ Bomb Group*. 380ᵗʰ Bomb Group Assn. 1946. Page 112.

135.   'The one enduring mystery...' The story of 'Beautiful Betsy' has been related in a number of publications, however research over many years by Australian, Col Tigwell, provided the majority of the material utilised in documenting the incident. Publications dealing with the incident include: Horton, pages 307-308; Livingstone, pages 80-81; Livingstone, Bob. 'A mystery no more'. *Flightpath* magazine. September 1994. Pages 92-95; Piper, Bob. In 'Betsy, where are you?' *Australasian Post*. 28 November 1985; and Powell, page 192. See also the Tigwell files held AHSNT/Alford Colln, including the report on the investigation of the crash site by the Joint POW/MIA Accounting Command (JPAC) based at Hickham AFB in Hawaii.

136.   'Whilst the Group Commander...' Horton, page 219. The incident was confirmed by both Lee Brissey and Virgil Stevens in discussion with the author at the 380ᵗʰ Bomb Group reunion, USA, 1991. Cole's message of congratulations is also related in this reference.

CHAPTER 11 LIBERATORS: The RAAF gets seven league boots.

Page 137.   'On 19 December 1941...' For Scott's message see Livingstone. *Under the Southern Cross*. Page 47.

'Other political games...' An excerpt of the RAF report summarising Kenney's attitude is in Powell, page 168.

'Thus through the intervention...' Jones' comment on the '6 part-used Liberators' is in Livingstone. *Under the Southern Cross*. Page 48.

138.   'Flight Lieutenant 'Mick' Jacques...' Nelms, page 43.

139.   'Those Australians posted to the 380ᵗʰ...' See 19 May 1944 entry in *Flying Log Book*. Flight Sergeant Les McDonald. Copy held AHSNT/Alford Colln.

'"Tommy' Thompson a 528th Squadron..." Pers comm. Thomson to author. 1988. On the occasion of the 380ᵗʰ Bomb. Gp reunion, Darwin.

'The Australians fitted in well...' Powell, page 170.

'The 380th Bomb. Gp had been advised...' Horton, pages 244-245.

'The U.S. Navy had requested...' Ibid. Page 298.

141.   'The 380th Bomb. Gp continued...' HQ, 380ᵗʰ Bomb Gp *Mission Evaluation Report*. September 1944. Copy held AHSNT/Alford Colln.

NOTES

'Number 82 Wing was declared...' For Roger Court's recollections see Court, Roger. *This Way. An Aviator's Journey Through War and Peace.* Self Published. Undated. Page 56.

142-143.   'Mosquito aircraft of 87 (PR) Squadron...' The comment relating to Kingwell's presence at Truscott is in correspondence, Anon of 14 February 2004 to Russ Brooks. Brooks' commentary is in extract of *Flying Log Book*, PltOff E.C.R. Brooks. Copies held AHSNT/Alford Colln. The destruction of the power houses remains a contentious issue in the B-24 Squadrons of Australia Association with a number of questions relating to Kingwell's role and claims of his destroying the targets remaining unresolved.

143.   'An attempt to complete the job...' Court, pages 59-60. For Court's commentary on the mission see Pages 58-60. Further commentaries on these missions are in: Nelms, pages 93-96; and Odgers, pages 401-402.
'Three days later they again flew...' Brooks and Anon correspondence.

143-144.   'RAAF navigators on B-24s...' For Ted Williams' comments on the use of Loran by the USAAF see correspondence to the author dated 24 October 2002. Copy held AHSNT/Alford Colln. Quoted in Alford. *ADF Facility...Bathurst Island.* Page 31.

144.   'Flying Officer Harry Seymour...' In correspondence to the author. 17 November 2002. Russ Brook's comments were made in conversation, 18 November 2002.
'The following day SqnLdr N. H. 'Fanny' Straus...' Ibid. Brooks.
'Truscott was being used extensively...' For Dave Sieber's comments on Truscott see extract of *Flying Log Book.* Copy held AHSNT/Alford Colln. For the history of Truscott see Beasy, John and Carol. *Truscott. The Diary of Australia's Secret Wartime Kimberley Airbase.* Australian Military History Publications. 1995.

145.   'Then Parker led the remaining Liberators...' Powell, page 172.

145-146.   'Roger Court recalled the Japanese fighters...'. Court, page 65. See also Nelms, page 102, in which the Japanese aircraft camouflage and markings are described by crew members involved in the mission.

146.   'They were picked up by a second Catalina...' Keith Shilling's experience is related in full in Odgers, pages 407-408. See also Piper. *Great Air Escapes.* Pages 128-135. The action of 6 April 1945 is also related in a number of publications including: Court, pages 61-68; Nelms, pages 103-106; and Odgers, pages 406-409.

146-147.   'Armed reconnaissance...' Odgers, page 433.
'In May four aircraft of 12 Squadron...' The mission of 8 May is summarised in Sieber's *Flying Log Book* entry for that day. Copy held AHSNT/Alford Colln.

148.   'Though arriving late in the war...' *Form A50 Operations Record Book.* No. 12 Squadron. Copy held AHSNT/Alford Colln. See also Alford. *Darwin's Air War.* Page 55.

CHAPTER 12 THE OFFENSIVE ROLLS ON: Moving north and boredom the enemy.

Page 149.   'Even with these movements...' The boredom of the correspondents is quoted in Alford. *Darwin's Air War.* Page 57.

150.   'The squadron was ably led...' Roy Goon's story including that of the award of an MID is related in; Darbyshire, Don. 'One of a Kind.' *Flypast* magazine. February 2002. Pages 22-26; correspondence by and in conversation with, Chris Alford who underwent his pilot training with the Victorian Aero Club in the mid-1930s with Goon as his instructor; and in Discussion with Roy Goon's niece, Kay Goon. Copies held AHSNT/Alford Colln.
'In the Darwin area the Spitfire squadrons...' *Form A50 Operations Record Book.* No. 452 Squadron. 27 July 1944. Copy held AHSNT.
'While training flights were the norm...' Ibid. 11 January 1944.

151.   'Gordon decided to carry out a test flight...' The admission of Gordon to the 1 MRS facility is related in the *Form A50* for 27 February 1944. Gordon's story is related in an article by Dennis Newton entitled 'Skywarriors: The old Firm Sqn Ldr Reginald 'Butch' Gordon and Flg Off Ronald Jordan'. *Aero* magazine. Issue 20. Pages 70-74.

151-152.   'The RAAF Spitfire squadrons...' The conditions at Potshot are described in Odgers, page 138.
'Searches by the Beaufighters and Mitchells...' Extract of *Flying Log Book.* Sergeant Doug Crosbie. Copy held AHSNT/Alford Colln.
'The Spitfire units had been more fortunate...' *Form A50 Operations Record Book.* No. 452 Squadron. 25 March 1944.

NOTES

153.   'Staging through Bathurst Island...' Public Relations, Directorate of, RAAF. *RAAF Saga*. Australian War Memorial. 1944. 'Darwin Fights Back'. Page 176.

154.   'Two crews of 1 Squadron were lost...' *Form A50 Operations Record Book*. No. 1 Squadron. 8 May 1944.

154-155.   'During May both RAAF Spitfire squadrons...' *Form A50*. No. 452 Squadron. 15 June 1944.

155.   'The mission of the 27th...' Extract of *Flying Log Book*. Warrant Officer Joe Gleeson. 27 June 1944. Copy held AHSNT/Alford Colln.

        'On 4 July a shipping strike...' *Form A50 Operations Record Book*. No 2 Squadron. 4 July 1944.

157.   'The third loss was on Boxing Day 1944...' Ibid. Entry for 26 December 1944 and pers comm. Joe Gleeson to author. 1987.

        'The Mitchell squadrons were resigned...' National Archives of Australia. Series 11312 Item 6/10/AIR. Correspondence Bostock to HQ NWA and 31 Squadron of 18 June 1943. See also *Form A50. Operations Record Book*. No. 31 Squadron. Commanding Officer's Reports. 1943. A number of comments appeared in the Operations reports for 31 Squadron in the latter half of 1944 alerting crews to their fuel states on return from strikes over the NEI and advising the use of Truscott.

        'For the Mitchells the situation wasn't so dire...' Extract of *Flying Log Book*. Sergeant John Marks RAAF. No. 18 NEI Squadron. Copy held AHSNT/Alford Colln.

159.   'Eric Coleman joined 31 Squadron...' In correspondence and response to questionnaire 'Can You Help?' 10 April 1989. See also 'Mentioned in Despatches Honours to Penrith Flying Officer'. *Nepean Times*. September 1945. Copy held AHSNT/Alford Colln.

159-160.   'Malcolm Philps, a wireless fitter...' In correspondence to the author, 1990. Copy held AHSNT/Alford Colln. See also Alford. *Darwin's Air War*. Page 62.

160.   'On 24 September 1944 two Beaufighters...' The disappearance of Beaufighters A19-192 and A19-208 is related in Powell, pages 153-154. Official reports include: Anon. *The Story of the last flight of Sqdn. Ldr. W. L. Wackett*. Transcribed from the original, 20 January 1987. Copy held AHSNT/Alford Colln; *Form A50 Operations Record Book*. No. 31 Squadron. Commanding Officer's comments for September 1944; National Archives of Australia. Series A705 Items 163/98/142 and 166/30/81 and A8681 Item 1944/4165; and RAAF Report, *Summary of events, crash of Beaufighter A19-208*. Copy held AHSNT/Alford Colln. See also Bowditch, Sharon. 'Lost wartime flyers' memorial'. *NT News*. 11 October 1980.

161.   'A total of 84 sorties were flown...' The comment by Keenan is quoted in Grantham, page 81.

        'Wireless Air Gunner Nerdan A. Chowns...' In correspondence from Chowns' brother to the author and extract of *Flying Log Book*. Copy held AHSNT/Alford Colln.

162.   'Again, AM Sir Charles Portal...' Powell, page 186.

        'Importantly, the raid...' See Nelson, Kenneth J. *Spitfire RCW The Wartime Exploits of Wing Commander Royce Clifford Wilkinson O.B.E., D.F.M. & Bar C. de G (France)*. Western Canadian Distributors. 1994. Page 136.

163.   'The following month the first of the RAAF units...' *Form A50*. No. 452 Squadron. 7 November 1944.

        'The departure of the RAAF squadrons...' The comment by the British official is quoted in Powell, page 187. 'The questions persisted...' Ibid. Page 187.

        'The RAF units continued their detachments...' Extract of the diary of Sgt Bill Nash provided to the author by Marjorie Nash as the 'Nash Collection'. Item held AHSNT/Alford Colln.

        'The personnel of 548 Squadron...' Wallis, Barry. 'Royal Air Force Squadrons No. 548 and 549. A Brief History'. *PAM News International*. Page 725.

164.   'An intruder was picked up...' Gadja, Stan. 'Dinah Recovery in Western Australia'. *After The Battle*. Battle of Britain Prints International. Issue 39. 1983. Page 42.

        'Those pilots were FltLts D. M. Gossland...' Extract of *Form 105 (A). Combat (Fighter) Report*. Narrative Section. 20 July 1944. Copies held by the author.

CHAPTER 13 GAME OVER: The unsung strength, victory at last and Darwin today.

Page 165.   'They fly through the air with a nonchalant air...' Quoted in Allen, G. U., with Shearman, Elizabeth. *Scotty Allen Australia's Flying Scotsman*. Clarion. 1992. Page 142. According to Clem Cerini, a flight engineer

NOTES

166.   with No. 11 Squadron, the song was adapted by the unit in 1943. In discussion with the author, Darwin, 1994.
       'On 25 November A24-45...' Honan, Robert. *That's That*. Self published. 1989. Page 78.
       'Missing the datum on the first run...' Ibid. Page 79.
       'The second pilot, Bob Honan...' Ibid. Page 85.

167.   'Darwin became a permanent Catalina base...' The Japanese shipping notice is cited in Vincent, David. *Catalina Chronicle*. Catalina National Committee. 1978. Page 59.

168.   'Doctors Gully also provided...' Honan, page 85.
       'Sergeant H. D. Davis, Flight Engineer...' Extract of *Flying Log Book*. Includes certification as both an Air Gunner and Flight Engineer. Copy held AHSNT/Alford Colln.

169.   'Staging through Woendi Island...' Bolitho's comments are related in Vincent. *Catalina Chronicle*. Page 73. Extracts of his report on the operation, along with the aircraft involved are on pages 72-73.
       'Over the next two days...' Ibid. Page 73.

1-170. 'Sorties were also flown against China...' Davis. Extract of *Flying Log Book*.

170.   'On 2 May 1945 SqnLdr M. Seymour...' Vincent. *Catalina Chronicle*. Page 79.
       'Fate intervened and A24-1 crashed...' The recollections of Harry Kirkhouse are in: Correspondence to the author of 14 May 1990; Kirkhouse, H. A. *A24-1 Air Crash at Darwin*. Undated; and Kirkhouse, H. A. Extract of *Flying Log Book*.

171.   'Perhaps the success of the Catalinas...' Vincent, page 75. Matsuzaki's comments are also related in part in Powell, page 175.
       'Another of the unsung units...' Introductory passage in *Form A50 Operations Record Book*. No. 6 Communications Unit. 20 June 1944. Copy held AHSNT/Alford Colln.

171-172. 'Fenton "...knew the Top End so well..."' McEwin, page 22.

172.   'The unit carried out a wide range of activities...' *Form A50*. No. 6 Comm. Unit. See also Alford. *Darwin's Air War*. Page 63
       'Jenkins was forced to dodge anthills...' Ibid.
       'Perhaps one of the more important...' *Form A50*. July 1945 entry.
       'At the time preparations were underway...' Ibid. *Form A50*.
       'Not all flights carried out...' Ibid.

173.   'August 1945 saw the cessation...' Ibid.
       'When peace did come, Fenton...' Ibid.
       'At the Loran site on Bathurst Island...' Williams, Joe. *AAF Army Airways Communication System Historical Data 1 June – 23 November 1945*. June-July 1945. Pages 1814-1815. Copy held AHSNT/Alford Colln. See also Alford. *ADF Facility Bathurst Island*. Page 36.

174.   'On 15 July A52-2 was flown to Biak...' Vincent, David. *Mosquito Monograph*. Self published. 1982. Page 137.
       'The long range flights staged through Truscott...' In correspondence to the author and quoted in Alford. *Darwin's Air War*. Page 64.

174.   'Whilst the new Mk XVIs were faster...' Vincent. *Mosquito Monograph*. Page 142.

175.   'The first fatality for 87 Squadron...' Ibid. Page 151.

176.   '"It is saddening to know that this month..."' Ibid. Page 152.

176.   'A52-609 set off as planned...' Coates, Graeme. 'Coomalie Creek Celebrations & the Last WWII Operation'. *Flightpath* magazine. September 2008. page 21. See also Burke, Terry. 'Coomalie Creek Airfield and Chapel – a Brief History'. *Aerogram. The Journal of the Friends of the RAAF Museum*. September 2008. Pages 6-7.

176-177. 'No doubt everyone in the NWA remembered...' The recollections of Austin Asche are related in 'Where were they on VP Day 1945'. *The Territory at War*. Australia Remembers NT Committee. 1995. Pages 90-94. A slightly different version is in Rayner, Robert. *Darwin and Northern Territory Force*. Southwood Press. 2001. Page 637.

177.   'Further north at the Loran Station...' Williams, pages 1815-1816.
       'This prompted Evatt to counter the British...' Hammond Moore, page 266.

NOTES

PILOT PROFILES

Page 180-186. The series of Pilot Profiles were completed in consultation with and concurrence of the subjects and utilised biographical notes, diaries, conversations and correspondence. Copies of the notes are held in AHSNT/Alford Colln.

APPENDICES

Appendix 1. **JAPANESE AIR OPERATIONS OVER THE NT, 1942-1944**

A range of sources was used in the preparation of the table, including: Alford notes and files held AHSNT/ Alford Colln; Alford notes. Held by the author; Australian War Memorial. *Darwin Air Raids (Excluding Recce Except Where Stated)*. Anti-Aircraft engagement records, per Ray Jackson, 1991; Australian War Memorial. *Enemy Air Raids on the Australian Mainland - Northern Territory - "Darwin Raids"*; Dunn, Richard L. Air Combat Australia – 1943. 2006. (Excerpts of manuscript with permission of the author) Chapters, *Japanese Army Raid* and *Fading Presence*; Foster. *Tally-ho!..*; Gillison. *Royal Australian Air Force*; Grant. *Spitfires over Darwin*; Kawano. *The Japanese navy's air-raid...*; Lockwood. *Australia under Attack* and *Australia's Pearl Harbour*; Odgers. *Air War Against Japan*; and Rogers, Edward. Correspondence of 29 November 2009.

Appendix 2. **MAJOR OPERATIONAL UNITS, NWA 1941-1945**

Alford. *Notes on Japanese air forces over the NWA 1942-45*. 2009; Lansdale, James F. *IJNAF Air Unit Code Prefixes*. 10 January 2008; and Pentland, Geoffrey. *RAAF Camouflage & Markings 1939-45. Vol 1*. Kookaburra Technical Publications. Page 141.

Appendix 3. **MAJOR OPERATIONAL AIRCRAFT, NWA 1942-1945**

Flightpath magazine. 'Museums of Aviation Guide.' May-July 2009 Issue; Francillon. *Japanese Aircraft...*; Long, James. Comments on Alford. *'Betty' bomber, Cox Peninsula Heritage Assessment Report*. Compiled for Heritage Conservation Services. In correspondence of 20 December 2006; *Pacific Wrecks* web site. Responses to queries re Catalina aircraft in Australia; and *Wikipedia* Encyclopaedia. Entries for Allied aircraft and remaining examples.

Appendix 4. **COMPOSITION OF JAPANESE AIR FORCES**

Alford. *Aviation Archaeology* and *Notes...*; Dunn. Correspondence of 23 May 2009; Hata, Ikochito, Izawa, Yasuho and Shores, Christopher. *Japanese Army Air Force Fighter Units and Their Aces 1931-1945*. Grub Street. 2002. Pages x-xii; Hata, Ikochito and Izawa, Yasuho. *Japanese Naval Aces and Fighter Units in World War II*. Airlife. 1989. Page xiv; Thorpe, Donald W. *Japanese Naval Air Force Camouflage and Markings World War II*. Aero Publishers. 1977. Page 12; and Thorpe, Donald W. *Japanese Army Air Force Camouflage and Markings World War II*. Aero Publishers. 1968. Page 13.

Appendix 5. **JAPANESE AIRCRAFT DESIGNATIONS AND ALLIED CODE NAMES**

Alford, Bob. *Japanese Aircraft Designations and Allied Code Names*. 2009; Collier. *Japanese Aircraft of World War II*. Pages 46-53; Dunn. *Japanese Aircraft Codenames in Perspective*. 2005; Francillon. *Japanese Aircraft...* Pages 46-60 and 534-566; Mikesh. *Japanese Aircraft Code Names...* Pages 10-24 and 164-181; Piper. *Souvenirs from Japan*; and Tagaya, Osamu. *Japanese Aircraft Type/Year Designations, Abbreviations & Notes*. 2008.

BIBLIOGRAPHY

BOOKS

Alcorn, John S. The Jolly Rogers. *History of the 90th Bomb Group during World War II.* Historical Aviation Album Publication. 1981.

Alford, Bob. *Darwin's Air War.* Aviation Historical Society of the Northern Territory. 1992.

Allen, G. U., and Shearman, Elizabeth. *Scotty Allen Australia's Flying Scotsman.* Clarion. 1992.

Appleton, Bill. *Rikai: A Guide to the Japanese War Cemetery Cowra NSW.* 1998.

Ballard, Geoffrey. *On Ultra Active Service – the story of Australia's signals intelligence operations during WWII.* Spectrum. 1991.

Beasy, John, and Carol. Truscott. *The diary of Australia's secret wartime Kimberley airbase.* Australian Military History Publications. 1995.

Bennett, John. Highest Traditions. *The History of No 2 Squadron RAAF. Australian Government Printing Service.* 1995.

Booth, George. *33 Days.* Greenhouse. 1988.

Bowman, Martin. *B-17 Flying Fortress Units of the Pacific War.* Osprey. 2003.

Brauns, John W., Col. U.S. Army. Retired. *History of the 43rd Engineers in the South-West Pacific.* 43rd Engineer Regiment. 1976.

Brace, Richard, *et al. World War II History of the 102nd Antiaircraft Battalion* (AW), New York National Guard of Buffalo, New York. (Buffalo and Erie County Historical Society 1961/1983).

Brereton, Lewis H. General. *The Brereton Diaries.* Morrow New York. 1946.

Brooks, Wilfred H. *Demon to Vampire: No. 21 Squadron History.* DemonVamp. 1986.

Callaghan, Peter. *With the RAAF at Gove.* National Trust (NT). 1988.

Carter, Kit C. and Mueller, Robert. *The Army Air Forces in World II. Combat Chronology 1941-1945.* Office of Air Force History. 1973.

Casey, Hugh J. Major General. *Airfield and Base Development: Engineers of the South Pacific 1941-1945. Volume VI.* Office of Chief Engineer, General Headquarters Army Forces, Pacific. 1951.

Clarke, Hugh V. *The Long Arm.* Roebuck Society. 1974.

Collier, Basil. *Japanese Aircraft of World War II.* Mayflower. 1979.

Court, W. Roger. *This Way: An Aviator's Journey Through War and Peace.* c. 1994.

Craven, W F. and Cate, J L. *The Army Air Forces in World War II. Plans and Early Operations, January 1939 to August 1942.* Office of Air Force History. 1963.

Edmunds, Walter D. *They Fought With What They Had.* Zenger. 1951.

Eisenhower, Dwight D. *Crusade in Europe.* Doubleday. 1948.

Farram, Steve. *Charles "Moth" Eaton Aviation Pioneer of the Northern Territory.* Charles Darwin University Press. 2007.

Foster, R W. With Franks, Norman. *Tally Ho!: From the Battle of Britain to the Defence of Darwin.* Grub Street. 2008.

Francillon, René J. *Japanese Aircraft of the Pacific War.* Naval Institute Press. 1987.

Frei, Henry P. *Japan's Southward Advance and Australia.* Melbourne University Press. 1991.

Gillison, Douglas. *Royal Australian Air Force 1939-42.* Australian War Memorial 1962.

Grant, Jim. *Spitfires Over Darwin 1943.* Techwrite Solutions. 2003.

Grant, Jim. *Spitfires Over Darwin 1943.* R J Moore. 1995.

Grantham, Sid. *The 13 Squadron Story.* Grantham/13 Squadron Association. 1991.

Griffith, Owen. *Darwin Drama.* Bloxhall and Chambers. 1946.

Hall, Bon. *A Saga of Achievement.* Bonall. 1978.

Hammond Moore, John. *Over sexed, Over paid & Over here.* Americans in Australia 1941-1945. University of Queensland Press. 1981.

BIBLIOGRAPHY

Hata, Ikochito, Izawa, Yasuho and Shores, Christopher. *Japanese Army Air Force Fighter Units and Their Aces 1931-1945.* Grub Street. 2002.

Hata, Ikochito and Izawa, Yasuho. *Japanese Naval Aces and Fighter Units in World War II: Airlife.* 1989.

Honan, Robert F. That's That. Honan. 1989.

Horikoshi, Jiro. *Eagles of Mitsubishi: The Story of the Zero Fighter.* Orbis. 1982.

Horton, Glenn. *The Best in the Southwest: The 380th Bomb Group in World War II.* Mosie Publications. 1995.

Horton, Glenn and Gary. *King of the Heavies: 380th Bomb. Group 1942-1945.* 1983.

Imai, Jai (Publisher) *General View of Japanese Military Aircraft in the Pacific War.* Compiled by the Staff of "Aireview". 1956.

Ind, Allison. Bataan: *The Judgement Seat.* MacMillan. London. 1944.

Livingstone, Bob. *Under the Southern Cross:The B-24 Liberator in the South Pacific.* Turner Publishing. 1998.

Lockwood, Douglas. *Australia under Attack: The Bombing of Darwin – 1942.* New Holland. 2005.

Lockwood, Douglas. *Australia's Pearl Harbour.* Cassell Australia. 1966.

McDonald, Kenneth Neal DFC. *Coomalie Charlie's Commandos.* Banner Books. 1996.

Matalof and Snell. *U.S. Army in World War II Strategic Planning for Coalition Warfare.* War Department. 1953.

Messimer, Dwight R. *In The Hands of Fate.* Naval Institute Press. 1985.

Mikesh, Robert C. *Japanese Aircraft Equipment 1940-1945.* Schiffer. 2004.

Mikesh, Robert C. *Japanese Aircraft Code Names and Designations.* Schiffer. 1993.

Mikesh, Robert C. and Tagaya, Osamu. *Moonlight Interceptor: Japan's "Irving" Night Fighter.* Smithsonian Institution Press. 1985.

Mitchell, John. *On Wings We Conquer.* G.E.M. Publishers. 1990.

Morehead, James. *In My Sights: The Memoirs of a P-40 Ace.* 2003.

Mrozek, Donald J., Higham, Robert and Newell, and Allen, Jeanne Louise. (Eds) *The Martin Marauder and the Franklin Allens.* Air Force Historical Foundation. 1980.

Nelms, Michael V. *Tocumwal to Tarakan. Australia and the Consolidated B-24 Liberator.* Banner Books. 1994.

Nelson, Kenneth J. Spitfire RCW. *The Wartime Exploits of Wing Commander Royce Clifford Wilkinson O.B.E., D.F.M. & Bar C. de G (France).* Western Canadian Distributors. 1994.

Noah, Joe, and Sox, Samuel L. Jr. George Preddy: *Top Mustang Ace.* Motorbooks. 1991.

NT Committee. *The Territory at War.* Australia Remembers Program. 1995.

Odgers, George. *Air War Against Japan.* Australian War Memorial. 1957.

Pajdosz, Waldemar and Zbiegniweski, Andre R. *3/202 Kokutai.* Kagero Studio. 2003.

Parnell, Neville. *Whispering Death.* Reed. 1980.

Pentland, Geoffrey. *RAAF Camouflage & markings 1939-45. Vol 1.* Kookaburra Technical Publications.

Perez, Father Eugene. *OSB. Kalumburu War Diary.* Artlook. 1981.

Piper, Bob. *The Hidden Chapters: Untold stories of Australians at war in the Pacific.* Pagemasters. 1995.

Piper, Bob. *Great Air Escapes.* Pagemaker. 1991.

Porter Hal. FltLt. *Adventures in Radar.* 1945. (Reprint 1991).

Potts, E Daniel and Annette. *Yanks Down Under 1941-45.* Oxford University Press. 1985.

Powell, Alan. *The Shadow's Edge.* Melbourne University Press. 1988.

Prange, Gordon W., Goldstein, Douglas M. and Dillon, Katherine V. *God's Samurai: Lead pilot at Pearl Harbour.* Brasseys. 1990.

RAAF, Public Relations, Directorate of. *These Eagles.* Australian War Memorial. 1942.

RAAF, Public Relations, Directorate of. *RAAF Log.* Australian War Memorial. 1943.

BIBLIOGRAPHY

RAAF, Public Relations, Directorate of. *RAAF Saga*. Australian War Memorial. 1944.

RAAF, Public Relations, Directorate of. *Victory Roll*. Australian War Memorial. 1945.

Rayner, Harry. *Scherger: a biography of Air Chief Marshal Sir Frederick Scherger*. AWM. 1984.

Rayner, Robert. *Darwin Detachment*. Rudder Press. 2002.

Rayner, Robert. *Darwin and Northern Territory Force*. Southwood Press. 2001.

Rayner, Robert. *The Army and the Defence of Fortress Darwin*. Rudder Press. 1995.

Rorrison, James. *Nor The Years Contemn*. Palomar Publications. 1992.

Sekigawa, Eiichiro. *Pictorial History of Japanese Military Aviation* (English Edition). Ian Allen Ltd. 1974.

Shores, Christopher and Cull, Brian with Izawa Yasuho. *Bloody Shambles: Volume Two: The Defence of Sumatra to the Fall of Burma*. Grub Street. 1993.

Simmonds, Ed. *Radar Yarns*. E.W. and E. Simmonds. 1992.

Simmonds, Ed. (Ed) *More Radar Yarns*. E. W. and E. Simmonds. 1992.

Southall, Ivan. *Bluey Truscott: Squadron Leader Keith William Truscott, R.A.A.F., D.F.C. and Bar*. Angus and Robertson. 1958.

Stagg, Ross Smith. *Caterpillar Club Survivor: Lost in the Top End, 1943*. C. Stagg. 2007.

Tagaya, Osamu. *Imperial Japanese Naval Aviator 1937-45*. Osprey Publishing. Undated.

Tagaya, Osamu. *Mitsubishi Type 1 Rikko 'Betty' Units of World War 2*. Osprey Publishing Ltd. 2001.

Thorpe, Donald W. *Japanese Naval Air Force Camouflage and Markings World War II*. Aero Publishers. 1977.

Thorpe, Donald W. *Japanese Army Air Force Camouflage and Markings World War II*. Aero Publishers. 1968.

USAAF. *The American Air Forces in Australia to the Summer of 1942*. AAF Historical Studies. 1944.

Venn, Walter. *Restore to Service*. Australian Military History Publications. 1999.

Vincent, David. *Mosquito Monograph*. 1982.

Vincent, David. *Catalina Chronicle*. Catalina National Committee. 1978.

Wernoth, Ron. *Beyond Pearl Harbor: The Untold Stories of Japan's Naval Airmen*. Schiffer. 2008.

Wilson, David. *Always First: The RAAF Airfield Construction Squadrons 1942-1974*. Air Power Studies Centre. 1998.

Woodgate, Fred. *Lion and Swans*. 1992.

Wray, Christopher. *Timor 1942*. Hutchinson Australia. 1987.

UNPUBLISHED MANUSCRIPTS, REPORTS AND RESEARCH PAPERS

Alford, Bob. *Japanese Aircraft Designations and Allied Code Names*. 2009.

Alford, Bob. *Japanese Air Forces over the NWA 1942-1945*. (In draft) 2009.

Alford, Bob. *33rd Pursuit Sqn (Provisional)*. 2009.

Alford, Bob. *Japanese Aircrew NWA, 1941-45*. 2009.

Alford, Bob. *Aviation Archaeology*. (In draft). 2009.

Alford, Bob. *Japanese losses over the North Western Area of Operations 1942-44 - rubbery figures?* 2009.

Alford, Bob. *General notes and files relating to Japanese aircraft, units, actions and individuals of the Japanese air forces in the NWA, 1941-45*. 2009.

Alford, Bob. *'Betty' Bomber, Cox Peninsula Heritage Assessment Report*. For Heritage Conservation Services. 2006.

Alford, Bob. *The Bombing of Darwin: A historic association*. Presentation paper to RAAF and American representative to the U.S. Ambassador. 19 February 2006.

Alford, Bob. *Report on Investigations Into the Origins of Aircraft Wreckage Located in Charles Darwin National Park, September 2005*. For Heritage Conservation Services, Office of Environment and Heritage, NT Government. September 2005.

Alford, Bob. *A Heritage Assessment of the proposed ADF facility at Point Fawcett, Bathurst Island, N.T. For URS*. 2002.

BIBLIOGRAPHY

Alford, Bob. *Heritage Assessment of the remains of B-24 Nothing Sacred.* For Heritage Conservation Services, Office of Environment and Heritage. 2004.

Alford, Bob. *49th Fighter Group, Darwin 1942. Aircraft/pilot allocations and brief historical data on individual aircraft.*

Anon. *The Story of the last flight of Sqdn. Ldr. W. L. Wackett.* Transcribed from the original, 20 January 1987.

Anon. *History of the Forty-Ninth Fighter Control Squadron* (Sep) Book II.

Anon. *Log of Events Since Leaving Williamtown.* (record relating to the 9th Squadron, 49th Fighter Group USAAF) 1942.

Australian War Memorial. *Enemy Air Raids on the Australian Mainland - Northern Territory - "Darwin Raids".*

Barnett, Clyde H. Jr. *War Memories 1941-1945.* c. 1992.

Birkett, Gordon. *Early USAAFP-40E/E-1 Operations in Australia.* Parts 3, 4 and 5. 2005.

Boniece, Robert J and Scott, Louis T. *Historical Record 49th Fighter Group USAAF. AAF Historical Office.* Historical Records Division. Maxwell AFB. 18 November 1946.

Bower, Coleen. *No. 1 Mobile Works Squadron: February 26th - October 6th 1942.* An Oral History as Recalled by Frank Beale and Syd James. January 1993.

Dalkin, Robert N. *Flying Fifty Years Ago and Other Experiences.* 1991.

Dermoudy, Peter. *Americans in the N.T.* Report for Museums and Art Galleries Board of the N.T. 1983.

D'Olier, Franklin. (Chairman) *United States Strategic Bombing Survey (Pacific) Japanese Air Power.* Military Analysis Division. July 1946.

D'Olier, Franklin. (Chairman) *United States Strategic Bombing Survey.* The Japanese Aircraft Industry. Aircraft Division. May 1947.

Dow, Wayne G. *Unit History – 27th Bomb Group (L).* Transcription of microfilm. 2007.

Dunn, Richard L. *Air Combat Australia – 1943. 2006.* (Excerpts of manuscript with permission of the author)

Dunn, Richard. *Japanese Aircraft Code Names in Perspective.* (Excerpts of manuscript) 2005.

Fisher, Cec. *Through the eyes of a young Airman.* 1987.

Glover, Lt Colonel Ralph C. *The History of the 808th Engineer Aviation Battalion.* Typewritten historical record held National Archives, Washington, D.C. USA.

Hesse, Charles. *World War II Report of Charles Hesse While a Member of the 90th Bombardment Group.* c. 1991.

Hitchcock, Charles I. Captain, 2nd BS, 22nd BG. Report entitled *B-26B (#41-17593) water landing of Nov. 3, 1942 in the Timor Sea.* Dated 3 May 1943.

Johnson, Paul E. *Excerpts from Diary of Paul E. Johnson Pilot 319th Squadron 90th Bomb Group From Feb 2, 1943 to Jul 9, 1943.* 1943.

Kawano, Teruaki. Captain. *The Japanese Navy's air-raid against Australia during the World War Two.* Military History Department of the National Institute for Defence Studies. August 29, 1997.

LeBaron, *Allan G. Interview with Admiral Thomas H. Moorer, USN (Rtd) 27 January 1978.*

McCoy, Frank T. Lt. Col., S.W.P.A. *Technical References to Inspected Enemy Airplanes. A.T.I.U. Memorandum No. 2.* HQ Allied Air Forces Directorate of Intelligence. 27 September 1943.

McEwin, Gavin. *Commentary on Darwin's Air War.* Comments providing additional personal recollections on Darwin's Air War publication. 1992.

Mason, John T. Jr. *The Pacific War Remembered.* An Oral History Collection. Annapolis Naval Institute Press. c. 1976.

Military Intelligence Division U.S. *Life of Japanese Aircraft Makers' Plates and Markings, Report No. 68 Life of Japanese Combat Airplanes.* 20 March 1945.

Moore, Murray. *The 80% Loss Raid.* 1998.

BIBLIOGRAPHY

Peaslee, Jesse. *2nd Lt. Air Corps. Operations Officer. Activities of the Ninth Pursuit Squadron.* c. 1945.

Piper, Bob. *Research paper entitled Japanese War Graves - Cowra N.S.W.* January 2005.

Royal Australian Air Force. *RAAF Index to Missing Aircraft.* c. 1947.

Royal Australian Air Force. *Summary of events, crash of Beaufighter A19-208.* 1944. Report.

Simmonds, Ed. *The RAAF on Bathurst Island in 1942.* 1991.

Tagaya, Osamu. *Japanese Aircraft Type/Year Designations, Abbreviations & Notes.* 2008.

Ward, Susan. *The Story of World War II Flying Ace George Preddy Jr. Stardust Studios.* 2002.

Williams, Joe. *AAF Army Airways Communication System Historical Data 1 June – 23 November 1945.* June-July 1945.

Yeaman, J. *Notes on Aerodrome Selection Programme in North Western Area as from 1st January 1942 and Aerodrome Development in the Northern Territory pre 1943. B/511.* From official RAAF records.

NEWSPAPERS, NEWSLETTERS AND MAGAZINES

13 Squadron Newsletter. RAAF 13 Squadron Association. Various editions.

380th Bomb Group Flying Circus. Newsletter of the 380th Bomb. Group Association. Various editions.

Advertiser, The. (Adelaide) Various editions.

Aero Australia. Various editions.

Aerogram. The Journal of the Friends of the RAAF Museum. September 2008.

After the Battle. Battle of Britain Prints International.

Age, The. (Melbourne) Various editions.

Argus, The. Weekend Magazine. (Melbourne) 'They Have Fought Homeless For Two Years.' 23 December 1944.

Army News. Various editions.

Austin American - Statesman. Metro & State. newspaper supplement. 'Their place in history. World War II veterans recount experiences in the Pacific.' 1 October 2000.

Australian Owner Pilots Association. AOPA magazine, June 1995. Piper, Bob. 'Souvenirs from Japan.'

Australasian Post. Various editions.

B-24 Squadrons Newsletter. B-24 Liberator Squadrons of Australia Association. Various editions.

Canberra Times, The. (Canberra) Various editions.

Courier Mail, The. (Brisbane) Various editions.

Darwin Defenders. Newsletters of the Darwin Defenders Association. Various editions

Flightpath. Alford, Bob. 'A Different Kind of Anzac Day.' Autumn 1992.

Flightpath. Gwynn Jones, Terry. 'Zeros Over Brisbane.'

Flypast. (UK). Various editions.

Forty Niner, The. Newsletter of the 49th Pursuit Group USAAF. 3 May 1942.

Hudson Squadrons Newsletter. RAAF Hudson Squadrons Association. Various editions.

Journal of the Australian War Memorial. Hiromi, Tanaka. 'The Japanese Navy's operations against Australia in the Second World War, with a commentary on Japanese sources.' Issue 30. April 1997.

Journal of the Australian War Memorial. Clayton, Mark. The North Australian Air War 1942-44. No 8. April 1986.

Journal of the Australian War Memorial. Powell, Alan. 'The Darwin 'Panic', 1942.' No.3. October 1983.

Katherine Times. (Katherine N.T.) 22 March 1985.

No. 18 Squadron NEI-RAAF Forces Association Newsletter. Osborne, Tom. 'The Morning I Bombed Darwin.' No 38, July 1992.

Nepean Times. September 1945.

BIBLIOGRAPHY

Northern Standard. (Darwin) Various editions.

Northern Territory News. (Darwin) Various editions.

Northern Territory News. (Darwin) Franklin, Matthew. 'Japanese flyer recalls bombing raids on Pearl Harbour and Darwin.' December 7, 1991.

PAM News International. Wallis, Barry. Royal Air Force Squadrons No. 548 and 549. A Brief History.

Spitfire Association Newsletters. Spitfire Association. Various editions.

Sun News-Pictorial, The. (Melbourne) 12 December 1942.

Sunday Mail, The. (Adelaide) 26 February 1972.

Sunday Territorian. (Darwin) Various editions.

Sunday Territorian. (Darwin) Franklin, Matthew. 'Bomber asks us to forgive him.' February 9, 1992.

Wartime. Official Magazine of the Australian War Memorial. Flying With Eagles. Issue 26.

Wings – Official Magazine of the RAAF. Various wartime editions.

Wings. Piper, Bob. 'Four Flew Out.' Winter 1997.

ARCHIVAL MATERIAL

National Archives of Australia. Various files including:

Series CRS M431 Item 1.

Series A705 Items 32/18/122, 163/98/142 and 166/30/81.

Series A816 Item 14/301/14.

Series A1196 Item 1/501/431.

Series A1564 Items 1/4/2 INTEL, 1/4/3 INTEL, 1/4/4 INTEL, 1/4/5 INTEL and 1/4/6 INTEL.

A11312 Item 6/10/AIR.

A5164 Item 1/4/2/INTEL.

Series A5954. Items 230/12 and 1082/7.

Series A8325 Items 21/4/1942 PART 1 and PART 2.

Series A8681 Item 1944/4165.

A9186 *(various unit records – Forms A50 and A51 Operations Record Book)*

Series A9695 Item 469.

Series A9696/1 Item 606.

Series A11093 Item 320/3J5

Series A11093 Items 000/093A and 373/8.

Series A11231.

Australian War Memorial. Series AWM 54, files 84/4/153, 86/5/1, 423/2/13, 423/2/51, 423/4/3 PART 1, 423/4/92, 812/3/16 and negative No. P02822.001.

Maxwell Air Force Base Historical Research Centre. Georgia, USA. File SQ-64-BOMB-HI.

Northern Territory Archives Service. File NTRS 2119.

RAAF Historical Section, Russell Offices. Canberra ACT. Various files.

DIARIES, LOG BOOKS AND CORRESPONDENCE

Aiken, David. Correspondence relating to Pearl Harbor raids and aircraft.

Akasaka, Susumu. Correspondence relating to 70 DCS Japanese Army Air Force.

Alford, Chris. Correspondence and discussion relating to Roy Goon.

BIBLIOGRAPHY

Appleton, Bill. Correspondence relating to Val 3304.

Baeza, Bernard. Correspondence relating to Japanese aircraft over the NWA.

Barnett, Clyde W. Diary extracts 1942 and correspondence relating to the 8th Squadron and Darwin operations of the 49th Fighter Group.

Beales, Bruce. Correspondence relating to 12 Squadron operations.

Boyce, Ralph J. Personal diary 1942. Transcribed to Vols. 1-III by Alford 1988.

Case, Jim. Correspondence relating to 90th Bomb. Group.

Coleman, Eric. Correspondence relating to 31 Squadron operations, Darwin and Morotai.

Cornfoot, Ron. Correspondence relating to Hudson operations.

Cunningham, J. Extracts from diary relating to the 8th Squadron. 1942.

Dakeyne, Dick. Correspondence relating to Section 22 and 380th Bomb. Group.

De Grussa, Len. Correspondence relating to B-17 crash at Batchelor.

Donalson, I. B. Jack. Correspondence relation to the Sauber/Preddy mid-air collision.

Dunn, Richard. Correspondence relating to Japanese operations over the NWA.

Eckert, Clarence E. Correspondence relating to the loss of Lady Millie – 90th Bomb. Group.

Evans, Harry. Correspondence relating to airfield construction.

Geary, Harry. Correspondence relating to 808th Engineers U. S. Army.

Glenn, Bob B. Lt. *Brigadier Patrick J. Hurley's Mission to Expedite Blockade Runner Ships to the Philippines.* Diary extracts. February 1942.

Goodwill, Stan. Correspondence relating to Val 3304 and Lt Brown incident.

Haggerty, Bill. Correspondence relating to 90th Bomb. Group.

Hickey, Larry. Correspondence relating to Japanese air raids.

Holyoake, Cyril. Correspondence relating to 5 Fighter Sector.

James, Ken. Correspondence relating to 457 Squadron operations and downing of Ki-46 *Dinahs.*

Johnson, Capt Paul E. Diary/recollections relating to the activities of the 90th Bomb. Group.

Kirkhouse, Harry. Correspondence relating to the crash of Catalina A24-1.

Kitazawa, Noritaka. Military History Dept. National Institute for Defence Studies. Correspondence to Bob Piper Canberra ACT, 27 November 2000.

Lambert, Des. Correspondence relating to Val 3304 and HMAS Sydney.

Long, James. Correspondence on deciphering Japanese data plates, manufacturer and construction numbers of Mitsubishi A6M Type 'O' fighter production, and production figures for the Aichi D3A *Val*, Mitsubishi G4M1 *Betty* and Mitsubishi Ki-46 *Dinah.*

McMahon, Robert F. Correspondence relating to the 33rd Pursuit Squadron and 19 February 1942.

McPherson, Cyril. Correspondence relating to 12 Squadron and Vultee Vengeance aircraft.

Morehead, James. Personal correspondence including combat reports of 25 April, 30 July and 23 August 1942.

Outhred, Len. Diary extracts, 1943 relating to 318 RDF radar operations and 20 June 1943 raid.

Pearce, Keith. Correspondence and notes relating to Japanese attacks on Fenton, 1943.

Philps, Malcolm. Correspondence relating to 31 Squadron.

Rogers, Edward. Correspondence relating to WWII air operations on the NT.

Sasaki, Muramitsu. *Personal History and War Service over Darwin.* Notes to author, 1991.

Selman, James. Correspondence relating to Lt. Livingstone's death.

Seymour, Harry. Correspondence relating to Loran and 24 Squadron operations.

Skillman, Tom. Correspondence relating to 43rd Engineer Regt. Manbulloo.

Stubbs, Alan. Correspondence relating to 8X2, Bathurst Island.

BIBLIOGRAPHY

Taylor, Cliff. Correspondence relating to 14 HAA Battery, Fannie Bay.

Taylor, Jack. Correspondence relating to 12 and 31 Squadrons.

Walker, Brian 'Blackjack'. Correspondence relating to A-24 aircraft and RAAF service.

Williamson, Ted. Correspondence relating to Loran and 380th Bomb. Group.

Woodnutt, Bill. Correspondence relating to 8X2, Bathurst Island.

INTERVIEWS AND ORAL HISTORIES

Boyce, Ralph. 49th Fighter Group.

Brooks, Russ. No. 24 Squadron.

Jackson, Ray. No. 52 OBU UXB team.

Knox, Ross. No. 1 MRS.

Lawson, Murray. No. 2 Squadron.

Lewis, Ted. No. 18 NEI Squadron.

McMahon, Robert F. 33rd Pursuit Squadron (Provisional).

Molyneux, Cyril. West Point Battery 1941-43.

Roberts, Peter. AIF East Point.

Robinson, Ron. No. 31 Squadron.

Thompson, Forrest E. 'Tommy'. 380th Bomb. Group.

Turnbull, George. No. 2 Mobile Oxygen Plant.

Vallance, George. No. 7 RSU.

Walker, Ben. No. 1 MWS.

Wicks, Gordon. Catalina operations.

UNIT OPERATIONS RECORDS - RAAF

A50 Forms. No. 1 Medical Receiving Station.

A50 Forms. No. 2 Squadron.

A50 Forms. No. 6 Communications Unit.

A50 Forms. No. 7 Repair and Salvage Unit.

A50 Forms. No. Stores Depot.

A50 Forms. No. 12 Squadron.

A50 Forms. No. 14 Aircraft Repair Depot.

A50 Forms. No. 18 NEI Squadron.

A50 Forms. No. 31 Squadron.

A50 Forms. No. 452 Squadron.

A50 Forms. No. 457 Squadron.

COLLECTIONS

The AHSNT/Alford Collection. Comprises publications, reports, manuscripts, correspondence, oral histories, documents, files and photographs. Held Aviation Historical Society of the Northern Territory.

RESEARCH FILES HELD AHSNT IN AHSNT/Alford COLLECTION

Alford, Bob. Various files including;

Allied Aircraft Losses Darwin 19 February 1942. 1991.

49th Fighter Group USAAF. Darwin Scoreboard 1942. 1991.

BIBLIOGRAPHY

Summary of Major Accidents 49th Fighter Group Period 14 MAR 1942-4 SEP 1942. 1987.

49th Fighter Group USAAF Personnel Losses in Australia 1942. 1987.

49th Fighter Group USAAF. Darwin Scoreboard 1942. 1991.

Japanese War Graves.

AL/33PS/1. *33rd Pursuit Squadron (Provisional).*

AL/49FG/- Series of files on 49th Fighter Group USAAF.

AL/A58/1-5. *Spitfire in Australia and RAAF Service.*

AL/70DCS/1-3 *70th DCS Japanese Army Air Force.*

AL/AKA/1 *Akasaka, Susumu. 70th DCS Timor.*

AL/USD/1 – *United States Service Deaths.*

Crash files *B-24 Liberator.* Vols. I and II.

Crash files. *Spitfire.* Vols. I and II.

Crash files. *Japanese aircraft.* Vols. I to V.

Crash files. Various types in Allied service. Six volumes.

INTERNET SITES

ADF Serials. Australian Military Aircraft Serials and Aircraft History.

J-aircraft and Pacific Air War History Associates.

Justin Taylan's Pacific Wrecks.

Peter Dunn's Australia @ War.

PRIVATE NOTES

Alford, Bob. Private notes and papers pertaining to and including Japanese air forces, aircraft, operations, code names and markings compiled in 2009 as used in the general text body and as Appendices 1, 4 and 5. © R. N. Alford

INDEX

Introduction.

End notes are denoted by *n* which refers to the page number in the Notes section itself. The page number of the reference in the main text body is in the left hand margin of the Notes section, pages 206 to 224.

INDEX

INDEX

INDEX

INDEX

INDEX

INDEX

INDEX

INDEX

INDEX

INDEX

INDEX

Pearce, Bill 26
Pederson, Capt Vic. Padre, Salvation Army 144, *145*
Piddington, Dr. J. 51
Powell, Alan 145
Roger 51
Sanz, Fr Serafin 57
Stokes, Mounted Constable Jack 24
Tapp, Russell 52, 212*n*
Thomas, Father 122
Ulm, Charles 165
Wackett, Sir Lawrence 160, *160*
Wade, G. C. Premier of New South Wales 10, 206*n*
'Willie', Tracker 62

British

Churchill, Winston. Right Honourable, the. Prime Minister 25, 43, 92, 98, 162, 210*n*, 216*n*, 217*n*

Dutch

Hekking, Dr. 74
Winckel, Yvonne 184

Japanese

Hata, Ikuhito 115, 218*n*
Hirohito, His Majesty, Emperor (Showa) 16, 115, 201
Kanoye, Prince 16
Kohama, Shozuke 96
Sasaki, Shunji – mother of 116
Saito, Shin'ya 93

MAJOR POWERS:

America (USA) 10, 15, 16, 17, 18, 22, 23, 25, 40, 62, 66, 68, 76, 78, 87, 107, 111, 137, 139, 177, 186, 206*n*
Australia 10, 13, 14, 15, 16, 17, 18, 22, 23, 27, 31, 32, 33, 40, 43, 45, 47, 69, 77, 87, 92, 98, 99, 110, 122, 125, 132, 135, 137, 149, 159, 162, 163, 165, 171, 177, 178, 180, 182, 184, 207*n*, 216*n*
Axis Powers 14, 16, 107
- Germany 14, 16
- Italy 14, 16
- Japan 10, 11, 14, 15, 16, 40, 94, 137, 148, 149, 176, 178, 184, 185, 186
Britain (Great Britain, British Commonwealth) 10, 15, 16, 27, 40, 92, 105, 137, 150, 162, 163, 177,
China 10, 11, 16, 17, 23, 78,
India 25, 40
Netherlands (Dutch) 16, 22, 25, 86, 103, 137, 147, 157, 177, 184
Vichy France 16

ALLIED UNITS, COMMANDS and OPERATIONAL AREAS

ABDACOM 22, 23, 25, 29
Allied HQ (Australia) 80, 87, 97, 204
European Theatre 15, 67, 137
HQ Allied Air Forces SWPA 203, 204
HQ CBI (China Burma India) Theatre 204
NWA 21, 26, 65, 68, 69, 72, 79, 83, 86, 87, 92, 94, 95, *96*, 97, 99, 100, 102, *102*, 107, 110, 110, 112, 115, *116*, 118, 119, 120, 122, 124, 125, 129, 131, 132, 139, 141, 142, 143, 144, 145, 147, 149, 150, 151, *151*, 153, 154, *154*, 161, 164, 165, 171, 173, 175, 176, *176*, 182, 185, 194, 200, 203, 205, 216*n*, 219*n*, 222*n*, 223*n*
SWPA (South West Pacific Area) 79, 107, 122, 131, 159, 186, 203, 204
TAIU (Technical Air Intelligence Unit) 78, 79, *79*, 122, 203, 204, 205, 215*n*, 219*n*
USAFFE (US Armed Forces in the Far East) 41, 45
USAFIA (US Armed forces in Australia) 30, 48, 211*n*

MILITARY FORCES

American – Army

43rd Engineer, General Service Regt *43*, 44, 76, 210*n*
102nd A-A Bn (Coastal Artillery) 52, 53, *53*, 55, 76, 212n
135th Medical Regt 65, 76, 77
147th Field Artillery Regt 23, 43, 63
148th Field Artillery Regt 23, 29
808th Engineer (Aviation) Bn 44, *44*, 51, 76, 210*n*, 212*n*
US Army 22, 78, 99, 186, 198, 203

American – Army Air Forces (USAAC and USAAF)

3rd Bomb. Group 41, 76, 86
3rd Pursuit Sqn (Provisional) 25, 27
4th Photographic Charting Sqn 174, 178
5th Air Force 68, 69, 127, 135, 136, 137, 139, 186
5th Bomb. Group Hawaiian Air Force 16
5th Fighter Command 69
7th Bomb. Group 23, 25, 30
13th Pursuit Sqn (Provisional) 27, *27*
14th Provisional Sqn Hawaiian Air Force 16
17th Pursuit Sqn (Provisional) 23, 24, 25, 41, 48, 207*n*
19th Bomb. Group 10, 16, 20, 22, *23*, 25, 26, *26*, 29, 31, 41, 47, 76, *77*, 78, 194, 211*n*, 215*n*
- 40th Sqn 47
- 93rd Sqn 22
- 435th Sqn 78
20th Pursuit Sqn (Provisional) 25
22nd Bomb. Group 81, 215*n*
- 2nd Sqn 82

INDEX

INDEX

INDEX

INDEX

INDEX

INDEX

INDEX

INDEX

INDEX

INDEX

INDEX

INDEX

INDEX

INDEX